Sati

Evangelicals, Baptist Missionaries,
and the Changing Colonial Discourse

Sati

Evangelicals, Baptist Missionaries, and the Changing Colonial Discourse

Meenakshi Jain

Aryan Books International
New Delhi

SATI
Evangelicals, Baptist Missionaries,
and the Changing Colonial Discourse

ISBN: 978-81-7305-552-2

Published in **2016** by

Aryan Books International

Pooja Apartments, 4B, Ansari Road, New Delhi-110 002 (India)
Tel.: 23287589, 23255799; Fax: 91-11-23270385
E-mail: aryanbooks@gmail.com
www.aryanbooks.co.in

Designed and Printed in India by
ABI Prints & Publishing Co., New Delhi

Contents

Preface   *vii*
List of Illustrations   *xxiii*

Section A

1. The Backdrop   3
2. Sati as Described in Foreign Accounts   25
3. Early British Appreciation of Indian Civilization   44
4. State of English Society at Home and in India   68
5. The Evangelical Movement   89
6. The Evangelical-Utilitarian Alliance   105
7. Baptists in Bengal   115
8. Evangelical-missionary Attack on Hinduism   146
9. Missionaries Gain Official Entry: 162
   The Charter Act of 1813
10. Missionaries and Sati   177
11. Abolition of Sati   200
12. Sati – An Infrequent Occurrence   213

Section B
SOME FOREIGN ACCOUNTS OF SATI

1. 326 BC to AD 1499   225
2. AD 1500–1699   233
3. AD 1700–1799   279
4. AD 1800–1845   316
5. Some Missionary Accounts   351
6. Sati – A Rare Phenomenon   390

Appendices
Appendix I: Translation of a Bewasta Received   399
    from Mutoonjoy, Pundit of the Supreme Court,
    Respecting the Burning of Widows, and Other
    Sacrifices Prevalent among the Hindoos.
    (Great Britain. House of Commons Papers. 1821)
Appendix II: Lord William Bentinck's Minute on   403
    Sati, 8th November 1829
Appendix III: Sati: Regulation XVII, AD 1829 of the   419
    Bengal Code
Appendix IV: The Commission of Sati (Prevention)   423
    Act, 1987 (No. 3 of 1988)

Select Bibliography   433
Index   459

Preface

And the Debate Continues

Though banned by the British Government in 1829 and subsequently, by the Government of independent India in 1956 and 1987, incidents of sati continue to be sporadically reported from various parts of India. The case of eighteen-year old Roop Kanwar in Deorala village, Sikar district, Rajasthan, which triggered the 1987 legislation, is perhaps the most well-known in recent decades (*Manushi* 1987: 15-25; *Seminar* 1988: 342; Upreti and Upreti 1991: 46-63). But instances of widows immolating themselves on the pyres of their husbands have occurred intermittently even thereafter.

On 6th August 2002, for instance, in Patna Tomali village in Panna *zila* (Madhya Pradesh), Kattubai immolated herself. As a punitive measure, the state administration imposed a fine on the entire village for allegedly abetting the act. Another incident took place in 2006, in village Baniyani in Chattarpur *zila*. In this case, the four sons of the widow were held accountable and sentenced to life imprisonment. In May, the same year, a thirty-five year old widow immolated herself in village Rari Buzurg in Fatehpur *zila*, Uttar Pradesh. And in

August, a forty-year old jumped on the pyre of her husband in Sagar *zila* (*Bhaskar* 12-10-2008). Bundelkhand witnessed four instances of widow immolation and ten attempts at the same in the preceding seven years (*Hindustan Times* 17-10-2008).

On 13th October 2008, the *Hindustan Times* reported that a seventy-year old woman had immolated herself on the pyre of her husband in Chechar village of Kasdol development block, about 120 km from Raipur, the capital of Chhattisgarh. Her seventy-five year old husband had died after a prolonged illness. Family members told police officials who rushed to the place that Lalmati Verma had been a devout woman but they had not expected her to take this extreme step. They discovered she was missing on returning from the cremation of her husband. When they began searching for her, some villagers informed them that they had seen her proceeding towards the cremation site. They hurried to the spot, but it was too late. This was the first case of sati in Chhattisgarh and created a sensation in the area. The *Times Of India* carried a news item the same day that a large number of people from neighbouring villages gathered at the spot to offer prayers to 'sati *mata*.'

In August 2009, the sixty-year old widow of Nanchhu Ram Meena of Kuchar village in Sikar district, Rajasthan, attempted to immolate herself, but was thwarted by her family, the village community, and the police, "after a lot of drama and tension" (*Mail Today* 11-8-2009; *Times Of India* 16-8-2009). In the same month, the forty-two year old childless widow of a temple priest in Chanderi, near Bhopal, allegedly committed suicide and was cremated with her husband. Neighbours, who viewed this as a case of sati, said they had seen the woman free the pet dog and cow after which she was missing (*Hindustan Times* 24-8-2009).

As recently as December 2014, *The Pioneer* reported the case of seventy-year old Gahwa Devi, who jumped into the funeral pyre of her husband in Parmania village in Saharsa district, Bihar (*The Pioneer* 15-12-2014). Clearly, sati remains a living subject.

Despite the ban on the glorification of sati, temples dedicated to sati *matas* (mothers) exist and continue to attract devotees particularly in Bundelkhand, Uttar Pradesh, and Rajasthan. Pargana in Bundelkhand has a thriving sati temple. In 1989, at Jari in Uttar Pradesh's Banda district, a huge temple was built in memory of Javitri, a fifteen-year old Brahmin widow who had immolated herself. The Rani Sati temple in Jhunjhunu district, Rajasthan, commemorating thirteen satis of the Jalan family, still draws large numbers (*Hindustan Times* 17-10-08; Upreti and Upreti 1991: 33). Sati veneration remains "a major aspect" of the religious lives of Rajput women (Harlan 1994: 79-80; Noble and Sankhyan 2001: 364-365). The state has over two hundred sati temples (Storm 2013: 135).

The reportage on each new incident of widow immolation generally results in furious condemnation of the rite and demands for more stringent laws against alleged abettors. Interestingly, the nationwide debate sparked off by Roop Kanwar's immolation was remarkably reminiscent of the colonial discourse in the nineteenth century. As in the colonial period, issues of *shastric* sanction, antiquity of the rite, and its forced or voluntary nature were raised and fiercely contested.

The Marxist-feminist scholar, Lata Mani, identified four types of responses to Roop Kanwar's immolation — the "liberal" position that criticized sati as "traditional," "religious," "barbaric," and as representing a failure of the project of modernization; the conservative stand which valourized sati's "religious" and "traditional" status and described it as a practice inaccessible to westernized, urban Indians; a third stance, critical of both approaches, represented by Ashis Nandy; and the "genuinely anti-imperialist position" taken by feminists (Mani 1990: 24-41).

Feminists viewed Roop Kanwar's immolation in the context of the general subordination of women in Indian society. They stressed the persistence of the custom a century-and-a-half after it was outlawed by the British, "One hundred and fifty years later we are having to remind ourselves that women are not for burning" (Bhasin and Menon *Seminar* 1988: 12).

Theories of patriarchy and class and caste ideologies were cited to explain why the custom had endured. Roop Kanwar's immolation was attributed to an alliance of religion, commerce, and patriarchy. The three upper castes—Brahmins, Banias, and Rajputs—were accused of having conspired to revive the practice in the area for their own gain (this was the first sati in Deorala in sixty-nine years). Sharda Jain, a scholar and activist based in Jaipur, for instance, stated, "The Banias have the economic power, the Rajputs the political power and the Brahmins the power of religious knowledge." These vested interests, she claimed, were controlling a woman's identity (Tully 1991: 223; Jain, Misra, and Srivastava 1987: 1891-94).

A team of the Women and Media Committee, which visited Deorala towards the end of September 1987, also held the union of religion, commerce, and patriarchy responsible for this "most violent of patriarchal practices" (Menon, Seshu, and Anandan 1987: 1-7). These arguments were elaborated by other scholars who dwelt on the collaboration between Brahmins, Rajputs, and Banias in creating a heady mix of ideological, ritual, and commemorative elements for periodic spectacles of sati (Vaid and Sangari 1991 *Economic and Political Weekly* WS-2 – WS-18).

The editors of *Manushi* pointed to the modernity of the incident. They described the Deorala event as "a modern day sati". Distancing themselves from the anti-sati campaign, they depicted Roop Kanwar's immolation as the creation of modern economic, political, and social forces. Deorala, they pointed out, was a modern village with modern amenities and a literacy rate of over seventy per cent. The pro-sati group in the village, they stated, consisted of men who were urban, educated, and in their twenties and thirties. The sati cult, in its current form, was primarily the product of "a phoney religiosity that is the accompaniment of new-found prosperity, harnessed by political leaders for their own vested interests." They countered the suggestion that it was "a traditional residue from the rural backwaters" (Kishwar and Vanita *Manushi*: Nos. 42-43, Sept-Dec 1987).

Ashis Nandy, a critic of the philosophy of modernization, viewed the search for grand spectacles of evil by metropolitan India as "a search for evidences of the inferiority of the other India." Those who declared the Deorala sati a pure case of murder, he said, attacked in the same breath "Indian traditions, village superstitions, even the *Mahabharata* and the *Ramayana*." Could a pure case of murder not involve pure greed and could it not be tackled under the Indian penal code, "without reference to the larger cultural factors." Nandy held that "the feigned panic and the hyperbole" that followed Deorala ignored the fact that in the post-independence era, cases of sati have mainly been confined to one state, and within it, to one region (Nandy 1994: 133).

While condemning the in-authenticity of sati in *kaliyuga*, Nandy stressed the need to respectfully admit "the authenticity of the values that speak through the acts of sati recorded in the epics and myths" (Nandy 1994: 138). He cited the example of Rammohan Roy, closely associated with the struggle against sati. Roy, he pointed out, appreciated the values underpinning the mythology of sati; the rite presumed "the superiority in the cosmos of the feminine principle over the masculine and recognized the woman's greater loyalty, courage, and firmness of spirit" (Nandy 1994: 140). The Tagore family, Nandy further stated, was in the forefront of the movement against sati, yet Rabindranath and Abanindranath presented awe-inspiring reverential depictions of sati with great sensitivity and sense of tragedy (Nandy 1994: 136).

M.P. Rege argued that a critical area of contestation between the pro- and anti-sati groups was the belief of the former in the possibility of a truly *"dharmic"* sati, in which the widow was not victim, but victorious. This was a viewpoint wholly rejected by the anti-sati bloc (Rege 1987).

Gayatri Chakravorty Spivak viewed the sati as the epitome of the mute female subaltern. She focused on the "profound irony" in locating a woman's free will in self immolation. The "sanctioned suicide peculiar to women," she stated, drew its ideological strength "by *identifying* individual agency with the supraindividual: kill yourself on your husband's pyre now, and you may kill your female body in the entire cycle of birth" (Spivak 1988: 303).

Rajeswari Sunder Rajan pointed to the absence of discussion on pain in the contemporary debate on sati. She said the subject of pain figured only in the language of the defenders of sati, "who speak with authority about the absence of pain felt by the sati (thus they are humane), or the transcendence of pain achieved by her spirit (thus they are reverent)." In the discourse of the anti-sati group, "while pain is undeniably everywhere present, it is nowhere represented" (Rajan 1993: 298-99). According to Rajeswari Sunder Rajan, there was a need to develop "both a phenomenology of pain and a politics that recognizes pain as constitutive of the subject" (Rajan 1993: 302).

Issues of female sexuality were also raised. Veena Talwar Oldenburg pointed to the problems Roop Kanwar's widowhood posed for her relatives. Roop could either go back to her parents with her substantial dowry and live the life of a widow or stay on in her matrimonial home. Either way, her sexuality would be a worry for both families. Immolation was a way to "convert impending shame into glory." The added advantage was that this was "a culturally acceptable solution" (Oldenburg 1994: 118-19).

Malavika Kasturi argued that in Rajasthan many powerful magnates linked themselves to Kshatriya genealogical tradition in a bid to strengthen their claims to kingship. The practice of sati became allied with the ideal of female virtue and Kshatriya tradition. The honour of brotherhoods was closely linked to that of their wives and daughters, who were viewed as property or instruments of exchange. The sexuality of women was controlled and they were mainly used to contract alliances. "This devaluation of women was mirrored in elite Rajput cosmology, which reinforced Rajput caste and gender stereotypes..." (Kasturi 2002: 103).

Beyond the immediate case of Roop Kanwar, scholars also studied sati in colonial times from the perspective of the British need to establish dominance over Indian society. Lata Mani examined representations of sati and the debate over its legal prohibition among colonial officials, missionaries, and the Hindu male elite in Bengal from 1780 to 1833. She argued that "a specifically colonial discourse on Indian society" informed the deliberations. The women who burned were neither the subjects nor even the primary objects of concern in this debate. Rather, they were the site of a complex struggle over Indian society and definitions of Hindu tradition. Mani held that the widow was buried under a welter of official deliberations on "Hindu law." She became "hostage" to colonial fallacy about the chaos that would presumably result from intervention in a practice "insistently coded as religious, despite evidence to the contrary." Mani stated that the debate on sati was concerned with testing the limits of legitimate interference in what had thus far been the un-colonized space of religion (Mani 1998: 1-2; 191-92; 1990: 24-41).

The missionary involvement in sati, Mani further argued, was also complex and ambivalent, "with horror being reserved primarily for fundraising material produced for a British public." For both British officials and missionaries, women were not really the issue, they "rather provided ground for the development of other agendas" (Mani 1990: 24-41). Mani's work undercut the colonial portrayal of the abolition of sati as the compassionate act of a caring regime.

The need to "modify" Lata Mani's analysis (as well as that of Gayatri Chakravorty Spivak) was made by Ania Loomba, who pressed for a more sophisticated study of female agency. She argued that we could "re-position the sati by looking not just at the widow who died but at those who survived to tell the tale." According to her, feminist theory was still working out the connections between social determinations and individual subjectivity (Loomba 1993: 223).

Gayatri Chakravorty Spivak discussed the representation of sati in the nineteenth century, but as Rahul Sapra argued, did not analyze or contextualize the changes in the English portrayal from the seventeenth to the nineteenth century. In the seventeenth century, the majority of white men glorified Hindu widows who immolated themselves as "martyrs." By the nineteenth century, the East India Company had emerged as the dominant power in the subcontinent. It was this historical backdrop, Sapra said, that allowed white men to endeavor to become liberators of brown women. It was not just a case of "white men saving brown women from brown men" (Sapra 2011: 100-01).

In her book, *Real and Imagined Women: Gender, Culture and Postcolonialism*, Rajeswari Sunder Rajan too dealt with the abolition of sati by the British. She alleged that the relocation of the concept of chivalry from "medieval and Renaissance Europe" to colonial India led British men to display their "valour and authority" and intervene in the practice of sati. She stated that "the colonizer's racial superiority ... had also to be demonstrated by acts of valour and authority." This made intervention in the custom of sati "both a test and a legitimization of British rule" (Rajan 1993a: 70). However, as has been pointed out, this seemed an inadequate explanation for British intervention; Englishmen did not display chivalric ideals in their encounters with sati in the seventeenth century. Rather, it was their transformation from a trading group to paramount authority that explained the changes in the British position (Sapra 2011: 106-07).

Andrea Major highlighted the heterogeneity of Western responses to sati while focusing on British interpretations of the rite. She argued that events and ideas of this period cannot be understood in isolation, but have to be viewed as part of an ongoing process of understanding that "builds both on previous British experiences and on an awareness of a longer tradition of European encounters with sati." Her study emphasized the interconnections between the colonial debate on sati and ideological changes and concerns within British society (Major 2006: 11). Major questioned why no other rite or custom "received the same degree of fascination and vilification accorded to sati." The sati debate, she pointed out, coalesced with metropolitan concerns over religious toleration (Catholic Emancipation was granted the same year as sati was banned), penal reforms, shifting legal and moral attitudes to suicide, and changing gender ideology. All these issues resonated in the sati debate and influenced British views of the rite (Major 2012: 71).

Traditional methods of empathetic understanding also regained importance, as was evident in Lindsey Harlan's *Religion and Rajput Women: The Ethics of Protection in Contemporary Narratives* (1992) and the works of Julia Leslie (Leslie 1989; 1991; 1993) which displayed an Indological approach (Fisch 2005: 517).

A thought provoking contribution was by Alaka Hejib and Katherine Young. In their essay, "Sati, Widow-hood and Yoga" (Sharma 1988: 73-84), they attempted to understand "what was Hindu about sati" (Sharma 1988: 74). They declared their intention to "restore the religious dimension to the description and interpretation of the proleptic models of the Hindu widow and sati" (Sharma 1988: 82). An analysis of the deep structure of the prolepyic models of the Hindu widow and sati, they argued, revealed a hidden religious dimension: yoga; though neither the widow nor the sati was conscious of the yogic dimension of her life (Sharma 1988: 82). The psychology of yoga was instilled, albeit inadvertently, in the traditional Hindu woman. This was manifest in the concept of *tapasvini*, a word that described the Hindu widow, as the word *tapasvi* denoted the yogi. Hejib and Young explained why the wife who immolated herself was viewed as a saintly figure, while the widow, despite her celibacy and austere life, was regarded inauspicious. The sati was a model wife and her voluntary death proclaimed the transcendental character of the conjugal relationship.

Catherine Weinberger-Thomas too attempted to see sati through Hindu eyes. She presented an experiential and psychoanalytic account of ritual self-sacrifice and self-mutilation in South Asia. The psychological landscape she uncovered, "with unconditional love and absolute fidelity in the foreground, and self-sacrifice as proof of that love and devotion in the background," was that which defined the innermost feelings and inherent nature of the sati. The Sanskrit word *sat* is associated with the idea of "goodness," or "virtue"; sati was thus the chaste and faithful "virtuous wife."

But *sat*, and its derivative *satya*, Catherine Weinberger-Thomas said, are also interconnected with a key concept in Indian thought—truth. *Sat* is also a substance—fire itself. According to belief, the pyre is ignited by the inner flame of *sat*. The earthly flames drawn from the domestic hearth at the time of the nuptial rite (and which are to be used, theoretically, in the cremation rite) erect around the satis a kind of enclosure that conceals the "true" spectacle of their death: an immediate death, with no burns to the body or physical suffering, by "self-combustion." Fire is not the agent of the satis death, but rather the essence of their being (Weinberger-Thomas 2000: 18; 20; 23).

Catherine Weinberger-Thomas drew attention to the belief that the fire will not burn a living woman and a dead man; "Such an act would (be) impossible for a Hindu to contemplate...." What burnt in the cremation fire was "a single body, comprising two indivisible halves, transformed into a sacrificial oblation and rice-ball—a *pinda*" (Weinberger-Thomas 2000: 216). The sati dies a happy wife whose husband is still alive (*suhagin*), and not a widow. She dresses herself as on her wedding day. "Death by fire becomes the mirror image of the marriage ceremony, with the pyre becoming the bed on which the couple was united for the first time" (Weinberger-Thomas 2000: 217).

GOVERNMENT REGULATION

In the wake of Roop Kanwar's immolation, the Government of independent India passed the Commission of Sati (Prevention) Act of 1987 (Section B: 423-32). The Act largely adhered to the colonial legislation on sati. Many colonial suppositions about the practice were rearticulated in the Government decree prohibiting the rite. The first paragraph of the preamble of the Act was, in fact, a verbatim copy of the opening lines of Lord William Bentinck's Regulation XVII of 4 December 1829 (Dhagamwar 1988: 34-39; Section B: 419-22).

The Regulation of 1829 had declared the practice of sati, or the burning or burying alive of Hindu widows, illegal and punishable by criminal courts. It also stated that persons convicted of aiding and abetting the act, whether it was voluntary or not, would be deemed guilty of culpable homicide, and punished by fine or imprisonment or both. Further, the death sentence would be passed on persons found guilty of using violence or compulsion, or of having assisted in burning or burying alive a Hindu widow while she was in a state of intoxication, or stupefaction, or other causes impeding the exercise of her free will (Section B: 419-22). The Regulation declared all satis criminal acts.

The Act of 1987 also proclaimed sati an offence whether it was "voluntary … or otherwise." Participation in sati ceremonies was declared a criminal offence, and the punishment enhanced from the colonial legislation. If immolation actually took place, the penalty was death or life imprisonment (Section 4.1). If the attempt at immolation was foiled, the penalty was life imprisonment (Section 4.2). In both cases there was no provision for a lighter sentence. The law also stipulated that any one involved in an incident of widow burning could not inherit the woman's property (Section 18). Glorification of sati was prohibited (Section 2.1), the penalty being between one to seven years imprisonment and a heavy fine (Section 5).

There were two deviations from the colonial Regulation. First, in case of abetment, the burden of proof fell on the accused (Section 16). Second, while the Regulation of 1829 only threatened punishment to the organizers, the widow was now included among the organizers and liable to one year imprisonment and a fine (Section 3).

Some scholars have argued that the Central Government legislation of 1987, as well as that of the state of Rajasthan in 1988, carried to "fruition" the suggestion made by the Bombay Government in the mid-1830s that the "act of suttee" should be made "criminal in the suttee." The Sati Acts of 1987–1988 transformed the widow "from a saint to a criminal." If she survived the ordeal she was liable to both imprisonment and fine (Cassels 2010: 109).

Be that as it may, legislation has not ended discussion on sati. A horrific new incident rekindles the debate.

ABOUT THIS BOOK

The deliberations on sati in the post-independence era have largely taken place within the parameters of Lord Bentinck's Regulation XVII of 1829. That Regulation, which declared sati a criminal offence, marked the culmination of a sustained campaign against Hinduism by British Evangelicals and missionaries anxious to Christianize and Anglicize India. The attack on Hinduism was initiated by the Evangelical, Charles Grant, an employee of the East India Company and subsequently member of the Court of Directors, who, as early as 1786, presented a *Proposal* for the establishment of a Protestant mission in Bengal and Bihar. In 1792, Grant prepared a draft of his famous treatise, *Observations on the State of Society among the Asiatic Subjects of Great Britain,* which elaborated the scheme sketched out in the *Proposal*. A harsh evaluation of Hindu society, it challenged the then current Orientalist policy of respecting Indian laws, religion, and customs set in motion by the Governor General, Warren Hastings (1772–1784). Grant argued that the introduction of the language and religion of the conquerors would be "an obvious means of assimilating the conquered people to them" (Grant 1832: 84-90). Grant was joined in his endeavours by other Evangelicals and Baptist missionaries, who began arriving surreptitiously in Bengal from 1793 onwards.

This is not a work on sati *per se*. It does not address, in any depth, issues of the possible origins of the rite; its voluntary or mandatory nature; the role, if any, of priests, or family members; or any other aspect associated with the actual practice of widow immolation. An introductory chapter briefly surveys the literature on these dimensions of the rite.

The primary focus of this work is the colonial debate on sati, particularly the role of Evangelicals and Baptist missionaries. It argues that sati was an "exceptional act," performed by a miniscule number of Hindu widows over the centuries. Its occurrence was, however, exaggerated in the nineteenth century by Evangelicals and Baptist missionaries eager to Christianize and Anglicize India. The "missionary assault on Hinduism" dramatized the practice of sati (Bayly 1991: 222).

Evangelical-missionaries wanted, firstly, to secure the consent of the British Parliament to operate in the East India Company's territories in India (which was denied to them till the Charter Act of 1813). Thereafter, to validate British presence in the country, they presented graphic accounts of the raging "ills" of Hindu society, among them female infanticide, *ghat* murders, and widow immolations. The "catalogue of horrors" was intended to shock and motivate the British public and also garner funds at home for missionary work in India (Major 2006: 124). Significantly, several contemporary non-missionary observers insisted that these "evil practices" were nowhere as rampant as alleged. It is pertinent that in missionary accounts the epicentre of these practices was the vicinity of Calcutta, the very area in which the Baptists operated and the seat of British power in India.

The Baptist presentation of sati marked a radical departure from earlier foreign accounts of the rite, beginning with that of Diodorus as far back as the first century BC. These accounts mostly resonated with awe and incredulity and speculated on the possible reasons for the custom. They also revealed how limited the practice actually was. It was only in the opening decades of the nineteenth century that Evangelicals and Baptist missionaries presented appalling figures of thousands of widows being burnt on the pyres of their husbands. Also, in contrast to earlier accounts which typically described sati as an act of voluntary martyrdom, missionary writings presented sati as murder or suicide (a mortal sin). This version of sati became dominant in the early nineteenth century.

Most studies have attributed the British drive for social reform in the nineteenth century to an ascendant liberal sentiment. The extent to which the reform agenda was invented by Evangelicals and Baptist missionaries eager to authenticate British presence in India has not been adequately emphasized.

Almost alongside, a change in the attitude of Company officials stationed in India began to be discernible (Sramek 2011: 43-46). From the 1790s onward, some Company men sought to maintain a distance from their native subjects and rule India as a "domination of strangers" (Wilson 2011). Early indicators were the decision of Lord Cornwallis to dismiss all Indians from Company jobs in 1793, the establishment of Haileybury College in 1806, and the appointment of moral thinker Thomas Robert Malthus as a professor in the College (Sramek 2011: 10-12). British colonial officials and authors of several India tracts began to blame Hinduism for the alleged Indian venality, corruption, deficiency in moral instructions, and lack of regard for truth. They contrasted Hinduism with Protestantism and its stress on the individual's personal moral responsibility for his actions. From their writings it almost seemed as if colonialism was "India's fault." "Control and reform" became the two facets of British presence in India (Robb 2007: 14-15).

The official British policy of religious neutrality and fear of missions gradually gave way, as "common interest" in the transformation of Indian society became evident. The convergence of missionary and official opinion focused on "the increasingly explicit association of Christianity, commerce, and civilization." The Baptist missionary, William Carey, in his *An Enquiry into the Obligations of Christians, to Use Means for the Conversion of the Heathens*, written in 1792, drew attention to British mercantile expansion as showing the way to the fulfillment of Isaiah's prophecies, "that *navigation*, especially that which is *commercial*, shall be one great mean of carrying on the work of God."

The growing confidence and assertiveness of Britain's governing classes following victory over Napoleonic France and territorial successes in India resulted in a refurbished British national identity. Missionaries were vital contributors to the "Protestant worldview," which permitted many Englishmen to view themselves as a distinct and chosen people.

List of Illustrations

1. The Changu Narayana temple inscription, Nepal, AD 464.
2. The Eran Stone Pillar Inscription, Sagar district, Madhya Pradesh, AD 510.
3. Sati of Dekkabe, in the time of Rajendra Chola; Belaturu Inscription, Saka 979 (inscription on reverse).
4. Mahasati Sthal at Chittorgarh Fort, where widowed queens of Mewar committed Sati.
5. Sati stone, AD 1206, Kedareshwar temple, Belligavi, Karnataka.
6. Sati memorial stone, 13th century AD, Penukonda, Andhra Pradesh (Government Museum, Chennai).
7. Sati memorial stone, 14th century, Bhopal State Museum, Madhya Pradesh.
8. Hampi Satikal.
9. Mandi Barsela (Sati pillars), of the royal family, 17th–18th century AD.
10. Sati stone of Sodha Rajputs, Nagarparkar, Sindh, Pakistan.
11. Sati stone of Sodha Rajputs, Berani village, Nagarparkar, Sindh, Pakistan.

12. Shiva carrying Sati on his trident, AD 1800.
13. Sati ceremony, Thanjavur, AD 1800.
14. Hindu widow having purification bath in preparation for immolation, by Robert Melville Grindlay, who served with the East India Company from 1804–20.
15. 'Sacrifice of a Hindoo widow upon the funeral pile of her husband,' Johann Zoffany (1733–1810).
16. Sati painting by James Atkinson (1780–1852).
17. Sati by Nandlal Bose, 1943, Philadelphia Museum of Art.

SECTION A

1

The Backdrop

There appears to be an inverse relationship between the rarity of the phenomenon of sati and academic writings on the subject. While forty-odd cases of widow-immolation have been reported since independence, sati figures prominently in recent works on India. The issue has especially occupied feminist writers. It is interesting that in colonial times, when the practice was allegedly at its peak, interest in sati was largely confined to Evangelical-missionary groups, which wrote copiously on the matter. Barring a few exceptions, sati then elicited little scholarly attention. From 1829, the year that Regulation XVII outlawed the practice, till 1947 also, it is difficult to enumerate academic works wholly focused on the issue. Ananda K. Coomaraswamy's "Sati: a vindication of the Hindu woman," published in 1913 (*Sociological Review* 6: 117-35), was a comprehensive article, not a monograph.

Edward Thompson's *Suttee: A Historical and Philosophical Enquiry into the Hindu Rite of Widow Burning,* published in 1928, was a notable exception to the general trend. But Thompson

(1886–1946), an academic and missionary, wrote at a time of growing political agitation against the British and ended his work with the lament that the vast majority of Indians were unable "to see anything amiss in Hindu civilization or anything that needs to be done in India except political agitation." He was convinced that attention should be directed to other issues, of which sati was symptomatic. "Sati is gone," he wrote darkly, "but its background remains" (Thompson 1928: 143-44).

In contrast to the pre-independence era, the post-partition decades, chiefly the recent few, have seen a sizeable corpus of literature on sati. Several fundamental questions have been raised in most works on the issue. Was sati a religious obligation? Was it a wide-ranging phenomenon? Was it forced? What was the state of mind of a widow who had resolved to immolate herself?

The indigenous sources on sati include literary works like the *Dharmasastras*, the Epics and *Puranas*, dramatic compositions, and general literature. In addition there are epigraphical records and memorial stones. But, surpassing all these in their sheer abundance are the accounts of foreign travellers to India. There was scarce a visitor who did not feel obliged to refer to the rite in his narrative on the country.

WAS SATI A RELIGIOUS OBLIGATION?
RELIGIO-LEGAL AND LITERARY TEXTS

For a considerable period, the religio-legal texts contained no definitive reference to sati. A case was fraudulently built for Vedic sanction of the rite by the substitution of the last word of the funeral hymn (*Rig Veda* 10.18.7) from *agre* ('earlier,' 'first') to *agneh* (fire). The forgery was commonly attributed to Raghunandana, the sixteenth century *Smriti* writer from Varanasi; but noted scholar, P.V. Kane, dismissed the accusation as "not sustainable." Kane ascribed the error to a corrupt printed text or an innocent slip (Kane Vol. II Part I 1997: 634-35).[1]

The hymn actually directed the widow to sit facing her dead husband, after moistening her eyes with *ghee*, then to rise and resume her place in the world —

> Let these unwidowed dames with noble husbands adorn themselves with fragrant balm and unguent.

> Decked with fair jewels, tearless, free from sorrow, first let the dames go up to where he lieth (*Rig Veda* 10.18.7).

> Rise, and come unto the world of life, O woman: come, he is lifeless by whose side thou liest.

> Wifehood with this thy husband was thy portion, who took thy hand and wooed thee as a lover (*Rig Veda* 10.18.8).

In 1795, H.T. Colebrooke, then a young scholar, wrote his maiden paper, "On the Duties of a Faithful Hindu Widow," for the Asiatic Society (*Asiatic Researches* IV 1795: 205-15). He cited the hymn from the *Rig Veda* as sanctioning widow burning, which William Jones immediately contested (Canon 1993 I: lxx). Colebrooke translated the end of the hymn as "let them pass into fire, whose original element is water." A quarter of a century later, the Orientalist, H.H. Wilson pointed out that the hymn had been distorted (Wilson 1854: 201-14; Cassels 2010: 89). Wilson translated the verse as per the reading corroborated by Sayana, the authoritative medieval commentator on the *Vedas*, and demonstrated that it did not refer to widow burning (Rocher and Rocher 2012: 24-25).

The *Brahmana* literature and the *Grihyasutras,* as also the Buddhist texts, made no mention of sati. Megasthenes, the Greek ambassador to the court of Chandragupta Maurya, and Kautilya, in his *Arthasastra*, too did not allude to the custom.

The authors of the *Dharmasutras* and writers of the early *Smritis*, while detailing the duties of wives and widows, did not exalt sati. Manu did not prescribe the rite. The *Manu Smriti* (placed by G. Buhler between the second century BC and the second century AD), stated that women are to be regarded as *pujarha grhadiptayah*, "worthy to be worshiped and the lamp that lights up the household" (*The Laws of Manu* V, 156-62; 165-66). They were to receive the protection of the father in childhood, the husband after marriage, and the son on the death of the husband (*The Laws of Manu* V, 148). Manu declared, "A virtuous wife who after the death of her husband constantly remains chaste, reaches heaven, though she have no son, just like those chaste men" (*The Laws of Manu* V, 160).

Yajnavalkya viewed wives as gifts of the gods who should be respected and valued. He laid down exacting duties for widows, but not self-immolation. The *Yajnavalkya Smriti* (dated variously between the first and fourth century AD; Lingat 2004: 99-100) stated that a widow,

> Deprived of her husband, she should not reside apart from her father, mother, son or brother, from her mother-in-law or father-in-law, or from her old maternal uncles. Otherwise she becomes infamous (*Yajnavalkya Smriti* LXXXVI).

The *Mahabharata* contained some references to sati. Madri, the younger wife of King Pandu, immolated herself on his pyre despite attempts of the assembled sages to deter her. They told her that her resolve would endanger the welfare of her young sons and that a pious woman led a life of austerity after the death of her husband. The *Mausalaparvan* mentioned two instances of widow immolations. In the first, four wives of Vasudeva (Devaki, Bhadra, Rohini, and Madira) ascended the pyre with him. In the second, on news of Krishna's death reaching Hastinapur, five of his wives (Rukmimi, Gandhari, Saibya, Haimavati, and Jambavati) immolated themselves in the absence of his body. The others survived him, and some like Satyabhama retreated to the forest to perform penance (some scholars have regarded this passage of the *Mausalaparvan* as a later interpolation; Agrawal 2004: 216-18). As against these cases, there were innumerable instances of widows who lived after their husbands. The Epic clearly affirmed that the widows of the fallen heroes remained behind and offered them funeral oblations. In the *Ramayana,* none of the wives of King Dasratha or Ravana immolated themselves.

Some incidents of widow immolation were cited in the *Puranas.* Sati was "gradually struggling into existence" in the early Christian era. Some *Smriti* writers had begun to refer to it, but recommended an ascetic life for the widow.

The *Vishnusmriti* (composed around the seventh century AD in Kashmir and the first *Dharmasastric* evidence for sati; Olivelle 2010. P.V. Kane, G. Buhler, and J. Jolly placed it several centuries earlier; Lingat 2004: 25-26) did not consider immolation a religious duty. It stated that "a good wife, who perseveres in a chaste life after the death of her lord, will go to heaven like (perpetual) students, even though she has no son" (*The Institutes of Vishnu:* XXX.17).

The *Vyasa Smriti, Parasara Smriti,* and the *Brihaspati Smriti* extolled the sati, but Brihaspati also proclaimed the rights of widows (Lingat 2004: 129-30). Vatsyayana, Bhasa, Kalidasa, and Sudraka mentioned sati. The poet Bana (AD 625), in his *Kadambari,* condemned widow-immolation,

> This following another to death is most vain! It is a path followed by the ignorant! It is a mere freak of madness, a path of ignorance, an enterprise of recklessness, a sign of utter thoughtlessness, and a blunder of folly. If life leaves us not of itself, we must not resign it. For this leaving of life, if we examine it, is merely for our own interest, because we cannot bear our own cureless pain. To the dead man it brings no good whatever. For it is no means of bringing him back to life, or heaping up merit, or gaining heaven for him, or saving him from hell, or seeing him again, or being reunited with him (*Kadambari* 1896: 135-38).

Medhatithi (among the oldest and most famous commentator on the *Manusmriti* variously placed between the ninth and eleventh centuries AD) compared the practice to *syenayaga,* which a man performed by way of black magic to kill his enemy. Others with similar views included Virata, who positively prohibited the practice, and Devanabhatta, the twelfth century writer from South India, who maintained that "the Sati custom is only a very inferior variety of Dharma and is not to be recommended at all." The Tantric sects and the Shakti cults expressly forbade the rite. They insisted that even in sacrifices female animals should not be burnt (Sharma 1988: 16-17).

But from about AD 700, some writers had begun to commend immolation for widows. Angira advocated concremation, "... there is no other duty but falling into the funeral pyre when the husband dies." A widow who followed her husband into death "dwells in heaven for as many years as there are hairs on a human body, *crores* of years" (*Yajnavalkya Smriti* LXXXVI: 167). Harita, who wrote a work of law, the *Haritasmriti*, contended that a woman could purify her husband of the deadliest sins if she immolated herself (Lingat 2004: 129).

The *Mitaksara* (a legal commentary on the *Yajnavalkya Smriti* written by Vignanesvara, an ascetic in the reign of Vikramaditya VI of the Chalukya dynasty who ruled from AD 1076 to 1127), referring to Manu, Yajnavalkya, the *Gita* and other sacred writings, as well as to Angira, Hirata, and Vyasa among others, expressed its reservations about the practice; "The widow who is not desirous of eternal beatitude, but who wishes only for a perishable and small degree of future fruition, is authorized to follow her husband."

By the late medieval period, when Raghunandana's *Smriti* appeared, the practice seemed not uncommon (Lingat 2004: 119-20). Digests like the *Nirnayasindhu* and the *Dharmasindhu*, written after the seventeenth century, described the procedures of the rite in considerable detail. Prior to that, even the few late *Smritis* that recommended the practice contained no instructions on the rituals to be followed (Altekar 1978: 133). But resistance to the rite continued (Bose 2000: 26).

An eighteenth century guide on the religious duties of women, the *Stridharmapaddhati*, by an orthodox *pundit* Tryambaka, in Thanjavur in South India, anxious to defend Hindu culture from Islamic encroachments, Christian missionaries, and European traders, recommended sati as a way of salvation for women. When practised by a devoted wife, it asserted, great blessings were conferred on both the husband and wife (Leslie 1989: 291-304). But despite his evident preference for sati, Tryambaka stated that the option of leading the life of a widow was open to a woman whose husband had died (Leslie 1993: 53-55). Around the same time, the author of the *Mahanirvanatantra* condemned the custom,

> Every woman, O Goddess, is your very form, your body concealed within the universe, and so, if in her delusion a woman should mount her husband's funeral pyre, she would go to hell (Bose 2000: 27).

WAS SATI WIDESPREAD?
LITERARY AND EPIGRAPHIC EVIDENCE

The earliest historical account of sati available is by Diodorus of Sicily (second half of the first century BC). Diodorus based his narrative on a text by Hieronymus of Cardia, who was probably an eyewitness to the event. Another foreign reference to sati is by Strabo, the Greek geographer and historian (b. 63 BC). On the basis of an account of Aristoboulos, Strabo stated that the Greeks under Alexander found the custom prevalent among the Katheae in the Punjab (*Hobson-Jobson* 1968: 879; Section B: 225-27). This indicated the antiquity of the rite and its existence prior to this period. Other writers to mention the rite include Propertius (first half of the first century BC) and St. Jerome (AD 340-420).

An inscription on a pot unearthed in a village in the Guntur region, in Brahmi characters of about the third century AD, referred to a case of *sahamarana*, "dying with." It read "*Ayamani/ Pustika.*" The pot probably preserved the relics of the husband,

Ayamani, and his wife, Pustika, who immolated herself on his pyre (Chakraborti 1974: 34-35).

The Gupta Inscriptions, edited by the British epigraphist, J.F. Fleet (1847–1917) in 1888, are among the early epigraphic records to mention sati. Fleet listed the Eran Stone Pillar Inscription in Sagar district, Madhya Pradesh, dated 191 of the Gupta era (AD 510), which was discovered by Alexander Cunningham in 1874–1875. The inscription is on a pillar that was later converted into a Shivalinga. It recorded that in the company of a powerful king, Bhanugupta, a chieftain, Goparaja, fought a battle with the Maitras, in which he was killed. The inscription commemorated the self-immolation of his widow,

> (There is) the glorious Bhanugupta, the bravest man on the earth, a mighty king, equal to Partha, exceedingly heroic; and, along with him, Goparaja followed ... (his) friends (and came here). (And) having fought a very famous battle, he (who was but little short of being equal to) the celestial (king Indra), (died and) went to heaven; and his devoted, attached, beloved, and beauteous wife, in close companionship, accompanied (him) onto the funeral pyre (Fleet *Corpus Inscriptionum Indicarum* Vol. III 1888: 92-93; D.R. Bhandarkar *Corpus Inscriptionum Indicarum* Vol. III 1981: 352-54).

The inscription of King Manadeva in the Changu Narayana temple, north-west of the Kathmandu valley, dated AD 464, is the earliest reference to sati in Nepal. Queen Rajyavati, widow of Dharmadeva, asked her son, Manadeva, to assume the reins of government so that she could follow her husband. She did not, however, immolate herself, as was evident from the last line of verse 11, "Observing the vows of sati, that is, with her husband in her heart, she lived very much like Arundhati" (Acharya 1996).

In AD 606, Queen Yasomati, the mother of Harsha and wife of King Prabhakaravardhana of Thanesar, predeceased her sick husband by consigning herself to the flames when it became apparent that he had little chance of survival. As her son tried to dissuade her, she said,

> I am the lady of a great house ... one whose virtue is her dower. Have you forgotten that I am the lioness mate of a great spirit, who like a lion has his delight in hundred battles? I cannot endure, like the widowed Rati, to make unavailing lamentations for a burnt husband. Not in the body, dear son, but in glory of loyal widows I abide on earth (*Harsacarita* 1897 V: 186-87).

Though Harsha could not deter his mother, he did succeed in persuading his sister, Rajyasri, the widowed queen of King Grahavarman of the Maukhara family, from immolating herself. Rajyasri lived and continued to pursue her interest in Buddhism and possibly influenced her brother's religious views (Rangachari 2009: 494). The wives of the Gahadawala king, Madanpala, also did not immolate themselves and actively participated in the administration (Rangachari 2009: 364).

The Belaturu Inscription of Saka 979, of the time of Rajendra Chola, referred to the immolation of a Sudra woman, Dekabbe, whose husband had been killed in battle against a Ganga king. Dekabbe immolated herself despite the strong opposition of her parents,

> When (her) father, mother and near relatives came, said: 'Daughter, do not die!; desist!,' and all embraced (her) feet, the blameless Dekabbe became angry... all united said: 'Do not (die)!; desist!;' (but) Dekabbe said: 'Speak not. But go!'; I will not desist;' and respectfully giving land, gold (-embroidered) clothes, cows and money as a present, she piously put the palms of (her) hands together (in obeisance) to the god of gods, entered the blazing flames... (*Epigraphia Indica* Vol. 6: 218-19).

Dekabbe's father, Raviga, erected the stone monument in her honour. This is perhaps the first inscription to be discovered regarding the self-immolation of a Sudra wife after the death of her husband (*Epigraphia Indica* Vol. 6: 213-19).

Up to AD 1000, satis were rare in the Deccan and an exception in the extreme south.[2] The utterances of the queen of Bhuta Pandya confirms that the norm was to dissuade widows from immolating themselves; "the practice was by no means encouraged, much less enforced." The "heroism and devotion" of the sati were commended, but a life of religious devotion in widowhood advocated (Sastri 1975: 91-92).

Among the Pallava, Chola, and Pandya ruling families no case was recorded till AD 900. The queens of Parantaka I (AD 907–955), Parantaka II (957–973), Rajendra I (1012–1044), and Kulotunga III committed sati. In the reign of Parantaka I, Gangamadeviyar, wife of the Kodumbalur feudatory Vira Chola Ilangovelar, immolated herself. She gifted a lamp to a temple before ascending the pyre (Sastri 1975: 553).

On the death of Sundara Chola (Parantaka II), his queen, Vanavan Mahadevi, committed *sahagamana*. Her daughter, Kundavai, installed an image of her mother in the Tanjore temple and endowed it with jewels to provide for its worship (Chandrababu and Thilagavathi 2009: 135-36). Her son, Rajaraja I (985–1016), recorded her immolation in the Thiruk-koyilur inscription. He also honoured her with a shrine in the Brihadeshvara Temple (Storm 2013: 132). Vanavan Mahadevi's action, though applauded, was "not often imitated" (Sastri 1975: 553). Sati was rare among the common people (Chandrababu and Thilagavathi 2009: 135; Sastri 1966: 315).

During the period AD 700–1100, the practice became more frequent in northern India and among the royal families of Kashmir. Kalhana in his *Rajatarangini,* written in AD 1148–49, referred to cases from the tenth to twelfth centuries.

Clusters of memorial stones found in various places reveal that from the end of the first millennium AD, at least in some regions, immolation was no longer confined to the upper castes. Fitzedward Hall, in the mid-eighteenth century, counted many such stones in a one-mile radius near the Narmada River in Central India, places near rivers being perceived as particularly auspicious for such rites (Fisch 2005: 228). Some stones found between the Narmada and Tapti dated to the thirteenth-fourteenth centuries, commemorated Bhil chiefs and their satis (Setter and Sontheimer 1982: 95).

Sati appeared originally to have been a Kshatriya custom; a heroic female complement to the warrior's death in battle. The *Brihaddaivata*, while recognizing the validity of the custom among Kshatriyas, doubted whether it could be permissible for other castes. The *Padmapurana* explicitly prohibited it for Brahmins, and stated that anyone assisting a Brahmin widow to the pyre would be guilty of the unpardonable sin of *brahmahatya* (Altekar 1978: 128). The discovery of sati memorial stones in the same localities as hero stones commemorating the dead in battlefield confirms that the rite was at first limited to martial communities (Setter and Sontheimer 1982: 185-87; Phadke 1996: 310). The rugged frontier zones of the west and northwest (in present day Karnataka, Maharashtra, Gujarat and Rajasthan), for centuries arenas of contests of warlike groups, contain a number of sati stones and shrines (Courtright 1994: 35).

From kings the practice spread among Brahmins. Around AD 1000, digest writers and commentators began to explain away the earlier ban on the practice by Brahmin widows (Leslie 1993: 57-58). The earlier stipulation, they said, was that Brahmin widows should not take the step under a temporary sense of overwhelming grief but after mature deliberation. Further, they stated, the prohibition was to immolation by a Brahmin widow on a pyre *different* from that of her husband. She was actually to burn with him on the same pyre (Kane Vol. II Part 1 1997: 627; 630).

The practice of widow immolation seemed to have gained currency in the medieval era. A distortion of the rite appeared to have taken place in warlike situations. Some scholars have linked sati to *jauhar*, the collective self-immolation by women in times of hostilities (Oldenburg 1994 163-166). It became particularly associated with Rajput ruling families (Horstmann 2000: 80). Lt. Col. James Tod wrote of *jauhar* at Jaisalmer in AD 1295 and at Chittor in AD 1533; in the first instance amidst bloody war with the Sultanate ruler Alauddin Khalji and in the second during resistance to Mughal troops led by Emperor Akbar (Tod I 2010: 249-50; II: 200-01).

The increasing incidence of sati has been attributed to contact with Muslim culture. Hindus subjugated and displaced by Muslim invaders, it is argued, displayed "an exaggeration of their traditional concern for female chastity" and a loss of their "cultural prestige led high-caste Hindus to kill girl babies and young widows." When Clive arrived in Bengal, he was viewed as a saviour from tyranny and "even hymned in some local ballads as Kalki," the tenth incarnation of Vishnu (Gupta and Gombrich 1984: 255-56).

RAJASTHAN

Though sati was gradually gaining adherents among royal families, few epigraphic records from North India refer to it. If such incidents had occurred, court panegyrists would certainly have mentioned them in their compositions. In fact, there is little epigraphic evidence even from Rajputana, which later became a stronghold of the practice. The earliest available record, the Dholpur inscription, dates to AD 842. It commemorates the immolation of Kanahulla, wife of Candamahasena. The next epigraphic evidence, the Ghatiyala inscription, dates to AD 890. It honours Samvaladevi, wife of Ranuka, who became a sati (Sharma 1935: 289-90). No other epigraphic evidence from Rajputana is available before AD 1000 (Altekar 1978: 129-30).

But the custom became established among Rajput ruling families of North India (Noble and Sankhyan I 2001: 349-58; Harlan 1994: 79-84; Major 2011: 32-35; Setter and Sontheimer

1982: 148). Rajput women seemed to require little urging to become satis (Harlan 1992). Those who were not with child, or not required to officiate as regents of their young offspring, ascended the pyre. The *Cyclopedia of India* noted, "Rajput women of rank seem to have been the most willing to accompany their husbands' remains to the funeral pile" (Thompson 1928: 53). Sir Lepel Griffin made a similar observation, "The proud Rajput women used to consider the disagreeable duty of burning themselves with their husbands a privilege attaching to their blue blood" (Griffin 1957: 65). Though no statistics for the period 1300–1800 are available, the incidence of sati appeared to have been as high as ten per cent among the warrior families of Rajasthan (Altekar 1978: 138).

In Marwar, from AD 1562 to 1843, that is, a period of 281 years, 47 queens, 101 concubines, 74 female slaves and others, and 5 men immolated themselves on the death of rulers, while 48 queens survived them (Datta 1988: 256).

In local lore, as many as eighty-four women are said to have ascended the pyre when Raja Budh Singh of Bundi was drowned. But, with time, the practice had begun to decline even in the princely states. James Tod, who spent many of his years in India in the courts of the ruling houses of Rajputana, highlighted the change,

> Budh Singh ... was one of the most intrepid generals of Aurangzeb; the period elapsed is about one hundred and twenty years. Mark the difference! When his descendant, my valued friend the Rao Raja Bishan Singh, died in 1821, his last commands were that none should give such a proof of their affection. He made me guardian of his infant heir. In a few days I was at Bundi, and his commands were religiously obeyed (Tod II 2010: 837-38).

CENTRAL AND SOUTH INDIA

In Mahakosala, sati stones near Sagar revealed that the rite was practiced by the weaver, barber, and mason groups between AD 1500 and 1800. The Karnataka inscriptions for the period AD 1000–1400, published in the *Epigraphia Carnatica,* confirmed eleven instances of sati. For the years AD 1400–1600, the number was forty-one, mostly from among the Nayakas and Gaudas, the fighting communities of South India. There were two Jains in the list, and a few Brahmins (Altekar 1978: 130-31).

THE MARATHA KINGDOMS

The earliest known sati stone inscription from the Maharashtra region dates to the sixth century AD. It was found at Sanski, a village in Kolhapur district (Kulkarni 1996: 178). Very few Maratha women of high rank ascended the pyres of their husbands. Jijabai, mother of Shivaji, changed her resolve to immolate herself on the censure of her son and pressure from other people. Only one wife of Shivaji (d. 1680) became a sati. One wife of his son, Rajaram (d. 1700), also immolated herself. The wife of Shivaji's grandson, Shahu (d. 1749), the childless and ambitious Sakwar Bai, felt compelled to immolate herself due to altered political equations (Sinha 1954: 257-60; Kulkarni 1996: 175).

Few cases of sati are recorded among Maratha ruling families at Satara, Nagpur, Gwalior, Indore, and Baroda. Among members of the Peshwa family, only Ramabai, widow of Madhavarao I, became a sati, in 1772, at the young age of twenty-six (Sardesai II 1958: 559). The custom did not become popular among the Marathas, who, in fact, tried to check it by individual persuasion. When the father-in-law of Peshwa Narayanrao died, his wife, who desired to immolate herself, was dissuaded by her relatives. Ahalya Bai Holkar, epitome of Hindu culture, did not become a sati and, in 1792, entreated her widowed daughter, Muktabai, in vain, not to immolate herself (Martin 1983a: 390; Section B: 305-06).

Shyamaldas Kaviraj, in his *Virvinod,* stated only one, or, at most, two per cent of all widows committed sati. He could not help but admire the women, "for be it as it may, the courage of women, who burn themselves out of love, has to be ranked even higher than that (required) at the time of battle" (Horstmann 2000: 91-92).

Bengal, which became the nucleus of the debate on sati in British times, witnessed few incidents in the early medieval era. No sati inscriptions from that period have so far been discovered. Kulluka Bhatta, the celebrated Brahmin commentator of the *Manu Samhita*, did not mention the practice. Jimutavahana, a Brahmin from Radha and a near contemporary of Vignanesvara, in his *Dayabhaga*, was also silent on the matter saying "a widow benefits her husband by the preservation of her person" (Jimutavahana's *Dayabhaga* 2002).

Jimutavahana stipulated that on the death of the father, the sons could not divide the parental property without the consent of the mother. The mother had to be given an equal share, provided no separate property had been allotted to her. In that case, she was entitled to half the prescribed allocation. Stepmothers with no male issue were also granted an equal portion. Jimutavahana asserted the right of the wife to her husband's property if he died without a male issue. The widow was, however, instructed not to squander the wealth inherited by indulging in luxuries (Jimutavahana's *Dayabhaga* 2002: 99, 198). Jimutavahana specified that in the matter of the widow's rights he followed a predecessor, Jitendriya (none of whose works have survived).

The *Brhaddharmapurana* (composed between the twelfth and fourteenth centuries), however, extolled sati. In the sixteenth century, the *Smriti* writer, Raghunandana, recommended it to every widow. Medieval Bengali literature contained accounts of sati [e.g. the *Manikchandra Rajar Gan* (twelfth century), the *Manasamangal* and the *Chandimangal* (sixteenth century), the *Dharmamangal* and the *Anandamangal* (eighteenth century), and the *Vidyasundar* (late eighteenth century)] (Ahmad 1968: 149-50).

WAS SATI FORCED?

This is a difficult question to answer. There could have been instances of unwilling immolations (Weinberger-Thomas 2000: 202-06). Kalhana recorded the cases of two queens of Kashmir who had bribed their ministers to induce them to come to the cremation ground to dissuade them from their seemingly voluntary decision to join their husbands on the pyre. Whereas Queen Didda was saved by this stratagem, in the case of the widow of King Uccala, Queen Jayamati, the wily minister delayed his arrival and the lady had to allow herself to be immolated. King Uccala's other Queen, Bijjala, was, however, apparently eager to ascend the pyre (*Rajatarangini* VI, 195; VIII, 363-67). Kalhana also cited the case of Utkarsa, whose concubine, Sahaja, burnt herself on his death, while Kalasa's concubine preferred to take another lover. In Book VIII, Kalhana referred to the performance of sati by women belonging to the non-royal strata of society.[3]

The Frenchman, Francois Bernier (who visited India from 1656 to 1668), referred to unwilling immolations (Section B: 267-70) but also witnessed incidents where he was struck by the "fortitude" displayed by the women. One case he saw, along with several English and Dutch men and the celebrated traveller Chardin, was as he was leaving Surat for Persia.

He observed, "the brutish boldness (and) ferocious gaiety depicted on this woman's countenance ... her undaunted step ... her easy air, free from dejection; of her lofty carriage ..." (Bernier 1994: 309-15).

Job Charnock, the founder of Calcutta, is believed to have rescued a widow from the funeral pyre and subsequently married her[4] (Hamilton II 1744: 8-9; Section B: 277). [Among other Europeans who contemplated freeing a sati were La De

Grandpre, an officer of the French Army who visited India in 1789 (Section B: 297-300) and Thomas Twining of the East India Company in 1792 (Section B: 307-12). Mariana Starke's *The Widow of Malabar* performed in Covent Garden in 1791, also ended with the rescue of an unwilling sati by a European].[5]

The romantic image of a grateful sati notwithstanding, not every widow wanted to be saved by a European. There were suggestions of cases where "the sati did not consider herself a damsel in distress" and showed aversion to intervention that "robbed her not only of the merit of the sacrifice, but her caste and honour" (Major 2006: 99; Elphinstone 1966: 187-89).

The number of widows who immolated themselves does not ever appear to have been large. Considerable epigraphic and other evidence indicates that relatives tried to discourage widows from performing the rite (Kane Vol. II Part I 1997: 635). In several accounts, Brahmins appeared in the role of "persons dissuading the widow from committing sati" (Sharma 1988: 25).

Tamil lyrics referred to an earthly bride "whom the Brahmans seek to dissuade from the sacrifice," but she answered that since her lord was dead, the cool waters of the lotus pool and the flames of the funeral pyre were alike to her. Muhammad Riza Nau'i wrote a poem in the reign of Emperor Akbar, on a Hindu girl whose betrothed was killed on the day of the marriage, and who wished to be burnt on his pyre. When informed, Akbar called the girl and offered wealth and protection, but she declined his offer and the counsel of Brahmans. She would speak or hear of nothing but Fire. Akbar reluctantly gave his consent to the immolation, but sent his son along who continued to discourage the girl. From amidst the flames she replied, "Do not annoy, do not annoy, do not annoy" (Coomaraswamy 1957: 127-29).

Foreign accounts of sati suggest that opinion on this issue underwent a significant change over time. The earlier sentiments of approbation and awe, which mostly stressed the voluntary nature of the rite, were replaced with condemnation and demands for intervention and abolition of the custom. In most missionary accounts, particularly those of the Baptists in the eighteenth-nineteenth centuries, "hungry Brahmins" were depicted as perpetrators of the rite. This was in contrast to several earlier accounts, in which Brahmins had pleaded against immolation (Sharma 1988: 8, 25).

STATE OF MIND OF THE WIDOW

Over the centuries, several foreign observers of immolation noted the conviction of the widows in afterlife. Bernier described an incident when travelling from Ahmedabad to Agra,

> I saw the fire catch the woman's garments ... it was said that she pronounced with emphasis the words five, two, to signify that this being the fifth time she had burned herself with the same husband, there were wanted only two more similar sacrifices to render her perfect, according to the doctrine of the transmigration of souls: as if a certain reminiscence, or prophetic spirit, had been imparted to her at that moment of her dissolution (Bernier 1994: 309-15).

In 1757, Abbe de Guyon observed, "This practice is founded on their notions of the metempsychosis, which passes among them as an undoubted truth ..." (de Guyon 1757: 57-58; Section B: 280).

The missionary journal, *Friend of India,* in September 1824, reported a case that had occurred in Cuttack the previous month. The widow claimed she had,

> been a Suttee in *three former births*, and must be so *four times more*, and then she should attain endless felicity ... From *joog* to *joog* (age to age), in this manner, with the same husband, she was to be born and die (Peggs 1984: 4; Section B: 367-70).

Dr. Richard Hartley, a surgeon in the Bombay Medical Service and later Inspector General for Hospitals in the Bombay Presidency, saw a sati in Baroda on 29th November 1825. He recorded,

> Her belief in the Pythagorean doctrine of transmigration was firm and fixed ... She declared that ...her soul ...had been thrice before on the earth; it had thrice been liberated from the earth by similar sacrifices: the present was her fourth cremation; and her destiny reserved for her a fifth ... (Courtright 1994: 44-46).

Several other observers confirmed that before the flames engulfed her body, the widow pronounced two numbers, whose sum total was always seven. The first denoted the amount of times she had immolated herself in previous births with the body of the same man (soul), the second the number remaining before she attained deliverance. The figure seven has been interpreted as a reference to the seven circumambulations of the sacrificial fire that unites the bride and groom in the wedding ceremony (Weinberger-Thomas 2000: 210). Sati, according to some scholars, reflected an exceptional approach to the matrimonial relationship of husband and wife. Marriage in the Hindu tradition was regarded a sacrament rather than a contract.[6]

SATI IN THE INDIAN TRADITION

Sati derived from the Sanskrit word *sat*, 'goodness' or 'virtue.' The original Sati, the virtuous wife of Lord Shiva, died in protest at the insult of her husband by her father, Daksha (Jocobsen 2011: 165-66).[7] Sati then denoted the chaste, faithful wife, and not the rite of widow-burning. The term carried with it associations of "great virtue, personal strength and religious autonomy" (Leslie 1993: 47-48). Among women who attained this status without immolating themselves were Sati Savitri, Sati Sita, and Sati Anusuya.

Sati was "an ideal worthy of worship" (Leslie 1993: 47-48), and not a religious obligation. Very few women felt disposed to attain that ideal. Indeed, because sati was of rare occurrence, those who practiced it were deemed extraordinary and aroused the deep reverence of traditional society. Sati stones or memorials (*sati-kal, masti-kal*) were erected in their honour. Such memorials depicted the raised right arm of the woman bent at the elbow, the palm facing forward in *abhaya-mudra* (blessing her family and friends before entering the pyre) and bangles adorning the wrist (signifying her married status). The deification was not individualized; the woman was not normally worshipped in her own name, but as part of the generalized *sati* goddess (Verghese 2000: 115).

The Sanskrit language had no specific term for the practice of widow immolation. Among the expressions used were "going with" (*sahagamana*), "dying with" (*sahamarana*), "dying after" (*anumarana*). In the late eighteenth or early nineteenth century, European travellers termed the rite of self-immolation 'widow burning,' which they called sati.[8] The term thenceforth began to be used for "both the practice and the practitioner" (Major 2012: 58).

END-NOTES

1. It has been pointed out that another Vedic text, the *Atharva Veda* (XVIII.3.1), indicated that the act of the widow lying beside her departed husband as a duty was already archaic by Rig Vedic times (Sharma 1988: 34-38).

2. Sati was referred to as *tippaidal* ('falling into flames') in South India. Tamil *Purananuru* poetry mentions sati as do the *Tolkappiyam*, the *Cilapattikaram,* and the *Manimekalai* (Storm 2013: 132). But Pallava, Chola, and Pandya inscriptions do not refer to sati before AD 900.

3. In some cases, the demise of a woman led to the death of several men. Suryamati's male attendants followed her on the pyre, as did Meghamanjari's cook, Teja (*Rajatarangini* VII: 481, VIII: 1224-25; Rangachari 2009: 160-61).

When Lachchala Devi, wife of the Calukya king, Tribhuvanamalla Vira Somesvara, died in AD 1189, a senior officer of the king gave his own head, so that he could accompany the queen (Aiyangar 1906: 129-31).

4. Alexander Hamilton, a free-trader who toured the East Indies from 1688 to 1723, described the incident (Hamilton II 1744: 8-9). Three children were born from this union. The eldest daughter married Charles Eyre, who was to succeeded Charnock as Governor of Bengal and head agent of the East India Company in the region. As the origin narrative of the founding of Calcutta, Job Charnock's story implied that British expansion was linked with "the rescue of local women and interracial intimacy." It foretold a nineteenth century construction of colonial officials as heroes saving Indian women from sati and other reprehensible local customs (Ghosh 2008: 246-47).

5. There are some accounts of the widow reaching out to the white man watching her; among them by William Hodges, Mandelso, and Thomas Bowery. Major Edward Moor, a soldier-scholar who served in the campaign against Tipu Sultan and was a founding member of the Bombay Branch of the Asiatic Society, wrote of a sati he witnessed while in Poona. He noted the widow was "a young and interesting woman, about twenty-five years of age." She beckoned him and proceeded to present him something. "She ... held her hand over mine, and dropped a pomegranate, which I received in silence, and reverently retired. I was sorry that it was not something of an unperishable nature, that I might have preserved it: some ornament, for instance" (Moor 1968: 319).

6. Ananda Coomaraswamy described sati as the "last proof of the perfect unity of body and soul" (Coomaraswamy 1957: 126).

7. The furious Shiva wandered the earth in a mad dance with Sati's dead body. The places where parts of her body fell became *Shakti Pithas*, holy seats of the mother goddess. Alf Hiltebeitel has argued that the three myths about goddesses who personified sati (Sandhya, Sati, and Bela, the folkloric heroine of the oral epic, *Alha*) were about daughters

in conflict with their fathers. The Goddess Sati, he says, was not mentioned in the *Mahabharata*. She was known to Kalidasa in the fourth or fifth century AD and also in some early *Puranas*. Her full story was most powerfully told only in medieval times, in the *Shiva Purana*. In the slightly later *Devibhagavata* and *Kalika Puranas*, her dismembered pieces were re-embodied "into India itself as an inviolable motherland." Hiltebeitel says these stories could be regarded as expressions of "the Hindu revivalist mix that responds to Muslim dominance" (Hiltebeitel 2011: 433-62).

8. Besides India, widow immolation was also practiced in several other cultures (Davies 1981: 103-07; Fisch 2005 Part I: Following into death outside India).

2

Sati as Described in
Foreign Accounts

316 BC–AD 1499

The earliest historical account of sati available, by Diodorus of Sicily, described an incident that occurred in 316 BC, after the death of Alexander the Great (323 BC). In a battle among his generals, at Gabiene in Asia, Antigonus triumphed over Eumenes, who had an Indian contingent among his troops. The commander of this contingent, Ceteus (Shashi Gupt?) was killed in the conflict. The assembled troops looked on in amazement as his two widows argued among themselves over who had the right to immolate with the body. Diodorus wrote of the younger widow, who ascended the pyre,

> to the great admiration of the people, who ran together to se the spectacle, she made her exit from life in heroic style ... (she) scorned to demean herself by uttering shrieks, even when the flames were raging around her — a sight which affected the onlookers variously. Some were filled with pity, others were profuse in their praises, while there were not wanting Greeks who condemned the institution as

barbarous and inhuman (Majumdar 1960: 240-41; Section B: 225-27).

From then, there was a long lull in foreign accounts of sati, which began to reappear only in the mid-ninth century AD. The Arabs, who now controlled the principal maritime trade routes, mentioned the rite. The *Akhbar al –Sin wa'l – Hind*, compiled in AD 851, referred to sati in Ceylon, "Sometimes when a king is cremated, his wife enters the fire and burns herself along with him, but if they do not wish, they do not do so" (Ahmad 1989: 53; Section B: 227).

Alberuni, writing in the early decades of the eleventh century, indicated that the custom was known in his time. He said that on the death of a husband, the wife could either choose to remain a widow as long as she lived or immolate herself. Wives of kings, however, "they are in the habit of burning ...to prevent any of them by chance committing something unworthy of the illustrious husband." An exception was made for women of advanced years and those who had children; "for the son is the responsible protector of his mother" (Sachau II 1989: 155; Section B: 228). Alberuni appeared not to have witnessed any case of widow immolation during his years in India.

The first new European account of India in centuries was by the Venetian traveller, Marco Polo, who visited the country on his return trip from China. The decline of the Roman Empire and the subsequent Muslim control of the seas had severed Europe's links with India. During this period a mythical image of India as "a land of miracles and monsters, of gold and heroism" had been implanted in the European mind (Metcalf 1995: 4). For some India "was the location of paradise, a living Garden of Eden, for others the abode of demons and perhaps of Lucifer himself" (Major 2006: 19).[1] Marco Polo's testimony could not dislodge the amazing image of India ingrained in the Western mind. Marco Polo made a brief factual reference to sati in Malabar,

... his wife, from motives of pious regard for her husband, throws herself upon the pile, and is consumed with him. Women who display this resolution are much applauded by the community, as, on the other hand, those who shrink from it are despised and reviled (Polo 1961: 339-40; Section B: 228).

Friar Odoric of Pordenone, in the early fourteenth century, also broadly stated that when a man died, they burnt his wife with him, "saying that she ought to go and keep her husband company in the other world. But if the women have sons by her husband she may abide with them, and she will" (Yule and Cordier II 1913: 138-40; Section B: 228).

Writing around the same time, the French Dominican monk, Friar Jordanus, confined himself to stating that on the death of a nobleman, or any person of substance, the wives, "for the sake of worldly glory, and for the love of their husbands, and for eternal life, burn along with them ...those who do this have the higher repute for virtue and perfection among the rest" (Sastri 1972: 203; Section B: 229).

The next definite eyewitness account of sati after Diodorus appears to have been by the Moroccan traveller, Ibn Battuta, who traversed the region between AD 1333 and 1347 (the first indisputable case of widow burning after Diodorus occurred in AD 510, in Eran, Sagar district). Ibn Battuta witnessed the self-immolation of three women near Dhar, Madhya Pradesh, whose husbands had died fighting the Sumras of Sind. He noted the fearlessness of the women, one of whom asked the attendants with a smile, "Do you frighten me with the fire? I know that it is a fire, so let me alone." Thereupon, he wrote, "she joined her hands above her head in salutation to the fire and cast herself into it." Ibn Battuta recorded that the rite was not obligatory (Gibb 1999: 191-93; Section B: 229-31).

There were some accounts of sati from Central and South India in the fifteenth century. The Venetian merchant, Nicolo Conti, was the first foreigner to visit Vijayanagar and write an account of it. He stated that two or three thousand women were selected as wives of the king "on condition that at his death they should voluntarily burn themselves with him," which they deemed an honour (Major 1992: 6; 24; Section B: 231-32). There is no epigraphic or literary evidence to corroborate that such large scale immolation actually took place.

The Genoese merchant, Hieronimo Di Santo Stefano, writing towards the close of the fifteenth century, generally noted that in the Coromandel "when a man dies and they prepare to burn him, one of his wives burns herself alive with him; and this is their constant habit" (Major 1992: 5-6; Section B: 232).

AD 1500–1699

The sixteenth and seventeenth century accounts of sati were more varied – alternating from admiration to condemnation. Among the earliest were those by the Venetian, Ludovico di Varthema, and Tome Pires, the first European to study Indian medicine. Both described ceremonies associated with sati (Varthema 1997: 77-78; Pires 2005: 59; Section B: 234-35). Varthema portrayed the priests present at immolations as "men clothed like devils, who carry fire in their mouths."

Duarte Barbosa, who arrived in India in 1501 with the Portuguese fleet of Pedro Cabral and remained in the Indian Ocean region for sixteen years, gave a detailed description of the rite. He wrote that before consigning herself to the flames the widow,

> ...tells the men who are with her on the scaffold to consider what they owe to their wives who, being free to act, yet burn themselves alive for the love of them, and the women she tells to see how much they owe to their husbands, to such a degree as to go with them even to death (Filliozat 2001: 307-11; Section B: 235-37).

Barbosa's report of widow immolation in the Vijayanagar kingdom was replete with generalizations. He stated that when a king died, four to five hundred women burnt with him. His colorful description of sati was included in the section of his travelogue describing "customs of the kingdom of Narasinga and of the inhabitants of the country," and appeared to be based on gossip and hearsay. Barbosa nowhere claimed to have himself been present at any immolation (Verghese 2000: 119).

The Portuguese horse trader, Fernao Nuniz's description of the rite in Vijayanagar (AD 1535) was again formulaic. He stated, "When a captain dies, however many wives he has they all burn themselves, and when the King dies they do the same." He added that the widow "casts herself into the fire with such courage that it is a thing of wonder..." (Filliozat 2001: 243-45; Section B: 238-40). Nuniz wrote in "a very generalized manner," and did not describe any incident he had observed (Verghese 2000: 120).

The number of memorial stones recovered at Vijayanagar indicates that widow immolation was not as widespread as the foreign accounts implied. The rite must have appeared "so dramatic and strange" that it was "occasionally exaggerated" in the writings of the visitors (Storm 2013: 134).

Anila Verghese's survey of the capital city of Vijayanagar reveals that less than a hundred memorial stones were raised as a tribute to women who became satis. The erection of memorial stones attests that the satis were "highly honoured and revered." Most memorial stones depicted one wife immolating with one man. Some showed two or more women, of whom only one was a sati. Sati appeared to have been performed voluntarily and not all wives followed the husband to the pyre. The highest number of women represented as satis on a memorial stone was four, contradicting foreign reports of hundreds of wives immolating with the dead husband (Verghese 2000: 123-38). The foreign narratives on sati in Vijayanagar appear "highly exaggerated" (Verghese 2000: 121-22).

Many royal ladies did not immolate themselves. The two principal queens (Tirumaladevi and Cinnadevi) of the Vijayanagar king, Krishnadevaraya, lived till long after him. Varada Devi, the widow of his successor Acyutaraya, as Queen Mother engaged in power politics to safeguard the Empire for her son (Venkataramanayya 1986: 77, 90).

Caesaro Federici, a trader from Venice who arrived in Vijayanagar two years after the battle of Talikota and stayed at a house en route to the cremation ground, claimed to have seen instances of widow-immolation (Filliozat 2001: 321-24; Section B: 240-42). Significantly, three other visitors to the city, the Persian envoy Abdur Razzak (1443), the Italian traveler Varthema (1505), and the Portuguese Domingo Paes (1520–21), made no reference to sati in their accounts of Vijayanagar.

As in the case of Vijayanagar, amazing figures of widow immolation were cited for the kingdom of Madurai. They ranged from three to four hundred (Dellon), to eleven thousand (Vincenzo), to three hundred (Baldaeus) (Fisch 2005: 231). The Jesuit missionary, Teixeira, claimed that four hundred wives of the Nayaka of Madurai burnt themselves on his death in 1611 (*Hobson-Jobson* 1968: 881; Section B: 247). As there are few literal descriptions of the funerals of rulers, the possibility of the accounts being based on gossip seems strong.

Sati had by then become one of the 'wonders' that had to be included in any account of India. The emergent genre of travel writing that gained popularity in Europe with the advent of print culture, the increase in literacy, and colonial expansion all created a demand for such works. Plagiarism was common; travellers freely copied the writings of others. This makes it difficult to assess the actual extent of the practice of sati and the regional variations, if any. The interest of the home audience as well as the voyeurism of the age in which executions were a form of public entertainment in Europe, made it almost mandatory for travellers to incorporate an account of sati in their works, even if second-hand or fabricated

(Major 2006: 27). The number of cases actually observed appears not to have been large.

Instances of sati continued to evoke awe among foreign viewers. The Jesuit missionary, Roberto de Nobili, who saw an incident on the death of the Nayaka of Madurai, Muttu Krishnappa, in December 1606, was struck by the courage of the women who demonstrated their fidelity in such a valiant manner. Theirs might be a mistaken ideal, he said, but their courageous striving after it was, nonetheless, magnificent. Should he ever succeed in inspiring them with the Christian ideal, they would show themselves, if the test came, heroic martyrs (Cronin 1959: 53-55; Zupanov 2001: 224; Section B: 243-44).

William Hawkins (1608–1613), captain of the first vessel to display the English flag on the coast of India, stated that he had seen many widows brought before the King, who tried to discourage them with promises of gifts but, "in my time no perswasion could prevaile, but burne they would. The King, seeing that all would not serve, giveth his leave for her to be carried to the fire ..." (Foster 1999: 119; Section B: 244-45).

Nicholas Withington (1612–1616), of the East India Company, recorded an incident he saw at Surat involving a girl of about ten, whose husband had died in battle. As she had never lived with him, the Governor refused to give his consent for the immolation. It was only after the receipt of a bribe that he could be persuaded to alter his decision. Withington stated,

> This was the firste that ever I sawe; at the sight wherof our Agente was soe greeved and amazed at the undaunted resolution of the younge woman that hee said hee would never see more burnte in that fashion while hee lived (Foster 1999: 219-20; Section B: 245-46).

Francisco Pelsaert, a factor in the Dutch East India Company (1620–1627), recorded a case where the Governor of Agra offered financial inducements to dissuade a young widow from immolating herself. Pelsaert wrote,

He could, however, produce no effect, but she answered with resolute firmness that her motive was not (the fear of) poverty, but love for her husband, and even if she could have all the King's treasures in this world, they would be of no use to her, for she meant to live with her husband ... (Pelsaert 2001: 78-79; Section B: 248-49).

Edward Terry, chaplain of Sir Thomas Roe who came to India during the reign of Emperor Jahangir, Reverend Henry Lord who arrived at Surat in 1624, and Alexander Hamilton who travelled in the East Indies from 1688 to 1723, while "distancing themselves from the custom of sati, end(ed) up glorifying and defending it" (Sapra 2011: 100). Terry wrote of widows who "marrie not; but after the losse of their husbands... spend all their life following as creatures neglected..." There were also young women, who were,

ambitious to die with honour (as they esteeme it), when their fiery love brings them to the flames ... of martyrdom, most willingly; following their dead husbands unto the fire, and there imbracing are burnt with them; but this they doe voluntary, not compelled (Foster 1999: 328; Section B: 247-48).

William Methwold recorded a case from Masulipatam in South India involving the widow of a goldsmith, who, denied permission by the Kotwal to ascend the pyre of her husband, hanged herself (Moreland 1931: 28-30; Section B: 250-51).

The Italian nobleman, Pietro Della Valle, who travelled in India between 1623 and 1624, noted the rarity of the rite,

....this burning of Women upon the death of their Husbands is at their own choice to do it or not, and indeed few practice it; but she who does it acquires in the Nation a glorious name of Honour and Holiness...

He was deeply moved by the conjugal fidelity of a sati. He described the immolation of a drummer's widow at Ikkeri, the capital of the local Nayakas, then still subordinates of Vijayanagar. The event was greatly talked about, indicating it was not a common occurrence. Pietro Della Valle went to see for himself, but did not witness the actual *sahagamana* of Giaccama (Della Valle 1991: 271). He wrote,

> She rode on Horse-back about the City with face uncovered, holding a Looking-glass in one hand and a Lemon in the other, I know not for what purpose ... She was follow'd by many other Women and Men on foot, who, perhaps, were her Relations; ... yet with a calm and constant Countenance, without tears, evidencing more grief for her Husband's death than her own, and more desire to go to him in the other world than regret for her own departure out of this: a Custom, indeed, cruel and barbarous, but, withall, of great generosity and virtue in such Women and therefore worthy of no small praise... (Della Valle 1991: 84-85; 266-67; Section B: 252-57).

An understanding very different from his was presented by Thomas Herbert. In his account written in AD 1627–28, Herbert described sati as "a just reuenge" for wives, who had "growne so audaciously impudent" that "to satiate their lustfull boldnesse," would poison their husbands to safeguard themselves from future dangers (an explanation also put forth in some earlier accounts).

Versions such as this one by Herbert countered the valiant image of the sati. She was not an emblem of the faithful wife, rather a reminder of female licentiousness. The idea of sati as a punishment for husband-murder was agreeable to some Europeans; "it explain(ed) a disturbing rite in familiar terms of crime and punishment and coincide(d) with the Christian sense of the sinfulness of women." It also provided an equivalent to the position of women under English law. At the time of the accession of James I, in 1603, women in England had no legal rights. If a wife intrigued to kill her husband, it was treated as treason and was punishable by the harshest form of death penalty – being burnt alive (Teltscher 1995: 55).

The French traveller, Jean Baptiste Tavernier, who first arrived in India in 1640–1641 and visited the country no less than five times, observed that sati "was usually a voluntary act and so powerful was the women's belief that only by burning could they win eternal happiness and bring blessings on their family that it was difficult to dissuade them" (Tavernier II 2000: 210). He recounted his experience at Patna, when he was at the residence of the Dutch Governor of the town. A young widow entered the reception room and asked for permission to immolate herself, which was outrightly refused. In the face of her insistence, however, a torch was brought to test her resolve. Tavernier observed,

> As soon as the woman saw the torch, which was well lighted, she ran in front of it, held her hand firmly in the flame without the least grimace, and pushed in her arm up to the elbow, till it was immediately scorched; this caused horror to all who witnessed the deed, and the Governor commanded the woman to be removed from his presence (Tavernier II 2000: 172; Section B: 261-63).

Missionaries usually condemned the rite (Fisch 2005: 354). The widow's funeral pyre was viewed as a foretaste of hell fire (unlike India, where fire has "a positive and purifying symbolism," in the Western tradition it is symbolically associated with the putative fires of hell; Storm 2013: 129). The title page of the Dutch missionary, Abraham Roger's work, showing the Demon over a burning widow, reinforced the association with Hell. The Jesuit, Athanasius Kircher, in his *China Illustrata* (1667), also wrote of the "... infernal troop of sacrificers ... who rather than conducting her to the Elysian Fields, as they believe, lead her into eternal flames to continue a never ending torture there" (Teltscher 1995: 55-56).

Also, the absence of overt references to witch burning (practised in varying degrees in contemporary Europe), in the travel narratives on India from AD 1500 on, was indicative of a desire to maintain the impression of Indian otherness (Banerjee 2003: 1-34). The last witch was burnt in Europe as late as 1780, while the burning of heretics had been fairly common.

The European counterpart of the Hindu reverence for sati took the form of literary tribute. Niccolao Manucci's editor, Catrou, stated that a description of sati was "as useful a Lesson of conjugal Fidelity, as the Constancy of the Heroes of Toxaris was among the Athenians of the Highest Friendship" (Teltscher 1995: 59-60).

Some European artists painted scenes of widow immolation; among them Tilly Kettle (1735–1786), James Atkinson (1780–1852), and Francois Baltazard Solvyns (Hardgrave 1998: 57-80). Tilly Kettle, the first British portrait painter of note to visit India (June 1769 to March 1776), portrayed a sati scene in Madras in 1770–1771. His romantic view of widow immolation was reiterated in a poem by a Madras Company servant, Eyles Irwin, who arrived in Madras in February 1768 at the young age of 17. His poem, *Bedukah or the self-devoted: an Indian pastoral,* composed in 1776, highlighted the conjugal fidelity of a young widow, who displayed no hint of self-pity (*'be'*-without, *'dukh'*-sorrow) as she ascended her husband's pyre (Archer 1979: 72, 105). Johann Zoffany (1733–1810) visited India from July 1783 to January 1789. His painting of a sati showed it "quite unambiguously as a heroic act." The widow was "not a sentimental figure inviting pity, but a moral exemplar to be admired" (Bayly 1991: 220-21; Archer 1979: 156, 176-77).

IMPORTANCE OF MARRIAGE AND CONJUGAL LOYALTY

Sati remained identified with marriage in the travel literature on India (Teltscher 1995: 59). Many travellers wrote about the centrality of the institution of matrimony and the degree of conjugal devotion they observed in India. Tavernier noted, "When married they are rarely unfaithful to their wives, adultery is very rare among them ..." (Tavernier Book III 2000: 196-98).

Manucci, who lived in India for almost six decades, commented on the importance of marriage, "To their idea, there is not in this world anything to compare in importance with getting married ..." (Manucci III 1999: 51-53).

The Englishman, John Ovington, writing in 1689, explained the love between a husband and wife,

> ... And thus being happily prepossessed with a mutual good liking, even as it were from the Womb, as if they had been Lovers, they are taken off from all Objects, and freed from the Disappointments of fickle Mistresses ... Which, besides others, may be some Reason why *Indian* Wives committed themselves with so much chearfulness into the Funeral Flames with their Dead Husbands; because their Sympathetick Minds, linked together from their Infancy, were then fed with such early Tastes of Love, as became the Seminary of those strong and forcible Inclinations in their riper Years, and made the Pains of Death become preferable to a Life abandon'd [by] the Society of those they so entirely lov'd (Ovington 1994: 189-90; Section B: 276-77).

AD 1700–1800

The "heroic constructions" of sati in foreign accounts of the eighteenth century left space for the idea of the widow as "the self-devoted author of her own fate." Allusions to the inherent chastity and marital commitment of Hindu women continued to be made. Some earlier adverse suggestions that sati was a retribution for husband-murder were rejected and the motivation presented in terms of the widow's conjugal loyalty. The French editor, Bernard Picart, wrote in 1733, "The horror of the raging flames seems so contemptible in their eyes, that one might venture almost to say, they would gladly suffer even more exquisite tortures, if possible, for their husband's sake" (Major 2011: 23).

On 20th November 1753, Alex Knox, in an account to David Doig, Lord Provost of Montrose, described the "great fortitude and unmatched resolution of the wives burning with the bodies of their dead husbands." They were not obliged to do so by the laws of their country, "as some people have suggested." On the contrary, "great entreaties and arguments (were) generally made use of, to break their resolution, but seldom to any purpose" (Dharampal 2000: 21-22).

John Grose, a writer in the East India Company, in *A Voyage to the East Indies: with an Account of the Mogul Government and of the Mahometan, Gentoo and Parsee Religion* (1757), attributed the Hindu women's "prodigious affection and veneration for their husbands," to early marriage. The parties,

> ...in the tenderness of that ductile age, are bought up until that of consummation, in the constant inculcation to them of mutual dearness, as a sacred point of religion. And the women especially retain such a strong impression of this doctrine, that notwithstanding the influence of a climate far from favourable to chastity, instances of infidelity are at least as rare among them as in any people of the world besides (Grose I 1772: 193-94; Section B: 280-81).

Luke Scrafton, Resident at Murshidabad, in *Reflections on the Government of Indostan* (1763), expressed a similar view,

> ... no women are more remarkable for their conjugal fidelity, in which they are distinguished beyond the rest of their sex, by that remarkable custom of burning with their husband. ... Let it be considered, they are brought up together from their infancy; the woman has no opportunity of ever conversing with any other man; her affections are centred solely on this one object of her love; she is firmly persuaded that by being burnt with him, she shall be happy with him in another world ... (Scrafton 1763: 9; Section B: 281).

Pierre Sonnerat, the French Orientalist, in his *A Voyage to the East Indies and China Between the Years 1774 and 1781*, commented, "however extravagant and atrocious this custom may appear, it is easy to give a reason for it. The extreme love of some women for their husbands, the despair at their loss, and the desire to follow them, was the first cause of this sacrifice..." (Major 2006: 79; Section B: 281-82).

European writings in the first three-quarters of the eighteenth century mostly viewed the sacrifice as voluntary (Major 2006: 97). John Z. Holwell, who served in the East India Company in Bengal and became Governor for a while in 1760, recorded an incident that occurred in 1742–1743, at the Company's factory at Cossimbuzaar when Sir Francis Russell was in charge. Rhaam Chund Pundit, a Maratha, died at the age of twenty-eight and his widow, between seventeen and eighteen years of age, immediately declared her resolve to immolate herself. Since the family was of considerable standing, the merchants of Cossimbuzaar, and her relations, tried their best to discourage her. Even Lady Russell made several appeals to her. But,

> When the torments of burning were urged in terrorem to her, she with a resolved and calm countenance, put her finger into the fire, and held it there a considerable time ... She was at last given to understand, she should not be permitted to burn; this for a short space seemed to give her deep affliction, but soon recollecting herself, she told them, death was in her power, and that if she was not allowed to burn, according to the principles of her cast, she would starve herself. Her friends, finding her thus peremptory and resolved, were obliged at last to assent (Marshall 1970: 94; Section B: 283-87).

Holwell compared sati with Christian martyrs stating that Europe's "... own history affords illustrious examples in both sexes of voluntary sacrifices by fire, because they would not subscribe even to a different mode of professing the same faith" (Major 2006: 93).

The Dutch traveller, J.S. Stavorinus, who observed an incident in 1770, wrote, "The wretched victim, who beheld these preparations making for her cruel death, seemed to be much less affected by it than we Europeans who were present. She underwent everything with the greatest intrepidity..." (Weinberger-Thomas 2000: 97-100; Section B: 288-91).

Nathaniel Halhed, the noted Orientalist, in a letter to Rev. George Costard in 1779, described the rite as generally voluntary. He wrote, "Most assuredly the act is generally voluntary on the part of the women; and it is equally certain that should they refuse, and persist in their refusal, their relations could not force them to submit" (Rocher 1983: 296; Section B: 292-94).

An American merchant, Benjamin Crowninshield, described with "great sensitivity" an immolation he had witnessed in Calcutta in 1789. He ended his sober account stating, "Whether it is right or wrong, I leave it for other people to determine... It appeared very solemn to me. I did not think it was in the power of a human person to meet death in such a manner" (Hardgrave 1998: 57-80).

Rev. William Carey, who subsequently categorized sati as murder and spearheaded the campaign against it, recounted a case had tried to stop in April 1799, at Noaserai, thirty miles from Calcutta. He recalled,

> I exhorted the widow not to throw away her life; to fear nothing, for no evil would follow her refusal to be burned. But in the most calm manner she mounted the pile, and danced on it with her hands extended, as if in the utmost tranquility of spirit (Carey 1934: 170-71; Section B: 354-55).

In 1802, Rev. William Tennant wrote,

> This resolution is formed with deliberation, and is declared to be voluntary and fixed, several times in the presence of relations. This is done that no advantage may seem to have been taken of the transient ebullition of frantic grief, and that the person devoting herself might have full time to reflect on the important sacrifice she is about to make to her affections, or to the custom of her country (Tennant 1802: 190-91; Section B: 365-66).

In the first decades of the nineteenth century, foreign accounts of sati suddenly assumed "monumental dimensions" (Fisch 2005: 213). Also, as Rahul Sapra has pointed out, the nineteenth century representations were at odds with most earlier accounts (he relates this change to the progression of the East India Company from a mercantile body to a colonial power; Sapra 2011: 100, 107).

While in earlier accounts anguish at the physical suffering of the widow was offset by a regard for her chastity and bravery, in the nineteenth century there was a near universal denigration of the rite. The widow, once almost compared to Christian martyrs, was increasingly portrayed as "a passive victim in both 'voluntary' and 'involuntary' satis." A correspondent of the *Asiatic Journal,* for instance, commented, "When martyrdom is mentioned, it could not for a moment be intended to compare that sacred cause to the heartless and senseless superstition of misguided Hindoo widows ..." (*Asiatic Journal* Vol. 14 1822: 127). The widow was denied "heroic autonomy;" she was to be pitied rather than admired. There was also a new emphasis on sati as a religious rite (Major 2011: 23-24; Major 2006: 125, 168).

Significantly, this was the period when Evangelicals and Baptist missionaries had launched a vigorous campaign for the right of proselytization in India. Sati was the most "gory" of the "wicked customs" of the Hindus they highlighted to press their case in London. While earlier accounts had mostly underlined the voluntary nature of the rite,[2] Baptist missionaries insisted it was almost always due to the forcible exertions of ravenous relatives and Brahmins. The widow's sacrifice was "shorn of its meritorious aspects" in the British imagination, and viewed as "an act of violence" against a vulnerable prey. The bulk of the anti-sati British literature stressed the use of drugs, the employment of poles and ropes to restrain the widow from fleeing the burning pyre, and insisted she was at that moment *non compos mentis* (not of sound mind) (Major 2011: 24-25). While several non-missionaries claimed that the rite was sporadic, the Baptists asserted it was rampant.

It is possible to divide foreign accounts of sati into two broad phases — a pre- and post- Baptist phase. With the advent of the Baptists, earlier sentiments of wonder and astonishment were almost entirely replaced by condemnation. Sati was labelled as murder or suicide (a heinous sin) and used as a moral justification for British rule.[3]

SOME LATER ACCOUNTS BY BRITISH ADMINISTRATORS

Well after sati had become a subject of fierce debate, some British officials recounted their own experiences of voluntary immolations. Sir Frederick Halliday, who rose to be the first Lieutenant-Governor of Bengal (1854–1859), narrated an instance he had witnessed while Magistrate of Hughli district. The widow, after silently listening to appeals to desist from the act, sought permission to proceed to the pyre. To demonstrate her resolve she asked for a lamp to be brought. After it was lit, she put her finger into the flame of the lamp. She then asked Halliday, "Are you satisfied?" To which he hastily answered, "Quite satisfied." She removed her finger from the flame saying: "Now may I go?" He gave his consent (Buckland 1976: 160-61; Section B: 334-36).

W.H. Sleeman, the well-known colonial administrator, described a similar failure to prevent a sati while serving in Jabalpur District. The incident occurred on the Narmada in November 1829. The widow said to him,

> My pulse has long ceased to beat, my spirit has departed, and I have nothing left but a little *earth*, that I wish to mix with the ashes of my husband. I shall suffer nothing in burning, and, if you wish proof, order some fire, and you shall see this arm consumed without giving me any pain.

After he was compelled to grant her permission to immolate herself, Sleeman stated,

> I must do the family the justice to say that they all exerted themselves to dissuade the widow from her purpose, and had she lived she would assuredly have been cherished and honoured as the finest member of the whole house. There is no people in the world among whom parents are more loved, honoured, and obeyed than among the Hindoos; and the grandmother is always more honoured than the mother. No queen upon her throne could ever have been approached with more reverence by her subjects than was this old lady by all the members of her family as she sat upon a naked rock in the bed of the river, with only a red rag upon her head and a single white sheet over her shoulders (Sleeman 2003: 17-22; Section B: 329-33).

Edward Thompson explained the willingness of widows to immolate themselves, "The intoxication was of the spirit, not the body ..." (Thompson 1928: 50-51).

END-NOTES

1. The write-ups on India long remained "mired in fantasy." As late as 1494, a pamphlet could "exhibit an extraordinary conception of India: there are one-eyed, dog-headed and headless men, pygmies, men and women with large feet used as parasol, a winged snake, a flying panther and other strange beasts, birds and insects." Sati was part of the lore of the Orient. No account of India could be regarded complete without it. A case in point was Sir John Mandeville's fictional narrative, *The Travels and Voyages of Sir John Mandeville*, which was regarded as authentic till the eighteenth century. His fantasy tale on sati was lifted from Friar Odoric (Major 2006: 20-21).

2. An English officer, in a letter to the Editor of the *Calcutta Journal* on 12th December 1822 narrated his successful endeavour to prevent a sati, in Buja village near Kotgurh, in which he was supported by the Hindus present. He urged the woman to desist "from the dreadful crime of self-immolation." He was "ably seconded in this good work by several of the Hindoos

who accompanied me, and by others who, (to their honor let it be said), to my joy and surprise, instantly stepped forward, supported my arguments, unsolicited, in a manner I little expected, and reasoned with the woman to comply with my wishes. Upon which soon after she gave a tacit assent..." (Ray 1985: 123-29).

3. Reports of forced immolation mostly came from Bengal, the centre of the debate on sati (Woodruff 1963: 255). W. Ewer, Superintendent of Police, Lower Provinces of Bengal Presidency, in a letter to W.B. Bayley, Secretary to the Government in the Judicial Department, on 18th November 1818, argued that in nine out of ten cases sati was not voluntary, "It is generally supposed that a Suttee takes place with the free will and consent of the widow, and that she frequently persists in her intention to burn, in spite of the arguments and entreaties of her relations. But there are many reasons for thinking that such an event as a voluntary Suttee very rarely occurs: few widows would think of sacrificing themselves unless overpowered by force or persuasion, very little of either being sufficient to overcome the physical or mental powers of the majority of Hindoo females... she is little prepared to oppose the surrounding crowd of hungry Brahmuns and interested relations ... Under these circumstances nine out of ten widows are burnt to death" (*Parliamentary Papers* Vol. 18 1821: 749).

3

Early British Appreciation of
Indian Civilization

The Evangelical-missionary condemnation of Hindu traditions was a significant departure from the earlier British laudation of Indian attainments. In the years immediately following the conquest of Bengal, a significant section of Englishmen had found in Indian culture "a deep and appealing wisdom" (Embree 1962: 148). The "enthusiasm for India," which continued into the early nineteenth century, was above all, "an enthusiasm for Hinduism," and Indian civilization "in most ancient times, prior to the coming of the Muslims" (Trautmann 2004: 63-65).

John Grose (1744–1771), a writer in the East India Company, in *A Voyage to the East Indies: with an Account of the Mogul Government and of the Mahometan, Gentoo and Parsee Religion* (1757), noted the liberal disposition of the Hindus in matters of faith. He wrote,

> Nothing appeared more paradoxical to me, than the violent tenaciousness of the Gentoos in their religion and customs; and yet at the same time their perfect acquiescence, humanity,

and toleration of others who differ from them in those points that are so sacred to them... (Grose Vol. I 1772: 182).

He elaborated,

As to that spirit of toleration in religion, for which the Gentoos are so singularly distinguished, it is doubtless owing to their fundamental tenet of it, of which the purport is; "that the diversity of modes of worship is apparently agreeable to the God of the universe: that all prayers put up to him from man, are all equally acceptable and sanctified to him, by the sincerity of the intention: that the true universal religion is no other than the religion of the heart; that the various outward forms of it are only accessories indifferent in themselves, and merely accidents of time, place, education or birth; and that therefore all change of religion is at best but a dangerous and needless experiment, since, according to them, every honest man is sure to be saved by his own.

Upon this principle, instead of persecuting and burning others for not being of it, or "of compelling them to enter," they will absolutely admit of no proselytes to theirs... (Grose Vol. I 1772: 183).

Luke Scrafton (?–1769), Resident at Murshidabad, in *Reflections on the Government of Indostan* (1761), stated that the Hindus,

... have undoubted claims to remote antiquity; for the earliest accounts we have of them represent them as cultivating all the useful arts in great perfection; and to judge by their slow progress among us, this seems to be the work of ages. Perhaps these eastern countries, peopled in the infancy of the world, never degenerated into that state of barbarism in which we were so long involved; the soil and climate were propitious to mankind, and the mind was a stranger to the fiercer passions, which arose from the stimulating necessities of our more northern climate (Scrafton 1763: 4).

Further, he said, that the Hindus,

... amidst all their errors, they agree to those truths which form the harmony of the Universe, that there is One Supreme God, And That He Is Best Pleased by Charity and Good Works. Their worship and ceremonies at the great temple of Jagernaut seem Instituted to remind them of this, for there the Bramin, the Rajah, the labourer, and mechanic, all present their offerings, and eat and drink promiscuously together, as if they would insinuate that all those distinctions are of human invention, and in the sight of God all men are equal (Scrafton 1763: 9).

John Z. Holwell (1711–1798), in *"The Religious Tenets of the Gentoos"* (the second part of his *Interesting Historical Events relative to the Provinces of Bengal and the Empire of Indostan*, 1767), declared that "the world does not now contain annals of more indisputable antiquity than those delivered down by the ancient Brahmins." He avowed that the people "from the earliest times have been an ornament to the creation if so much can with propriety be said of any known people upon earth." Holwell believed that the Hindu texts predated the Flood and that "the mythology, as well as the cosmogony of the Egyptians, Greeks and Romans, were borrowed from the doctrines of the Bramins..." He dismissed modern writers who denigrated the Hindus as "chiefly of the Romish communion ... Popish authors ..." (Marshall 1970: 46; 48).

Holwell said the Brahmins were,

so famed ...in the earliest known times for the purity of their manners, and the sublimity of their wisdom and doctrines, that their converse was sought after, and solicited universally by the philosophers, and searchers after wisdom and truth. For this character of them, we have the concurring testimony of all antiquity...At what period of time, Indostan was visited by Zoroaster and Pythagoras, is not clearly determined by the learned; we will suppose it, with the generality of writers, to have been about the time of Romulus. That these sages travelled, not to instruct, but, to be instructed; is a fact that may be determined with more precision; as well as, that they were not in Indostan together. As they both made a long residence with the Bramins North West of the Ganges (for the name of *Zardhurst*, and *Pythagore* retain a place in the Gentoo annals 'as travellers in search of wisdom') it is reasonable to conclude they might in some degree be instructed in the Sanscrit character, and consequently, in the doctrines and worship instituted by the *Chatah* and *Aughtorrah Bhades* (Atharva Veda)... (Marshall 1970: 61-64).

Alexander Dow (1735–1779), Lt-Colonel in the Company's military service, and author of the three-volume *The History of Hindostan* (1770), stated that the primeval truths of the Hindus owed nothing to Jews or Christians. The Brahmins, he declared, invariably believed in the unity, eternity, omniscience and omnipotence of God; "the polytheism of which they have been accused, is no more than a symbolical worship of the divine attributes ..." (Dow I 1973: lxxiv). Further,

The system of religion which they profess is only perfectly known in the effect which it has upon the manners of the people. Mild, humane, obedient, and industrious, they are of all nations on earth the most easily conquered ... Revolution and change are things unknown; and assassinations and conspiracies never exists. Penal laws are scarce known among the Hindoos; for their motives to bad actions are few ... it is to the ingenuity of the Hindoos, we owe all the fine manufactures in the East (Dow III 1973: xxxv-xxxvi).

Dow was struck by the "astonishing formation" of the Sanskrit language. He said,

It ...bears evident marks that it has been fixed upon rational principles, by a body of learned men, who studied regularity, harmony, and a wonderful simplicity and energy of expression. Though the Shanscrita is amazingly copious, a very small grammar and vocabulary serve to illustrate the principles of the whole. In a treatise of a few pages, the roots and primitives are all comprehended, and so uniform are the rules for derivations and inflections, that the etymon of every word is, with facility, at once investigated (Dow I 1973: xxx-xxxi).

Robert Orme (1728–1801), who arrived in India in 1742 and served as a Factor, wrote the early history of the East India Company in India in 1782. He said of the Hindus,

A people believing in metempsychosis, who are forbid by their religion to destroy the smallest insect; a people continually assembling to celebrate the festivals of their gods, who believe that acts of charity to the poor can atone for all their sins, who are fond to excess of the enjoyment of a domestic life, and extremely solicitous in the cares of it — such a people must acquire humane and gentle manners.

The Gentoos are very affectionate parents, and treat their domestics with great mildness. They are charitable, even to relieving the necessities of strangers: and the politeness of their behaviour is refined by the natural effeminacy of their disposition ...

Slavery has sharpened the natural finess of all the spirits of Asia. From the difficulty of obtaining, and the greater difficulty of preserving it, the Gentoos are indefatigable in business, and masters of the most exquisite dissimulation in all affairs of interest. They are the acutest buyers and sellers in the world, and preserve through all their bargains a degree of calmness, which baffles all the arts that can be opposed against it... (Orme 1978: 276-77).

George Forster (d. 1792), an employee of the Company who travelled through Northern India beginning in 1782, wrote,

When this empire, its polished people, and the progress which science had made amongst them, are attentively considered; when, at the same period, a retrospective view is thrown on the states of the European world, then immersed in, or emerging from, ignorance and barbarity, we must behold Hindostan with wonder and respect; and we may assert without forfeiting the claims of truth and moderation, that, however far the European world now outstrips the nations of the East, the followers of Brimha in the early period of life, were possessed of a fund amply stored with valuable materials of philosophy and useful knowledge. The humane mind will naturally feel a sense of sorrow and pity for a people, who have fallen from so conspicuous a height of glory and fortune, and who probably have contributed to polish and exalt the nations, who now hold them in subjection...

Let me conclude this comparative view, with observing, and I trust dispassionately, that when we see a people possessed of an ample stock of science of well digested ordinances, for the protection and improvement of society — and of a religion whose tenets consist of the utmost refinement, and variety of ceremony — and, at the same time, observe amongst other Asiatic nations, and the Egyptians of former times, but partial distributions of knowledge, law, and religion — we must be led to entertain a supposition, that the proprietors of the lesser, have been supplied from the sources of the greater fund ... (Forster I 1970: 60-61; 65-66).

THE ORIENTALISTS

Towards the end of the eighteenth century, following the British ascendancy in Bengal, individual efforts to acquire access to Indian philosophy and literature were replaced by the systematic endeavours of a number of officials of the East India Company. The great patron of Indic studies was Warren Hastings, the first Governor General of Bengal (Governor and Governor General 1772–1784). He exhibited deep interest in Hindu religion and philosophy and enjoyed going "pundit-hunting" to Banaras, as his contemporaries put it. Rev. William Ward (1769–1823) recorded in his journal that the Brahmins of the Kalighat temple had told him that Warren Hastings used to go there every Sunday to worship the Goddess[1] (Sen Gupta 1971: 56). An interesting entry in Hastings' notebook attests to his favourable perception of Indian culture and religion. "Is the incarnation of Christ more intelligible than... those of Bishen?" he questioned. He attributed the European triumph over non-Europeans not to the superiority of Christianity, but to secular reasons like "a free government, cold climate and printing and navigation." Christianity, he argued, did not make people "better" (Trautmann 2004: 72).

Hastings, representative of a new kind of civil servant in India, believed that an understanding of Indian culture was imperative for sound administration. He strove to create an Orientalized service elite competent in the Indian languages and sensitive to Indian traditions. The select group that gathered around him included Charles Wilkins who came to Bengal in 1770; Nathaniel Halhed and Jonathan Duncan who assumed duty in 1772; and William Jones, the most famous of the Orientalists, who arrived in 1783. Together with H.T. Colebrooke, H.H. Wilson, and James Prinsep, they made notable contributions in the fields of Indian religion, philology, philosophy, archaeology, and history.[2]

Warren Hastings was an advocate of indigenous institutions.[3] His personal experience had convinced him that ancient Indian institutions were commendable and practicable. In his plan for the administration of justice, issued in 1772, he declared his wish to reinstate the ancient constitution of the Indian people within an improved "modern" judiciary (Dodson 2011a: 20-21). Hastings explained his policy in a communication to the Court of Directors in November 1772, "We have endeavoured to adapt our Regulations to the Manners and Understanding of the People, and Exigencies of the Country, adhering, as closely as we are able, to their Ancient Usages and Institutions" (Stokes 1982: 35-36).

Subsequently, in a correspondence with the jurist, Lord Mansfield, in March 1774, Warren Hastings stressed the right of a great nation to preserve its own laws. He said,

They have been in possession of laws, which have continued unchanged, from the remotest antiquity. ...the Mahomedan government ... suffered the people to remain in quiet possession of the institutes which time and religion had rendered familiar to their understandings and sacred to their affections[4] (Gleig I 1841: 399-404).

As a result of Hastings' appeal, Brahmins versed in the *Shastras* gathered at Fort William and drafted a comprehensive treatise on Hindu law, the *Vivadarnavasetu,* in the year 1772.[5] This was subsequently translated into Persian and, in 1776, into English by Nathaniel Halhed as *A Code of Gentoo Laws* (Derrett 1968: 237-42).[6]

In his Preface to the work, Halhed (1751–1830) stated that Hindus had ever "laid claim to an antiquity infinitely more remote than is authorized by the belief of the rest of mankind" (Halhed 1776: xxxvii). This proposition was refuted, in 1778, by Rev. George Costard, clergyman and writer of the history of the earliest times, and family friend of Halhed (Rocher 1983: 58-59, App B; Trautmann 2004: 73-74).

In 1778, Halhed published a *Grammar of the Bengali Language,* rated among the earliest and finest introductions to the scientific study of the language. Hastings not only helped Halhed meet the costs of employing a *pandit,* but also arranged for the Company to sponsor publication of the work (Rocher 1983: 241). In his forward, Halhed described Sanskrit as the source of all other languages. He wrote,

> The grand Source of Indian Literature, the Parent of almost every dialect from the Persian Gulf to the China Seas, is the Shanscrit; a language of the most venerable and unfathomable antiquity; ... I have been astonished to find the similarities of Shanscrit words with those of Persian and Arabic, and even of Latin and Greek: and these not in technical and metaphorical terms ... but in the main ground-work of language, in monosyllables, in the names of numbers, and the appellations of such things as would be

first discriminated on the immediate dawn of civilization (Halhed 1778: iii-iv).

Further, he argued that to Sanskrit,

> ... every word of truly Indian original in every provincial and subordinate dialect of all Hindostan may still be traced by a laborious and critical analysis; and all such terms as are thoroughly proved to bear no relation to any one of the Shanscrit roots, I would consider as the production of some remote and foreign idiom, subsequently ingrafted upon the main stock... (Halhed 1778: viii).

The Bengali language, Halhed said, was "intimately related to the Shanscrit both in expressions, construction and character" (Halhed 1778: xiv). Halhed's attempts to extract the "authentic" Bengali language from Persian and Portuguese influences, led directly to the renaissance in Bengali language and literature (Kopf 1969: 18-20; Rocher 1993: 229; Dodson 2011a: 21).

With Hastings' backing Charles Wilkins (1749–1836) also engaged in the study of Sanskrit. Wilkins had been the first to discover, and, in 1778, to use, methods of engraving, casting, and setting Bengali characters for printing. In 1784, he translated the *Bhagwat Gita*, the earliest translation in a European language directly from a Sanskrit text (Moon 1947: 352). In a letter introducing the work to the Chairman of the East India Company, Warren Hastings described the *Bhagwat Gita* as "a performance of great originality; of a sublimity of conception, reasoning, and diction, almost unequalled ..." (Marshall 1970: 187; Dodson 2011a: 22).

Wilkins also translated the *Hitopadesa.* He described the translation as,

> ... a faithful portrait of a beautiful work, which ... is the Sanskreet original of those celebrated fables, which after passing through most of the Oriental languages ... at length, were introduced to the knowledge of the European world...

Sir William Jones says: '... the fables of Veeshnoo-Sarma, whom we ridiculously call Pilpay, are the most beautiful, if not the most ancient collection of Apologues in the world' (Willson 1964: 45).

Wilkins pioneered the use of inscriptions to reconstruct the history of the Pala dynasty of Bengal. His *A Grammar of the Sanscrit Language* was hailed as the best Sanskrit grammar on its publication. Wilkins said Samskrta, when analyzed according to the rules of *vyakarana*, "denotes a thing to have been composed, or formed by art, adorned, embellished, purified, highly cultivated or polished, and regularly inflected, as a language" (Wilkins 1808: 1). He also noted the connection between Sanskrit and the vernacular languages;

the several dialects confounded under the common terms Hindi, Hindavi, Hindostani, and Bhasha, deprived of Sanscrit, would not only lose all their beauty and energy, but, with respect to the power of expressing abstract ideas, or terms in science, would be absolutely reduced to a state of barbarism (Wilkins 1808: x-xi).

Warren Hastings' encouragement of oriental scholarship led to the establishment of the Asiatic Society of Bengal, in 1784, for the study of the Indian heritage. For over half a century, it remained a centre of learning that took the shape of a host of translations of texts and other scholarly endeavours (Kejariwal 1988). After Hastings refused its presidency, William Jones (1746–1794) was selected for the post. In 1788, the journal, *Asiatic Researches,* was started for the dissemination of knowledge on Indian culture.[7]

William Jones' translation of Kalidasa's *Shakuntala* into English (1789) went through five reprints in England in the two decades immediately following its first publication and greatly impressed the German poet, Goethe (who proclaimed, "When I mention *Shakuntala,* everything is said," Schwab 1984: 59; Dasgupta 2007: 26-27).[8] In his introductory remarks Jones stated,

Dramatick poetry must have been immemorially ancient in the Indian empire ... By whomsoever or in whatever age this species of entertainment was invented ... it was carried to great perfection in its kind ... in the first century before Christ ... at a time when the Britons were as unlettered and unpolished as the army of Hanumat (satyrs or mountaineers who participated in a great Hindu battle) (Willson 1964: 44-45).

In 1792, came Jones' translation of the *Gita Govinda*. In his view, Indian literature was on par with Greek literature; it was not only "sublime and beautiful in a high degree," but also "perfectly original," whereas Latin literature derived from the Greek (Cannon 1970: 716).

Jones made a lyrical declaration of his estimation of Indian religion, philosophy, and literature. He confessed,

I am in love with Gopia, charmed with Crishen (Krisna), an enthusiastic admirer of Raama and a devout adorer of Brimha (Brahma), Bishen (Visnu), Mahiser (Mahesvara); not to mention that Judishteir, Arjen, Corno and other warriors of the M'hab'harat (Mahabharata) appear greater in my eyes than Agamemnon, Ajax and Achilles appeared when I first read the Iliad (Mukherjee 1968: 117).

He was the first to propose that India's golden period as a culture lay in a remote period in history. He viewed the philosophy of *Vedanta* as a unique manifestation of the "Aryan genius." It was not possible for him, he said, "to read the Vedanta or the many fine compositions in illustration of it, without believing that Pythagoras and Plato derived their sublime theories from the same fountain with the sages of India" (Kopf 1969: 34-39; Mukherjee 1968: 117-19; Canon 1990: 320).

Hailed as the father of Indology, William Jones is popularly credited with the discovery of the common origins of what came to be known as the Indo-European family of languages (Mukherjee 1968: 91-121). He described Sanskrit as, of a wonderful structure; more perfect than the Greek, more copious than the Latin, and more exquisitely refined than either, yet bearing to both of them a stronger affinity, both in the roots of verbs and in the forms of grammar, than could possibly have been produced by accident; so strong indeed that no philologer could examine them all three, without believing them to have sprung from some common source ... (*Asiatic Researches* Vol. 1: 348-49).[9]

Jones also contributed to the study of comparative mythology and drew a parallel between the classical gods and goddesses of the West and those of Indian tradition (Kejariwal 1988: 40-41). In a succinct summing up of the contributions of the Hindus, Jones, in his Third Anniversary Discourse delivered on 2 February 1786, stated,

The Hindus are said to have boasted of three inventions, all of which, indeed, are admirable, the method of instructing of apologues, the decimal scale adopted now by all civilized nations, and the game of chess, on which they have some curious treatises; but, if their numerous works on grammar, logick, rhetorick, musick, all which are extant and accessible, were explained in some language generally known, it would be found, that they had yet higher pretentions to the praise of a fertile and inventive genius. Their lighter poems are lively and elegant; their epick, magnificent and sublime in the highest degree; their *Puranas* comprise a series of mythological histories in blank verse from the Creation to the supposed incarnation of Buddha; and their *Vedas*, as far as we can judge from that compendium of them, which is called *Upanishat*, abound with noble speculations in metaphysicks, and fine discourses on the being and attributes of God. Their most ancient medical book, entitled *Chereca* [Charak], is believed to be the work of Siva; for each of the divinities in their Triad has at least one sacred composition ascribed to him; but, as to mere human works on history and geography, though they are said to be extant in Cashmir, it has not been yet in my power to procure them. What their astronomical and mathematical writings contain, will not, I trust, remain long a secret: they are easily procured, and their importance cannot be doubted. The philosopher, whose works are said to include a system of the universe founded on the principle of attraction and the central position of the sun, is named Yavan Acharya, because he had travelled, we are told, into Ionia: if this be true, he might have been one of those, who conversed with Pythagoras; this at least is undeniable, that a book on astronomy in Sanscrit bears the title of *Yavana Jatica,* which may signify the Ionick Sect; nor is it improbable, that the names of the planets and Zodiacal stars, which the Arabs borrowed from the Greeks, but which we find in the oldest Indian records, were originally devised of the same ingenious and enterprizing race, from whom both Greece and India were peopled ... (*Asiatic Researches* Vol. 1: 354-55).

Jones' *Institutes of Hindu Law: Or, The Ordinances of Menu* which was to aid in the administration of justice, was posthumously published in 1794 (it was completed by H.T. Colebrooke). In his opening remarks, Jones stated,

> ...a spirit of sublime devotion, of benevolence to mankind, and of amiable tenderness to all sentient creatures pervades the whole work; the style of it has a certain austere majesty, that sounds like the language of legislation and extorts a respectful awe; the sentiments of independence on all beings but God, and the harsh admonitions, even to kings, are truly noble; and the many panegyricks on Gayatri, the Mother as it is called, of the Veda, prove the author to have *adored that divine and incomparably greater light*, to use the words of the most venerable text in the Indian scripture ... (Jones 1796: xv-xvi).

Some scholars have argued that the practices of Orientalism were devoted, primarily, to the progression and empowerment of the colonial state. Jones's translation of *Shakuntala* and the *Gita Govinda*, however, had no application in government; nor did his study of Indian music or the game of chess. They "added to the documentation of India's brilliant past" (Rocher 1993: 233-34). Indeed, even towards the end of the eighteenth century when the British were ruling over a sizeable native population, "contemporaries were not thinking in terms of Kipling's 'White Man's Burden.'" A considerable proportion of Company servants were "aficionados of Indian culture" (Rocher 1993: 216, 219).

H.T. Colebrooke (1765–1837), ranked the greatest Orientalist after Jones, arrived in India the same year as him. He was associated with three important institutions – the *Sadr Diwani* and *Nizamat Adalats,* Fort William College, and the Asiatic Society. He translated *Kosha or Dictionary of the Sanskrit Language* by Amara Singh. Reflecting on the antiquity and evolution of Indian culture, Colebrooke stated,

> Whatever may be the true antiquity of this nation, whether their mythology be a corruption of the pure deism we find in their books, or their deism a refinement from gross idolatry; whether their religious and moral precepts have been engrafted on the elegant philosophy of the Nyaya and Mimansa, or this philosophy been refined on the plainer text of the Veda; the Hindu is the most ancient nation of which we have valuable remains, and has been surpassed by none in refinement and civilization; though the utmost pitch of refinement to which it ever arrived preceded, in time, the dawn of civilization in any other nation of which we have even the name in history (Colebrooke 1873a: 61).

Colebrooke's *A Digest of Hindu Law* was published in 1797. In 1810, he translated and annotated a work on Hindu law, *Dayabhaga and Mitaksara. Two Treatises on the Hindu Law of Inheritance.* Among his other works were *Algebra, with Arithmetic and Mensuration: From the Sanscrit of Brahmegupta and Bhascara.* Colebrooke was the first systematic expounder of Indian philosophy. His *Essays on the Religion and Philosophy of the Hindus,* written after thirty years of study and experience, was widely read in scholarly circles in Europe.

Colebrooke identified Sanskrit as the fount of Indian civilization and asserted that "civilization had its origin in Asia" (Kopf 1969: 39; Dodson 2011a: 37-39). He was perhaps the first European to recognize that Hindi had existed prior to, and separate from, Persianized Urdu. He differed from William Jones, who in his Third Anniversary Discourse (*Asiatic Researches* Vol. 1: 343-55), had argued that pure Hindi was primeval in Upper India and Sanskrit was introduced by conquerors from other kingdoms in some remote age. Colebrooke correctly maintained that Hindi did not predate Sanskrit but descended from it ("The Sanscrit and Prakrit Languages," *Asiatic Researches* Vol. 7: 199-231). Together with Jones, Colebrooke created a "Sanskritocentric" vision of Indian culture that celebrated Sanskrit and the Vedas and decried the state of contemporary Hinduism (Ballantyne 2002: 30-32).

Meanwhile, in 1791, Jonathan Duncan (1756–1811), Resident at Banaras, founded the Sanskrit College in the city for the preservation and cultivation of Hindu laws, literature, and religion (Cohn 1985: 318-19; Kopf 29-30). Writing to Lord Cornwallis, then Governor General (1786–1793), Duncan pointed out that though "... learning has ever been cultivated at Benares, in numerous private seminaries, yet no public Institution of the kind here proposed ever appears to have existed." He also noted the considerable difficulty of collecting complete treatises on Hindu religion, laws, arts, and sciences, which could be removed with the establishment of a permanent college. This would help accumulate "a precious library of the most ancient and valuable general learning and tradition now perhaps existing on any part of the globe" (Sharp 1920: 10-11).

H.H. Wilson (1786–1860), who joined the Company's medical service in 1808, became Secretary of the Asiatic Society of Bengal in 1811, and served till he left India in 1832 to become the first Boden Professor of Sanskrit at Oxford. He translated Kalidasa's *Megha Duta (Cloud Messenger)* in 1813, and prepared

A Dictionary in Sanskrit and English in 1819. This was followed by *Selected Specimens of the Theatre of the Hindus* (1827), which was a survey of Indian drama, the translation of six full plays and short accounts of twenty-three others. Wilson subsequently published a translation of the *Vishnu Purana* and the first book of the *Rig Veda*. His *Essays and Lectures on the Religion of the Hindus* was published after he had left India.[10]

OTHER VOICES

Admiration for Indian culture existed outside this official circle as well. The Scottish philosophical historian, William Robertson (1721–1793) in his *An Historical Disquisition Concerning Ancient India* (1791) categorically stated, "Many facts have been transmitted to us, which, if they are examined with proper attention, clearly demonstrate that the natives of India were not only more early civilized, but had made greater progress in civilization than any other people ..." (Robertson 1981: 197). It was from their ancient writings, he said, that they derived "the most liberal sentiments which they entertain at present, and the wisdom for which they are now celebrated has been transmitted to them from ages very remote" (Robertson 1981: 277).

Quintin Craufurd (1743–1819), in his *Sketches Chiefly Relating to the History, Religion, Learning, and Manners of the Hindoos* (1792), claimed that India, not Egypt was the original home of the arts and sciences and that the Hindus were "a polished and civilized nation" (Craufurd I 1977: 71-74).

William Macintosh, who visited India in the third quarter of the eighteenth century, wrote,

> All history points to India as the mother of science and art. This country was anciently so renowned for knowledge and wisdom that the philosophers of Greece did not disdain to travel thither for their improvement...The tranquility of their minds, even in the most trying circumstances, is expressed by a constant smile that sits gracefully on their

placid countenances...the Hindoos are naturally the most inoffensive of all mortals... In Asia, particularly in India, both on this side and beyond the Ganges, there is a scrupulous tenacity of ancient customs and manners... In refinement and ease [the Hindus] are superior to any people to the westward of them. In politeness and address, in gracefulness of deportment, and speech, an Indian is as much superior to a Frenchman of fashion, as a French courtier is to a Dutch burgo-master of Dort... (Willson 1964: 25-31).

Captain Thomas Williamson (1790–1815), author of *East India Vade-Mecum; or, Complete Guide to Gentlemen intended for the Civil, Military, or Naval Service of the Hon. East India Company* (1810), wrote from his experience of twenty years residence in the Bengal Presidency in the military service of the Company. Decrying the hostile depictions of the missionaries, he stated,

[Indians were, on the whole], a race whose intellectual qualities, whatever may be said by ignorant or designing men, are at least on a par with those of Europeans. (Not that they did not have a share of human depravity, but they were not) so debased, so immoral, or so vindictive, as they have been represented by many gentlemen, especially some divines who have lately returned from the East, and whose opinions breathe by no means the spirit of that sublime religion they would coerce the natives to adopt. Taking all points into consideration, and viewing the nature of the country conjointly with the nature of their laws, and of their former government, I think we have by far more to admire than to censure, in a race of people, who, notwithstanding some highly remarkable instances of depravity, may be classed among the most innocent, and most industrious, of worldly inhabitants!!! (Dyson 1978: 157).

Maria Graham (1785–1842), daughter of the Commissioner for Navy in Bombay, who arrived in India in 1808, was also critical of missionary attacks on Hindus. She wrote,

Our missionaries are very apt to split upon this rock, and in order to place our religion in the brightest light, as if it wanted their feeble aid, they lay claim exclusively to all the sublime maxims of morality and tell those they wish to convert, that their own books contain nothing but abominations, the belief of which they must abandon in order to receive the purer doctrine of Christianity. Mistaken men! Mistaken men! Could they desire a better opening to their hopes than to find already established that morality which says, it is enjoined to man even at the moment of destruction to wish to benefit his foes, 'as the sandal tree in the instant of its overthrow sheds perfume on the axe that fells it.' ...

In short I consider morality like the sciences and arts, to be only slumbering not forgotten in India; and that to awaken the Hindus to a knowledge of the treasures in their own hands is the only thing wanting to set them fairly in the course of improvement with other nations.

Everywhere in the ancient Hindu books we find the maxims of that pure and sound morality which is founded on the nature of man as a rational and social being ... (Graham 1814: 85-88).

CONTRIBUTIONS TO SCIENCE

India's contributions in the realm of science were readily acknowledged by early Englishmen. In astronomy, mathematics, and medicine in particular, Hindus were regarded as having been remarkably advanced well before the commencement of the Christian era, and being the source of discoveries and techniques later incorporated into Western civilization (Arnold 2007: 3). One admirer declared "The Asiaticks had climbed the heights of science before the Greeks had learnt their alphabet" (Kopf 1969: 102).

In 1777, Sir Robert Barker, presented a paper to the Royal Society in which he praised the "mathematical exactness" of the stone instruments at Raja Jai Singh's observatory at Banaras.

He said, "The signs of the Zodiac must ... have originated with them ..." (Dharampal 1983: 65-66).

John Playfair (1748–1819), Professor of Mathematics at Edinburgh University, in a paper, "Remarks on the Astronomy of the Brahmins," presented in 1790, reiterated,

> These tables [of the Brahmins of Tirvalore, a small town on the Coromandel Coast] go far back into antiquity. Their epoch coincides with the famous era of the Calyougham, that is, with the beginning of the year 3102 before Christ. When the Brahmins of Tirvalore would calculate the place of the sun for a given time, they begin by reducing into days the interval between that time, and the commencement of the Calyougham, multiplying the years by 365^d 6^h 12', 30"; and taking away 2^d 3^h, 32', 30", the astronomical epoch having begun that much later than the civil. They next find, by means of certain divisions, when the current began, or how many days have elapsed since the beginning of it, and then, by the table of the duration of months, they reduce these days into astronomical months, days, etc. which is the same with the signs, degrees and minutes of the sun's longitude from the beginning of the zodiac. The sun's longitude, therefore, is found.

> Somewhat in the same manner, but by a rule still more artificial and ingenious, they deduce the place of the moon, at any given time, from her place at the beginning of the Calyougham. This rule is so contrived, as to include at once the motions both of the moon and of her apogee, and depends on this principle, according to the very skilful interpretation of M. Bailly, that, 1,600,894 days after the above mentioned epoch, the moon was in her apogee, and 7^s, 2°, 0', 7", distant from the beginning of the zodiac; that after 12,372 days, the moon was again in her apogee, with her longitude increased, 9^s, 27°, 48', 10"; that in 3031 days more, the moon is again in her apogee with 11^s, 7°, 3', 1" more of longitude; and, lastly, that, after 248 days, she is again in her apogee, with 27°, 44', 6", more of longitude. By

means of the three former numbers, they find, how far, at any given time, the moon is advanced in this period of 248 days, and by a table, expressing how long the moon takes to pass through each degree of her orbit, during that period, they find how far she is then advanced in the zodiac. This rule is strongly marked with all the peculiar characters of the Indian astronomy. It is remarkable for its accuracy, and still more for its ingenuity and refinement; but is not reduced withal, to its ultimate simplicity (Dharampal 1983: 82-83).

By then, the powerful Evangelical movement that took birth in England had begun to impinge on India.

END-NOTES

1. Many Company-men also felt that granting Indians freedom in religious matters was a realistic response. It would be difficult for a few Europeans, aided mainly by a sepoy army, to control the millions of native subjects. By the 1780s, or even earlier, the Company had become increasingly involved in Hindu festivals and temples. Warren Hastings mentioned the supervisory role played by Company officials at the Gaya pilgrimage. In 1784–85, the Company permitted the Collector of Gaya to collect the pilgrimage tax as part of the excise tax. In 1788, the Collector of Beerbohm himself assumed direct management of the Deoghar temple. In 1803, the Company took over the administration of the Jagannath temple at Orissa (Carson 2012: 15-16).

2. Even John Shore, who later joined the Clapham Sect and supported the Anglicist and missionary cause, worked as a young civil servant, in 1784, on a Vedantic text, *Yogavasistha*, in Persian translation (Rocher 1993: 219).

3. Subsequently, a group of Company officials, called the Paternalists, also argued for retaining indigenous institutions to the greatest extent possible. Thomas Munro (1761–1827) was a consistent proponent of "native agency" and native institutions. Munro's ideas were endorsed by friends like Mountstuart Elphinstone (1779–1859) and John Malcolm (1769–1833), and later, by officials like Charles Metcalfe

(1785–1846) and Henry Lawrence (1806–1857). They opposed the form of government introduced in India by Lord Cornwallis, which was in accordance with British constitutional principles. This was essentially an application of Whig political philosophy to governance.

4. David Washbrook asks why the East India Company state almost at its birth created the theory of race/culture/history that argued for the common origins of the colonizer and the colonized. Equally, why did it decide to rule India according to Indian laws and customs, rather than import those of an allegedly superior Europe? He says this decision was not informed by conservatism, but upheld by Enlightenment opinion of the times. Adam Smith ranked India with Britain at the highest state of civilization, a "commercial society" that already possessed all it needed to prosper economically. William Robertson, of the Scottish Enlightenment, held that Indian culture had the capacity for its own "improvement" (Washbrook 2004: 483).

5. Hastings was successful in enlisting the services of the renowned Radhakanta Tarkavagisa (Rocher 1989). Several factors forced Brahmins to rethink their stance towards the British. The famine of 1770, and its recurrence in 1783, had greatly reduced indigenous patronage; ecological changes due to shifts in the riverine system of Western Bengal weakened many provincial centres, leading to a migration of people to Calcutta; some Brahmins who migrated, established Sanskrit schools in the city, some joined Company service. Pandits from the Radh region, west of the river Hughli, were particularly prominent in the intellectual life of colonial Calcutta (Ballantyne 2002: 24). Subsequently many Indians were employed in Fort William College, among them Tarinicharan Mitra in the Hindustani department and Mritunjay Vidyalankar in the Bengali department.

6. It has been argued that as a consequence of British support, Hindu law extended its sway over sections of society that had not known it in the past. The "brahminization of Hindu law" had far-reaching consequences for social life.

7. Rev. Thomas Maurice (1754–1824), a prolific writer on Asian history and mythology, who never visited India, derived most of his knowledge from the accounts of Orientalists resident in India, including contributors to *Asiatick Researches*. Maurice prepared two substantive works, *The History of Hindostan* (2 vols.; 1795–1798) and *Indian Antiquities* (7 vols.; 1793–1800), and, following the lead of William Jones, launched "forth into the warmest strains of admiration on the survey of the virtues, learning, fortitude, and industry of this innocent and secluded race of men" (Marshall 1970: 41). Concerned chiefly with upholding the Biblical narrative, especially Mosaic chronology, his enthusiasm for Asia has been described by Trautmann as "Christian Indomania" (Trautmann 2004: 75, 80; Dodson 2011b: 56-57).

8. Georg Foster (1754–1794) introduced *Shakuntala* to the German intellectual world. He brought *Shakuntala* with him in 1790 from a stay in England. *Shakuntala* set the classically inclined German literary world aflame. Foster never had the opportunity of seeing India for himself. In a letter of 23rd July 1790 he wrote, "I have brought with me from England: *Sacontala* or The Fatal Ring, an Indian drama, translated by Sir W. Jones from the Sanskrit and written by Calidas [Kalidas], a famous Indian poet, 1,900 years ago! The qualities of this play make it worthy of close attention. It embodies subtlety, sentiment and poetic fervour despite its childlike innocence of the as yet unformed art of drama."

In his foreword to *Sakontala*, Georg Forster stated, "(The fascination of the work did not lie in) its having five or seven acts, but in the fact that the tenderest emotions of which the human heart is capable could have been as well expressed on the Ganges by dark-skinned people as on the Rhine, the Tyber or the Ilissus by our white race." He sent a copy to Herder, who wrote the Preface to the second edition of Forster's work. Writing to Whilhelm Humboldt on 17th December 1795, Forster declared enthusiastically that "in the whole Greek antique" there were "*no poetic portrayal of beautiful womanhood and beautiful love*" that came anywhere near *Shakuntala* (Leifer 1971: 77-79).

9. Jones did not state that Sanskrit was the mother of Indian and European languages or the source of all civilization. His argument was that there was a fundamental unity in human thought and belief beneath the surface of linguistic differences (Ballantyne 2002: 29-30; Majeed 1992: 15). Jones reconciled his belief in the harmony of Indo-European languages with the Genesis account of Creation that formed the basis of Western understanding of languages and human development. According to this account three distinct races emerged after the Flood – the Persians and Indians (including the Greeks, Romans, Goths, Egyptians, and probably also the Chinese and Japanese), the Jews and Arabs, and the Tartars. These three broadly defined races were associated with the three sons of Noah and were also defined linguistically; the first were descendants of Ham, the second of Shem, and the third of Japheth (Ballantyne 2002: 27-29). Trautmann (Trautmann 2004: 42-47) has shown that Jones's theory was a reworking of Jacob Bryant's *Analysis of Ancient Mythology* (1774–1776), which had stated that the Egyptians, Greeks, Romans, and Indians were descendants of Ham. Later 19th century theorists regarded the Aryans (Indians, Europeans, and Polynesians) as sons of Japheth.

10. Wilson attempted to reverse the educational plans of William Bentinck-Thomas Macaulay for India. In a lengthy article in the *Asiatic Journal* (*Asiatic Journal* 1836: 1-16) he argued, "It is not by the English language that we can enlighten the people of India; it can only be effected through the forms of speech which they already understand and use. These must be applied to the purpose, either by direct translation, or which is preferable, by the representation of European facts, opinions, and sentiments, in an original native garb" (Zastoupil and Moir 1999: 46, 225-41).

While Boden Professor at Oxford, Wilson corresponded with Ramcomul Sen, Native Secretary to the Asiatic Society and later Dewan of Calcutta Mint. In a letter dated 20th August 1834, Wilson wrote, "If Sanskrit is discouraged in India, the Pundits must adjourn to Europe; but neither Lord William, nor Mr. Trevelyan, know what they are doing when they seek to dis-countenance it. Upon its cultivation depends the means of the native dialects to embody European learning and science. It is a visionary absurdity to think of making English the language of India. It should be extensively studied, no doubt, but the improvement of the native dialects, enriching them with Sanskrit terms for English ideas, and to effect this, Sanskrit must be cultivated as well as English" (Mittra 1880: 16-17).

In another letter, dated 25th September 1835, Wilson reiterated, "...I saw no incompatibility between the cultivation of the classical languages of India and English, and I am still of the opinion that real improvement — the elevation of the minds of the people — cannot be effected without both classes of languages being studied" (Mittra 1880: 19).

4

State of English Society at Home and in India

W hile the apparently degenerate state of Hindus and Hinduism was a cause of concern for the Evangelicals, English society in the eighteenth century has been described as in a state of "spiritual torpor." The general quality of life was low and cynicism about religion and Church palpable at all levels. The French thinker, Montesquieu (1645–1725), after a visit to the country, had remarked that in the higher circles "everyone laughs if one talks of religion." Most prominent public figures were "distinguished for the grossness and immorality of their lives" (Green 1875: 717). Faithfulness to marriage vows was not in vogue. The King, the Prime Minister, and the Prince of Wales all lived in open adultery at the time of Robert Walpole's ministry (1721–1742; Balleine 1951: 12). Lord Chesterfield, in letters to his son, initiated him on the art of seduction as part of his education (Green 1875: 717).

At the other end of the social scale, the masses were "ignorant and brutal" to an extent difficult to visualize. The introduction of gin gave "a new impetus to drunkenness"

(Green 1875: 717). London gin shops invited customers to get "Drunk for 1 D, dead drunk for 2 D, clean straw for nothing!" (Balleine 1951: 11).

The peasantry, pauperized by the misuse of Poor Laws, was bereft of moral or religious guidance. The Evangelist, Hannah Moore, later recalled, "We saw but one Bible in the parish of Cheddar and that was used to prop a flower-pot" (Green 1875: 717). The baptism registers indicated the unbridled dissipation in the villages. Immorality was accompanied by a love for brutality. Cock-fighting and bull-baiting ranked among popular amusements.

In the absence of an effective police, mobs pillaged towns at will. The criminal code was draconian in the belief that it would deter crime. People were threatened with the gallows "for every offence about which there was a temporary panic." During the reign of George II (1727–1760) and a considerable part of that of George III (1760–1820), capital offences increased at a rate exceeding two a year. The arbitrary list of two hundred crimes punishable by death did not even have "consistent severity to recommend it." It was death sentence for stealing from a boat on a navigable river, but not from a boat on a canal. It was a capital offence to cut down trees in a garden and slit a person's nose; but a vicious attack in which the victim managed to survive with nose intact was not so categorized (Trevelyan 1944: 31).

The pillory was a common punishment. Men and women were whipped through the streets. Public executions were a popular enjoyment, "All London turned out on Mondays for the Tyburn hangings" (Balleine 1951: 12).

The English clergy then was among the most inactive in Europe, "the most remiss of their labours in private, and the least severe in their lives" (Green 1875: 717). The archbishops, bishops and their subordinates had all abandoned celibacy. They were the direct nominees of the Crown, which ensured that the selection was political. A considerable number of the appointees were of aristocratic birth (Halevy 1949: 390; 393).

The lower clergymen were chosen, not by the episcopates, but by the Crown or lay persons. In the few instances where the archbishop or the bishop could make appointments, he distributed the patronage among his relatives, first among his sons and sons-in-law. With the disbanding of the monasteries, the parochial patronage was transferred to the colleges at Oxford and Cambridge, the public schools of Eton and Winchester (as they were the direct heirs of the former religious houses), or to the Crown, or the families of great landowners. The landed gentry were thus, "masters equally of the ecclesiastical as of the civil administration" (Halevy 1949: 390; 393-94).

England was then perhaps the only country in Christendom where candidates for ordination were not tested for their knowledge of theology. They were all selected from Oxford and Cambridge; neither University having a special institute for imparting the Christian doctrine. At Oxford, applicants were asked a single question on divinity at the examination. At Cambridge, there was no test in theology and one could directly advance to clerical status (Halevy 1949: 391).

The dual practices of pluralities and non-residence had rendered the Church of England almost static. The sale of benefices by public auction was common, but whether he obtained the benefice as a favour or by purchase, there was "nothing whatever of the 'priest' about the English clergyman" (Halevy 1949: 395). A person could concurrently hold several benefices, in one instance a person held as many as eight.

The priest performed his religious duties in his parishes by appointing a deputy at a low stipend and keeping the rest of the income. If the parishes were nearby, he performed the duties himself in a perfunctory manner. He would hurry from one Church to another every Sunday morning, and rush through an abbreviated service. Hundreds of parishes had only one service a week and none during bad weather. The churches were rundown, almost empty barns, where the village children played their marbles, and "the beadles hatched out their chicken" (Halevy 1949: 397-98).

STATE OF BRITISH SOCIETY IN CALCUTTA

Englishmen in Calcutta lived no differently from their compatriots back home. As far back as November 1699, Parson Benjamin Adams, appointed to the Bay (Hughli), narrating some of the scandals, said, "I might instance in several things of this nature which occur daily, to the great scandal of our Christian profession ..." (Wilson I 1895: 200-02).

Captain Alexander Hamilton (who journeyed between the Cape of Good Hope and Japan from 1688 to 1723 and published an account of his experiences in 1727), recorded various stories then current about Job Charnock, the Company's head agent, and his Indian wife. In addition, he detailed the corrupt practices of President Weltden who's "term of governing was very short," but, who "took as short a way to be enriched by it, by harassing the people to fill his coffers. ... I could give many instances of the force of bribing both here and elsewhere in India, but am loath to ruffle the skin of old sores" (Wilson I 1895: 202-03).

CORRUPTION IN COMPANY SERVICE

Corruption and nepotism were pervasive at the East India Company's headquarters in London itself. All appointments to Company service were made by nomination by the Court of Directors. The importance of the patronage powers of the Directors increased dramatically after the battle of Plassey, when immense opportunities for misappropriation arose.

The Directors used their patronage first to provide for their own families. Lawrence Sulivan, for instance, sent his three brothers and only son to India. Some utilized this privilege to get a direct fiscal return by sale of appointments. In 1772, Charles Grant, in a letter to his uncle, stated that he had acquired his selection as a Writer for "no less than five thousand pounds" from Director, Henry Savage, who gave it to him on the plea of Richard Becher. During the debate on Fox's India Bill in the House of Commons, Sir William Dolben pointed out that there had been advertisements in the press offering 1,000 pounds for a Writership in Bengal. William Hickey narrated an incident when Lord Cornwallis asked Colonel Auchmuty how he had managed to get his sons in the Company. The Colonel replied, "I gave the lads of Leadenhall Street (the Directors) five thousand guineas ... for the writerships in Bengal for my two eldest whelps, and so in the generosity of their hearts they threw a cadetship into the bargain for my youngest spalpeen" (Ghosh 1998: 20-21).

In the second half of the eighteenth century, the Directors distributed the patronage among themselves according to their seniority in the Direction. The Chairs and the nine senior members of the Court of Directors who served on the Committee of Correspondence got the largest share. In 1776, for instance, the Chairman and his Deputy each got two Bengal and two Madras Writerships, the nine members of the Committee of Correspondence got one Bengal Writership each, eight Directors got one Madras Writership each, and five one Bombay Writership each.

The Board of Control, established in 1784, was also given a share of the patronage. Thus, William Pitt obtained one Bengal Writership in 1791, and one in 1792. In 1794, he received two Bengal Writerships and Henry Dundas one. After 1794, the share of the Board was raised to four and all were given to Henry Dundas. He availed of the opportunity to send young Scotsmen to India, to the disapproval of some members of the Board. The second Earl of Minto stated that there was hardly a gentleman's family in Scotland, of whatever politics, that had not received some Indian appointment or some act of kindness from Dundas (Ghosh 1998: 17-18).

Several secret enquiries were conducted on the sale of patronage. At the time of the renewal of the Company's

Charter in 1793, Parliament imposed an oath that each Director had to take within ten days of election to the Direction. He had to pledge that he would not derive any pecuniary advantage from the use of his patronage. But the old practice appears to have continued for some time (Ghosh 1998: 22).

The patronage was also used to secure a position in Parliament. From 1758 to 1800, there were 126 persons who sat in the Direction, of whom 34 sat in the House of Commons during the period covered by the Parliamentary elections between 1761 and 1802 (Ghosh 1998: 24; Cohn 1966: 106). A Director's patronage was helpful in winning support in a constituency. David Scott, elected in 1796, for instance, used his patronage to satisfy demands from his electorate. As the patronage at the disposal of a Director was limited, he borrowed from his friends in the Direction and also maintained a "Book of Patronage," whereby he tried to grant a Writership or Cadetship according to the seniority on the list. Scott admitted his use of Indian patronage to maintain his seat in Parliament in a letter to Collins Salisbury,

> I ... have a just sense of your kind Offices in my election, and if I had a Cadetship in my gift, you should have it immediately — When I left the Direction (out by rotation) last year, I was too much committed for patronage and the late Contest (of 1796) has increased exceedingly my obligations to my Friends — on my list of Cadets there are 11 not one of which can be struck off unless by themselves on finding my inability to serve them (Ghosh 1998: 24-26).

MISUSE OF *DASTAKS*

As regards India, there had been allegations of corruption among Company servants employed in its commercial business in the first half of the eighteenth century. In 1752, the Directors charged that Europeans had collected a ten per cent commission from those to whom they farmed markets or the collection of dues (Marshall 1976: 160-62). The situation changed noticeably after Plassey, which opened the floodgates for Company officials to make personal fortunes. They blatantly resorted to extortions and misuse of *dastaks* (customs duty exemption passes granted to the Company) for their private trade.[1]

RECEIPT OF PRESENTS

These gains were, however, a trifle compared to the enormous amounts collected by highly placed Company servants. From the mid-eighteenth century, the British in Bengal were in a position to decide who would be the Nawab and made the claimants pay handsomely for their support. On the eve of the battle of Plassey, Mir Jafar, a contender for the Nawab-ship, formally pledged to award huge sums to the Company and make large presents to its officials. He by and large kept his promises. Subsequently, the Select Committee of the House of Commons compiled a list of presents worth 1,238,575 pounds that were distributed in 1757[2] (Marshall 1976: 165-66).

In October 1760, just three years after Plassey and within months of Clive's departure, there was another change in the Nawab-ship of Bengal. The Governor, Henry Vansittart, replaced Mir Jafar with his son-in-law, Mir Kasim. The new Nawab was forced to recompense for his accession with grant of the districts of Burdwan, Chittagong, and Midnapur to the Company and payments to individuals. The Select Committee of the House of Commons, on the basis of incomplete information, later concluded that presents worth 200,000 pounds were taken after the "revolution" of 1760.

When Mir Kasim was defeated in 1763 (following determined efforts to protect his authority from fresh British encroachments) and Mir Jafar brought back as Nawab, he, too, was confronted with demands for money. Officers in the army also applied for personal remuneration for their role in the overthrow of Mir Kasim. Major Hector Munro, who commanded the army at the battle of Buxar, for example, demanded two lakhs in compensation for the award of a *jagir* in Bengal (Marshall 1976: 169-72).

The grant of the *Diwani* of Bengal, Bihar, and Orissa to the Company in 1765 considerably worsened the situation.[3] Clive, who returned to Calcutta in May 1765, described the situation,

> I shall only say, that such a scene of anarchy, confusion, bribery, corruption, and extortion was never seen or heard of in any country but Bengal; nor such and so many fortunes acquired in so unjust and rapacious a manner. The three provinces of Bengal, Behar, and Orissa, producing a clear revenue of 3,000,000 pounds sterling, have been under the absolute management of the Company's servants, ever since Mir Jafar's restoration to the subaship; and they have, both civil and military, exacted and levied contributions from every man of power and consequence, from the Nawab down to the lowest zemindar.

> The trade has been carried on by free merchants, acting as gomastas to the Company's servants, who, under the sanction of their names, have committed actions which make the name of the English stink in the nostrils of a Hindu or a Mussulman; and the Company's servants themselves have interfered with the revenues of the Nawab, turned out and put in the officers of the government at pleasure, and made every one pay for their preferment (Malcolm II 1836: 379-80).

In 1765, the Directors sent orders prohibiting receipt of presents. However, on Mir Jafar's death that year, Company officials made the new Nawab, Najm-ud-daula, a young boy of sixteen, pay for his appointment. The contenders for the office of chief minister were also forced to disburse cash. Muhammad Reza Khan, who served as *Naib Subehdar* from 1765 to 1772, was alleged to have generously rewarded the Residents at Murshidabad and the Governors at Calcutta. He later produced lists of money he had distributed to senior

Company officials. The recipients did not deny the allegations, but insisted that they had not solicited the money. They said, "we more than once told him (the Nawab) we wanted no such offer if it was not entirely with his own inclination, which he repeatedly assured us it was." They also denied putting any pressure on Muhammad Reza Khan (Marshall 1976: 172-75).

In the twelve years between 1757 and 1769, it was virtually guaranteed that a Company servant in Bengal would return home with a fortune. William Watts, who had played a vital part in the Plassey revolution, was, on his death, said to have left an estate valued at 110,000 pounds. Clive's successor as Governor, Holwell, worth 20,000 pounds when he assumed charge, had amassed 96,000 pounds when he demitted office a few months later. Henry Vansittart, on return home, bought a valuable estate in Berkshire and got himself into Parliament. John Johnstone was worth 300,000 pounds when he went back to Scotland and purchased three estates (Marshall 1976: 234-43).

There were several Parliamentary investigations into the crimes in the East. In 1772–1773, the Select Committee of the House of Commons conjectured that "presents" worth over two million pounds had been distributed in Bengal between 1757 and 1765 (Dirks 2007: 10). The most significant investigation concerned the acquisitions of Robert Clive. In a letter to his father, in August 1757, Clive had acknowledged the magnitude of the gifts he had received from Mir Jafar. He wrote, "His (the Nawab's) generosity has been such as will enable me to live in my native country much beyond my most sanguine wishes" (Muir 1971: 59). In 1759, eighteen months after Plassey, Clive had decided to add a permanent income from India to his already substantial assets. He secured from the Nawab a *jagir* worth roughly 27,000 pounds a year (Marshall 1976: 165-66). Clive had left Bengal in 1760 with the greatest fortune ever made by an individual in India. In 1767, he calculated his total stock at 401,102 pounds.

In his defense, in 1772, Clive stressed his relative virtue as compared to those of his Company colleagues. He declared,

> A great prince was dependent on my pleasure, an opulent city lay at my mercy; its richest bankers bid against each other for my smiles; I walked through vaults which were thrown open to me alone, piled on either hand with gold and jewels! Mr. Chairman, at this moment I stand astonished at my own moderation (Muir 1971: 60).

The *Annual Register* reported that Clive "may with all propriety be said to be the richest subject in the three kingdoms" (Dirks 2007: 48).

Robert Orme, official historian of the East India Company, stopped his account of the Company in 1762 due to his growing alarm about writing the history of scandal. A painstaking chronicler of mid-eighteenth century events, who began as a supporter of Clive, he said, "I have looked forward into the subject far enough to see that the Bengal transactions will not do my countrymen so much honour as they have received from the first volume"[4] (Dirks 2007: 247).

As a growing number of Company servants who returned to England with fortunes invested in property, titles, "rotten boroughs" and seats in Parliament, there were apprehensions that the corruption, greed, vice, and misrule of the East would be brought home and undermine traditional values and virtues. Lord Chatham expressed concern that, "The riches of Asia have been poured in upon us, and have brought with them not only Asiatic Luxury, but, I fear, Asiatic principles of government. Without connections, without any natural interest in the soil, the importers of foreign gold have forced their way into Parliament by such a torrent of private corruption as no hereditary fortune could resist" (Lawson 1993: 120).

Clive used his massive personal fortune not only to become an Irish peer, but also to command a troop of seven MPs elected under his patronage (Travers 2008: 39). In Samuel Foote's play, *The Nabob,* first produced in 1772 at Haymarket Theater, the country gentleman and MP, Sir Thomas Oldham, complained to Sir Matthew Mite, a returned Nabob, that "your riches by introducing a general spirit of dissipation, have extinguished labour and industry, the slow, but sure source of national wealth" (Travers 2008: 52).

The Regulating Act of 1774, ostensibly an effort to control the Company, was itself an indication of the extent to which Parliament had come under the sway of "Nabob" money. In lending the Company over one million pounds to avert bankruptcy, the Act was a demonstration that many sitting members had shares and proprietary interests in the Company (Dirks 2007: 15). In the 1760s, about twenty-three per cent of MPs held Company stock (Travers 2008: 39).

A Supreme Court was established in Calcutta to protect the natives from oppression. But that did not materially transform the situation. Twelve years after the passage of the Regulating Act, Sir John Shore claimed that he could have amassed 10,000 *l.* a year if he did not have scruples (Marshman 1859: 40-41). Records in the India Office labelled *Europeans in India* (vols. i-xxiv) contain detailed accounts of European misdeeds in Bengal during the years 1766–1800 (Spear 1980: 192-94).

STATE OF RELIGION AMONG ENGLISHMEN IN INDIA

In 1775, a year after his arrival in India, Alexander Mackrabie, brother-in-law of Philip Francis (member of the Supreme Council), described the state of the clergy in a letter to Rev. S. Baggs. He said,

> We are upon excellent terms with the clergy here. They are not numerous, but thoroughly orthodox. One rivals Nimrod in hunting, a second supplies bullocks for the army, another

is a perfect connoisseur in Chinese gardening. I endeavour to obtain some light from them all; but the fear of God is not the kind of wisdom most in request in Bengal (Busteed 1972: 127).

James Hickey, who started *Hickey's Bengal Gazette* in 1780, wrote of the army chaplain, Mr. Blunt,

This incomprehensible young man got abominably drunk and in that disgraceful condition exposed himself to both soldiers and sailors, running out stark naked into the midst of them, talking all sorts of bawdy and ribaldry, and singing scraps of the most blackguard and indecent songs, so as to render himself a common laughing stock (Kincaid 1973: 105).

Eustace Carey, nephew of Rev. William Carey, observed,

By the almost total absence of an Evangelical ministry, and, in many remote stations, the total destitution of all means whatever of religious improvement, there was nothing to restrain the exorbitancy of human passions, or prevent renunciation of principle...

He added,

A practical assimilation to heathenism soon obliterated the influence and almost the recollection of a nominally Christian education; and 'the filthiness of the flesh' made way for 'the filthiness of the spirit,' and, by their mutual corroboration, both became fearfully rancorous. Men feared to read their Bible, because it denounced their crimes and awakened their punishments. The next thing was, to hope the Bible they had neglected was not true; then to feign to think it false; and soon, being able to believe the lie which depravity had led them to forge, they openly impugned and denounced it. Hence Hinduism was 'a most beautiful religion,' Mahommedanism had but little in it objectionable; but Christianity was as revolting to the prevailing habits and tastes of that day as was its Holy Founder to that of the generation who witnessed his incarnation and ministry, and in whose esteem he was without form and comeliness (Carey 1836: 352-53).

Sabbath was rarely observed. In the army the flag was hoisted, and those who saw it knew it was Sunday, "Is it Sunday? Yes; for I see the flag is hoisted" (Spear 1980: 111). But the work-table and the card-table were availed of as on week-days.

CONCUBINES

The majority of Europeans in and out of service lived with native females. In 1790, there were only 250 European women in Calcutta compared to 4,000 men (Nevile 2010: 18). A favourite after-dinner toast changed the traditional lament, 'Alas and alack-a-day,' into 'A lass and a *lakh* a day,' illustrative of the desire to acquire huge sums and a *bibi*, or Indian companion (Ballhatchet 1980: 2).

Young civilians were told on their arrival that among their first duties was to "stock a *zenana*" and that the mistress was the best *moonshee* (accountant) in the country. In 1780, Asiaticus (Philip Stanhope) calculated the expenses of the seraglio "... for those whose rank in the service entitles them to a princely income" (Spear 1980: 36-37). Innes Munro pointed out that it was easier to support "a whole *zenana* of Indians than the extravagance of one English lady."

Captain Thomas Williamson, who came to Bengal in 1778, in his *The East India Vade Mecum* (1810), devoted a section to the cost of maintaining native mistresses. He estimated it would cost forty rupees a month per female, "which must certainly be considered no great price for a bosom friend, when compared with the sums laid out upon some British damsels" (Nevile 2010: 21-22). He narrated the story of an elderly gentleman who kept a harem of sixteen, and when asked how he looked after such a large number, replied, "Oh, I give them a little rice and let them run about." Among those who had Indian mistresses were Philip Francis and John Shore.

It was in Calcutta that Mrs. Sherwood found the material for her account of "the splendid sloth and the languid debauchery of European Society in those days ..." (Kincaid 1973: 90-91). Mrs. Sherwood was particularly disturbed by the influence of native dancing girls on her compatriots,

> All these English-men who were beguiled by this sweet music had had mothers at home, and some had mothers still, who, in the far distant land of their children's birth, still cared, and prayed, and wept for the once blooming boys, who were then slowly sacrificing themselves to drinking, smoking, want of rest, and the witcheries of the unhappy daughters of heathens and infidels (Dyson 1978: 81).

GLUTTONY

There are plentiful accounts of Company servants having gargantuan fifteen course meals for dinner and supper, accompanied by drinks on the same lavish scale (Spear 1980: 12). A visitor to Calcutta in 1761, wrote,

> It is a frequent observation that the English gentlemen, finding unexpectedly this country to produce what is common to them in England, are too apt to indulge their appetites; so it is become a saying that they live like Englishmen and die like rotten sheep. Of 84 rank and file, which our company consisted of on our arrival, we had but 34 remaining in three months ... (Nair 1984: 133).

Eliza Fay noted the food at dinner, the heaviest meal of the day, "A soup, a roast fowl, curry and rice, a mutton pie, a fore-quarter of lamb, a rice pudding, tarts, very good cheese, fresh churned butter, fine bread, excellent Madeira" (Fay 1908: 181).

Most people of all classes drank too much, "the income of the drinker determining only the quality and not the quantity of the drink" (Spear 1980: 18-19). Philip Francis's wine book revealed that in one month in 1774, 268 bottles of wine had been drunk in his household (Ghosh 1998: 124). A lady wrote from Calcutta a few years before the arrival of Rev. William Carey (1793), "Wine is the heaviest family article, for whether it is taken fashionably or medicinally, every lady drinks at least a bottle per day, and the gentlemen four times that quantity" (Annett: 42). Rev. Tennant commented that gentlemen would often finish "the whole chest of claret" while judging its quality at the dinner table (Ghosh 1998: 125).

COST OF HOUSEHOLD

A lot of money was spent on maintaining a household. Mackrabie, in a letter to his father in 1775, described the size of his establishment, "One hundred and ten servants to wait upon a family of four People. Oh monstrous! And yet we are economists" (Ghosh 1998: 111). William Hickey, not affluent by Calcutta standards, had a staff of sixty-three (Nevile 2010: 2). William Carey was struck by the "profuse way of living" of Europeans in India (Annett: 43).

LOW MORALITY

Rev. James Long (1814–1887), of the Church Missionary Society, who arrived in Calcutta in 1840, was, as member of the Government Record Commission, given access to the early records of the East India Company in Bengal. He wrote of British society prior to his arrival, "...the state of Morals in Calcutta ... was low among all classes ... Enormous fortunes were made by no creditable means ...'" (Nair 1983: 26). Rev. Long elaborated on the state of English society,

> Religion was at a low ebb in Calcutta last century, but so it was throughout England, and particularly among the middle and lower classes ... Talk of religion — there was not even common morality in high quarters. Tippoo styled the English of his day 'the most faithless and usurping of mankind.' ... Half a dozen palanquins or carriages about

1790 were sufficient to convey persons on Sunday to St. John's Church ... persons proceeded from Church direct to join the company at a Durga Puja Nautch ... These were days when we find a Colonel submit to be circumcised in order to get possession of a Mussulmani who would not on other terms submit to be his mistress (Long 1974: 106-08).

Fortunes were lost on cards in a single night. The stakes were high, but the club remained crowded every evening. Philip Francis won 20,000 pounds in a single sitting, while Richard Barwell, Commercial Resident at Malda, lost 40,000 in another. Mackrabie noted the huge sum he lost in a night. "Oh," ran an entry in his diary on 9th March 1776, "I lost seven rubbers running. Oh sad, sad, sad" (Kincaid 1973: 92).

Some improvement in the moral ambiance became visible after Lord Cornwallis (1738–1805) assumed charge as Governor General in 1786. Cornwallis had the advantage of an aristocratic background, unlike earlier Governors who had humble beginnings in India. He was a person of exceptional honesty and also benefited from the secure base created by Warren Hastings. But John Kaye (1814–1876) stated, "there was little real Christianity in India. ... Living in a heathen land, they (the Englishmen) were still contented to live as heathens... Christianity cantered to the races in the morning and in the evening drove to a nautch." Any talk of divine worship was dismissed. One lady claimed to be a venerator of the Sabbath, because she read the Church service while her *ayah* combed her hair. Another, who had lived in Calcutta for twelve years, said she had never been to the Church because no gentleman had offered to escort her (Kaye 1859: 121-22). When Cornwallis assumed charge, Calcutta had only one church. A new church, St. John's Church, was completed in 1787. It had several empty pews every Sabbath.

John Shore, who served as Governor General from 1793 to 1798, was a Christian man but could do little for Christianity in India. Lord Wellesley, Governor General from 1798 to 1805, elaborated on the new principles of administration introduced by Cornwallis and "gave them a religious basis." He was the first Governor General who "made a point of regular and official church attendance." In 1800, he attended a Nile thanksgiving ceremony and heard the discourse of Rev. Claudius Buchanan against the revolutionary forces in France. It was relayed among the official community along with orders against Sunday racing (Mayhew 1929: 74). But there was no immediate discernible change. Rev. Long wrote,

> An anecdote is recorded of Lord Wellesley traveling up the country. He halted for a Sunday at a civil station when he requested the judge to read the Church service, — but he was informed there would be some difficulty as there was not a Bible in the 'station;' — last remnants of the days when Europeans left their religion behind them at the Cape of Good Hope to be resumed when they returned from India (Long 1974: 108).

Rev. Daniel Corrie (1777–1837), who arrived as a chaplain in 1806, also found a general indifference to religion. "The state of society among us is such," he remarked, "as would make rivers of water run down the face of a man of David's spirit" (Hough IV 1845: 357).

Lord Hastings, who assumed office as Governor General in 1813, allowed Rev. T.T. Thomason to accompany him on a state tour through the provinces as Chaplain. Rev. Thomason was, however, dismissed from the camp in June 1814, because he protested at "the general profanation of the Lord's Day, and finding that his public notice of it was disregarded, he thought proper to remonstrate with the Governor-General against such a dereliction of Christian duty." His censure gave much offence, though the order of dismissal was soon revoked. The "desecration of the Sabbath, and other improprieties of conduct remained unaltered" (Hough IV 1845: 383).

William Adam (who came to Bengal as a Baptist missionary in 1817 but left the Baptists in 1821 and wrote the famous *State of Education in Bengal*) remarked, in 1824, that "The low state of religion and morals among Christians tends to the discredit of the Christian cause" (Sen Gupta 1971: 63). Frederick John Shore (son of Sir John Shore), who came to India in 1818, commented that there was,

> little in the conduct of the English, whether the Government or individuals be concerned, which should induce the people of India to respect the religion professed by us ... The mass of people, indeed, consider the English as a low tribe, who have no religion, and that to become of the same persuasion with ourselves, they have only to throw off the trammels of caste, to drink wine, not forgetting occasionally to get drunk, and eat beef or pork (Penner and MacLean 1983: 192-93).

However, public debate over the renewal of the Company's Charter turned the focus on the "scandals" in India rather than on the personal excesses of Englishmen in the country. The shift in the attention of William Wilberforce and the Evangelicals from slavery to sati, symbolized "the more general displacement of scandal from colonizer to colonized." Practices like sati, female infanticide, and hook swinging became the subject of intense debate. They warranted British rule. In the writings of the Empire in the nineteenth century, almost "sacred status" was accorded to the atrocity tale of the Black Hole of Calcutta[5] (Dirks 2007: 34).

The changed perception of the British role in India, the "moral swing to the East," demanded that imperial presence be justified not in terms of economic gains but the advantages it conferred on the native population. Sati became a major validation of the civilizing mission.

END-NOTES

1. In 1717, the Company had obtained a *farman* (imperial edict), from the Mughal Emperor, Furrukhsiyar, granting it customs-free trading privileges. A *dastak,* signed by the head of an

English factory, shown at a toll-house secured the Company's goods from all duties. After Plassey, as the stature of the Company increased, its servants misused the *dastaks* for their private trade.

Henry Vansittart, Clive's eventual successor, described the situation, "... our influence over the country was no sooner felt than many innovations were practiced by some of the Company's servants or the people employed under their authority. They began to trade in the articles which were before prohibited, and to interfere in the affairs of the country" (Vansittart 1976: 24).

Harry Verelst, the next Governor, similarly observed, "A trade was carried on without payment of duties, in the prosecution of which infinite oppressions were committed. English agents or Gomastahs, not contented with injuring the people, trampled on the authority of government, binding and punishing the Nabob's officers whenever they presumed to interfere" (Verelst 1772: 48).

The gross misuse of *dastaks* forced the Nawab to complain to the English Governor in March 1762. In May, he again protested at being deprived of the duties "...I suffer a yearly loss of nearly twenty-five lakhs ..." (Dutt I 1970: 13; 15).

Warren Hastings, then member of the Governor's Council, was among the few (along with Vansittart) to object to the unashamed abuse of *dastaks* for the private trade of Company officials.

In a bid to allow Indian merchants the same privilege as Englishmen, the Nawab, Mir Kasim, abolished all inland duties. But Company servants demanded the restoration of inland duties for everyone except themselves. The matter led to war in 1763 in which Mir Kasim was defeated. In a fit of anger, he had the English prisoners at Patna massacred and then left his kingdom. Mir Jafar was again placed on the throne but died soon after, and was succeeded by his illegitimate son.

Clive, on his return to Bengal in1765, reduced the opportunities for plunder by abolishing most of the *aurungs* (up country factories) and recalling their staff, but the problem persisted. He made inland trade in salt, betel, and tobacco a monopoly, the profits of which were to be divided among Company servants according to their rank. The Company itself was to receive an *ad valorem* duty of 35 per cent. Though not sanctioned by the Directors, this scheme continued till 1768 (O'Malley 1931: 13-16).

However, the problem persisted till 1775, when the Governor, Warren Hastings stopped the use of *dastaks*. The Regulating Act had meanwhile prohibited private trade for all Company servants engaged in revenue collection or the administration of justice, though it was still permitted for those whose duties were purely commercial (Blunt 1938: 27-28).

2. John Clark Marshman (1794–1877), son of the missionary Rev. Joshua Marshman, described the state of affairs after the battle of Plassey. He wrote, "A boundless field was suddenly opened before them for the gratification of ambition and cupidity, and every thought was absorbed in the accumulation of wealth, without any qualms of conscience as to the mode of its acquisition..." He affirmed that the "influence of Christian principle" was almost extinct in European society and "a deadly taint of impiety pervaded the whole community... Calcutta presented a scene of such unblushing licentiousness, avarice, and infidelity as had never been witnessed before under the British flag. England had subdued Bengal, and Bengal had subdued the morals of its conquerors" (Marshman 1859: 39-41).

3. From the time the Company secured the Diwani of Bengal, Bihar and Orissa, a progressively increasing drain of Indian resources commenced. The land revenue collected by Mughal agents in Bengal in 1764–1765 was valued at 818,000 pounds. In 1765–1766, the first year of the Company's Diwani, it rose to 1,470,000 pounds. By 1790–1791, it had further increased to 2,680,000 pounds, and it was on this basis that the Permanent Settlements were made (Beauchamp 1934: 24). The Fourth Report of the House of Commons (1773) on the revenues and expenses of Bengal during the first six years of the Company's administration showed that the gross revenue grew from approximately 2,260,000 pounds in 1765–1766 to 3,800,000 pounds the following year. After the payment of tribute to the Mughal Emperor, collection charges, and all the

Company's civil and military expenses there was a balance of 1,250,000 pounds to be remitted home (Beauchamp 1934: 25; Dutt I 1970: 30-31).

This annual drain of nearly one-third of the net revenue did not reveal the total depletion of Bengal. Vast sums were taken out by English officials who made great fortunes. Harry Verelst, Governor of Bengal (1767–1770), compiled figures of imports into and exports from Bengal for the years 1766, 1767, and 1768. These showed that Bengal sent out about ten times what it imported (Beauchamp 1934: 25-26; Dutt I 1970: 30-31). Holden Furber was perhaps the first professional historian who tried to quantify the extent of the annual drain of wealth from India to Britain. For the period between 1783 and 1793, he estimated the figure to be 1.8 million pounds (Furber 1970: 310).

4. There were many instances of Company men borrowing large sums of money from Indians. In 1824, the Bengal Government ordered an inquiry regarding 33 Bengal covenanted servants who had been appointed between 1808 and 1810. The inquiry revealed that 16, or roughly half the covenanted servants, were still in debt almost fifteen years after their arrival in India; twelve, or slightly more than a third, severely so. In 1823, the Bengal Government promulgated Regulation VII prohibiting district officials throughout India from borrowing money from individuals under their authority (Sramek 2013: 50-52).

5. According to the standard account, the Nawab of Bengal after capturing the English fort at Calcutta, in June 1756, forced the remaining 146 Europeans into a dingy detention cell 18 by 14 foot space, known as the Black Hole, which had only two small windows. Most of the prisoners died. Brijen K. Gupta has examined the various accounts of the incident and shown that the number of Europeans who may have actually died in the Black Hole was 18 of 39 taken prisoners (Gupta 1966: 70-80).

5

The Evangelical Movement

By all accounts, widow immolation appears not to have been a regular occurrence in pre-British India. In the early nineteenth century, however, it suddenly assumed the appearance of a pervasive practice, which demanded intervention by the colonial Government. What brought about this abrupt and unexpected change? A significant development took place in the year 1803, when Rev. William Carey and his colleagues at the Serampore mission engaged ten people to record all cases of sati that occurred within thirty miles of Calcutta. Who were the Serampore missionaries, and why did they get so interested in sati as to commission a private survey? The answers to these questions can be found in the rise of the Evangelical movement in Britain.

Towards the close of the eighteenth century, a movement known as Evangelicalism spread among the upper classes in Britain partly in response to the revolution in France (Halevy 1949: 433-34). Indeed, the French Revolution and its Napoleonic aftermath determined much of what happened in England between 1789 and 1815. As the Whig lawyer, Alexander

Cockburn, put it, "everything was connected with the Revolution in France, which for twenty years, was, or was made, all in all, everything; not this thing or that thing, but literally everything was soaked in this one event" (Briggs 1967: 129).

Evangelicalism derived much of its motive force from hostility to the French Revolution. The Evangelicals felt that the root of the crisis in France lay in the irreligion propagated by Voltaire. They endeavoured to prevent a similar outburst in England by a religious movement designed to make the lower classes religious and reverent. The Evangelicals promoted voluntary organizations like the London Missionary Society in 1795, the Church Missionary Society in 1799 (Tomkins 2010: 176-77) and the British and Foreign Bible Society in 1804 (Tomkins 2010: 191-93).

While the threat of invasion hung over England, Bibles were considered the best antidote and distributed in thousands. The *Christian Observer* wrote in 1812, "If the security of the state depends upon the loyalty and morals of its people, by what other means (than Bible reading) can you contribute so essentially to the preservation of order, to the authority of the law, and the stability of government?" The *Morning Chronicle*, contrasting the two nations, observed "It is to the cultivation of the moral qualities that England is indebted for her power and influence. From the want of them France may be mischievous, but she will never be great" (Briggs 1967: 172-74). The Evangelicals emphasized that the Bible was the key to British success in other countries as well.

The intellectual centre of the Evangelical movement was the University of Cambridge. There it had among the clergy, two leading men of the movement — Isaac Milner and Charles Simeon. Milner, who occupied the chair of John Newton, was president of Queen's College and Dean of Carlisle. Simeon was Vicar of Holy Trinity for over half a century. It was from Trinity Church and Simeon's own College rooms that "radiated so much of that apostolic spirit," that was directed towards India. He was the "spiritual father" of many who ventured to that land — Revs. David Brown, Henry Martyn, John Sargent, Thomas Thomason, and Daniel Corrie — to name a few (Kaye 1859: 128-36).

THE CLAPHAM SECT

The Cambridge set was supported by a group at Clapham, a village near London. Here in close proximity lived a group of affluent men, who linked the Evangelical clergy with the world of politics and business to which they themselves belonged. Their leader was William Wilberforce, who resided at Clapham from 1795 to 1808. The anti-slavery movement was the first of several campaigns associated with the Clapham Sect (Tomkins 2010: 43-50). Many activists in the forefront of the campaign against slavery also highlighted the issue of widow immolation in India, men like Wilberforce and Thomas Fowell Buxton. The latter introduced the first Parliamentary motion calling for the abolition of slavery and presented the first petition to Parliament demanding the suppression of sati (Zastoupil 2011: 60).

Among others at Clapham, the most illustrious was the Thornton family. John Thornton was an uncle of Wilberforce. His three sons, Samuel, Robert, and Henry, were all to become Members of Parliament. The Clapham Sect began to form around them. In 1756, Henry Venn, a distinguished Evangelical, began his ministry there. In 1792, John Venn, son of Henry Venn, and an ardent Evangelical like his father, was invited to settle at Clapham. He remained there till his death in 1813, the religious guide of the brotherhood.

Zachary Macaulay (father of Thomas Macaulay), a Scot, went to Clapham in 1803, and stayed till 1819. His sister was married to Thomas Babington, a man of Evangelical fervour who linked Zachary Macaulay to Clapham.

Two young Scotsmen, Charles Grant and John Shore, employed with the East India Company, also developed intimate links with Clapham. John Shore lived at Clapham from 1802 to 1808 after his return from India where he where he served as Governor General from 1793 to 1798. Charles Grant and James Stephen, a Scottish lawyer, stayed for certain spells. Also in residence were William Smith, Charles Elliott (who married John Venn's sister), and Edward Elliot, brother-in-law of William Pitt (Howse 1960: 15-17).

Thomas Gisborne, a college friend of Wilberforce and clergyman at Staffordshire, too became closely associated with the Sect and resided at Clapham for a considerable part every year. He married the sister of Thomas Babington, and introduced Babington to Wilberforce.

Others of importance to the Clapham Sect included Claudius Buchanan, a Scot who came under the influence of John Newton, a friend of the Sect; Henry Martyn; Josiah Pratt, first editor of the *Christian Observer* and one of the founders of the Church Missionary Society (CMS); Thomas Fowell Buxton (Member of Parliament); and Hannah More, poetess and Evangelical laywoman. Several marriages took place within the group further cementing ties (Howse 1960: 18-19). Reginald Coupland wrote of the Clapham Sect,

> It was a remarkable fraternity, remarkable above all else, perhaps, in its closeness, its affinity. It not only lived for the most part in one little village; it had one character, one mind, one way of life... It was doubtless this homogeneity, this unanimity that gave the group its power in public life. They might differ on party issues; but on any question of religion or philanthropy the voice of the "Saints" in Parliament or in the press, was as the voice of one man. It was, indeed, a unique phenomenon — this brotherhood of Christian politicians. There has never been anything like it since in British public life (Coupland 1945: 251).

The Claphamites aimed at "saving souls" through political action. Two great objectives of the Clapham Sect were abolition of the slave trade and the opening of India to missionary enterprise (Till 1813, the East India Company did not permit missionaries to operate in its territories in India, for fear of an adverse impact on its trading activities).

THE EVANGELICAL MOVEMENT IN INDIA

Towards the close of the eighteenth century, the Evangelists began to make inroads into India. Leading the charge was Charles Grant, Commercial Agent of the East India Company at Malda (Bengal). He was perhaps the first British official to argue for the Christianization and Anglicization of India.

CHARLES GRANT AND THE DEMAND TO CHRISTIANIZE INDIA

Charles Grant (1746–1823) has been called "the father and founder of modern missionary effort in Great Britain's Indian Empire" (Morris 1904: 395). It was due to him, than to any other individual, that Protestant Missions and Missionary Societies of the Church of England commenced their activities in Bengal and North India. Grant had converted to Evangelical Christianity in 1776 following a series of personal tragedies, including the death of two infant children within a span of nine days (Morris 1904: 56-64). For some years after his conversion, he lived quietly in India (he had arrived in 1767 in a humble capacity), where he became a close friend of John Shore (later Lord Teignmouth). Grant also befriended William Chambers, brother of the Supreme Court judge Robert Chambers and an intimate associate of the Danish missionary Frederick Schwartz.[1] William Chambers originally belonged to the Madras Civil Service; but in 1773 joined his brother at Calcutta and became Interpreter in the Supreme Court. Grant described him as "a man whom religion animates and directs" (Morris 1904: 64-65).

In December 1780, Grant was appointed Commercial Resident at Malda, where he resided for six years. Among his many assistants was George Udny, an Evangelical, who became a valued ally. During the latter part of his stay at Malda, Grant acquired a large share in an indigo factory at Gumalti, a village near Gaur, the ancient capital of Bengal. In January 1787, he was appointed Fourth Member of the Board of Trade, and at his suggestion, George Udny was nominated his successor at Malda.

EARLY EFFORTS FOR CHRISTIAN MISSIONS

The first recorded instance of Grant's interest in matters of religion came in the context of St. John's Church (afterwards the Cathedral of the Metropolitan of India). A Church built near the Old Fort in the early eighteenth century had been destroyed in 1756. Efforts to construct a new Church began in 1782 and Grant actively involved himself in the project (Morris 1904: 93).

Grant also displayed interest in Rev. John L. Kiernander's Mission in Calcutta. Rev. Kiernander, a Danish missionary from Cuddalore associated with the Society for the Promotion of Christian Knowledge (SPCK), had arrived in Calcutta in September 1758 at the invitation of Robert Clive, after his mission in South India was dismantled by the French armies (Sen Gupta 1971: 18).

Kiernander started a school in December 1758 and in 1767 began to build a Mission Church, contributing a substantial sum from his personal assets. The Church, which opened for worship three years later, was the only one in Bengal till 1784. In 1787, however, his son was unable to pay a surety that Rev. Kiernander had given. Consequently all Rev. Kiernander's properties were confiscated and put up for sale.

Charles Grant stepped forward and redeemed the Church and the school and handed them to the SPCK. Three trustees of the properties were appointed, William Chambers, Rev.

David Brown (the Evangelical chaplain of the East India Company who had arrived in India in 1786) and Charles Grant himself. An urgent appeal was made to the SPCK to send missionaries, but "the Church at that period was sunk in the selfishness of mere home exertions, and *no one* volunteered, except the Rev. T. Clarke, of Cambridge, who left England for the Mission Church in 1789" (Long 1848: 9-16).

Rev. Clarke was the first English Missionary in Bengal. In 1790, however, while still employed with the Mission, he accepted the post of Superintendent of the Free School Society and subsequently left the Mission altogether to become a chaplain of the East India Company. The Mission Church would have closed down had Rev. Brown not stepped forward and carried on the religious services. It was apparent that there was then little enthusiasm in the Church of England for missionary enterprise (Sherring 1875: 68). Men of missionary zeal like Rev. David Brown, Rev. Claudius Buchanan (who arrived in Calcutta in 1797), and Rev. Henry Martyn (who arrived in 1805) entered the country as chaplains of the East India Company, not as missionaries.

A PROPOSAL FOR ESTABLISHING A PROTESTANT MISSION IN BENGAL AND BEHAR

In 1786–1787, along with Rev. David Brown, William Chambers and George Udny, Grant drafted the plan for a *"Mission to Bengal."*[2] It envisioned the division of the province into eight missionary circles, each with a clergyman of the Church of England. The clergyman was to setup schools, superintend catechisms, and establish churches. Government support was deemed essential for the success of the project. As Rev. David Brown stated, "It requires only to live a month in Bengal to be convinced of this fact: the Governor of Bengal is like the head to the body in a more clear and intimate manner than is perhaps known in any other country. Whatever is undertaken without his permission, or some sort of provision, must wither and die" (Marshman 1859: 31-32).

It was necessary to acquaint the Governor General, Lord Cornwallis, of the plan by "gentle gradations, and therefore (Rev. David Brown) pressed the idea of native schools as preparatory to the main business of giving Christian light to this land sitting in heathen darkness" (Hyde 1901: 217). Cornwallis, however, dismissed the scheme (Marshman 1859: 32-33).

David Brown wrote to Charles Simeon, "He has no faith in such schemes, and thinks that they must prove ineffectual; but he has no objection that others should attempt them, and promises not to be inimical." Brown elaborated their immediate plans,

> It is proposed that forthwith two young clergymen be sent as missionaries to India. They will come immediately to Bengal, and remain with us a few months at Calcutta. It will then be advisable that they move to that famous seat of Hindoo learning, Benares. There they will spend about three years in study, and furnish themselves with languages. After which they may begin their glorious work of giving light to the heathen with every probability of success (Kaye 1859: 137).

It was planned that each missionary would be given 300 rupees a month from a public fund, if such a fund could be raised. Meanwhile, Charles Grant would bear the costs. Copies of the *Proposal* were sent to fourteen persons in England, including Revs. Romaine, Newton, Foster, Cecil and Simeon, Thomas Raikes (a Russian merchant and Governor of the Bank of England during the financial crisis of 1797; also a friend of William Wilberforce and William Pitt), the Archbishop of Canterbury, the Bishops of Llandaff and London and William Wilberforce (among the most forceful parliamentarians of the time).

In a letter to Wilberforce from Calcutta, on 17th September 1787, Charles Grant stressed the imperial benefits of conversion,

> ...the people are universally and wholly corrupt, they are as depraved as they are blind, and as wretched as they are depraved, and to govern them and render them obedient and orderly upon right principles is no easy Work. There has been much inquiry concerning the best system of managing the Country. It seems to us clear that no system which has not the Reformation of the morals of the People for its basis can be effective; for they are lamentably destitute of those Principles of Honesty, Truth, and Justice which are necessary to the Well-being of Society. And to reconcile them to a Foreign dominion like Ours, it seems equally clear that We and they ought to have some *strong common Principles*; at present they are united to us neither in Interest nor in Sentiment...

> *Religion* is that *common Principle*, the only just and durable one that can be established between us; not the Religion of Error, but the Religion of Truth. If they were once converted to that, they would of course be freed from many ties which now connect them with their neighbours... And as we are inclined to believe that there has been more of the appointment of God than of the Injustice of Man in bringing the Country under subjection to Great Britain, so we are persuaded that the only thing it has *not* to fear, is the communication of its Religion; and that even in a political view, there is more danger of losing the Country from leaving the dispositions and Prejudices of the People, in their present state, than from any change that the Light of Christianity and an improved state of Civil Society would produce in them ... (Morris 1904: 108-14).

This seems to be the first occasion when Wilberforce's attention was drawn to the issue of missions in India. For the next decade and a half he devoted himself to the cause. As David Brown wrote to Charles Simeon, "Our hopes are particularly fixed on Mr. Wilberforce. It is to his influence alone that we hope the minister will regard such a project, and ask for it the countenance of majesty" (Howse 1960: 69). Wilberforce took the proposal to William Pitt and both he and Charles Simeon made the introduction of Christianity in India one of their principal concerns (Morris 1904: 120-121).

A PRIVATE MISSIONARY STATION AT GUMALTI

Meanwhile, in the absence of any immediate outcome, Grant established at his own expense, a private missionary station at Gumalti, where he had setup a factory for the cultivation of indigo. He engaged Dr. John Thomas (1757–1801), a surgeon with a missionary zeal who had twice before been to India, as the first Baptist missionary at Gumalti. Grant was, however, compelled to abandon the mission soon after.

CHARLES GRANT IN ENGLAND

Grant left India in 1790, after over twenty years of stay, and continued to work for the cause of missions in England. There he soon established contact with William Wilberforce and Henry Thornton (a leading light of the Clapham Sect, Member of Parliament, and the first treasurer of the Christian Missionary Society), who became his closest associates.

OBSERVATIONS ON THE STATE OF SOCIETY AMONG THE ASIATIC SUBJECTS OF GREAT BRITAIN

In 1792 (at the height of English hysteria over events in France and on the eve of the renewal of the Company's Charter that was mandatory every twenty years), Grant prepared a text specifically for Henry Dundas, President of the Board of Control, wherein he developed the plan outlined in the *Proposal*. Grant realized that if the Company and the Government were to be persuaded to take action, Dundas' support was critical. Many merchants and politicians then perceived the relationship between Britain and India in economic terms and felt it was beyond their purview to attempt change.

Grant sought provisions for private trade and missionary work in the new Company Charter. His manuscript was circulated among a small group that included Wilberforce, Thornton, and Hannah More, though, as Grant told David Scott, in November 1793, it was written in a hurry and needed "corrections and elucidations." He also showed it to Rev. Claudius Buchanan, one of his appointees as chaplain of the Company, prior to the latter's departure for India. Five years later, in 1797, when Grant occupied a seat in the Direction of the East India Company, he formally placed it before the Court of Directors. Titled *Observations on the State of Society among the Asiatic Subjects of Great Britain*, it was printed as a Parliamentary Paper on the eve of the Company Charter debates of 1813 and 1833. It underwent considerable elaboration and expansion from its first appearance in 1792.

Grant's *Observations* "gives a fair exhibition of the Evangelical mentality" (Stokes 1982: 29). It invented the reform agenda for the British and thereby provided a justification for British rule in India (Trautmann 2004: 101). After a detailed survey of the state of Hindu society, Grant concluded,

> Thus, we trust, it has been evinced ... the moral character and condition of the natives ... is extremely depraved, and that the state of society among that people is, in consequence, wretched. These evils have been shewn to lie beyond the reach of our regulations, merely political power, however good; they have been traced to their civil and religious institutions; they have been proved to inhere in the general spirit and many positive enactments of their laws, and more powerfully still in the false, corrupt, impure, extravagant, and ridiculous principles and tenets of their religion. ... A remedy has been proposed for these evils; the introduction of our light and knowledge among that benighted people, especially the pure, salutary, wise principles of our divine religion ... (Grant 1832: 120).

PERMANENCY OF BRITISH RULE

The Evangelist, Grant was among the first to plead for the permanence of British rule in India. There was no way in the foreseeable future, he said, "in which we may not govern our Asiatic subjects more happily for them than they can be governed by themselves" (Embree 1962: 142-43).

Till then not many administrators who had served in India had advanced such an argument. Warren Hastings, for instance, had pointed to the fragility of British rule. He noted,

> The dominion exercised by the British Empire in India is fraught with many radical and incurable defects, besides those to which all human institutions are liable, arising from the distance of its scene of operations, the impossibility of furnishing it at all times with those aids which it requires from home, and the difficulty of reconciling its primary exigencies with those which in all States ought to take place of every other concern, the interests of the people who are subjected to its authority. All that the wisest institutions can effect in such a system can only be to improve the advantages of a temporary possession, and to protract that decay, which sooner or later must end it (Gleig II 1841: 149-59).

John Malcolm (1769–1833), who had served in several senior positions, expressed similar sentiments. Noting that a *crore* of men had been excluded from high rank and fame, he calculated that the Empire "should last fifty years." If the British could keep up a number of Native States without political power, as royal instruments, the British could stay as long as they maintained their naval superiority in Europe, "beyond this date it is impossible" (Kaye II 1856: 370-72).

Grant, however, argued that since the Company profited from India, it ought to give good government to the people, "in order that we might continue to hold the advantage we first derived from them." Moreover, the Company "as part of the Christian community," should work for the millions under it. The dual arguments of self-interest and religious imperative were the hallmarks of the Evangelical position.

The same year that Grant wrote the first draft of his *Observations*, he arranged for John Shore (back from India) to meet Wilberforce. Together he and Wilberforce persuaded John Shore to return to India as Governor General (where he served from 1793 to 1798). Shore was an eminently Christian man but could do little for the missionary cause in India (Kaye 1859: 144). As Governor General, he was particularly concerned about the sentiments of the Company's sepoys. He told Henry Dundas that it was good pay and "an indulgence to his habits, whether religious or otherwise," that ensured the loyalty of the Company's native troops. If there was any disrespect shown towards their religious beliefs "the bond of attachment would soon be dissolved, and disaffection and aversion be substituted for subordination" (Teignmouth Vol. I 1843: 280-81).

PARLIAMENT AND RENEWAL OF THE COMPANY CHARTER – 1793

Grant looked forward with anticipation to the renewal of the East India Company's Charter. He hoped that the Charter would contain some provisions for the improvement of India that he had been advocating. The India Bill, introduced in 1793 by Henry Dundas, however, provided for every interest except religion. After the bill had been discussed Wilberforce proposed two resolutions, believed to have been drafted by Grant.

> First, — That it is the opinion of this House that it is the peculiar and bounden duty of the legislature to promote, by all just and prudent means, the interests and happiness of the inhabitants of the British dominions in the East; and that for these ends such measures ought to be adopted as may gradually tend to their advancement in useful

knowledge and to their religious and moral improvement (Marshman 1859: 7).

The second resolution referred to the provision of religious instruction for all Protestants in India and the maintenance of a chaplain on every ship of 500 tons burden upwards (Marshman 1859: 7).

Wilberforce's standing enabled him to carry these resolutions. Emboldened, he added an extra clause, that the Directors of the Company be empowered and required to send out "fit and proper persons" to act as "school-masters, missionaries, or otherwise." This too was passed. Wilberforce wrote in his journal on 19 May,

> The hand of Providence was never more visible than in this East Indian affair. What cause have I for gratitude, and trust, and humiliation! How properly is Grant affected! Yet let me take courage. It is of God's unmerited goodness that I am selected as the agent of usefulness. I see His overruling power (Morris 1904: 182-83).

The insertion of the clause on missionaries and schoolmasters, however, alarmed the Directors of the Company, who resolved to stop the move (Carson 2012: 37-38).[3] The most opposed were those who had served in India. So great was the resistance to the "Pious Clause" that when the Charter Bill came up for the Third Reading, Dundas withdrew his support.

He disagreed in Parliament with the unsympathetic portrayal of Hindus and instead argued that they were a harmless and orderly people. He further said that "the same imputation which was urged against them, as a plea for the establishment of Christianity, applied in a great measure to those nations by whom the benefits of that religion were already enjoyed" (Embree 1962: 154-55; Carson 2012: 38).

Dundas's *volte face* could be explained by the fact that he was also Home Secretary and Britain was then at war with

France. He wanted the bill passed speedily and was unwilling to go against the strong sentiments of the Company. East Indian votes were important for Pitt's government. Dundas also wanted approval for other parts of the bill, particularly the provision extending private trade. The "Pious Clause" was not opposed by the Company alone. Charles James Fox stated that all forms of proselytization were wrong in themselves and resulted in abuse and political mischief (Embree 1962: 154-55; Carson 2012: 38).

Wilberforce's protestation that the objective was not "to break up by violence existing institutions, and force our faith upon the natives of India; but gravely, silently, and systematically to prepare the way for the gradual diffusion of religious truth," was of no avail. He wrote to Gisborne, "The East India directors and proprietors have triumphed, all my clauses were last night struck out on the third reading of the Bill, and ... twenty millions of people ... are left ... to the providential protection of — Brama" (Howse 1960: 71-72).

Writing to a friend in India, Grant described the situation,

> I was in the gallery of the House when the question came on, and had one melancholy pleasure, that of seeing Mr. Wilberforce in the face of that House stand forth as the bold, zealous, animated and able champion of Christianity, and of the propriety and duty of communicating its blessings to our heathen subjects. But the success was less than the cause and his eloquence deserved (Marshman 1859: 48).

Grant's hopes for a mission patronized by the Company and Government were dashed, because there was "no missionary spirit in the nation ... The East India Charter Act of 1793 was the true reply to the Calcutta plan of 1787" (Howse 1960: 72).

But the Clapham Sect had learnt valuable lessons from the incident. Wilberforce concluded that they had overly depended on the assurances of Pitt and Dundas, and they should in future ensure the support of voluntary organizations in the country. The Sect also recognized it was an error to expect the Company to maintain missionaries. When the next chance came in 1813, their methods, and the content of their proposals were appropriately modified (Embree 1962: 155-56).

Meanwhile, in 1794, Grant was elected Director of the East India Company, his candidature having the strong backing of Henry Dundas and the Prime Minister. Before long, he became Deputy Chairman and, in 1805, Chairman. He used his authority to get suitable men appointment as chaplains. Among the twenty sent to India between 1793 and 1813 (selected with the help of Rev. Charles Simeon) were Claudius Buchanan, Henry Martyn, Thomas Thomason, David Corrie and Daniel Wilson.

END-NOTES

1. Schwartz (1726–1798) was the most renowned of the Tranquebar missionaries. He arrived in 1750 from Halle in Germany and spent 48 years in India without once visiting home. He acquired fluency in Tamil, Telugu, Sanskrit, Marathi, Dakhni, Persian, and Portuguese. He was Regent Protector to Maharaja Serfoji of Tanjore (Neill 1985: 45-58).

2. In 1772, George Livius, a close friend of Charles Grant, had discussed with the Moravians the prospect of setting up a mission in Bengal. A mission was indeed set up in the Danish colony of Serampore, but abandoned in 1792. In 1783, the Methodist leader, Thomas Coke, also communicated a plan for a mission to India. *A Proposal for Establishing a Protestant Mission in Bengal and Behar* (1787) was significant as it came from Company officials who were also members of the Established Church (Carson 2012: 27-28).

3. While the British Parliament was debating the Pious Clause, in India, Lord Cornwallis and his Council passed Bengal Regulation III of 1793, which promised to "preserve to (Indians) the laws of the Shasters and Koran in matters to which they have been invariably applied, and to protect them in the free exercise of their religion" (Carson 2012: 41).

6

The Evangelical-Utilitarian Alliance

T he Evangelical attack on India was fortified by an alliance with the Utilitarians, who had emerged as an influential group in Britain. The political language of Utilitarianism was articulated, above all, by Jeremy Bentham (1748–1832) and James Mill (1773–1836). Its prime target was the conservatism of the period (represented, above all, by Edmund Burke and itself a response to the threat posed by the French Revolution). The nature of British rule in India became an area of contest between the Conservatives and the Utilitarians (Majeed 1992: 2).

Many commentators argued that the only way to counter the French threat was to extend and perpetuate the British Empire. The period of the French wars indeed witnessed the greatest expansion of British imperial dominions. By 1820, twenty-six per cent of the world population lived in British territories. The global conflict with France, and the expansion of the British Empire in response to the French threat, ensured that colonial and domestic issues were inextricably linked (Majeed 1992: 8).

JAMES MILL

The Utilitarian, James Mill, attempted to define an idiom for the British Empire to replace the conservative trend. It was perhaps not entirely accidental that Charles Grant became Chairman of the East India Company in 1805, and Mill began work on his *History of British India* in 1806. It was published a decade later in six volumes, by when the Company's position in India had changed dramatically as it "began to solidify an ever-growing and valuable empire in India" (Knowles 2011: 41). Mill's work appeared at an opportune moment.

A Scotsman like Grant, Mill had been educated for the ministry and licensed to preach by the Presbyterian Church. He, however, exchanged his faith for the Utilitarianism of Bentham, which believed in progress and the principle of the greatest good of the greatest number (Trautmann 2004: 117). Why did Mill, who had no personal experience of India, venture on the *History* project? Was he commissioned to write the work? Who gave him direct access to the records of the East India Company? (Frykenberg 1999: 194-95). Was the project in any way linked to the Fort William versus Haileybury College controversy? Was it intended to counter the "Brahminization" of young Company officials in India and inculcate a "superiority complex" in British administrators? Was Mill trying to justify the British conquest of India as the destiny of a decadent Hindu society?

Mill's views on India were "so unremittingly dark, often so pathetically foolish," that it is difficult to believe he would have spent ten years of his life gathering them unless he was motivated by "a more serious purpose" (Mehta 1999: 90).

Mill wrote his *History* in the "specific context" of the admiration for civilizations of the East due to the work of the Orientalists. He made "a decisive and transforming contribution" in reversing this trend (Mehta 1999: 89). Mill rebuffed the Orientalists by taking a firm anti-empiricist stance and denying that "observing and ... acquisition of languages" were necessary for a correct evaluation of Indian history. He censured the "particular respect" that Orientalists like William Jones had for the "legendary tales of the Hindus". Mill regarded these as "Hindu fictions" and "marks of a rude age", for the Hindus were "perfectly destitute of historical records". According to Mill, "rude nations seem to derive a peculiar gratification from pretensions to a remote antiquity." The true history of this "rude age" could only be written from an English point of view, by a "critical" or "judging history" that distinguished between real and false causes and effects (Pels 1999: 85; Mehta 1999: 13, 90).

Mill's *History of British India* represented the starting point for "the theoretical repositioning" of India in relation to Europe following the growth of industrial capitalism. It was an attempt at the intellectual subordination of India to the "universalist principles" of European social theory that accompanied European imperial expansion (Ludden 1993: 263-64).

In 1844, the Orientalist, H.H. Wilson, who edited an edition of *History of British India*, defended his own work and that of his colleagues against Mill's "disdain of the early records of nations," which "may sometimes be suspected to veil a distaste for dry, laborious and antiquarian research." However, despite providing an empiricist critique, Wilson's remarks on Mill's "historical incompetences" were relegated to a Preface and elaborate footnotes to the text. In his Preface, Wilson in fact described the *History of British India* as "the most valuable work on the subject which has yet been published" (Pels 1999: 86; Ludden 1993: 269-70).

Mill applied the Utilitarian doctrine of his friend and master, Bentham, to the governance of India. Mill had been attracted by the references to India in Bentham's *Treatise on the Influence of Time and Place in Legislation*, and resolved "to provide for British India, in the room of the abominable existing system, a good system of judicial procedure." In the process he designed a scale of civilizational development to simplify the legislator's task of prescribing for every society on each rung of the scale. The scale would inform the legislator what was below and above any civilization under discussion. It would eliminate the need to engage with local conditions. For instance, once it was established that "the savage is listless under every climate," this could be conveniently factored for necessary consideration. Mill said, "To ascertain the true state of the Hindus in the scale of civilization ... is to the people of Great Britain ... an object of the highest practical importance." If India was on a low rung, then the policies the British should adopt would be very different from those recommended by the Orientalists. Mill categorized Hindu civilization as representing the "rudest and weakest state of the human mind" (Mehta 1999: 13, 93-94; Mill I 1840: 115).

The *History of British India* played a major role in the transformation of Utilitarianism into a "militant faith". It provided the theoretical basis for the programme to "emancipate India from its own culture" (Majeed 1992: 123,127). Wilson wrote of the book, "... its tendency is evil: it is calculated to destroy all sympathy between the ruler and the ruled...a harsh and illiberal spirit has of late years prevailed in the conduct and councils of the rising service in India, which owes its origin to impressions imbibed in early life from the *History* of Mr. Mill" (Mill I 1840: xii-xiii).

It was significant that Mill, a Utilitarian, depended on missionary writings on Hindu society. Wilson commented on Mill's sources, "As missionaries ... they see the errors and vices of a heathen people through a medium by which they are exaggerated beyond their natural dimensions, and assume an enormity which would not be assigned to the very same defects in Christianity" (Mill I 1840: 523).

The *History of British India* became a standard work for East India Company officials, and eventually a textbook for candidates for the Indian Civil Service. It was also the official course book of the Company's College at Haileybury. It held

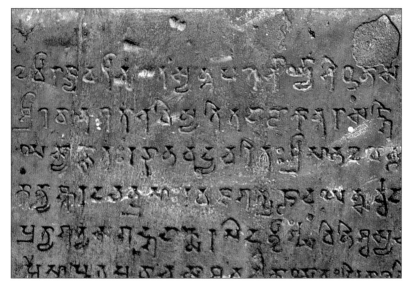

1. The Changu Narayana temple inscription, Nepal, AD 464.

2. The Eran Stone Pillar Inscription, Sagar district, Madhya Pradesh, AD 510.

3. Sati of Dekkabe, in the time of Rajendra Chola; Belaturu Inscription, Saka 979 (inscription on reverse).

4. Mahasati Sthal at Chittorgarh Fort, where widowed queens of Mewar committed Sati.

5. Sati stone, AD 1206, Kedareshwar temple, Belligavi, Karnataka.

6. Sati memorial stone, 13th century AD, Penukonda, Andhra Pradesh (Government Museum, Chennai).

7. Sati memorial stone, 14th century, Bhopal State Museum, Madhya Pradesh.

8. Hampi Satikal.

9. Mandi Barsela (Sati pillars), of the royal family, 17th-18th century AD.

10. Sati stone of Sodha Rajputs, Nagarparkar, Sindh, Pakistan.

11. Sati stone of Sodha Rajputs, Berani village, Nagarparkar, Sindh, Pakistan.

12. Shiva carrying Sati on his trident, AD 1800.

13. Sati ceremony, Thanjavur, AD 1800.

14. Hindu widow having purification bath in preparation for immolation, by Robert Melville Grindlay, who served with the East India Company from 1804-20.

15. 'Sacrifice of a Hindoo widow upon the funeral pile of her husband,' Johann Zoffany (1733-1810).

16. Sati painting by James Atkinson (1780-1852).

17. Sati by Nandlal Bose, 1943, Philadelphia Museum of Art.

the field for decades, being reprinted in 1820, 1826, 1840 and 1844.

The Utilitarians became closely associated with Indian affairs. In 1819, soon after the publication of his *History*, James Mill (followed shortly by his son) was appointed Assistant Examiner of Indian correspondence, and, in 1830, Examiner. This placed him in a position to implement the Utilitarian principles, as he admitted in a letter written in the early period. He said,

> The time of attendance is from 10 till 4, six hours, and the business, though laborious enough, is to me highly interesting. It is the very essence of the internal government of 60 millions of people with whom I have to deal; and as you know that the government of India is carried on by correspondence; and that I am the only man whose business it is, or who has the time to make himself master of the facts scattered in a most voluminous correspondence, on which a just decision must rest, you will conceive to what extent the real decision on matters belonging to my department rests with the man who is in my situation (Carter and Harlow 2003: 47-48).

When accepting the office of Examiner at India House in 1819, James Mill wrote to Zachary Macaulay of his willingness to subordinate his own will and ideas to those of Charles Grant. He stated, "I differ in many things from him; but the nature of the office implies that I consciously become an instrument in his hand" (Morris 1904: 250).

Jeremy Bentham's papers confirm his keenness to have a say in framing the system of laws for India. His interest revived with Mill's entry into India House. Subsequently, with the appointment of William Bentinck as Governor General, Bentham's influence seemed complete. At a farewell dinner, Bentinck feasted on "the pure milk of the Benthamite word." There he said to James Mill, "I am going to British India, but I shall not be Governor-General. It is you that will be

Governor-General." Bentham directed "our friend James Young" (the radical head of the Calcutta house of the agency, Alexander & Co.) to expound the details of Benthamic principles to Bentinck. Young soon acquired an influence over the Government and access to classified papers that senior administrators like John Malcolm regarded improper (Stokes 1982: 49).

This was another instance of the alliance between the Evangelicals and Utilitarians. Bentinck had been a member of the British and Foreign Bible Society at least since 1811, indicating an interest in missionary work. His wife and her family had become deeply involved in the Evangelical movement soon after her marriage (Rosselli 1974: 57-64).

G.M. Young described the power of the new union, "in discipleship or reaction no young mind of the thirties could escape their (the Utilitarians') influence. Bentham's alliance with James Mill, Mill's friendship with Malthus and Ricardo, had created a party, almost a sect, with formularies as compact as the Evangelical theology and conclusions not less inexorable" (Ghosh 2001: 54).

Meanwhile, Bentham, then almost eighty years old, had begun to correspond with Rammohan Roy, whom he addressed as the "intensely admired and dearly beloved Collaborator in the service of mankind." Bentham wrote to him,

> Now at the brink of the grave (for I want but a month or two of four score) among the most delightful of my reflections is the hope, I am notwithstanding feeding myself with, of rendering my labours of some considerable use to the hundred millions, or thereabouts, of whom I understand that part of your population which is under English governance or influence is composed (Singh 1987: 210).

THE EVANGELICALS AND UTILITARIANS

The earlier British admiration for Indian culture and civilization, described as British Indomania, was killed in the early nineteenth century by Evangelicals and Utilitarians, its chief architects being Charles Grant and James Mill. The defining texts in the vilification of India were Charles Grant's *Observations* and James Mill's *History* (Trautmann 2004: 99). Mill's *History*, particularly the ten chapters "*Of the Hindus*," was "the single most important source of British Indophobia and hostility to Orientalism." It was in many ways "a kind of secularized version" of Grant's *Observations* (Trautmann 2004: 117). It presented an even darker picture of India than Grant's *Observations* (Embree 1962: 155-56). It became a cornerstone "for establishing discourses of colonial difference that supported the colonial civilizing mission" (Knowles 2011: 37).

Despite their dissimilarities, the Evangelicals and Utilitarians had little difficulty working together. Both believed that India was in urgent need of change. Grant urged reform to make Britain's association with India permanent and indissoluble. Mill stressed the need to give to the government of India "the benefit of men capable of applying the best ideas of their age to the arrangement of its important affairs." Both the Evangelical and Utilitarian movements were products of the rising middle class in business and the professions and shared the same goal: the Utilitarians wished to improve morals by reforming society; the Evangelicals hoped to improve society by reforming morals (Hutchins 1967: 9-10). Though the reform agenda of the Utilitarians did not include religion, like the Evangelicals, they needed a rationalization for their social reform programme.

INDOPHOBIA REPLACES INDOMANIA

In his efforts to belittle Hindu achievements, James Mill viewed Sir William Jones as his "intellectual nemesis" (Knowles 2011: 47). He charged Jones of being "promiscuous" in his use of the term civilization. It was unfortunate, Mill stated, "that a mind so pure, so warm in the pursuit of truth, and so devoted to oriental learning, as that of Sir William Jones, should have adopted the hypothesis of a high state of civilization in the principal countries of Asia" (Trautmann 2004: 121-22). Mill criticized Jones' portrayal of the life of the Hindus as far surpassing the "rhapsodies of Rousseau on the happiness and virtue of savage life" (Mukherjee 1968: 111).

Both James Mill and Charles Grant maintained silence over Jones' central thesis regarding the kinship between Europeans and Indians and the similarity between Sanskrit, Latin, and Greek (Trautmann 2004: 121-22). Grant feared that Jones' works could be cited to argue that India had no need for Christianity. He was, therefore, anxious to project Jones as a devout Christian and "a strenuous advocate for the diffusion of the Gospel in the East" (Embree 1962: 148-49). John Shore's biography of William Jones, published in 1805, reflected Grant's desire to present Jones as a friend of the missionaries. Shore, an Orientalist and protégé of William Jones in Calcutta, had become a member of the Clapham Sect on returning to England.

Shore relied on some stray passages in Jones' writings to claim that, "the conversion of the Hindus to the Christian religion, would have afforded him (Jones) the sincerest pleasure ..." (Teignmouth II 1976: 244). Shore's endeavours have been castigated by later scholars as "a patent fraud" (Arberry 1960: 83; Trautmann 2004: 99-101).

The change in British perception, exemplified by the ascendancy of the Evangelicals and Utilitarians, can also be attributed to mounting self-confidence following a series of military successes in India and triumph over Napoleonic France by 1815. The abolition of the slave trade in 1807 was an added factor.

The Governor Generalship of Lord Wellesley had made it abundantly clear that the British would soon emerge as the paramount power in the subcontinent. In 1798, the Nizam of Hyderabad had been compelled to sign a subsidiary treaty by which his troops were brought under British control and he himself ceased to be an independent ruler. In 1799, the East India Company vanquished Tipu Sultan of Mysore; and in 1801 forced Awadh to cede half its territories. The Marathas were worsted in a series of battles across the Deccan and North India during the Second Anglo-Maratha War. In 1803, British forces entered Delhi and ousted the Marathas from the imperial capital. A final win in the Third Maratha War in 1817–1819, during the Governor Generalship of the Marquis of Hastings (1813–1823), ensured that no political rivals remained. On 1st December 1815, the Marquis declared, "The British Government stands pre-eminent among the Powers of India ..." (Desika Char 1983: 195-97).[1]

Several other forces were at work to turn the tide against India. The growing technological and scientific advancement of Europe reduced the admiration for Indian culture. India was seen as a land of the past that needed to be reformed. The policy of non-interference with Indian tradition, a British byword in the eighteenth century, was abandoned in favour of change through the induction of British values. Evangelicals and Utilitarians identified Hinduism as the source of many ills that allegedly plagued Indian society. India was to become not just a part of a *Pax Britannica* but also of a *Civilis Britannica* (Washbrook 1999: 395).

END-NOTES

1. The growing political ascendancy of the British in India dampened the early exuberance for Indic studies, though discoveries continued to be made in numismatics, epigraphy, and archeology. In 1825, the Frenchman, Joseph Guigniaut stated that he depended more on German than English works for information on Hindu religion. He said, "The route mapped by Jones, Robertson, and the learned Thomas Maurice was soon abandoned in England, and the Christian missionaries contributed, through their often tainted picture of the moral and religious state of these people, a great deal to the diffusion of a host of false ideas about the ancient religion of the Hindus."

The German, Wilhelm Schlegel complained to H.H. Wilson in 1827 about the English not taking enough interest in Indian culture (Schwab 1984: 43-44). The resistance of the English elite to the revelation of India became pronounced in the 1830s. In 1835, the colonial Government also stopped funding the Asiatic Society of Bengal.

Also, while the Asiatic Society of Bengal was founded in 1784, just a couple of years after the British conquest of Bengal, a chair in Sanskrit was established in England only in 1833. Though William Jones had made a contribution to comparative philology in his oft-quoted address to the Asiatic Society in 1786, the Philological Society was established in London in 1842, well after the discipline had attained maturity in France and Germany.

The late renewal of Britain's interest in Indology and the newly emerging disciplines appears to have been linked to the nascent German nationalism and the emerging German-French rivalry. Indology played a pivotal role in buttressing German nationalism. The rising German nationalism allied with British imperialism against the common foe, France. The alliance was also dictated by Germany's dependence on England for access to Indian literary works. The arrival of Chevalier Bunsen as ambassador of Prussia to England in 1841 signalled Anglo-German collaboration on the intellectual and political plane. The following year the Philological Society was founded in England, to be followed, in 1843, by the Ethnological Society. Bunsen was instrumental in bringing Max Muller to England, who did much to popularize the Aryan race and invasion theory. Britain used German scholars in an understated manner to further her imperial designs in India.

A view was also developing among a section of British missionaries that Sanskrit could aid in the conversion of high caste Hindus. Colonel Joseph Boden, who established the chair of Sanskrit at Oxford, hoped that the translation of the Bible into Sanskrit would facilitate the evangelization of India.

7

Baptists in Bengal

Till the nineteenth century, the East India Company had displayed little interest in sponsoring missionary activity in its territories in India. In 1658, the Court of Directors had for the first time resolved to appoint a chaplain for the spiritual well-being of their employees in their Indian factories. But the chaplains were not missionaries and hence not obliged to preach outside their community.

EARLY PROTESTANT MISSIONARIES

The first Protestant missionary in Bengal was Rev. Kiernander from the Royal Danish Mission (Long 1848: 5-16). His successor, Rev. Clarke (who arrived in 1789), was the first Englishman to come to Bengal as a missionary (Hyde 1901: 212). In 1783, John Thomas, a Baptist doctor with missionary zeal, arrived in Calcutta as surgeon of a Company ship. He believed in the paramount importance of religion, and, on arrival, inquired about devout Christians. He learnt of two gentlemen, Charles Grant and William Chambers, but they were too far up the country for him to establish contact. He placed an advertisement in the *Indian Gazette* inviting co-operation for a plan "for the more effectual spreading of the knowledge of Jesus Christ, and His glorious Gospel, in and about Bengal." He received two responses but was unable to pursue the matter before his return to England (Hough IV 1845: 92-93).

In 1786, John Thomas sailed to India a second time and rejoiced to find Rev. David Brown, Charles Grant and William Chambers in Calcutta. Grant offered support if he desired to stay on as a missionary. Thomas thereupon gave up his job as a surgeon and commenced missionary work at Gumalti in 1787. But his unstable ways and the heavy debts he incurred led to a break with Grant in 1791. During these years, Thomas studied Bengali, and, with the help of a native, translated portions of the Old and New Testament into that language. In 1792, he went back to England, where he tried to create a fund for a Mission in Bengal and find a companion to accompany him to India for proselytizing work (Hough IV 1845: 93-95).

From 1793 missionaries started coming to Calcutta without valid licenses, due to the encouragement of Charles Grant and his Evangelical friends in England.

THE SERAMPORE TRIO

On the right bank of the Hughli, sixteen miles above Calcutta, in the town of Serampore, the Danes, in October 1755, raised their flag on a twenty acre plot of land they had purchased from local owners. Among the early Governors of this settlement was Colonel Ole Bie, who, while an official of the Danish Government at Tranquebar, had imbibed the missionary spirit from Rev. Frederick Schwartz. During the years the English East India Company forbade missionaries from operating in its territories, Colonel Bie opened his doors to them. William Carey, William Ward, and Joshua Marshman, the three early Baptist missionaries in Bengal, popularly known as the Serampore trio, all found refuge in the Danish colony.

William Carey (1761–1834), the oldest of the three and the first to arrive, belonged to a poor family of Northampton and had been apprenticed to a shoemaker (Smith 1885).[1] In 1792, he was appointed to the five member committee of the newly founded Baptist Missionary Society (BMS) and volunteered to go to any country in service of Christ. The committee's attention was directed to India by John Thomas, who was in seeking a co-worker to go with him to the country. "We saw", said Andrew Fuller, Secretary of the BMS, "that there was a gold mine in India, but it was deep as the center of the earth. Who will venture to explore it?" Carey responded, "I will venture to go down, but remember that you must hold the ropes" (Holcomb 1901: 70-71). Thomas was introduced to his future colleague (Carey) and, "they fell on each other's necks and wept" (Hough IV 1845: 96).

Due to the ban on missionary activity in Company territory, missionaries had to proceed clandestinely or in some other capacity, for on landing they risked immediate deportation. Carey found it impossible to secure a license permitting him to travel to India. He was removed from a ship that had set sail with him on board, but eventually obtained passage in a Danish vessel.

William Ward (1769–1823), the second of the Serampore missionaries, was the son of a carpenter. He did not follow his father's trade and instead apprenticed with a printing establishment on leaving school. After his training, he edited the *Derby Mercury*. Some years later, Ward gave up journalism and began to prepare for the work of spreading the Gospel. He presented himself to the Baptist Society, hoping that they might employ him in the printing of the Scriptures. His offer was immediately accepted (Holcomb 1901: 75-76). In 1799, the Baptist Missionary Committee sent him to India along with Joshua Marshman.

Joshua Marshman (1768–1837), the third of the Serampore group, was the son of a weaver. He was educated at the village school and served as an assistant at a bookshop. He too volunteered his services to the Baptist Society (Holcomb 1901: 76-77).

SERAMPORE MISSION

William Carey and John Thomas landed in India on 11th November 1793 and immediately paid a visit to Rev. David Brown. Soon after, Carey shifted to the Sunderbans. In March 1794, George Udny, "a wonderfully Christian planter ... (with) a thirst for souls," and Commercial Resident of the Company in the area, offered Carey the superintendence of his indigo factory at Mudnabatty, about thirty miles north of Malda and Thomas that of a second factory at Moypaldiggy, seventeen miles further ahead (Mayhew 1929: 64-65).

The involvement of Charles Grant in these developments cannot be ruled out. Udny, together with Rev. David Brown and William Chambers, had assisted Grant in drafting *A Proposal for Establishing a Protestant Mission in Bengal and Behar*, in 1786. Grant's prior acquaintance with John Thomas is also recorded. As noted earlier, Grant had, in 1787, engaged Thomas at the private missionary station he had established at Gumalti, near Malda.

The superintendence of the indigo factory gave the missionaries enough spare time to undertake missionary tours, study Bengali, and engage in other activities in furtherance of their proselytizing objectives. Indigo establishments then required just three months of careful attention during the rainy season. Carey remained at Mudnabatty for five years. There were around ninety workmen employed in the factory, to whom he imparted Christian teaching. He also preached the Gospel in two hundred villages in the vicinity.

Carey started his first school at Mudnabatty in 1794. His forays in the field of education were directly linked to his religious goals. The subjects taught at the school included reading, writing, arithmetic, the local accounting system, and

Christianity. In January 1795, Carey outlined "a plan for erecting two colleges (*chowparries* Bengalee) ... they are to be taught the Shanscrit, Bengalee and Persian languages. The Bible is to be introduced there, and perhaps a little philosophy and geography." Though the plan could not then be implemented, it eventually led to the foundation of the Serampore College in 1818 (Laird 1972: 63).

In addition to the school, Carey worked on a translation of the Scriptures into Bengali. He learnt that a wooden printing press was on sale in Calcutta and decided to purchase it. It was, however, gifted to the mission by Udny. In 1799, Udny had to abandon the indigo factory which had proved financially unviable. Carey was, therefore, compelled to look for a new residence and occupation.

Around this time, in October 1799, four English missionaries arrived in the Hughli. They came at a time when the French National Assembly was dispatching sympathizers in many directions. Lord Wellesley's government had detected several of them in India and, hence, carefully screened all arrivals (Hough IV 1845: 103). Before landing his passengers, the ship's captain was asked to declare their occupations in writing. After some thought, the missionaries decided to admit their missionary purpose, where after they immediately proceeded to the Danish settlement at Serampore and placed themselves under the protection of its Governor. When the ship's papers were presented to British officials in Calcutta, it was resolved to deport the missionaries to England and seize the ship until the Government's orders were complied with. The Danish Governor was, however, unwilling to hand them over (Sherring 1875: 69-71). Wellesley refrained from pursuing the matter on the recommendation, it was believed, of the Company chaplain, Rev. Claudius Buchanan (Hough IV 1845: 104).

The Danish Governor now proposed that the missionaries establish themselves permanently at Serampore, start schools for Hindu youth, set up a printing press for the publication of the Scriptures and engage in any other work they thought fit. William Ward went to Malda to discuss the matter with William Carey and they decided to establish the Baptist Mission in the Danish colony (Sherring 1875: 69-71). Carey arrived at Serampore in 1800. The printing press, brought from Mudnabatty, was soon set up. Carey had completed a translation of the Bible in Bengali and Ward printed the work within a year. The Bengali New Testament was hailed as "the first stroke of the axe leveled at the banyan-tree of India's superstitions" (Carey 1934: 198). A copy was sent to King George III at Windsor (Mayhew 1929: 66-67).

FORT WILLIAM COLLEGE AND THE CHURCH OF ENGLAND

By some fortuitous coincidence, the Governor General, Lord Wellesley (1798–1805), was at that time planning to set up a college for training Company officers in the vernaculars, and the laws and customs of India (Kopf 1969: 45-49).[2] The College, known as the College of Fort William, was formally established in August 1800. The statutes of the College declared that it was founded on the principles of the Christian religion and intended,

> not only to promote the knowledge of oriental literature, to instruct the students in the duties of the several stations to which they may be destined in the government of the British Empire in India, and to strengthen and confirm, within these possessions, the attachments of the civil servants of the East India Company to the wise laws and happy constitution of Great Britain; but also to maintain and uphold the Christian religion in this quarter of the globe ...

It was specifically stated that "Divine service shall be performed in the College chapel at such times as the Provost shall appoint, at which all the students shall attend." Further,

It shall be the peculiar province and sacred duty of the Provost governing the College at Fort William, to guard the moral and religious interests and character of the institution, and vigilantly to superintend the conduct and principles of all its members (Martin II 1984: 732-34).

The connection of Fort William College with the Church of England was underscored by the appointment of Rev. David Brown and Rev. Claudius Buchanan as Provost and Vice-Provost respectively. Claudius Buchanan (additionally appointed Professor of Classics) himself recorded his pivotal position at Fort William in a letter to a friend, "The whole direction of the college lies with me; every paper is drawn up by me; and every thing that is printed is revised by me" (Pearson I 1819: 226).

In a correspondence with Charles Grant soon after his appointment as Vice-Provost, Claudius Buchanan enunciated the objectives of the Governor General, "Lord Wellesley wants some persons of distinguished ability in science and classics to superintend in college, and thinks, properly, that they should, if possible, be clerical men. He has asked me for names..."[3] (Pearson I 1819: 221). Writing to a friend in 1801, Buchanan expressed the hope that Fort William would prove a religious and literary institution to its pupils (Pearson I 1819: 224).

Buchanan oversaw the publication of several works while at Fort William. Among those published under his supervision were several volumes of *Primitiae Orientales*. They contained essays and theses prepared by students of the College and public disputations on matters of contemporary interest. Among the topics of debate in 1803 was the burning of Hindu widows (Chaplain 1803–1804; Pearson I 1819: 254; Das 1978: 150).

In 1804, while Vice-Provost at Fort William, Buchanan instituted prizes in seven public schools and universities in England, awarding a hundred pounds each for the best compositions by students. The essays selected were on subjects like "the best means of civilizing the subjects of the British Empire in India, and of diffusing the light of the Christian religion throughout the eastern world." In 1805, Buchanan set up two larger prizes of five hundred pounds each at Oxford and Cambridge for the finest works on spreading the Gospel in the East (Pearson I 1819: 313-14).

Also while at Fort William, Claudius Buchanan prepared *A Memoir of the Expediency of an Ecclesiastical Establishment for British India.* The design of the *Memoir*, Buchanan afterwards said, was suggested to him by Bishop Porteus who had "attentively surveyed the state of our dominions in Asia" and expressed his "conviction of the indispensable necessity of an ecclesiastical establishment for our Indian empire." He was also encouraged "by subsequent communications with Marquis Wellesley, to endeavour to lead the attention of the nation to this subject." The manuscript was transmitted to England in the spring, and published in the autumn, of 1805 (Pearson I 1819: 312).

The *Memoir* discussed the expediency of an ecclesiastical establishment both as a means of "perpetuating the Christian religion among our own countrymen, and as a foundation for the ultimate civilization of the natives." The first part of the *Memoir* demonstrated the inadequate state of the ecclesiastical establishment in India for purposes of the instruction and religious communion of resident Englishmen. The second section described the degraded condition of the Hindus. The concluding segment argued the feasibility of improving their lot by providing instances of progress already made among native Christians on the Malabar Coast. The *Memoir* was dedicated to the Archbishop of Canterbury. In the appendix were detailed a variety of superstitions of the Hindus, to counter the general perception of them as a mild, humane, and inoffensive people (Buchanan 1805).

Meanwhile, Wellesley, who had founded Fort William College without waiting the approval of the Court Of Directors, was directed to shut the College by a letter dated 27th January 1802. The Directors had found his scheme too elaborate and expensive, and ordered closure of the College, permitting only a truncated establishment for teaching oriental languages. Writing to the Archbishop of Canterbury towards the end of 1805, Buchanan stressed the importance of the College for the Christian mission. He said it was a mistake to believe that the sole objective of the College was to instruct the Company's writers. He stated,

> Our hope of evangelizing Asia was once founded on the college of Fort William ... Had the college ... been cherished at home with the same ardour with which it was opposed, it might in the period of ten years have produced translations of the Scriptures into all the languages from the borders of the Caspian to the Sea of Japan.

> An idea seems to have gone forth in England, that Lord Wellesley founded his college merely to instruct the Company's writers. Lord Wellesley founded the college of Fort William to enlighten the oriental world; to give science, religion, and pure morals to Asia; and to confirm in it the British power and dominion ...The toleration of all religions, and the zealous extension of our own, is the way to rule and preserve a conquered kingdom[4] (Pearson I 1819: 374-75).

MISSIONARIES AT FORT WILLIAM — TRANSLATION OF THE SCRIPTURES

Soon after the establishment of the College, Wellesley invited Rev. William Carey to serve as Professor of Bengali. Carey joined Fort William in May 1801 and the, "interlocking work of the Serampore missionaries and Fort William College began..." (Laird 1972: 57). Interestingly, Ram Basu, a convert made by John Thomas, was appointed to assist Carey (Mayhew 1929: 67).

Carey realized the "missionary possibilities" of his position at Fort William. He was not only brought in touch with the most learned Europeans in Bengal, but also many gifted Indian scholars of various languages, fifty of whom the College appointed. With their assistance Carey could translate the Scriptures into all the major Indian languages (Carey 1934: 229; Farquhar 1967: 10; Laird 1972: 56-57). This was of the utmost importance for "... the evangelization of the country must be accomplished through the vernacular tongues" (Drewery 1978: 177).

Carey wrote to Andrew Fuller, Secretary of the BMS, at the end of 1803, "If we are given another fifteen years, we hope to translate and print the Bible in all the chief languages of Hindustan. We have fixed our eyes upon this goal" (Carey 1934: 232). The first versions of the Gospel in Persian and Hindustani printed in India were from the press of Fort William College (Pearson I 1819: 305-06).

At the beginning of 1804 and three months before the establishment of the Bible Society in England, the Serampore missionaries sent home a plan for the translation of the Scriptures, or portions of them, into the languages of the East, stating that Carey's links with the College "furnish(es) us with the best assistance from Natives of the different countries" (Hough IV 1845: 130-31). They asked for 1,000 pounds a year by way of financial assistance. Fuller showed great interest and raised 1,300 pounds for the project (Carey 1934: 232). Carey also decided to translate the Scriptures into Sanskrit with the help of the pandits at the College. He said,

> Sanskrit was the vehicle by which the learned shared their literary information; the depository of their records, and of all the science they possessed. It had, too, a sacred character, as the tongue in which were treasured the stories of their theology, the rites of their religion, the exploits of their gods. To translate the Scriptures there into would be to deposit them in the country's archives, and to secure for them a

degree of reverence in the Indian people's eyes (Carey 1934: 233).

Rev. M.A. Sherring was to later observe,

In no country in the world, and in no period in the history of Christianity, was there ever displayed such an amount of energy in the translation of the Sacred Scriptures from their originals into other tongues, as was exhibited by a handful of earnest men in Calcutta and Serampore in the first ten years of the present century ... (Sherring 1875: 85-86).

As a result of their endeavours, portions of the Bible, mainly of the New Testament, were translated and printed in thirty-one Indian languages and dialects. At the same time, the translation of certain texts, like the *Ramayana*, from Sanskrit into English was also undertaken. The objective, Carey explained in a letter, was to expose those "mysterious sacred nothings" that had "maintained their celebrity so long merely by being kept from the inspection of any but interested Brahmans" (Sen Gupta 1971: 127).

The translation of the Bible into Chinese also commenced. Marshman devoted fifteen years to the task. The work, though imperfect, was "a monument of diligence and perseverance almost without parallel" (Holcomb 1901: 82-83).

Buchanan used his position as Vice-Provost to aid the work of translation by the missionaries and create public interest in the project.[5] In 1806 he drew up a *"Proposal for a Subscription for translating the Holy Scriptures"* into fifteen oriental languages. Copies of the Proposal were "distributed liberally" in India and England. Buchanan acknowledged,

The plan of these translations was sanctioned at an earlier period by the Most Noble the Marquis, the great patron of useful learning. To give the Christian Scriptures to the inhabitants of Asia is indeed a work which every man who believes these Scriptures to be from God, will approve (Pearson I 1819: 391-94).

EXPANSION AND EVANGELIZATION

Soon after the establishment of the Serampore Mission, the Baptists began to cautiously expand their activities beyond their small enclave. Late in 1800, they learnt from Claudius Buchanan that they would not be troubled by the Government if they commenced missionary work in Calcutta and that they were free to preach "anywhere in the Town" except "before the Government House which would have been indecent" (Potts 1967: 27). Missionary work in Calcutta gathered pace, and missionary stations were established at Dinagepore, Cutwa, and Jessore.

After the hurdles they faced in forming out-stations, the missionaries approached the Government for a general license "to itinerate in the country and to form stations, and if that was refused, for a license renewable from year to year" (Marshman 1859: 249). George Barlow (1762–1847), temporarily appointed Governor General after the departure of Lord Wellesley, had proceeded to the North-West Provinces and the administration of Calcutta was in the hands of Udny, Carey's old friend. The previous year Carey had presented a statement on the subject to Udny, which stated,

> Our ultimate plan is to settle missionary stations throughout Bengal and Orissa, and in several parts of Hindoostan Proper. These stations are to be at the distance of 100 or 150 miles from each other, and to be managed by a European missionary. Surrounding each of these as a center, we wish to settle seven or eight native preachers, or catechists, at proper distances from each other, who will be under the management and control of the European minister. The places at which we desire to settle missionaries are at or near to Cawnpore, Benares, Dinagepore, Goalpara, Chittagong, Jessore, Cutwa, Dacca, and Juggernath. At present we are only able to occupy three of the above stations, viz.: Dinagepore, Cutwa and Jessore. To each of these places we wish to send a person immediately ...

We wish for no privileges or exemptions, but merely for leave to settle, preach the Gospel, and distribute Bibles, or other religious tracts, among the natives, without molestation or prohibition from the magistrate of the district; and for a general license to itinerate for this purpose in any part of the British dominions in India ... (Marshman 1859: 249-50).

Carey pressed the subject anew on Udny, arguing that the Government's consent was most essential. Udny's own views were in accord with Carey's, and he sent the plan to George Barlow with his recommendation. Barlow stated that though he favoured missionary efforts, he did not have the power to sanction missionary establishments in the country and could not act against the known views of the Court of Directors. Udny communicated these views with regret to Carey, who said that however great the respect of the missionaries for the Government's wishes, "they *must* form stations," and were prepared to face the consequences (Marshman 1859: 250).

They resolved, therefore, without further hesitation to send Felix Carey and Rowe to Benares, Mardon to Juggernath, and Biss to Dinagepore. They had decided upon Patna as another station but on learning that Rev. Henry Martyn was to be posted in the neighbourhood as chaplain, dropped the idea (Marshman 1859: 250).

Despite these efforts, the Baptists could boast of only thirty-one converts in their first ten years in the region (Mani 1998: 111). In a letter, dated 2nd January 1797, William Carey wrote of a congregation telling him, "Every people have their own *shasters*, and their own kind of holiness; attend to the proper work recommended by the *shasters* of your own country." William Ward recorded an instance, on 30th May 1800, when a man "asked why we came, and said if we could employ the natives as carpenters, blacksmiths, &c. it would be very well, but *they did not want* our holiness." In another incident, in August the same year, "An old man, who was drunk, was rather rough with Brother C. on Lord's Day morning while he was talking to the natives. He said – You English have taken the whole country and now you want the people to receive your religion. They would be great fools if they did."

Carey, in a letter dated 29th December 1800, admitted, "Often the name of Christ alone is sufficient to make a dozen of our hearers file off at once and sometimes to produce the most vile, blasphemous, insulting and malicious opposition from those who hear us." Ward noted, in June 1804, that the tracts given by the missionaries were sometimes refused and "many out of ill-will have torn them in pieces & scattered them thro' the streets" (Mani 1998: 102-05).

THE VELLORE MUTINY

On 10th July 1806, a mutiny broke out among the Sepoys at Vellore, ninety miles from Madras. The Sepoys attacked the British garrison late at night, killing over a hundred officers and men. This was the most serious armed uprising against the British after the Bengal Nawab Siraj-ud-Daula's sack of Calcutta in 1756. The Mutiny created great alarm in Government circles. John Malcolm wrote that it made him "tremble for India," while the Governor of Madras, William Bentinck, reported that Europeans in Madras "went to bed in the uncertainty of rising alive" (Sramek 2011: 76).

The Commander-in-Chief at Madras, Sir John Cradock, had drawn up orders that had been sanctioned by William Bentinck, introducing certain changes in the appearance of sepoys. These pertained to their distinguishing caste marks, dress and turbans, and the quantity and shape of their facial hair. The sepoys interpreted these as an attack on their religion. General H.G.A. Taylor explained in his memoirs that at the time of the Mutiny, "There had been an unpleasant feeling in the Native army of Madras, from the introduction of an obnoxious turban, and interference with the marks of the Hindoos, clipping of beards, whiskers, & c ..." (Crowell 1990: 268).

The presence of Christian missionaries in the region strengthened their apprehensions (In 1806, there were fourteen Protestant missionaries working in South India, Vellore itself was an SPCK outstation; Carson 2012: 76-77). Rev. Claudius Buchanan, who left Madras Presidency on 29th June, barely ten days before the Mutiny, referred to native fears in a letter to Henry Thornton in September 1806. "A rumour has for some months pervaded India," he wrote, "that all castes are to be made Christians" (Kaye 1859: 247). The presence at Vellore of the exiled family of Tipu Sultan added to the turmoil.

Many senior Company officials viewed the Mutiny as a fall-out of missionary propaganda. Sir George Barlow was convinced that "preaching Methodists and wild visionaries disturbing the religious ceremonies of the Natives will alienate the affections of our Native troops" (Porter 1999: 230). The Governor General-in-Council sent a dispatch to the Secret Committee on 7th December 1807 wherein it was stated that,

> although Mr. Buchanan, on the ground of his personal communications with some of the natives on the coast, is of opinion that the insurrection at Vellore had no connexion with the Christian religion, directly or indirectly, immediately, or remotely, we are compelled to form a different judgement, from the mass of authentic evidence and information on that unhappy event recorded in the public proceedings of government; and we are satisfied that a persuasion (a most erroneous one, indeed, but a firm and sincere persuasion) in the breasts of a great proportion of the sepoys who were thus betrayed into the execution of the massacre of Vellore, and of those who subsequently manifested a spirit of insurrection, that a design existed on the part of the British government to operate a general conversion of the inhabitants of India to Christianity (Malcolm II 1970b: 444).

The missionaries were ordered not to preach to the natives, nor distribute pamphlets among them, or take any steps to induce them to embrace Christianity. The missionaries described their plight in a communication to the BMS,

> We are in much the same situation as the apostles were, when commanded not to preach in His name ... To act in open defiance of the will of the Governor-General might occasion a positive law against evangelizing the heathen, and at once break up the Mission, which has been settled at so great an expense. On the other hand, if we yield a little to the present storm, it may soon blow over, and we may not only preserve our present privileges, but obtain the liberty which we have so long wished for (Marshman 1859: 260).

There was a great uproar in England.[6] The majority of the Directors were disposed to agree with the views of Francis Baring, Sweny Toone, and Thomas Twining that the Mutiny was the outcome of missionary activities. Sweny Toone wrote to Warren Hastings, on 27th May 1807, "If the question were put to the Court (of Directors), it would result in an order to send all missionaries home" (Philips 1961: 160).

It was fortunate for the Evangelicals that Charles Grant and Edward Parry were back as Chairman and Deputy Chairman of the East India Company in 1807. They tried to refute charges of missionary culpability, and argued that both Cradock and Bentinck had acted recklessly (Parry was a member of the Clapham Sect; fellow-Director, Sweny Toone, described him as "a man who has infinite kindness in his character and mad upon one subject — religion," Philips 1961: 154; 161). Grant privately told Rev. David Brown, on 20th June 1807, of the opposition of the Court of Directors to sending missionaries to India. He said,

> There has been an eager propensity to send out strong orders at once to restrain the missionaries, or, at least, to confine them to Serampore, and encourage our Government in the discountenance it has of late shown them. It is lamentable

to see many men of parts and respectable in society so little sensible of the nature of Christianity, and of the obligations of nations ... For the present we hope the idea of sending out strong orders is given up, and it is not a small point to have gained time ... The tide was so strong that, if God had not been pleased to use two well-intentioned, though weak, instruments, in situations in which my colleague and I are, orders of a very different kind would, in all probability, have been transmitted (Morris 1904: 301).

GOVERNMENT OPPOSITION TO MISSIONARIES

The Government in India took immediate steps to curtail missionary activities. In August 1806, two new missionaries from England were ordered to quit the country immediately (Sherring 1875: 79).

The anger against missionaries revived with the arrival of Lord Minto as Governor General (1807–1813). The first news he received on landing in India was of the Vellore Mutiny. Soon after, a missionary tract was brought to his notice in which Mohammad was called a pretender. Carey claimed that the sentence had been inserted without his knowledge by a Muslim convert. The tract was withdrawn and Carey agreed to submit all Baptist publications to the Government for approval. That was not the end of the matter. Lord Minto put pressure on the Danish Governor of Serampore to ban the pamphlets.

A report on missionary pamphlets and activities was also received from Blaquiere, a Calcutta magistrate. He found eleven Baptist pamphlets, containing "strictures on the Hindu deities tending to place them in a hateful or disgusting light" and "exhortations to embrace Christianity." Additionally, a preacher was found casting aspersions on the lives of Brahmins and claiming that the religious festivals of the Hindus were sinful. Sir George Barlow had also informed Lord Minto that he had received reports that a Baptist missionary (probably William Ward) was "in the habit of preaching publicly in the streets of Calcutta in terms abusive of the Hindoo religion" and that on "several occasions the populace had manifested signs of irritation, and on one occasion especially had proceeded to acts of violence" (Carson 2012: 91).

The Governor General-in-Council decided to forbid all preaching in Calcutta in the native languages, proscribe the issue of any publication from the Society of Missionaries at Serampore, and shift the press to Calcutta (Marshman 1859: 315-16).

On receipt of the note Carey said,

> such a letter was never written by any Government before. Roman Catholics have persecuted other Christians under the name of heretics, but no Christian Government, that I know of, has prohibited attempts to spread Christianity among the Heathen (Marshman 1859: 316).

In a communication to the Chairman of the East India Company, in 1807, Lord Minto detailed the activities of the missionaries that had created unrest. He drew attention to,

> ...the principal publications which have issued from the Serampore press, in the native languages, the sole effect of which was not to convert, but to alienate, the professors of both religions prevalent amongst the natives of this country. Pray read especially the miserable stuff addressed to the Hindus, in which... without proof or argument of any kind, the pages are filled with hell fire, denounced against a whole race of men for believing in the religion which they were taught by their fathers and mothers, and the truth of which it is simply impossible it should ever have entered into their minds to doubt... A total abolition of caste is openly preached... Is it possible that your Government should be required to countenance public exhortations addressed to a Hindu nation to efface at once, not a little spot of yellow paste from the forehead, but the whole institution of caste itself, that is to say, their whole scheme of civil polity as well as their fondest and most rooted religious tenets? This is to

be accomplished by coarse and scurrilous invective against the most revered order of Hindu society and addressed to that order itself.

Lord Minto added,

... I am no enemy at the progress of Christianity in India. It is the way, I observe, of some who are personally engaged in the work of conversion ... I do not think we should be justified in refusing the dispensation of the Christian revelation to this great country for our interest or security, but I am not equally ready to sacrifice the great interests which are confided to me to a blind principle of complaisance towards every indiscretion which zeal or negligence may commit (Muir 1971: 251-52).

Though Minto eventually cancelled the order for the transfer of the press, he retained a tight control over its publications and for several years forbade all preaching in British territory. In an interview with William Carey, he asked, "Don't you think it wrong, Dr. Carey, to try and make Indians Christians?" However, as a result of the persistence of his visitor, Minto, four years later, openly assisted in the inauguration of a mission station at Agra. Carey (whose first wife had died) was by now married to a relative of the Danish Governor (Mayhew 1929: 71).

In November 1807, Claudius Buchanan memorialized Lord Minto on the changes in policy from the time of Wellesley. His litany of complaints included — withdrawal of government patronage for translation of the Scriptures into Oriental languages; efforts to suppress the translations; attempts to conceal encomiums of the Court of Directors on the missionary, Schwartz; and endeavours to restrain Protestant missionaries in Bengal from exercising their functions and establishing an imprimatur for theological works. He was also asked by the Chief Secretary to submit for scrutiny the sermons he had delivered on the Christian prophecies, which he declined to do (Martin 1983b: 513).

The Government continued to be nervous about the missionaries. Efforts were also made in London to uproot the Serampore Mission, the Danish influence having ended with the cession of Serampore to the English in 1808. On 30th April 1808, Robert Dundas, in a long letter to Minto, listed eight priorities of the Board of Control, of which the second was a strong determination to "adopt the most effectual measures of enforcing the laws against unlicensed persons landing or settling in India, and particularly against their traversing the Country." On missionaries, he said that the British occupation of Serampore "will have left you at full liberty to enforce any regulations you may think expedient." He,

> had no doubt in thinking that, next to restraining the missionaries from any acts which may be dangerous to the public tranquility, it is most desirable that the Government should not appear to be a party in any of their proceedings, even of the most inoffensive description (Carson 2012: 98).

Meanwhile, three Baptists who arrived in 1811 were allowed to stay only because they were trained in printing. In 1812, there was a raid against the missionaries in Bengal. In 1813, several missionaries from different societies were ordered to quit India without delay. One in particular, William Johns, was told that if he did not take his passage immediately, he would be forcibly carried on board a ship (Martin 1983b: 513).

PAMPHLET WAR BETWEEN PROPONENTS AND OPPONENTS OF PROSELYTIZATION

In the wake of the Vellore Mutiny, a pamphlet war broke out on the issue of missions in India in which over two dozen writers participated (Philips 1961: 163; Fisch 1985: 22-68). It was described as "a contest between the friends of Christianity and the advocates of Heathenism" (Kaye 1859: 159).

Thomas Twining (son of the opulent tea-dealer), employed for thirteen years in various departments of the Civil service of the Bengal Presidency, opened the attack with *A Letter to the Chairman of the East India Company on the danger of interfering in the religious opinions of the Natives of India* (1807). It was written in response to Claudius Buchanan's *Memoir of the Expediency of an Ecclesiastical Establishment for British India* (1805). Twining said his *Letter* was a precursor to a motion he intended to bring before the Court of Proprietors for expelling all Christian missionaries from India. He stated,

> ... Notwithstanding the extraordinary observation of Mr. Buchanan, that the natives are not particularly attached to their religious opinions, I will venture to say, that there is not, in the world, a people more jealous and tenacious of their religious opinions and ceremonies, than the native inhabitants of the East. Sir, the people of India are not a political, but a religious people. In this respect, they differ, I fear, from the inhabitants of this country. *They* think as much of their Religion, as *we* of our Constitution. *They* venture their Shastah and Koran, with as much enthusiasm as *we* our Magna Charta.

> As long as we continue to govern India in the mild and tolerant spirit of Christianity, we may govern it with ease: but if ever the fatal day shall arrive, when religious innovation shall set her foot in that country, indignation will spread from one end of Hindostan to the other; and the arms of fifty millions of people will drive us from that portion of the globe, with as much ease as the sand of the desert is scattered by the wind ... (Marshall 1968: 189-90).

A critic of Twining commented on his tract, "no such letter was ever before written in a Christian country, under a Christian king, by a gentleman professing the Christian religion" (Kaye 1859: 152).

Among those who joined the attack on the missionaries was Major Scott Waring, who had gone to India in military service of the Company in 1765, and subsequently served on the personal staff of Warren Hastings. Major Scott Waring became one of the principal adversaries of the missionaries in the pamphlet war. He proclaimed,

> Whenever the Christian religion does as much for the lower orders of society in Europe, as that of Brahma appears to have done for the Hindus, I shall cheerfully vote for its establishment in Hindustan (Long 1848: 14).

A "Bengali Officer," Col. Stewart, known in India as "Hindoo Stewart," who had lived in the country for twenty-seven years, also wrote in defense of Hinduism (*Vindication of the Hindoos*, 1808). He professed,

> I would repose the Hindoo system on the broad basis of its own merits; convinced that, on the enlarged principles of moral reasoning, it little needs the meliorating hand of Christian dispensations, to render its votaries, a sufficiently correct and moral people ...Wherever I look around me, in the vast region of Hindoo Mythology, I discover piety in the garb of allegory: and I see Morality, at every turn, blended with every tale; and as far as I can rely on my own judgment, it appears the most complete and ample system of Moral Allegory, that the world has ever produced ... (Marshman 1859: 337-45, 349-53, 354-60).

The Hindus, Stewart declared, had developed a much higher and purer concept of God than the Greeks and Romans ever had, so "that there is scarce a single bearer, who carries the Palankeen in India, who has not as exalted a notion of God as ever Socrates entertained." The credit for the doctrine of the immortality of the soul should, Stewart stated, go to India,

> To India then, as the true source of this glorious doctrine, let us turn, with becoming reverence, and pay due homage at the shrine of that profound genius which unfolded this great truth — and, divesting our minds of unworthy prejudices of education, ever hostile to improvement, let us contemplate with awe and with respect, that remote period, when this

sublime tenet ... irradiated the eastern hemisphere, and exhibited the pious Brahmins as the most enlightened of the human race (Fisch 1985: 43-45).

On sati he said,

Every feeling mind must lament that infatuation that urges the Hindoo widow to burn herself with the corpse of her deceased husband; it is an instance of deluded heroism that we cannot but admire, while we condemn (Marshman 1859: 354-60).

Another critic of the missionaries, Sydney Smith protested bitterly against "consecrated cobblers" (Howse 1960: 80-81). He wrote in the *Edinburgh Review*,

The missionaries complain of intolerance. A weasel might as well complain of intolerance when he is throttled for sucking eggs. Toleration for their own opinions — toleration for their domestic worship, for their private groans and convulsions, they possess in the fullest extent, but who ever heard of toleration for intolerance? Who ever before heard men cry out that they were persecuted because they might not insult the religion, shock the feelings, irritate the passions of their fellow-creatures, and throw a whole colony into bloodshed and confusion?

He added, "The wise and rational part of the Christian ministry find they have enough to do at home ... But if a tinker is a devout man, he infallibly sets off for the East" (Marshman 1859: 373-76).

The missionary response came principally from Rev. John Owen (of the Foreign and Bible Society) and Andrew Fuller (Secretary of the Baptist Missionary Society). Fuller, in his *Apology* asked,

Is giving the Scriptures, then, to the natives, in their own languages, and offering to instruct them in their leading doctrines, opposed to the mild and tolerant spirit of Christianity? ... The question which Mr. Twining proposes to submit to a General Court of Proprietors, whatever be the terms in which it may be couched, will not be, whether the natives of India shall continue to enjoy the most perfect toleration, but *whether that toleration shall be extended to Christian Missionaries* ... (Marshman 1859: 347-49, 353-54).

Around this time also appeared an *Essay on the duty, means, and consequences of introducing the Christian religion among the native inhabitants of the British dominions in the East.* Written by one Cunningham, it had formed part of a work submitted to the University of Cambridge for the prize instituted by Claudius Buchanan. It listed superstitions of the Hindus and stressed the Britain obligation to communicate that divine system, which alone could improve native character (Pearson II 1819: 184-85).

Lord Teignmouth's pamphlet, *Considerations of the practicability, policy, and obligation of communicating Christianity to India* (1808), was the most important contribution to the missionary cause. He viewed the demand for a prohibition of the translation and circulation of the Scriptures and the recall of missionaries as the "most fatal prognostics with respect to the permanency of the British dominion in India." He considered it strange that,

> while every other religion in India is left undisturbed, while the doctrines of the Koran are freely circulated, and those of the Vedas and Shasters left unmolested, the Government of a country professing the Christian religion is called upon to exert its power for barring out every scattered ray of that religious and moral light which, through the endeavours of any charitable individuals among us, might otherwise shine upon the inhabitants of that benighted land ...

He concluded,

> I have no wish to limit that toleration which has hitherto been observed with respect to their religion, laws, and customs. On the contrary, I hold a perseverance in the system

of toleration, not only just in itself, but as essentially necessary to facilitate the means used for their conversion (Marshman 1859: 368-73).

After tempers cooled, Grant, in 1809, thought it safe to demand a re-examination of the Vellore Mutiny and the responsibility of the missionaries. He pointed out that unpopular orders regarding the sepoy's appearance alone could not have caused the outbreak. "The underlying cause," he said, "was Muhammadan political disaffection, and advantage was taken of the unpopular orders to provoke the mutiny." The Court of Directors accepted his appraisal, and a resolution exonerating the missionaries was sent to India. This was the "necessary preliminary" for the insertion of a clause in the Charter Act of 1813 permitting missionaries to operate in India (Philips 1961: 168-69).

END-NOTES

1. Carey had studied the Scriptures at an early age. At thirteen, he appeared in the pulpit for the first time. He married the sister of his former master before he was twenty, but the marriage proved a mismatch, his wife having little sympathy for her husband's goals. Soon after his marriage, Carey was invited to preach regularly to a small congregation at Earl's Barton. He preached there for three and a half years on the Sabbath, working at his cobbler's stall during the week.
   At twenty-four, Carey accepted ministerial charge of a Baptist church at Moulton. Around this time he came across Cooke's *Voyages Around the World*, and began to think about the "spiritual degradation" of a large number of the world's inhabitants. Rev. Andrew Fuller later recalled that he had once gone to Carey's little shop and seen hanging on the wall, a large map with several sheets pasted together. Against each country Carey had written the information he had acquired about its population, religion, and government (Holcomb 1901: 66-68). Carey's mind was "appalled" at the "darkness of heathendom" and his spirit became "heavily burdened" (Annett: 20-21).

Not many then shared his certainty that it was a Christian duty to spread the Gospel among non-Christians. At a ministerial meeting in Northampton, the Baptist divine, Mr. Ryland (senior) invited the audience to suggest a topic for discussion. Carey proposed, "The duty of Christians to attempt the spread of the Gospel among heathen nations." The astonished Ryland responded, "Young man, sit down. When God pleases to convert the heathen He will do it without your aid or mine" (Holcomb 1901: 68-69).

Carey shifted to Leicester at the age of twenty-eight to take charge of a church there. In 1792, while at Leicester, he prepared a treatise entitled, "*An Enquiry into the Obligation of Christians to use means for the Conversion of Heathens in which the Religious State of the Different Nations of the World, the Success of Former Undertakings, and the Practicability of Further Undertakings, are Considered.*" This has been described as "the most significant apologia for Protestant missions to emerge at the beginning of the modern era" and was one of the factors that led to the formation of the Baptist Missionary Society some months later (Oddie 2006: 136).

In the work Carey accepted that there was much spiritual work to be done in England itself. But he argued,

"... Our own countrymen have the means of grace, and may attend on the word preached if they chuse it ... faithful ministers are placed in almost every part of the land, whose spheres of action might be much extended if their congregations were but more hearty and active in the cause: but with them the case is widely different, who have no Bible, no written language... no ministers, no good civil government, nor any of those advantages which we have. Pity therefore, humanity, and much more Christianity, call loudly for every possible exertion to introduce the gospel amongst them" (Carey 1792: 13).

Carey made every effort to convince fellow-ministers. Fuller recalled,

"He would also be frequently conversing with his brethren on the practicability and importance of a mission to the heathen, and of his willingness to engage in it. Some of our most aged and respectable ministers thought ... that it was a wild and impracticable scheme that he had got into his mind, and therefore gave him no encouragement. Yet he would not give it up, but would converse with us, one by one, till he had made some impression on us."

Carey's sister provided similar testimony, "He was always, from the first, remarkably impressed about heathen lands... I never remember his engaging in prayer, in his family or in public, without prayer for those poor creatures" (Annett: 22). After delivering a sermon at a minister's meeting in Nottingham, on 31st May 1792, Carey drew two principles from the text, "Expect Great Things From God; Attempt Great Things For God." He urged his colleagues to help set up a society to spread the Gospel.

As a result, in Kettering, in October 1792, aided by Andrew Fuller, the pastor of the local Baptist church, the Baptist Missionary Society was founded. Carey was part of the five member committee of the Society, and Fuller its Secretary. A collection was made in support of foreign missions. Carey volunteered to go to any country to spread the Gospel (Holcomb 1901: 69-70).

2. Despite its growing responsibilities, till the early nineteenth century there was no provision for training Company servants either at home or in India. Candidates were selected when they were between 15 and 18 years of age, and immediately set sail for India. Warren Hastings had proposed that after candidates had received their appointment, they be permitted to complete their studies in branches of European knowledge and also learn Persian (then the language of administration in India). He suggested that a seminary be established by the East India Company to encourage Persian learning. He recalled, "I formed a plan for such an institution ... my plan was to obtain professors from India (for teaching Persian at the institute)" (Beveridge 1978: 37). But the proposal received little interest. It was only with Lord Wellesley that the regular training of Company officials was seriously taken up.

Wellesley, an imperialist, declared that the Indian possessions "must be considered as a sacred trust and a permanent possession." For governing India on a permanent basis, "we shall require a succession of able magistrates, wise and honest judges, and skilful statesmen properly qualified to conduct the ordinary movements of the great machine of Government" (Martin II 1984: 339). Wellesley elaborated his plan in his famous Minute of 10th July 1800, which established Fort William College for training English officers in the vernaculars, laws, and customs of India. According to Wellesley's plan, every candidate nominated to Company service would be required to undergo three years training at Fort William College. The College would "fix and establish sound and correct principles of religion and government in their (the candidates) minds at an early period of life" and serve as "the best security which (could) be provided for the stability of the British power in India" (Martin II 1984: 346).

3. Wellesley had been friendlier with the missionaries than any other Governor General, but Grant regretted that he had stopped short of actual assistance. In a letter to Wellesley in 1801, when the controversy over private trade and Fort William College was at its peak, Grant stated,

"If you had seen fit to recommend the diffusion of (the Christian religion) among the heathen, no one could have done this with so much effect; and though diversities of opinion on some other Indian subjects... unhappily prevail, yet in the true glory of espousing such an object, all the best judgments of the present and future times I am convinced would be agreed" (Embree 1962: 222-23).

Even six years later, after many bitter differences, Grant acknowledged Wellesley's contribution. In a letter to David Brown, he wrote,

"... I lament that the successors of Lord Wellesley did not imitate him in countenancing ministers of religion and ministerial labours. If anything could have bribed me to wink at enormous faults in his administration, this would" (Morris 1904: 302).

4. A leading critic of the College was Charles Grant, Member of Parliament and of the Court of Directors. While agreeing on the need for their further education, Grant feared that if young boys of 15 were given intensive training in India before they were old enough to fully appreciate their European heritage, they could succumb to the "disease of Indianization," that

had claimed so many Company servants in the eighteenth century. That would negate Grant's vision of the Company servant as "the vital spearhead of Western cultural and Christian change."

A letter, dated 29th January 1804, from Canton had suggested that because of the ill effects of climate upon boys of 15, Writers should not be sent out for China till they were 19 years old. The period between their nomination and that age could be devoted to "a completion of education ... under the direction of the Honourable Court [which] might form them to be more capable servants of the Company and give them a chance to become more distinguished members of Society than they could be when quitting Europe at the very early age they frequently do." The Plan was accepted by the Court of Directors. Accordingly, in 1806, Hertford Castle, located twenty miles from London, was selected as the temporary site of the East India College. Subsequently, in 1809, the College was shifted to a new location and building at Haileybury. The prospectus of 1806 stated, "The object of this establishment is to provide a supply of persons duly qualified to discharge the various and important duties required from the civil servants of the Company in administering the government in India" (Blunt 1938: 35). The curriculum, approved by the Court of Directors, emphasized religious teaching and morality. A religious bias in the education of civil servants was intended to shield them from the declared principles of the French Revolution, which the Directors believed were founded on atheism.

The staff at Haileybury College had "a distinct religious orientation." Many teachers were ordained as Anglican priests and some were active Evangelicals, a manifestation of the preferences of Charles Grant and other "Saints" in the Company (Cohn 1966: 119; 132). One of the rules was that the Principal "shall be a divine of the Church of England." Rev. Samuel Henley (1740–1815), a Cambridge graduate and clergyman of the Church of England, was appointed the first Principal. Besides general supervision of the conduct of students, he was required to teach the classics and deliver lectures "within moderate limits" on "the principles, obligations, value and sanctions of religion and morals, elucidating with particular attention the evidences of Christianity." Of the six professors appointed, four were clergymen, including Rev. T.R. Malthus, Professor of History and Political Economy (Misra 1959: 400). William Dealtry, Professor of Mathematics, was an active Evangelist. The Bishop of London was appointed ex-officio Visitor to the College.

There was also a strong Utilitarian influence on the College; Bentham's ideas were disseminated among the students via William Empson, a staunch Utilitarian, who taught at Haileybury for over thirty years (Stokes 1982: 52; Campbell I 1893: 10).

Henry Melvill, one of the foremost evangelical preachers of the Church of England, served as principal from 1844 to 1857. On the last "graduation" he said that in the years to come many would "look back to Haileybury with gratitude and affection and trace to some lesson received within its walls much of their usefulness as men and their consistency as Christians" (Penner 1986: 240-41). While in Central Africa the missionaries opened the path for empire, in India "the empire paved a way for mission" (Penner 1986: 243).

5. The Brahmin pandits of Fort William College together rose against J.B. Gilchrist (1759–1841), when he proposed, in 1804, that there be a debate on the topic that the natives of India would embrace the Gospel as soon as they were able to compare the Christian precepts with those of their own books. There were such strong protests that Gilchrist had to eventually resign (Das 1974: 15).

6. Officials were not just concerned about the internal threat from the native population, but also fearful of French designs. William Elphinstone, Chairman of the Company in 1806, in a Minute on the missionaries, expressed the apprehension that the French would take advantage of the situation to throw out the British. Elphinstone compared the Company to James II, "a fool who exchanged three kingdoms for a Mass", while the Company "have exchanged the Mogul Empire for a Chapter in the New Testament." He stated that the Company "certainly are canting and preaching away their authority in India." Robert Dundas, who became President of the Board of Control

in April 1807, was also alarmed by the French. He told Lord Minto, the new Governor General, that the overthrow of the British in India was a "constant object of Bonaparte's hostile ambition" (Carson 2012: 73-74).

8

Evangelical-missionary Attack on Hinduism

The Evangelist, Charles Grant had fired the first salvo in the endeavour to Christianize and Anglicize India. His *Observations* was a scathing attack on the morals and religion of the Hindus. Therein Grant described them as,

> a race of men lamentably degenerate and base, retaining but a feeble sense of moral obligation, yet obstinate in their disregard of what they know to be right, governed by malevolent and licentious passions, strongly exemplifying the effects produced on society by great and general corruption of manners, and sunk in misery by their vices ... (Grant 1832: 41).

Grant's denunciation, indicative of the wider shift from Orientalist to Anglicist policies, was reiterated by Baptist missionaries. The Baptist missionary journal, *Friend of India*, for example, stated that "The infelicity of (India's) inhabitants arises not from ungenerous soil, but from an unnatural system of morals; and from rites and customs, which though deemed to be sacred, are inimical to human happiness" (Major 2006: 126).

STREET PREACHING

From 1793 to 1804, William Carey, William Ward, and Joshua Marshman actively engaged in street preaching, during which they openly condemned Hindu religion and customs. They recorded their experiences in letters, diaries, and journals. Writing to Andrew Fuller of the BMS in January 1795, Carey narrated,

> I had occasion to go and preach to a company of people who were worshipping Sarosaudi (Saraswati), the patroness of literature. The general opinion of the learned is, that the idols are only images, having no power in them; but that it is well pleasing for God to worship them in honour of the persons they represent, who they say, were eminent for virtue or goodness to men: The Brahman however who attended this ceremony, told me plainly that *this image was God*. When I asked him, by what authority he did this? He said, That the *shasters* commanded it. I enquired, What *shasters*? He said, The Bee Accorn (*vyakaran*), which I knew to be only a *grammar*. I was much drawn out in love to their souls, and was enabled to warn them against the devices of their teachers (Mani 1998: 92).

Carey's attempt was to demonstrate the "ignorance" of the Brahmin priest and his own superior knowledge of Hindu texts. Undermining the status of Brahmins appeared particularly important for the missionaries. In a letter soon after his arrival in India, Marshman wrote,

> The influence of the brahmans also is almost inconceivable to them who do not live within the light of it. They are Sacred, nay in some instances they are almost regarded as Deities. I have often seen people falling at their feet in the most profound reverence. If there are any who do not wish thus (to) respect them out of love, yet they stand in the greatest awe of them, not for their number, for perhaps they are not above a 20th part of the nation, nor indeed are they vested with any real power, but merely on account of their sanctity

tho' perhaps there is not a set of worse men in the Earth (Mani 1998: 96).

A pronounced anti-Brahmin sentiment was palpable in missionary writings (Dalmia 2007: 66). Carey shared Marshman's assessment of Brahmins, regarding them an obstacle to proselytization. The missionaries made all efforts to undermine the status of Brahmins. Carey once challenged a Brahmin to prevent the sun from setting, as Brahmins were formerly said to have done. In another case he recorded,

A young Brahman came after me. I stopped & asked him if he could read. He looked at the printing, but he could not read it. I then told him, that this poitou (sacred thread) bore false witness. It said that he was wise; but he was as ignorant as a sooder (sudra) (Mani 1998: 96-97).

ABHORRENCE OF HINDU PRACTICES

From the time of their arrival, the Baptists displayed disapproval for Hindu practices. William Carey's journal abounds with entries indicating prejudice. He wrote at one place,

I told them (the natives) that their books were like a loaf of bread, in which was a considerable quantity of good flour, but also a little very malignant poison, which made the whole so poisonous that whoever should eat of it would die; so, I observed, that their writings contained much good instruction mixed with deadly poison (Carey 1836: 232-33).

In a letter to John Williams, leading Baptist minister of New York, on 9th December 1800, Carey said,

It is not to be thought that the moral character of a people should be better than that of their gods. Men make themselves idols after their own hearts, and therefore to look for good morals among idolaters is the height of folly...

the Hindoos ... are literally sunk into the dregs of vice (Williams 1892: 61-62).

To another friend Carey stated,

Never was such a combination of false principles as here. In other heathen lands conscience may often be appealed to with effect. Here God's law is erased thence, and idolatrous ceremony is engraved in its stead. The multitude pay a thousandfold more deference to the Brahmins than the people did to the priests in the Papacy's darkest days. And all are bound to their present state by caste, in breaking whose chains a man must endure to be renounced and abhorred by his wife, children, and friends. Every tie that twines the heart of a husband, father, and neighbour must be torn and broken ere a man can give himself to Christ (Carey 1934: 190).

A correspondence by the Serampore missionaries with the BMS in October 1800 described their annoyance at,

...those amazing barriers which Satan has thrown in the way of the destruction of his kingdom in this country ... Here the multitude believe that the Ganges can wash from iniquity: what need then of the blood of Christ? Here Brahmuns unblushingly declare that God is the author of sin, and that the world is merely his show: so that sin is no longer feared. Here it is commonly believed that this is not a state of probation, but of rewards and punishments: the doctrine of a future general judgment, therefore, appears wholly false. Here the multitude believe that hell is a place of temporary punishment merely: so that no one much fears, though he may think he is going there ... (Carey 1836: 402-07).

IDOLATRY

Image-worship was an anathema for the missionaries. William Carey noted in his journal in August 1794,

The last of these days was Lord's-day; I spent it in reading to and praying with my family. Towards evening I went out, when the workmen who have built the works came to me, and said that, as I was to begin making indigo tomorrow, it was much their wish that I would make an offering to Kally, the goddess of destruction, that I might have success in the work. This Kally is the most devil-like figure that can be thought of: she stands upon a dead man; her girdle is strung with small figures of human skulls, like beads upon a bracelet; she has four arms, and her tongue hangs out of her mouth below her chin; and in short, a more horrible figure can scarcely be conceived of. I took the opportunity of remonstrating with them upon the wickedness and folly of idolatry, and set my face as much as possible against their making any offering at all, and told them that I would rather lose my life than sacrifice to their idol; that God was much displeased with them for their idolatry, and exhorted them to leave it and turn to the true God. But I had the mortification of seeing, the next day, that they had been offering a kid; yet I doubt not but I shall soon see some of these people brought from darkness to the marvelous light of the gospel (Carey 1836: 196-97).

William Ward expressed a similar aversion. He wanted,

to feel and avow a just abhorrence of idolatry, and to deplore it as one of the greatest scourges ever employed by a Being, terrible in anger, to punish nations who have rejected the direct and simple means which nature and conscience supply of knowing himself ... (Ward IV 1990: 126).

Eustace Carey, nephew of William Carey, listed the malevolent consequences of image-worship,

While in all countries in which idolatry exerts its influence, it produces, in the human mind, cruelty, lust, hatred to God and Divine things, which completely justifies the description given us of the heathen character in the Word of God; it is our lot to labour among a people in whose character are united all the above features, and added to cunning and fraud, which render our work peculiarly painful... We have begun a warfare with the empire of Satan in this country, which we hope not to relinquish till death, nor till some signal success shall have been granted ... (Carey 1857: 270-71).

In an entry in his journal, in November 1822, Eustace Carey cited an occasion when he saw a few persons making an offering to Kali. He wrote,

We called them to us and began by interrogating them as to what they could expect from such devotions. Some of them turned it off with a smile, and said that was the way they had been taught. I tried to impress upon them the heinous sin of idolatry (Carey 1857: 279).

"EVIL PRACTICES"
HOOK-SWINGING

Among the native practices to first attract William Carey's attention was hook-swinging. While in the Sunderbans, in April 1794, during the *charak puja* celebrations, he wrote in his journal, "Today the cursed mode of Self-torturing was varied, a large pole was erected, and a Bamboo fixed across the top, and the swinging by Hooks fixed in the Back was attended to. I went out to see it." Next day, he added,

Their horrid and idolatrous transactions have made such an impression on my mind as cannot, I think, be easily eradicated. Who would grudge to spend his life and his all, to deliver an otherwise amiable people from the misery and darkness of their present wretched state! (Oddie 2006: 142; 153).

While at Mudnabatty, he again described "the wickedness of the horrid practice of swinging" and "the horrid self tormenting mode of worship ... as falling on spikes of iron, dancing with threads or bamboos thrust through their sides, swinging, &c" (Carey 1836: 229-30).

INFANTICIDE

In 1794, William Carey, riding near Malda, saw the remains of an infant who had died from exposure. William Ward, in his account of the Hindus, referred to people "frequently offer(ing) their children to the goddess Gunga," and to a custom of sacrificing female children (Ward IV 1990: 122-24). Claudius Buchanan also stated that women who had no children "vow to sacrifice their first-born to the goddess Gunga" (Buchanan 1805: 59).

In October 1801, George Udny was promoted to the Supreme Council. A "warm and steady friend of the missionary cause" (Marshman 1859: 157), he drew Lord Wellesley's attention to the practice of sacrificing children in fulfillment of religious vows at the Ganga Saugor, and suggested its suppression. Wellesley was the first Governor General to depart from the policy of non-interference in the religious practices of the natives. He asked William Carey to prepare a report on the matter.

Carey wrote to Andrew Fuller,

> You may be sure that I shall make my report as full as possible, do it with the greatest pleasure; for I consider that the burning of women, the burying them alive with their husbands, as in the case of many jogees, the exposure of infants, and the sacrifice of children at Saugor, ought not to be permitted, whatever religious motives may be pretended because they are all crimes against the State (Marshman 1859: 158).

Carey recommended immediate stoppage of the practice. A regulation was accordingly enacted in August 1802. This was the first instance of intervention and to the surprise of "the whole body of Christian alarmists," it created no rebellion (Marshman 1859: 159). The obvious explanation would seem to be that incidents of child sacrifice were not commonplace. The issue appeared part of a missionary campaign to impress the British public on the reforming role of a Christian state and prepare the ground for proselytization.

The assertions of Carey and his friends were, in fact, challenged by H.H. Wilson, among the greatest Sanskrit scholars of his time and Secretary of the Asiatic Society. In a letter to the Military Secretary of the Government, Wilson said the sacrifice of infants at Sagor was neither countenanced by the religious orders nor the people at large. It was, moreover, "of rare and restricted occurrence." The practice of female infanticide, too, was a "very limited observance, being confined to a few castes in one or two districts" (Majumdar 1941: 134).

Earlier, the Orientalist, Sir William Jones had regarded infanticide and sacrifices to Kali as unrepresentative of Hinduism, "comparable to the claims that the Virgin Mary had appeared in Italy in 1294, which did not invalidate Christianity" (Canon 1990: 321).

Yet Rev. Claudius Buchanan asserted that in one month alone at Sagar (January 1801), 23 children had been sacrificed (Buchanan 1849: 24).

VOLUNTARY SUICIDES, *GHAUT* MURDERS

Among the "evil practices" of Hinduism, William Carey listed *ghaut* murders, the exposure of the sick on the banks of the Ganges. In a graphic account, he stated,

> The custom of half immersing persons supposed to be dying, undoubtedly occasions the premature death of many, and the multitudes destroyed in other methods would swell the catalogue to an extent almost exceeding credibility... How much should every friend of the Redeemer, and of men, desire the universal spread of that gospel, which secures glory to God in the highest, and peace on earth (Oddie 2006: 158).

William Ward wrote of voluntary suicides. He claimed that a native informed him that in the year 1806 he had spent two months at Prayag,

> ...during which time he saw about thirty persons drown themselves! Almost every day he saw or heard of one or more *sunyasees* who thus terminated their existence; and several instances occurred in which a man and his wife, having no children, drowned themselves together, praying for some blessing in the next birth (Ward IV 1990: 118).

The missionary, William John, presented a striking description of the practice of "Exposing the Sick and Aged." He wrote,

> The Hindoo character is in many essential points defective, and led by deep-rooted prejudices, and barbarous customs, to the commission of crimes which ought not to be sanctioned by any moral or religious code. How often is the aged Hindoo parent deemed an encumbrance and an unnecessary expense by the family; and carried a living victim, devoted to die on the margin of the Ganges, or some other holy stream: there his own children fill his mouth and nostrils with mud; and, thus cutting off every prospect of recovery, they leave the author of their being to be carried away by the stream, as food for alligators and vultures! Although sanctioned by the Brahmuns, and perhaps sometimes voluntary on the part of the aged victim, no religion should tolerate such a sacrifice; that it is not always voluntary we have many undeniable proofs. The fatal consequence of not submitting to this extraordinary viaticum, or of eluding its effect, by returning to his family in case of a rescue or recovery, is so provided for, by the brahminical laws, that death is far more desirable than the continuance of life on such terms (John 1816).

DEATHS CAUSED BY PILGRIMAGES

The Baptists expressed outrage at the number of deaths purportedly caused by Hinduism. In a note to a friend in 1812, William Carey stated,

> Idolatry destroys more than the sword. The numbers who die in their long pilgrimages, either through want, or fatigue, or from dysenteries, and fevers, caught by lying out, and want of accommodation, is incredible.

He conservatively estimated the mortality caused by pilgrimage to the Jagannath temple alone at an astonishing 120,000 a year (Oddie 2006: 158).

William Ward also made a rough calculation of the number of Hindus who perished annually as "the victims of superstition." He claimed that those who had seen these figures felt they fell "far below the real fact." They nevertheless presented "a horrible view... of the effects of superstition." He concluded,

> Since the commencement of the bramhinical system, millions of victims have been immolated on the altars of its gods; and, notwithstanding the influence of Europeans, the whole of Hindoost'hanu may be termed 'a field of blood unto this day' (Ward IV 1990: 126-29).

EVANGELICAL-MISSIONARY WRITINGS ON HINDUISM

The Evangelical-missionary treatises on Hinduism were designed to sway public opinion at home and compel Parliament to concede the right to proselytization in Company territories. In a letter to the Archbishop of Canterbury, towards the end of 1805, on the promotion of Christian knowledge in India, Rev. Claudius Buchanan said,

> How India is to be preserved in time to come must be submitted to the wisdom of the Imperial Parliament. If the Scriptures be from God, our nation does not deserve at his

hand to retain possession of this 'paradise of nations' a year longer; so greatly have we abused our sacred trust. We have, in one word, 'withheld the revelation of God; and permitted the libation to Moloch of human blood.' In the course of the two last months, the Rev. Mr. Brown, the senior of the English clergy now in India, has witnessed the burning alive of eight women at the place of sacrifice, in the suburbs of Calcutta, as he passed casually on his way from his country-house to the church in town. How can the minister of the altar approach without trembling to his holy office, when he reflects on such scenes, and on their connexion with the sin of his country! ...

... I would now impress the mind of your Grace with a just sentiment of our present state in India, in order that your Grace may deliberate on the means of promoting the welfare of the hundred million of souls which Providence has committed to our charge.

One observation I would make on the proposed Ecclesiastical Establishment. A partial or half will have no effect. A few additional chaplains can do nothing towards the attainment of the great object in view. An Archbishop is wanted for India...

Spiritual power with means of instruction, is wanting, to awaken to life this sluggish and inert race. Vegetating in ignorance and passive misery, they want a guide, who shall take them by the hand, and lift them up, and look them in the face, and express some interest in their happiness. The success of the solitary missionary demonstrates what would be the powerful effect of the Church ... (Pearson I 1819: 373-81).

In 1805, Claudius Buchanan wrote a *Memoir of the Expediency of an Ecclesiastical Establishment for British India*, arguing for a properly organized ecclesiastical establishment.[1] He was concerned that Baptists were marching ahead of the established Church of England in their efforts in India. The *Memoir* was intended, Rev. Hugh Pearson said, "from the peculiar subjects of which it treated, to excite general attention, and to provoke both discussion and animadversion" (Pearson I 1819: 320).

Buchanan's arrival in Britain in 1808 gave a new momentum to the Evangelical cause. In his first public appearance in February 1809, Buchanan preached his celebrated sermon, *"The Star in the East,"* where he declared that the time had come for the "day-star to arise" on the benighted inhabitants of Asia. In 1810, he delivered the annual address before the Church Missionary Society, titled *"The Light of the World."* He reminded his Christian listeners that as victory had been won for humanity in Africa, so another must be won for Christianity in India.

Buchanan was also invited to give two commencement discourses by the University of Cambridge. The subject was the same as in the earlier sermons he had delivered and made a deep impact on the undergraduate students, many of whom later became active in promoting the missionary cause (Hough IV 1845: 181-85).

In 1811, Buchanan published *Christian Researches in Asia*, based on his findings while on a tour outside Bengal in 1806–07. It was his thirteenth work in three years (Hough IV 1845: 186). In the introductory note, Buchanan stated,

> The principal objects of this tour were to investigate the state of superstition at the most celebrated temples of the Hindoos; to examine the churches and libraries of the Romish, Syrian, and Protestant Christians... and to discover what persons might be fit instruments for the promotion of learning in their respective countries, and for maintaining a future correspondence on the subject of disseminating the Scriptures in India (Pearson II 1819: 3).

The work "aroused probably the greatest interest in Indian affairs that had ever been felt in England." The first edition of 1700 copies was soon sold out, and three more editions were printed the same year. A year later, the eleventh edition was brought out. The work included a detailed account of

Buchanan's visit to the Jagannath temple at Puri. Buchanan described the visit to Rev. David Brown in June 1806,

> I have lived to see Juggernaut; the scene at Buddruck is but the vestibule to Juggernaut; no record of ancient or modern history can give, I think, an adequate idea of the valley of death; it may be truly compared with 'the valley of Hinnom.' The idol called Juggernaut, has been considered as the Moloch of the present age; and he is justly so named, for the sacrifices offered up to him by self-devotement, are not less criminal, perhaps not less numerous, than those recorded of the Moloch of Canaan (Buchanan 1849: 12).

In subsequent letters he reported,

> At twelve o'clock of this day, being the great day of the feast, the Moloch of Hindoostan was brought out of his temple amidst the acclamations of hundreds of thousands of his worshippers; when the idol was placed on his throne, a shout was raised, by the multitude ... The throne of the idol was placed on a stupendous car or tower, about sixty feet in height, resting on wheels ...

A high priest mounted the car in front of the idol, and pronounced his obscene stanzas in the ears of the people; who responded at intervals in the same strain. Buchanan wrote,

> These songs are the delight of the God: his car can only move when he is pleased with the 'song.' The car moved on a little and then stopped. A boy of about twelve was then brought fourth to attempt something yet more lascivious, if per-adventure the God would move; the 'child perfected the praise' of his idol with such ardent expressions and gesture, that the god was pleased, and the multitude emitting a sensual yell of delight, urged the car along. — After a few minutes it stopped again. An aged minister of the idol then stood up, and with a long rod in his hand, which he moved with indecent action, completed the variety of this disgusting exhibition.

Later, challenged on these points and asked how he knew what the priests were saying, Buchanan responded that he had two translations of the language, one from "the indecent gestures of the priest," whose behaviour interpreted his words, and the second from his servants "who could translate every word he uttered" (Ingham 1956: 35-36; Oddie 2006: 80-81).

Buchanan continued his account,

> I felt a consciousness of doing wrong in witnessing it. I was also somewhat appalled at the magnitude and horror of the spectacle. I felt like a guilty person, on whom all eyes were fixed, and I was about to withdraw; but a scene of a different kind was now to be presented. The characteristics of Moloch's worship are obscenity and blood. We have seen the former — now comes the blood!

> After the tower had proceeded some way, a pilgrim announced that he was ready to offer himself a sacrifice to the idol. He laid himself down in the road before the tower as it was moving along, lying on his face, with his arms stretched forwards; the multitude passed round him, leaving the space clear, and he was crushed to death by the wheels of the tower. A shout of joy was raised to the God; he is said to *smile* when the libation of the blood is made; the people threw cowries, or small money, on the body of the victim, in approbation of the deed. He was left to view a considerable time, and was then carried by the *Hurries* to the Golgotha, where I have just been viewing his remains. How much I wished that the proprietors of India stock could have attended the wheels of Juggernaut, and seen this peculiar source of their revenue... (Buchanan 1849: 15-16).

Closing his narrative of the visit, Buchanan noted,

> It was the morning of the Sabbath; ruminating long on the wide and extended empire of Moloch in the heathen world, I cherished in my thoughts the design of some 'Christian Institution,' which being fostered by Britain, my Christian

country, might gradually undermine this baleful idolatry, and put out the memory of it for ever (Buchanan 1849: 18).

Extracts from the work were published in several missionary journals. The editor of the *Missionary Register* stated that "Dr. Buchanan's affecting representations, in his *Christian Researches*, of the abominations attending the worship of this Idol [Jagannath] have made a general and deep impression." The *Baptist Magazine* (1811) and the *Missionary Papers* (1814, 1816 and 1817) also reproduced excerpts from Buchanan's account.

Another significant literary attack on Hinduism came from Rev. William Ward, who had begun work on his project soon after arrival in India. In 1811, he published from Serampore, *Account of the Writings, Religion and Manners of the Hindoos*, in four volumes. This became an important source of information on Hindu religion and society in England. After the success of the first edition, Ward brought out a single volume of the work in 1815. At least five two-volume editions under slightly different titles were published in London between 1816 and 1818. These were followed by two four-volume editions. A three-volume edition was published in 1822, just before Ward's death. Such was the popularity of the work, that Ward rivaled James Mill as one of the most widely-read European commentators on India in the first quarter of the nineteenth century (Oddie 2006: 160).

Subsequently, Ward's work was criticized by several observers of the Indian scene. Rev. J. Long, in a speech delivered to the Family Literacy Club in 1860, remarked that in Ward's book,

> the character of the Bengalis is drawn so darkly that many men rise from it with the feeling — 'What a set of brutes these Hindus are, they have only such good qualities as are common to quadrupeds (Oddie 1999: 187).

Rev. Long quoted F.D. Maurice, a sympathetic critic of Hinduism, as saying,

> Mr. Ward can see only the hateful and the devilish; of what good it may be the counterfeit, what divine truth may be concealed in it, and may be needed to supplant it, he had not courage to enquire (Long 1848: 494).

To gain public support in Britain, the Parent Societies periodically published accounts of the activities of their missionaries in India. The information provided by the missionaries, in their letters and journals, was carefully edited before extracts were published (Sen Gupta 1971: 42). Lord Minto commented on the overstatements in missionary writings, "some allowance must be made for the exaggeration of men partial to their own pursuits" (Sen Gupta 1971: 43). Claudius Buchanan, in a letter to the Court of Directors on 25th May 1813, admitted that, "an ardent zeal for the diffusion of the blessings of religious will, in some cases ... produce too high colouring statements and narrators may make mistakes in description" (Sen Gupta 1971: 43-44).

END-NOTES

1. Till the first decade of the nineteenth century, the Company employed only thirteen chaplains for the whole of India (Sramek 2013: 86).

9

Missionaries Gain Official Entry: The Charter Act of 1813

As the Charter of the East India Company was due for renewal in Parliament in 1813, the Evangelicals readied for battle. The "Saints" of Clapham launched a well orchestrated campaign, inside and outside Parliament. William Wilberforce proclaimed that he looked forward to the renewal of the Charter as the moment when friends of Christianity would wipe out what was "next to the Slave Trade, the foulest blot on the moral character of our country" (Hole 1896: 185). He was "busily engaged in reading, thinking, consulting, and persuading." He was determined to "call into action the whole force of the religious world," willing to "abolish the East India Company altogether" than to refrain from providing India "a passage for the entrance of light, and truth, and moral improvement and happiness." "We are all at work," he wrote, "about the best mode of providing for the free course of religious instruction in India" (Howse 1960: 82-83).

Lord Liverpool was then the Prime Minister and Lord Castlereagh the Foreign Secretary and leader of the House of

Commons. The Earl of Buckinghamshire (Lord Hobart) was President of the Board of Control. The Prime Minister was believed to be more disposed than his colleagues to the promotion of Christianity in India. Claudius Buchanan wrote to a friend in July 1812,

> Be so good as to tell — and — that I have received a letter from Colonel Macaulay this morning, informing me that a deputation of Messrs. Wilberforce, Grant, Babington, &, had waited on Lord Liverpool, on the subject of evangelizing India, and that his Lordship surprised them by offering almost more than they wished. He intimated his intention to carry the three following important measures: — 1st. To establish a seminary at each presidency in India for instructing natives for the ministry; 2nd. To grant licenses to missionaries, not from the Court of Directors, but from the Board of Control; 3rd. To consecrate bishops for India (Kaye 1859: 268).

To fortify their efforts, Buchanan drafted a prospectus for the proposed episcopacy in India. It was at this time that Grant's *Observations* in its present form came to public light. He placed it before the House of Commons which ordered its publication. Macaulay undertook to prepare circulars to be dispatched all over the country (approximately 100,000 were indeed sent out, Carson 2012: 136), while Babington was asked to organize hundreds of petitions for which the circulars would pave the way. Daily consultations took place at Clapham (Howse 1960: 83).

But despite these endeavours, the Clapham Sect discovered that the people were not as enthused about heathen Indians as they were about enslaved Negroes. Wilberforce admitted, "I am sadly disappointed in finding even religious people so cold about East India Instruction." The group, however, continued their work. In April 1812, they enlisted the services of the Missionary Society, a special meeting of which was convened and attended by about four hundred men.

Babington, Stephen, Thornton, and Wilberforce addressed the gathering which ended with the Society's pledge to exert itself for Christianity in India (Howse 1960: 84).

In January 1813, Josiah Pratt, the first editor of the *Christian Observer*, launched the *Missionary Register* to promote interest in missionary work. On 19th February 1813, Wilberforce placed before the House a petition of the Scottish SPCK that the Charter Bill makes the propagation of Christianity in India legal. On 22nd March, on the motion of Lord Castlereagh, the Commons went into Committee of the Whole House on the East India Company's affairs. Wilberforce, William Smith, and Stephen participated in the debate, but the results were not heartening.

Wilberforce confessed,

> The truth is, and a dreadful truth it is, that the opinions of ... a vast majority of the House of Commons would be against any motion which the friends of religion might make ...But I trust, it is very different in the body of our people; and petitions are to be promoted with a view to bring their sentiments and feelings to bear upon the opposite tenets and dispositions of the members of parliament (Howse 1960: 85).

Buchanan concurred with the assessment. He wrote to a friend in April 1813, "If every city or town in England and Scotland were to petition, (which is practicable,) the business would acquire a new complexion before the end of May." In the following month, he wrote again,

> Many thanks for your 'Christianity in India.' It is drawn up in the manner I entirely approve, which I could not say of the former summaries. It comes in well after the petitions; and its perspicuity and brevity will fix and fascinate the careless eye. I begin almost to sympathize with your Indian opponents, the battering of religious Britain has been so tremendous (Pearson II 1819: 304-05).

Wilberforce also requested his friends to organize petitions to the House of Commons. In a missive to Hannah More he said,

> You will agree with me that now the Slave Trade is abolished, this (the denial of religious light to the East Indians) is by far the greatest of our national sins... But all this is to lead you to stir up a petition in Bristol, and any other place.

He implored an associate,

> You petitioned in the case of the Slave Trade, and those petitions were eminently useful: so they would be now; and what is more, after having been talked of, their not coming would be highly injurious; so lose no time.

To another he pleaded,

> Can you venture to add your sanction to the opinion ... that our East Indian Empire is safer under the protection of Brahma with all his obscenities and blood, than under that of God Almighty? (Howse 1960: 86).

But despite Wilberforce's labours, "the spirit of petitioning" spread slowly. In a countermove, on 22nd and 23rd April 1813, John Bebb, a former director of the Company, sent two letters to the Court of Directors expressing concern at the number of public meetings being organized by missionary societies to propagate an actively Christian policy in India (Ingham 1956: 36).

Meanwhile, the House of Commons began to examine witnesses. Among those called were former Governor Generals, Warren Hastings and Lord Teignmouth. Contradicting the missionary view of the Hindus, Warren Hastings described them as,

> gentle, benevolent, more susceptible of gratitude for kindness shewn them, than prompted to vengeance for wrongs inflicted, and as exempt from the worst propensities

of human passion as any people upon the face of the earth; they are faithful and affectionate in service, and submissive to legal authority; .... Gross as the modes of their worship are, the precepts of their religion are wonderfully fitted to promote the best ends of society, its peace and good order (*Parliamentary Debates*, 30 March 1813, 25, col. 553).[1]

Lord Teignmouth helped the Evangelicals as much as possible by his replies to the questions put to him. Wilberforce entreated his personal friend, Lord Wellesley, almost convincing him that the anti-Christian party was attacking the former Governor General's own system. He wrote on 6th April 1813,

> I know not whether your Lordship has heard of the unreasonable clamour that has been raised by the Anglo-Indians in the House of Commons, against all, even the most prudent, attempts to convert the natives of India; and more especially against missionaries. Now let me hope ... that your Lordship will tomorrow use your just authority in putting to flight these vain fears. The rather because the alarmists are enemies of the *system which your Lordship certainly established, and which I trust, you will confirm and revive, that I mean of diffusing useful knowledge of all sorts among the natives of India; and I confess for my part that I have always held and still retain the opinion that education, the translation and diffusing of the Scriptures and advancement in general knowledge, would be far the most powerful agents in the great work of Christianizing the natives of India* (Pearce II 1989: 298-99).

Wellesley had till then been mostly absent from the Select Committee of which he was a member. In his speech on 9th April 1813, Wellesley endorsed a more respectable footing for the ecclesiastical establishment, which "would tend to elevate the European character in the eyes of the natives." But, he cautioned that this was a matter of considerable "delicacy" and care ought to be taken not to alarm the people.

Any attempt should "not appear to be recommended by the authority of the government because in India the recommendation of the government is supposed to be almost equivalent to a mandate." He suggested combining religion with education, preferably via Fort William College. Wellesley described the efforts he had made for the spread of Christianity in India, with respect to putting the ecclesiastical establishment on a proper footing, with a Bishop at its head, and the encouragement given to discreet missionaries. He concluded saying,

> he had thought it his duty to have the Scriptures translated into the languages of the East, and to give the learned natives employed in the translation the advantages of access to the sacred fountains of Divine truth: he thought that a *Christian* Governor could not have done less, and knew that a British Governor ought not to do more (Martin V 1984: 143).

Thomas Munro, in his evidence on 12th April 1813, stressed the high level of civilization in India. He went so far as to state,

> if civilization is to become an article of trade between (Britain and India), I am convinced that this country will gain by the import cargo...With regard to civilization I do not exactly understand what is meant by the civilization of the Hindoos; in the higher branches of science, in the knowledge of the theory and practice of good government and in an education, which, by banishing prejudice and superstition, opens the mind to receive instructions of every kind, from every quarter, they are much inferior to Europeans: but if a good system of agriculture, unrivalled manufacturing skill, a capacity to produce whatever can contribute to convenience or luxury; schools established in every village, for teaching reading, writing and arithmetic; the general practice of hospitality and charity amongst each other; and above all, a treatment of the female sex, full of confidence, respect and delicacy, are among the signs which denote a civilized people, then

the Hindoos are not inferior to the nations of Europe (*Parliamentary Papers* 1812-13, 122, vii I: 131).

The great majority of Parliamentarians appeared opposed to sending missions to India. Not more than a hundred members were present throughout the proceedings (Philips 1961: 190). During the course of the Parliamentary debates, several speakers criticized Claudius Buchanan as "the calumniator of the Hindoos, and as having given to the world a false, or at least an exaggerated, statement of their cruel and immoral superstitions" (Pearson II 1819: 308). Among them were Sir Henry Montgomery, Sir Stephen Lushington, and Charles Marsh.

Sir Henry Montgomery, an old India hand, declared that during his twenty years of residence in the country, he had,

> ... never known an instance of any convert being made to Christianity, nor had he ever heard of any, except one, who was converted by that very responsible individual, Mr. Schwartz... The attempt to introduce Christianity had never succeeded; but it had been productive of endless massacres and mischiefs ... The religion of the Hindoos was pure and unexceptionable... [Dr. Buchanan's account of its ceremonies was] an imposition upon England, and a libel upon India.

He further stated, "If we wished to convert the natives of India, we ought first to reform our own people there, who at present only gave them an example of lying, swearing, drunkenness, and other vices." The practice of women burning themselves on the pyres of their husbands, he pointed out, "(was not) any more a religious rite than suicide was a part of Christianity" (*Parliamentary Debates* 1813 Vol. 26: 830).

Sir Stephen Lushington (Governor of Madras) viewed missionary activity in India as politically dangerous, impractical, and undesirable. He described the missionaries already in India as "tub preachers," incapable of debating with the "intelligent Hindoo." Sir Stephen defended the Hindus as a moral and virtuous people and stressed that sati was not sanctioned by the scriptures but is "a species of overstrained interpretation of its duties." He suggested that the reformist energies of the Evangelists might be best employed in ameliorating English society (*Parliamentary Debates* 1813 Vol. 26: 1018-51).

Charles Marsh, a former barrister at Madras, was incredulous at the attack on the Hindus as a people destitute of civilization, and degraded in the scale of human intellect. He said,

> ... when I turn my eyes either to the present condition, or ancient grandeur, of that country; when I contemplate the magnificence of her structures, her spacious reservoirs, constructed at an immense expense, pouring fertility and plenty over the land, the monuments of a benevolence expanding its cares over remote ages; when I survey the solid and embellished architecture of her temples, the elaborate and exquisite skill of her manufactures and fabrics, her literature, sacred and profane, her gaudy and enameled poetry, on which a wild and prodigal fancy has lavished all its opulence; when I turn to her philosophers, lawyers, and moralists, who have left the oracles of political and ethical wisdom, to restrain the passions and to awe the vices which disturb the commonwealth; when I look at the peaceful and harmonious alliances of families, guarded and secured by the household virtues; when I see, amongst a cheerful and well-ordered society, the benignant and softening influences of religion and morality; a system of manners, founded on a mild and polished obeisance, and preserving the surface of social life smooth and unruffled — I cannot hear without surprise, mingled with horror, of sending out Baptists and Anabaptists to civilize or convert such a people, at the hazard of disturbing or deforming institutions, which appear to have hitherto been the means ordained by Providence of making them virtuous and happy (Marshall 1968: 191-92).

The Saints faced another rout. Wilberforce began relentless interviews, "He was the link between the most dissimilar allies, Bishops and Baptists found in him a common term." Grant, Teignmouth, and Buchanan complemented his endeavours with their pamphlets. "Cabinet Councils" at Clapham coordinated their efforts. The 1813 anniversary of the Missionary Society was converted into a mass meeting for their campaign. William Dealtry, a like-minded clergyman who was subsequently chosen as John Venn's successor by the Clapham Sect, preached the anniversary sermon. It was so exhilarating that it was ordered to be printed "instantly" to add to the campaign literature. "The whole Christian world seems stirred up, almost as you would expect it to be in the Millennium," reported Rev. Charles Simeon. When the preliminary resolutions were introduced, there was willingness to concede an Episcopal establishment for the White residents in India, but not missionaries for the natives. William Smith, Thornton, and the two Charles Grants (father and son) all advocated their cause (Howse 1960: 87-88).

Wilberforce presented a colorful account of India's ills and the urgent need for Christianity,

> ... the evils of Hindostan are family, fireside evils: they pervade the whole mass of the population, and embitter the domestic cup, in almost every family. Why need I, in this country, insist on the evils which arise merely out of the institution of Caste itself ... Again in India we find prevalent that evil, I mean infanticide, against which we might have hoped that nature herself would have supplied adequate restraints ...

He referred to the rising incidents of widow immolation,

> Another practice (sati) ... has increased since the country came under our dominion. Great pains were taken by the missionaries a few years ago to ascertain the number of widows which were annually burnt in a district thirty miles

round Calcutta, and the House will be astonished to hear that in this comparatively small area 130 widows were burnt in six months. In the year 1803 within the same space the number amounted to 275, one of whom was a girl of eleven years of age. I ought to state that the utmost pains were taken to have the account correct; certain persons were employed purposely to watch and report the number of these horrible exhibitions; and the place, person, and other particulars were regularly certified. After hearing this you will not be surprised on being told that the whole number of these annual sacrifices of women who are often thus cruelly torn from their children at the very time when from the loss of their father they must be in the greatest need of the fostering care of the surviving parent, is estimated, I think, in the Bengal provinces, to be 10,000...

Turning to other practices, he said,

And now, Sir, I shall do little more than allude to another class of enormities, which by that very enormity, are in some measure shielded from the detestation they would otherwise incur: I allude to the various obscene and bloody rites of their idolatrous ceremonies, with all their unutterable abominations... A gentleman of the highest integrity, and better qualified than almost any one else to form a correct judgment in this instance; I mean Dr. Carey, the missionary, has calculated, that, taking in all the various modes and forms of destruction connected with worship at the temple of Jaggernaut in Orissa, the lives of 100,000 human beings are annually expended in the service of that single idol....

Sir, I am persuaded, that in all who hear me, there can be but one common feeling of deep commiseration for the unhappy people whose sad state I have been describing to you; together with the most earnest wishes that we should commence, with prudence, but with zeal, our endeavours to communicate to those benighted regions, the genial life and warmth of our Christian principles and institutions ... (*Parliamentary Debates* Vol. 27: 831-72).

This time round, Wilberforce had whipped up militant fervour in the country. Altogether, nine members of the CMS delivered speeches. The missionary clauses were included in the Charter despite the opposition of the House of Commons and many members of the Company by pressurizing Parliament through an extraordinary mobilization of public opinion. A staggering 908 petitions bearing more than half a million signatures were presented to Parliament (Carson 2012: 3). The numbers, unmatched on such a subject, made an impact. Wilberforce himself stated, "The petitions, of which a greater number than ever known, have carried our question instrumentally, the good providence of God really" (Howse 1960: 93).

The bill reflected the efforts of Wilberforce and his party of twenty Evangelicals in the Commons who had insisted on the moral obligations of the British in India. Parliament also sanctioned an Anglican establishment for India, with a bishop in Calcutta and archdeacons in the Presidencies of Bombay and Madras (Philips 1961: 191; the East India Company also failed to protect its monopoly of trade to India and had to surrender to powerful new commercial interests that had gained ascendancy).

The public support that the Clapham Sect whipped up came from Methodists, Baptists, and the Evangelical clergy of the Church of England, sections of the population not highly rated for their intelligence or social status. John Bowen wrote, "Their well-drilled riders ... (were) dispatched with commercial punctuality to lay an unsuspecting credulity under contribution." Wilberforce was aware of this criticism and confessed,

> Both Mr. Grant and I have been afraid lest the Anglo-Indians, who are among the most intelligent members of the higher circles, should be able to produce an impression that we carried our point in the House of Commons by availing

ourselves of a popular delusion, contrary to reason (Embree 1962: 274).

Sir John Malcolm expressed regret that the "numerous petitions to Parliament" forced the Government's hand (Potts 1967: 154). Observing the triumph of Grant's views, Warren Hastings wrote to the Marquis of Hastings,

> Our Indian subjects having been represented as sunk in grossest brutality and defiled with every abomination that can debase humanity; and it is therefore said that as we possess the power, so it is our duty to reform them, nay to 'coerce' them into goodness by introducing our faith among them. If the debasement of their moral character is the only plea for the positive intervention of our Government to bring about their reformation, indeed, my Lord, it will be better to leave them as they are, especially that race of them, the Hindoos, against which these aspersions are particularly fulminated. These I dare to pronounce, and your Lordship will have ample means of knowing with what truth, are as exempt from the worst propensities of human nature as any people upon the face of the earth, ourselves not excepted. They are gentle, benevolent, more susceptible of gratitude for kindness shewn them than prompt to vengeance for wrongs sustained, abhorrent of bloodshed, faithful and affectionate in service and submission to legal authority. They are superstitious; but they do not think ill of us for not behaving as they do. Coarse as the modes of their worship are, the precepts of their religion are admirably fitted to promote the peace and good order of society; and even from their theology arguments, which no other can afford, may be drawn to support the most refined mysteries of our own. The persecuting and intolerable spirit of Mohammedanism has spared them through a course of three centuries, and bound them into union with its own professors: the least therefore that can be expected from the most liberal and enlightened of all nations, that which providence has appointed the guardian of their civil rights, is to protect their persons from wrong, and to leave their religious creed

to the Being who has so long endured it, and who will in his own time reform it (Moon 1947: 349-350).

Claudius Buchanan pondered on another aspect, "And now we are all likely to be disgraced. Parliament has opened the door, and who is there to go in? From the Church not one man!" (Pearson II 1819: 307-08).

Despite the passage of the Charter Act, the Court of Proprietors continued to have misgivings about missionary activity. Till at least the mid-1820s, they questioned applications from Evangelical missionary societies. In 1815, they sent a dispatch on the requests of Lord Minto, and his successor, Lord Moira (Lord Hastings), on the policy to adopt vis-à-vis missionaries who had arrived without valid licenses in 1812. They ordered that "no persons must in future be allowed to enter and remain in any part of the Company's possessions without producing a certificate, agreeably to the said act." That would prevent "improper persons" from settling in Company territories. The Governor General was also directed "to keep a strict watch" over them and "in the event of any impropriety occurring in their conduct immediately to withdraw protection from them" (Carson 2012: 153).

Company officials in India also demonstrated a resolve to control missionaries. The Governors of most provinces remained convinced that India could be held only as long as the natives believed there was no danger to their religion. Lord Hastings and Lord Amherst encouraged missionary educational efforts but not attempts at proselytization.

END-NOTES

1. Asked for his views on the political consequences of a Church establishment for India, Warren Hastings expressed his fears in measured tones,
    "May I say, without offence, that I wish any other time had been chosen for it? A surmise has gone forth of an intention in this Government to force our religion upon the consciences of

the people in India, who are subjected to the authority of the Company. It has pervaded every one of the three establishments of Bengal, Fort St. George, and Bombay, and has unhappily impressed itself with peculiar force upon the minds of our native infantry, the men on whom we must depend, in the last resort, for our protection against any disturbances, which might be the effect of such surmises. Much would depend upon the temper, conduct, and demeanour of the person devoted to that sacred office. I dare not say all that is in my mind on this subject; but it is one of great hazard" (Kaye 1859: 263-64).

Several Company officials in India, concerned about the durability of the Empire and the desire to ensure continuous flow of revenue, were also not in favour of proselytization. They were not against missionary activity, but opposed State sponsored attempts at conversions.

Thomas Munro, in a Minute dated 15th November 1822, reiterated that it was the declared intention of the Legislature and the Court of Directors that the people of India be permitted to enjoy their ancient laws and institutions and be protected against the interference of public officers in their religion. Such a system was the wisest that could be adopted, "whether with regard to the tranquility of the country, the security of the revenue, or the improvement or conversion of the natives" (Gleig II 1830: 37-45).

Mountstuart Elphinstone feared the zeal of the missionaries would endanger British possessions in India. He stated,

"I have often considered the state of our Empire in India & it has always appeared to me that notwithstanding the small numbers of those who uphold it & its want of a root in the feelings of the people, it would probably stand for a long time unless chance should raise up some false prophet who should unite a plan for the reformation of the existing religion with one for the deliverance of the country from foreigners. Against such a storm as an able & enthusiastic man might raise by these means, I do not think our power could stand one moment & this is exactly what attempts at conversion are likely to produce" (Ballhatchet 1957: 248-49).

John Malcolm was also against all links between the Company and missionaries in the interests of the safety of British power. He held that the Company was bound to provide the Christian inhabitants of their territories the means of spiritual instruction,

"But in every effort we permit beyond this, for the propagation of our faith among a people who are attached to the religions transmitted to them from their forefathers, and which, however false, are rendered venerable in their eyes by their connexion with the great principles of morality and social duty, we should be guided by our experience of the past, and knowledge of the present, and use that caution which is alike recommended by regard for the safety of the state, and for the ultimate accomplishment of our hopes for the enlightening of our Indian subjects" (Malcolm II 1970b: 144).

Malcolm attributed the downfall of the Portuguese, the first European settlers in India, to "that bigoted spirit with which they endeavoured to introduce their religion." The French, in their heydays under Dupleix and Lally, "allowed the most sacred usages of both (the Hindus and Muslims) to be frequently violated." The British, by contrast, took great care to avoid "the great errors of their rivals." Should the British deviate from this policy, "the consequence may be fatal to our power."

Malcolm noted that the Act of 1813 gave "a new impulse" to missionaries in India. But, he argued, there could be no hope of conversion until "a foundation has been laid by a more general diffusion of knowledge." On the possibility of the safe conversion of natives he cautioned, "...generations must pass away before it can be accomplished" (Malcolm II 1970b: 151-53).

Finally, Malcolm said, "We may and ought to be grateful that superior knowledge has removed us far from the ignorance and errors of our Hindu subjects, but we should be humbled to think in how many points, in how many duties of life, great classes of this sober, honest, kind, and inoffensive people excel us" (Malcolm II 1970b: 154).

10

Missionaries and Sati

The Evangelical-missionary critique of Hinduism spotlighted the issue of widow immolation.[1] The entire campaign was directed by a handful of Evangelical-missionaries, who included Charles Grant, William Wilberforce, George Udny, William Chambers, John Shore, and Revs. William Carey, William Ward, Joshua Marshman David Brown, and Claudius Buchanan.

Sir Charles Malet, Resident at the Court of the Peshwa at Poona, had been among the early British officials to refer to sati. In 1787, he sent to the Government an eye-witness account of immolation by a Brahmin widow narrated by a Mr. Cruso. The following year, Jonathan Duncan, Resident at Banaras, dispatched a report on an occurrence in the neighbourhood of Mirzapur. In 1789, the Collector of Shahabad reported a case he had prevented. From then on, till the year 1812 there had been little official notice of sati, except for casual and brief reports in the years 1793, 1797, and 1805 (*Calcutta Review* XCII).

It is pertinent that sati did not figure in the 1793 Parliamentary debates on the renewal of the Company Charter. Was that because many of the missionaries arrived in India only thereafter? If sati was rampant, why did it fail to invite the ire of earlier Englishmen in Calcutta? Also, the first two accounts of sati by Baptist missionaries (by John Thomas in 1789 and William Carey in 1799) stated that the incidents were voluntary, and despite their best efforts, they could not dissuade the widows from immolating themselves (Lewis 1873: 142-44; Smith 1885: 107-09; Section B: 351-55).

William Carey first witnessed a widow immolating herself six years after his arrival in India. Sati had, however, seized his attention well before this event. In a letter to his church in Leicester in 1793, soon after arriving in India, Carey wrote, "Burning women with their husbands is a practice too frequent. We were at Nuddea [Nadia] last Lord's day, and were informed that about a month ago two women devoted themselves in this manner" (Oddie 2006: 143).

Further, in a correspondence with John Sutcliffe (member of the first committee of the Baptist Missionary Society), on 10th October 1798 from Mudnabatty, Carey had described sati as the "most singular and striking circumstance in the customs of this people." In 1800, he attempted to frighten a group assisting a sati near Serampore by claiming that the Governor General had "threatened to have the first man hanged who was proved to have kindled one of these fires" (Potts 1967: 145-46).

In 1802, Carey was asked to submit a memorial to Lord Wellesley's government on infanticide. Carey hoped that the information he had included on other murders committed under "the pretence of religion," would lead to some action. George Udny, member of the Governor General's Council, asked Carey to provide complete information on the practice. Claudius Buchanan, Vice-Provost of Fort William College, also sought Carey's advice "respecting the way of putting a stop to women burning" so that he could put forward concrete suggestions to Wellesley (Oddie 2006: 150; 153; Potts 1967: 146).

Carey used his position at Fort William College to enquire from the pandits about *Shastric* injunctions on the matter. He concluded that the rite was religiously ordained, provided that the widow concerned had no young children, was not pregnant or 'impure', and was willing. Carey was probably aware of H.T. Colebrooke's article published in the *Asiatick Researches* in 1795, wherein the latter had cited several texts to argue that sati had religious sanction but was rarely practiced (*Asiatick Researches* IV 1795: 205-15). That the issue was under discussion at Fort William is further attested by the fact that in 1803 the motion debated was, "The suicide of Hindoo widows, by burning themselves on the decease of their husbands, is a practice repugnant to the natural feelings, and inconsistent with moral duty."

The Evangelical-missionary campaign against sati falls into two phases — the first, from 1803 to 1813 when the case was prepared (and also discussed in Parliament during the Charter renewal debates); the second, from 1813 to1829 when awesome figures were marshalled to demonstrate that it was a raging practice. The sati issue was the most forceful created by the Evangelical-Utilitarian alliance to validate British rule in India.

MISSIONARIES AND THE CAMPAIGN AGAINST SATI – THE FIRST PHASE

In 1803, Carey with his colleagues at Serampore and Fort William College, attempted to collect data on the prevalence of sati. Ten people were engaged to record all cases that occurred within 30 miles of Calcutta. They were to gather information on the number of widows who had immolated themselves in the previous twelve months, their age, and the number of children they had left behind. Each informant had to cover an area of roughly 800 square kilometers. It was believed that he would get to know of every incident that occurred in his vicinity even if he could not personally be present on each occasion (Fisch 2005: 232).

VARYING RESULTS OF MISSIONARY SURVEY

Citing the results of the survey, Claudius Buchanan stated that 275 cases were recorded in 1803; between 15th April and 15th October 1804 there were 115 cases. Explaining these figures, Buchanan said,

> no account was taken of burnings in a district to the west of Calcutta, nor further than twenty miles in some other directions; so that the whole number of burnings within thirty miles round Calcutta must have been considerably greater than is here stated (Buchanan 1849: 21-22).

William Ward wrote, "From actual enquiry at all the villages & towns for 30 miles around Calcutta it appears that no less than 438 widows have been burnt with their husbands in this circuit during the last year." This was the precise area in which the Baptists lived and preached (Mani 1998: 145-46).

The missionaries placed the data before George Udny. Carey believed that the figures were "rather below the truth than above it" and pressed the government to take action. Udny's submission was "the first official notice regarding female immolation which had appeared in the records of government" (Marshman 1859: 222).

HORRIFIC FIGURES

Applying the figures collected to the rest of the country, the missionaries presumed that several thousand widows were burnt every year. Claudius Buchanan in his *Memoir* wrote, "... it was calculated by the late learned Mr. William Chambers, that the widows who perish by self-devotement in the northern provinces of Hindostan alone, are not less than ten thousand annually" (Buchanan 1805: 61). William Carey, in a letter to a friend, in 1812, cited similar figures, "... I calculate that 10,000 women annually burn with the bodies of their deceased husbands" (Oddie 2006: 158).

William Ward, in his *History*, listed several instances of widow immolation "voluntarily" narrated to him by natives, most of who claimed to have been eye-witnesses to the events. The earliest instance recounted to him occurred in 1789 (Ward IV 1990: 101; Section B: 356-63). On the basis of the information collected from his informers, Ward asserted that "instances of children of eight or ten years of age thus devoting themselves are not uncommon" (Ward IV 1990: 108). Ward further stated,

> ...on enquiring among the bramhuns, and other Hindoos employed in the Serampore printing-office, I found that these murders were much more frequently practiced than I had supposed: almost every one had seen widows thus buried alive, or had heard of them from undoubted authority.

He added that he could,

> easily increase the number of these accounts so as to form a volume; but I am not anxious to swell this work with more facts of this nature: these are sufficient to fill the mind of the benevolent with the deepest compassion for the miserable victims of this shocking superstition (Ward IV 1990: 111).

Ward was particularly critical of the role of priests. He said,

> The conduct of the brahmuns at the burning of widows is so unfeeling, that those who have represented them to the world as the mildest and most amiable of men, need only attend on one of these occasions to convince them, that they have greatly imposed on mankind (Ward IV 1990: 113).

Alluding to the results of Carey's initial survey, Ward concluded,

If within so small a space several hundred widows were burnt alive in one year, how many thousands of these widows must be murdered in a year — in so extensive a country as Hindoost'han! So that, in fact, the funeral pile devours more than war itself! How truly shocking! Nothing equal to it exists in the whole work of human cruelty! (Ward IV 1990: 114-15).

Calculating the total number of victims sacrificed annually to the altar of Hindu gods, Ward gave the following breakup —

Widows burnt alive	-	5000
Pilgrims perishing on the roads and at sacred places	-	4000
Persons drowning themselves in the Ganges or buried or burnt alive	-	500
Children immolated, including the daughters of Rajputs	-	500
Sick persons whose death is hastened on the banks of the Ganges	-	500
Total		- 10,500

(Ward IV 1990: 127).

However, on the very next page, he doubled the number of satis from five to ten thousand, arguing,

Supposing there to be five thousand towns and large villages in Hindoost'hanu, and that one widow is burnt from each of these places in one year, no less a number than five thousand helpless widows are annually burnt alive in this country; but if we are guided by the calculation made at Calcutta it will appear, that at least two widows in every village must be murdered annually, including all the large towns in the same ratio. If so, instead of five thousand murders, the number must be doubled; and it will appear that ten thousand widows perish on the funeral pile in the short period of twelve months (Ward IV 1990: 128).

Ward's *History* went through at least eight editions between 1811 and 1822 and was repeatedly cited in evangelical publications.

Rev. David Brown, in a letter to Rev. Robert Robinson of Cambridge wrote on the subject of immolations,

> My very learned friend, Mr. William Chambers, has computed that about 50,000 widows are, in these provinces burnt annually with their husbands! ... In 1803, an enquiry was set on foot by Dr. Carey; and, by an actual enumeration, it was found, that, in a small district round Calcutta, 275 burnings took place within six months; and it was therefore estimated that in all the Bengal provinces no fewer than 10,000 persons were thus consigned to death in the course of a year (Lewis 1873: 141).

Charles Grant, in his *Observations*, hypothetically placed the number of widow immolations in Hindustan annually at around 33,000 and added, "... let the proportion be reduced to the lowest probable scale, the annual immolation of human victims to a dire superstition, will appear an enormity under which language must sink" (Grant 1832: 62). How Grant arrived at this supposed figure is difficult to say. It is possible that the *Observations*, ostensibly written in 1792, was considerably revised and updated before it was printed as a *Parliamentary Paper* on the eve of the Charter debates of 1813 and 1833, and that this figure reflected the numbers then being bandied by Baptist missionaries.

The "consolidation of missionary discourse" on sati occurred in a number of overlapping ways (Mani 1998: 122). The figures collected by the missionaries on satis in Bengal in 1803 and 1804 were cited by Claudius Buchanan in his widely read *Christian Researches in Asia* (1811). In 1813, he informed the Court of Directors that on the basis of further data supplied by the Serampore missionaries and the official estimates of the population of India, he had calculated that about 10,000 satis took place annually. The figure appeared a gross overstatement. But there was no one was sufficiently informed to contradict it, and it served to create an impression of enormity.

Further publicity was given to the Baptists' figures in the House of Commons in 1813, when William Wilberforce included them in his speech on the renewal of the Company Charter. He also inserted in the printed record of his speech a gruesome account of a sati witnessed by the missionary, Joshua Marshman (Ingham 1956: 47). He described the incident most eloquently,

> That which added to the cruelty was the smallness of the fire. It did not consist of so much wood as we consume in dressing a dinner: no, not this fire that was to consume the living and the dead! I saw the legs of the poor creature hanging out of the fire while her body was in flames. After a while, they took a bamboo ten or twelve feet long and stirred it, pushing and beating the half consumed corpses, as you would repair a fire of green wood, by throwing the unconsumed pieces into the middle. Perceiving the legs hanging out, they beat them with the bamboo for some time, in order to break the ligatures which fastened them at the knees, (for they would not have come near to touch them for the world). At length they succeeded in bending them upwards into the fire, the skin and muscles giving way, and discovering the knee sockets bare, with the balls of the leg bones: a sight this which, I need not say, made me thrill with horror, especially when I recollected that this hapless victim of superstition was alive but a few minutes before. To have seen savage wolves thus tearing a human body, limb from limb, would have been shocking; but to see relations and neighbours do this to one with whom they had familiarly conversed not an hour before, and to do it with an air of levity, was almost too much for me to bear (*Parliamentary Debates* Vol.: 860-62; Section B: 364-65).

The outcome of the debate being inconclusive, the missionaries felt compelled to further publicize their data. The *Missionary Register* (a publication of the Church Missionary Society started in London in January 1813 to coincide with impending renewal of the Company's Charter) and the

Missionary Papers circulated accounts of satis sent by missionaries in India. In June 1813, at the peak of the Parliamentary debate, the *Missionary Register* published an extract on sati from Ward's *History*. Its motive in reproducing the passage was to,

> Let every Christian Woman who reads the following Statement, pity the wretched thousands of her sex who are sacrificed every year in India to a cruel superstition, and thank God for her own light and privileges, and pray and labour earnestly for the salvation of these miserable fellow subjects (*Missionary Register for the Year 1813* Vol.1: 215-18).

The following month, it published another passage from Ward's account on sati under the title, "Instance of the Cruelty of Hindoo Superstition" (*Missionary Register for the Year 1813* Vol. 1: 268-69). The *Missionary Register* also carried reports titled, "Groans of India for Christian teachers" (*Missionary Register for the Year 1813* Vol. 1: 214-15) and "India Eager to receive the Holy Scriptures" (*Missionary Register for the Year 1813* Vol. 1: 218-21).

The objective was to raise funds for missionary work through consistent "exposes" of Hindu superstitions and to convince British readers of the enormity of, and necessity for, evangelical work. Appeals were particularly directed towards women. Fifteen per cent of the subscribers of the Baptist Missionary Society in 1800 were females. The figure rose to seventeen per cent in 1825. In the Church Missionary Society, the proportion was twelve per cent in 1801 and twenty-nine per cent in 1823 (Mani 1998: 141-44). Sati was the first "political" issue in which British women were directly involved to gather support for their luckless "sisters" in India (Major 2012: 66).

In the volumes covering the period 1812–1814, the *Periodical Accounts* (a series of edited compilations of letters and journals received from Baptists in India) reprinted three instances of sati from letters of the BMS, each of which concluded with comments like, "The scene was calculated to strike the mind with inconceivable horror." The "high profile" sati assumed in missionary writings suggests that the "spectre of sati (was deployed) to convert British Christians to Evangelism" (Mani 1998: 147, 151).

Charles Lushington, Chief Secretary to Government, on the basis of figures collected by Government surveys in the Bengal Presidency from 1815 to 1818, described the figures of the Baptist missionaries as "one of the most preposterous misrepresentations that ever proceeded from credulity or ignorance" (Lewis 1873: 141).

REGISTRATION BY THE GOVERNMENT — 1815–1828

The registration of cases of sati by the Government began in 1815 and continued till 1828. It covered the three Presidencies of Bengal, Bombay, and Madras. The Bengal Presidency then included besides Bengal (now Bangladesh and the Indian state of West Bengal), most of what are today the states of Bihar and Orissa and the eastern parts of Uttar Pradesh.

The data collected by the Government revealed a curious picture. In the ten years between 1815 and 1824, 6,632 cases were reported for the three Presidencies. Of these, an astonishing 5,997 (90.4 per cent) occurred in Bengal. The heavy preponderance of cases in Bengal, a region not historically associated with the rite, raises uncertainties about the reliability of the data.

In the Madras and Bombay Presidencies, during the years 1815 and 1820, the average number of satis recorded was below fifty. In Madras, it was less common in the central region, and unknown in the west and south, except in Tanjore and one estate in Kanara (Thompson 1928: 68-69).

The Judge of Cuddapah, in a letter dated 1st April 1820, reported that four cases of sati had taken place since 1816; such instances were generally rare, and unknown in the neighbourhood of Cuddapah. The Judge of Trichinopoly informed around the same time that he could trace no instance of widow immolation for the previous ten years in his district, except the case of the widow of a pleader in his own Court (*Calcutta Review* XCII).

The Judge of South Malabar notified that the practice was entirely absent in his area. There had been two attempts at sati, but the opposition of the people had forced the funeral parties to take their widows to Coimbatore for performance of the rite. Since then there had been no attempt, nor would the natives permit it on the soil of Malabar (*Calcutta Review* XCII).

In Bombay Presidency, instances of widow immolation were even more uncommon than in Madras. One solitary case had occurred in the district of Ahmedabad. In Southern Concan, the custom had been rare under native rule, and had not occurred at all during the colonial administration. In 1817, two cases had taken place in the territories conquered from the Peshwa (*Calcutta Review* XCII).

The average figures for all India were far less than in the Lower Provinces of the Bengal Presidency or in Calcutta Division. If one in 150 widows immolated herself in Calcutta Division, the ratio for the entire Bengal Presidency was roughly 1: 400 and for India as a whole between 1: 800 and 1: 1000 (Fisch 2005: 242). This raises the query whether the allegedly high incidence of satis in Bengal was a missionary manufacture.

GOVERNMENT STATISTICS FOR BENGAL

According to Government figures, of the 8,134 widows immolated in Bengal in the fourteen years between 1815 and 1828, 5,119 (almost 63%) were from Calcutta Division, followed by the Banaras (1153), Dacca (710), Patna (689), Murshidabad (260), and Bareilly (203) Divisions. Within Calcutta Division, Hughli district topped the list almost every year, with the district of Burdwan coming next. The number of satis in the

24 Parganas or the suburbs of Calcutta was much less than in Hughli or Burdwan (Mukhopadhyay 1957: 108). The high incidence of sati in the area around Calcutta was surprising, given that the city was the harbinger of the Bengal Renaissance.

Even outside Calcutta Division the frequency of sati varied from place to place. Shahabad witnessed 39 cases in 1821, while the five districts of Patna Division (Patna city, Tirhoot, Bihar, Ramgar, and Mungher) together witnessed 14. In 1825, there were 63 incidents in the district of Backarganj and 2 in the adjacent Dacca Jalalapur. The same year there were 21 cases in Ghazipur district and none in bordering Jaunpur (Mukhopadhyay 1957: 108).

Christopher Bayly has noted that the Government figures revealed "how limited the number of satis were." Between 1817 and 1827, 4,323 cases were reported for a population of about 160 million for the whole of British India. The practice was mostly restricted to Bengal, particularly the environs of Calcutta. Between 1815 and 1820, the annual average for the Bombay and Madras Presidencies was under fifty. The concern with sati, he said, reflected "a more general movement of Anglo-Indian opinion, rather than its incidence or statistical significance." Sati was seen as an "irrefutable justification for the continued British presence in India." The attack on sati also implied a rejection of those officials who opposed the Anglicization of education and the missionary vilification of Hindu culture (Bayly 2001: 153; 2010: 22).

The British obsession with sati "was boundless." Thousands of pages of parliamentary papers dealt with 4,000 immolations while the death of millions from famine and starvation was mentioned "only incidentally — sometimes only because it tended indirectly to increase the number of widows performing the 'horrid act'" (Bayly 2001: 153).

ANALYSIS OF GOVERNMENT DATA

Though census surveys for the entire country were conducted only from 1872, relatively reliable estimates of the population for the Bengal Presidency, especially for the Lower Provinces, are available for the second and third decades of the nineteenth century, based on house counts.

John Herbert Harington (1764–1828), a judge and a civil servant of considerable experience, in 1823 estimated the Hindu population of Bengal Presidency at about 50 million. He assumed a death rate of 1: 33, i.e. 30 per thousand annually, which meant that 1.5 million people died annually. Harington assumed that with every sixth death a wife became a widow. Of the roughly 250,000 widows, therefore, one in 430 would have burned herself on an average, according to Government figures, for the years 1815 to 1828. In 1818, the year with the highest frequency, it would have been one in 298.

Given the figures of about 2.3 (3.4) per thousand of all cases in which wives became widows, and of about 0.4 (0.6) per thousand of all cases of death, widow immolation was statistically almost insignificant. In the district with the highest number of immolations, Hughli, with a population of 1,239,150, one in 43 widows immolated herself in 1818, the year in which the highest number of cases — 141 — were registered. From 1815 to 1828, it was one in 66, on an average. Here, therefore, 23.3 (15.1) per thousand widows would have immolated themselves. With respect to all cases of death it would have been 3.8 (2.5) per thousand deaths.

The frequency was greater in the suburbs of Calcutta, although the absolute figures were lower here. With a population of 360,360 there were, on an average, 39 widow immolations per year; in 1819 there were 51. This meant that between 1815 and 1828, one in 47, and, in 1819, one in 36 widows burnt to death (21.3 or 27.8 per thousand respectively). With respect to the total number of deaths, it was 3.6 (4.7) per thousand deaths. Such figures did not occur in other parts of India. The region around Calcutta, with 62.9 per cent of the cases, constituted the real nucleus of the rite (Fisch 2005: 236-39). This again raises questions about the role of Evangelicals and missionaries in the official exercise.

CASTE BREAKUP OF DATA

A caste wise analysis of the Government data for Bengal proper for the period 1815–1827 reveals that Brahmins, who comprised between 5 and 8 per cent of the population, accounted for 38.4 per cent of the cases of sati (5,388 cases). Kshatriyas constituted 14.8 per cent of the cases and Vaishyas 3.9 per cent. Given that Kshatriyas comprised 3.1 per cent of the population according to the Census of 1881, they too were over-represented. Altogether Brahmins, Kayasthas, Vaidyas, Sadgops, and Kaibarthas accounted for 64 per cent of Government recorded instances of sati between 1815 and 1827. The figures also show that the rite was practiced by all castes (Roy 1987: 36-48, 148-66). In 1823, for instance, of the 575 cases reported, 41 per cent were Brahmins, 6 per cent Kshatriyas, 2 per cent Vaishyas, and 51 per cent Sudras. The diversity in the caste composition does not corroborate the argument of scholars who interpret sati as the expression of a rudderless, upper class Bengal gentry seeking to anchor itself in an era of flux by resorting to a "traditional" practice (Nandy 1975: 171-74).

AGE OF VICTIMS

In several respects, the Government data contradicted missionary accounts. Most missionary narratives had emphasized the tender age of the widows. Government statistics, however, claimed that almost half the satis were in the age group of 50 and above, and two-thirds 40 and above. Less than five percent of all satis between 1815 and 1829 were in the age group of eleven to twenty. Overall, sixty per cent of the widows who immolated were over forty-one years of age. The official report concluded, "a great proportion of these acts of self-devotion have not taken place in youth, or even in the vigor of age; but a period when life, in the common course of nature, must have been near its close" (Yang 2007: 41; Roy 1987: 48-49; 167; *Parliamentary Papers* 1821 Vol. 18: 222). Between 1815 and 1820, 62 child widows (below 18 years) were immolated in the whole of Bengal, which was less than two per cent of the total number (Mukhopadhyay 1957: 114).

NUMBER OF WIDOWS ON THE PYRE

Government figures also revealed that of the 8,132 widows who immolated themselves in the Bengal Presidency, 8,004, i.e. 98 per cent mounted the pyre alone. Only 128, i.e. 1.6 per cent burnt to death with one or several widows of the same man. In fifty-two cases there were 2 women, in four cases 3, and in three cases 4. The survey did not mention a single instance of more than four widows immolating with one man (Fisch 2005: 259-60).

Here too, there was a discrepancy between Government and missionary accounts. William Ward, in his *History*, cited several instances of a large number of widows burning with one man. He mentioned one occasion in which 13 widows immolated with one man, another involving 37 widows of a man, another 12 widows, and yet another in which 18 widows burnt with one man (Ward 1990 IV: 101-06).

Claudius Buchanan in *An Apology for Christianity in India* referred to a case related by a native employee of the Serampore press. The native claimed to have witnessed a sati in 1799, in which 22 of the 100 wives of a Kulin Brahmin immolated themselves and the fire was kept kindled for three days! (Buchanan 1814: 14-16; Section B: 366-67). Such statements, not borne out by the Government data, raise misgivings about the authenticity of missionary accounts.

WHY BENGAL?

KULINISM

The high incidence of sati in Bengal was linked in some accounts to *kulin* Brahmin polygamy.[3] Claudius Buchanan, in his *Memoir*, gave instances of *kulin* Brahmins who had over a hundred wives (Buchanan 1805: 71). However, Rammohan Roy, in his *A Second Conference between an advocate for and an opponent of the practice of burning widows alive*, pertinently asked, "How many *kulin* Brahmins are there who marry two or fifteen wives for the sake of money, that never see the quarter number of them after the day of marriage, and visit others only three or four times in the course of their life?" (Anand 1989: 10).

The geographical distribution of sati also did not substantiate the connection with *kulin* polygamy. The incidence of sati was higher in West than in East Bengal (more in Calcutta than in Dacca Division), whereas *kulinism* was more prevalent in East than in West Bengal (Yang 2007: 38; Gupta and Gombrich 1984: 256; Mukhopadhyay 1957: 108).

DAYABHAGA SCHOOL

The frequency of sati in Bengal was also attributed to the Dayabhaga School, associated with Jimutavahana, a Brahmin from Radha. Dayabhaga, viewed as a reformed School of Hindu Law as compared to the orthodox Mitaksara, allowed women greater access to their deceased husband's property for their maintenance. Ludo Rocher has, however, argued that Jimutavahana cannot rightly be regarded the founder of a reformed Bengal School of inheritance. The legal principles characteristic of that School were not typically Bengali, and were closer to the ancient *Smriti* texts than those of Mitaksara. He further says that H.T. Colebrooke, who translated the Dayabhaga and Mitaksara into English in 1810, (*Dayabhaga and the Mitaksara. Two Treatises On the Hindu Law of Inheritance*), was the first to speak of two principal schools of Hindu law (Rocher 2002: 20-32).

That apart, Jimutavahana introduced Dayabhaga to Bengal in the twelfth century, whereas incidents of sati increased only in the decades preceding its abolition, when first the missionaries, and then the British Government presented statistics on the extent of the custom (Phadke 1996: 312-13). Dayabhaga also does not explain the great variance in the incidents of sati in the different districts and cities of Bengal (Bayly 2001: 154).

It is, however, a fact that in eighteenth century Bengal and Bihar, both Hindu and Muslim women had often been substantial property holders. In some instances, they possessed and managed assets for their male relatives. There were cases where they held land in their own right after the death of their husbands. In the years preceding British rule, women held far greater property than in the nineteenth century, though it was vulnerable to opposing claims by locally powerful men. Hindu jurists, for example, debated whether Hindu widows could adopt new heirs and transfer property to them without the (prior) approval of their deceased husbands. Many did so (Wilson 2010: 4-5).

Further, the First Judge of the Calcutta Court of Circuit mentioned the significant fact that he had no less than 57 civil suits pending involving property worth four *lakh* rupees, to which Hindu women were parties. It was thus "clearly possible for widows not to follow their husbands to the pile, to fill respectably their own positions in society, and to manage their own affairs" (*Calcutta Review* XCII).[4]

CONSEQUENCE OF FAMINE OR CHOLERA?

The prevalence of sati cannot also be linked to the scarcities that occurred in Bengal after the famine of 1770. For if sati was "a primitive Malthusian means of population control in famine-ridden Bengal" (Nandy 1975: 171), Morris Carstairs rightly argues "it would surely have resulted in higher rates among the poorer castes, less well protected against starvation, than among the gentry" (Yang 2007: 38-39).

The major increase in the incidence of sati in the years 1817–1818 was attributed to the high mortality rates due to a cholera epidemic. The Judges of the Calcutta Court of Circuit in a letter to the Registrar of the Nizamat Adalat, however, did not endorse the link between cholera deaths and the increased instances of sati (Mukhopadhyay 1958: 26). In Backerganj, in 1825, the year of the cholera outbreak, 25,000 persons died within a few months, yet the official figure of satis was 63 (Mukhopadhyay 1957: 105).

MISSIONARIES AND THE CAMPAIGN AGAINST SATI – SECOND PHASE

The entire colonial debate on sati centred on figures provided by the missionaries and the Government, each set of which suffered from serious flaws. But the figures seem seldom to have been questioned during the course of the campaign the Evangelicals and missionaries unleashed.

In 1815, the second edition of William Ward's *View of the History, Literature and Mythology of the Hindoos* was issued by the Serampore Press. It contained a chapter citing the Baptists' figures on sati in the Calcutta area and included descriptions of the most offensive cases known to Ward.

In 1816, the first known major pamphlet on the subject, *A Collection of Facts andOpinions Relative to the Burning of Widows with the Dead Bodies of their husbands and to other Destructive Customs Prevalent in British India*, was published in England by William Johns, a missionary expelled by the British from Serampore in 1812. He based his write-up mainly on the second edition of Ward's *History*. Johns protested that, in this country we appear to have retrograded, for whilst we have legislated to prevent cruelty to animals, we allow a portion of the human race, nay even of our own subjects, to have cruelties practiced upon them at which humanity shudders (Johns 1816: 28-29).

William Ward, on a visit to England during the years 1819–1820, personally confirmed missionary accounts of sati. While in England, he delivered a number of speeches, the substance of which was published in the form of *Farewell Letters* to his friends. In a letter to Miss Hope of Liverpool, a long-time activist of the British and Foreign Bible Society, he claimed,

> By an official statement that I brought with me from India, it appears that every year more than seven hundred women (more probably fourteen hundred) are burned or buried alive in the Presidency of Bengal alone. How many in other parts of India? Your sex will not say that in the roasting alive of four widows every day there is not blood enough shed to call forth their exertions? (Ward 1822: 51-59; Ward made explicit appeals to British women to participate in the campaign against sati, Zastoupil 2011: 63-64).

The following month, writing to Rev. Steadman, Ward proffered different figures. He claimed that between eight and nine hundred widow immolations took place every year in the Bengal Presidency alone. He said,

> Let us suppose that in each of the other Presidencies 400 each year are immolated and then we have the awful spectacle of Two Thousand widows burnt or buried alive every year in India (Ward 1822: 84-85).

Robert R. Pearce, in the *Memoirs and Correspondence of the Most Noble Richard Marquess Wellesley,* stated that it had been calculated that between 1756 and 1829 no less than 70,000 widows were immolated within the British dominions in India (Pearce II 1989: 307).

The Baptists kept up the attack through the *Samachar Darpan* and *Friend of India* (both started in 1818). In 1819, *Friend of India* cited the figure of 100,000 (10, 000?) satis per year. In 1829, the journal claimed that the custom had claimed over one million lives in Bengal alone! (*Friend of India NS 1*: 366; Fisch 2005: 234).

The quarterly *Friend of India* (started in June 1820 by Joshua Marshman), published a series of articles on sati in 1822-23. Most unsigned ones were believed to have been penned by Marshman. They were reprinted in England in 1823, by the Baptists as part of a series, *Essays Relative to the Habits, Character and Moral Improvement of the Hindoos*. English periodicals like the *Oriental Herald* and *Quarterly Review* reproduced large portions of the articles, as did the *Bengal Hurkaru* and other Calcutta periodicals.

John Adam (acting Governor General in 1823) advised that the quarterly *Friend of India* "should be suppressed" because of the Baptist impudence in publishing a provocative article on sati. Lord Hastings, however, found the article contained "nothing obnoxious, and that he wished the practice could be abolished" (Potts 1967: 149-51; Mani 1998: 151; Mukhopadhyay 1958: 34). J.H. Harington, Chief Judge of the Nizamat Adalat, in a Minute on sati submitted to the Governor General on 28th June 1823, acknowledged his debt to a "well-written paper" (by Marshman) in the *Friend Of India* (Potts 1967: 151).

In 1825 Rev. T.S. Grimshawe wrote a pamphlet, "*An earnest appeal to British humanity on behalf of Hindoo widows.*"

The Utilitarian, James Silk Buckingham, editor of the *Oriental Herald and the Journal of General Literature,* urged immediate abolition of sati. He said,

> According to the last returns there are about on an average two women burnt to death every day of the year; so that this Tophet of British India may be considered as never

extinguished, but continually smoking with human sacrifices (*Oriental Herald* Vol. 8).

The January-March 1826 number of the *Oriental Herald and the Journal of General Literature* devoted twenty pages to widow-burning (earlier issues had also highlighted sati). It argued,

> While we boast of being the most enlightened and civilized of nations, should we not afford our Indian subjects the benefit of that mental superiority in the exercise of that power which we have usurped over them? ... it would be some compensation for having deprived them of the power of self-government, if we were to employ our ascendancy to deliver them from the ferocious tyranny of a custom, which their degraded and darkened minds are too weak to shake off (*Oriental Herald* No. 25 January 1826: 1).

In 1828, the General Baptist missionary, James Peggs (who had returned to England in 1825 after some years of missionary work in Orissa), published a booklet, *Suttee's Cry to Britain.* Among his other tracts was *India's Cries to Britain*. He also formed an association at Coventry, The Society for Promoting the Abolition of Human Sacrifices in India. "Let Britain 'plead for the widows,'" he said by petitioning Parliament to abolish sati and other forms of human sacrifice in the colony (Zastoupil 2011: 67-69).

In addition, several public meetings were held in Britain, beginning in 1823. In 1827, a convention was held at York at which only supporters of abolition were permitted to speak. The details were published in a leaflet, *An account of the proceeding at a public meeting held at the City of York, on the 19th January 1827, to take into consideration the expediency of petitioning Parliament on the subject of Hindoo widows in British India.* Another open meeting was held in 1829.

END-NOTES

1. Sati had been prohibited earlier. The Portuguese Governor, Albuquerque, had banned it in the Portuguese territory of Goa, in 1510. The Mughals, too, opposed the practice and prior official sanction was mandatory for performance of the rite. Contemporary European travellers noted that the permission of Mughal governors was easily procured by payment of bribes.

   Official approval was a requisite in some Hindu kingdoms and probably dated to the time when only leading families were permitted to perform the rite.

   The third Sikh Guru, Amar Das (1552–1574), condemned sati. But after the transformation of the Sikhs into a fighting force, the Sikh aristocracy began following martial traditions (Altekar 1978: 132). On the death of Maharaja Ranjit Singh, one of his wives (a Rajput and the natural daughter of Raja Sansar Chand), and three ladies of his household, ascended the pyre (Section B: 342-45). One of the *chadar dalna* (marriage to a deceased brother's wife) wives died with Ranjit Singh's son, Maharaja Kharag Singh. Two wives of Ranjit Singh's grandson, Nao Nihal Singh, became satis on the latter's death (Griffin 1957: 65).

   Though instances of sati were reported from among the Marathas, they attempted to prohibit the custom. The celebrated queen, Ahalya Bai (d. 1795) discouraged it, and vainly tried to dissuade her widowed daughter from mounting the pyre. Before the century ended, two Maratha states — the Peshwa's personal dominions and Tanjore — had prohibited sati.

   The Raja of Tanjore described sati as "a barbarous and inhuman rite." He told his wife not to sacrifice herself when he died. He forbade the rite wherever he could (Carey 1907: 132). The prohibition was not entirely effective. Tanjore relapsed and became one of the few centers of the custom in the Indian peninsula. A third Maratha state, Savantvadi, was mentioned in a letter of the Governor of Bombay, in May 1821, as having abolished the practice a decade earlier (Thompson 1928: 57-59).

In 1798, the Supreme Court of Calcutta refused to permit widow immolation within its jurisdiction. Charles Metcalfe, Resident at Delhi (1811 to 1819), had banned the rite in the imperial capital in 1811, eighteen years before Lord Bentinck (Spear 2003: 108). At the opening of the nineteenth century, the Dutch prohibited sati in Chinsura; the French in Chandernagar, and the Danes in Serampore. But sporadic acts of immolation did take place.

2. William Ward's journal had only nine entries on sati in the twelve-year period from October 1799 to October 1811, during which he kept a regular diary. This was surprising, given the importance the issue assumed for the Baptists (Mani 1998: 145).

3. *Kulin* signified the highest order of Bengali Brahmins. *Kulin* grooms were much in demand and it was considered a pious act to give a daughter in marriage to a *Kulin* Brahmin (Ahmed 1976: 17-18).

   It is not clear when *Kulinism* was introduced in Bengal, but it seems that "it was a protective device to maintain the purity of the high castes during the Muslim invasions" (Mukherjee 1982: 158; Majumdar 1973: 224-225). The ruler, Ballal Sena is traditionally credited with introducing *kulinism* in Bengal. Since *Radi* Brahmins were in close contact with Muslims, that could account for the practice of *kuilinism* among them (Mukherjee 1982: 159-60).

4. Among the cases that came up before the Mayor's Court (set up in 1772), two related to the property of widows. In the first, the brother-in-law of an issueless widow had taken control of all his dead brother's possessions and offered maintenance to the widow. After enquiring about local practices, the Court decreed in June 1728,

   "as it is the custom of the country to allow a wife all her jewels and half the husband's estate in case of no children, in case she insists upon it – that Monick (the brother-in-law) be obliged to deliver up Krishna (the widow) all her jewels and half her husband's effects and pay all costs and charges." The order was complied with. In another property case in March 1733, the Court again ruled in favour of the widow (Panda 2008: 42-43).

11

Abolition of Sati

Though the Court of Directors remained diffident on the issue of abolition of sati, the efforts of the missionaries began to produce results elsewhere. In 1812, Thomas Fowell Buxton, M.P. for Weymouth and an important leader of the Clapham Sect, moved the House of Commons for the publication of all correspondence relating to sati. The proposal was accepted.

It was, however, only in 1821 that sati was placed on Parliament's agenda. Most speakers were against immediate abolition. That year, Parliament issued the first Blue Book on the subject. Sati was again debated in 1823. Buxton urged complete and total abolition of the practice, but, with the exception of Wilberforce, received no vocal support.

A motion in Parliament in 1825, to appoint a committee to investigate the matter was rejected when Sir Charles Forbes and Sir Hyde East attributed the increase in incidents of sati to Indian religious fears, and to "shoals of missionaries which had been allowed to go in among them" (Potts 1967: 152-53). In March 1830, Buxton again placed sati on Parliament's schedule, to learn that it had been abolished in December 1829 (Fisch 2005: 406-07).

RESPONSE OF EARLIER GOVERNOR-GENERALS

The history of legislation on sati is relatively brief. In all, four circulars were promulgated between February 1789 and December 1829. In January 1789, a widow asked M.H. Brooke, the Collector of Shahabad, for permission to immolate herself, which he refused. Brooke wrote to the authorities in Calcutta justifying his act. The Government of Lord Cornwallis approved his conduct, but added that though it was,

> desirous he should exert all his private influence to dissuade the natives from a practice so repugnant to humanity and the first principles of religion, they do not deem it advisable to authorize him to prevent the observance of it by coercive measures, or by any exertion of his official powers; as the public prohibition of a ceremony, authorized by the tenets of the religion of the Hindoos, and from the observance of which they have never yet been restricted by the ruling power ... (*Parliamentary Papers* 1821 Vol. 18: 22).

In 1797, the Acting Magistrate of Midnapore also tried to prevent an immolation and informed the Governor General, John Shore. Though his conduct was against the policy of non-interference, the Government endorsed his act (*Parliamentary Papers* 1821 Vol. 18: 23). In 1805, J.R. Elphinstone, Acting Magistrate of Gaya, who was successful in dissuading a widow from immolating herself, complained of lack of orders on sati (*Parliamentary Papers* 1821 Vol. 18: 23).

In January 1805 therefore, Lord Wellesley asked the judges of the Nizamat Adalat, the supreme criminal court, to ascertain from pundits how far sati "is founded on the religious opinion of the Hindoos," so that he could decide, "whether this unnatural and inhuman custom could be abolished altogether." It is argued that the British thereby "virtually orchestrated the articulation of a textual tradition and scriptural sanction for widow immolation" (Loomba 1993: 212).

The judges reported that voluntary immolations had definite religious sanction and that abolition "would be highly inexpedient," though hopes could "reasonably [be] entertained that this very desirable object may be gradually effected, and at no distant period of time" (Potts 1967: 147; Fisch 2005: 371-72). Wellesley left India before he could take up the matter further, and the Vellore Mutiny of 1806 strengthened the position of officials who opposed direct Government interference. These included men like H.T. Colebrooke, Mountstuart Elphinstone and Colonel Sutherland.

Lord Minto (1807–1813) stated that he was "sorry to say" that sati was prevalent, but he was too "charitable" towards India's religion to take action (Potts 1967: 147). On 5th December 1812, his Government issued a Circular Order wherein it declared that sati would be permitted in cases approved by Hinduism, and prohibited in all other instances (*Parliamentary Papers* 1821 Vol. 18: 29-30).

On 29th April 1813, the Government issued guidelines to all police officers that certain cases of immolation were "contrary to the *Shaster* (Hindu law), and perfectly inconsistent with every principle of humanity." A sati would be deemed illegal if the widow was pregnant, not yet sixteen years of age, under the influence of drugs, had a small child, or if her decision was not voluntary (*Parliamentary Papers* 1821 Vol. 18: 749).

Based on the experience of two years, additional instructions were issued in 1815. Anyone assuming responsibility for bringing up a widow's infant children was required to sign a "Form of Engagement." Further, a widow could withdraw from the flames at the last moment (*Parliamentary Papers* 1821 Vol. 18: 41-43). Lord Hastings (1813–1823) later stated, "...he would have suppressed it (sati) if he had been sure of support from home." In the absence of that backing, all he could do was stop sati within the limits set by law (Potts 1967: 149). Meanwhile, state registration of cases of sati commenced in 1815.

In a letter to the Court of Directors, on 3rd December 1824, Lord Amherst (1823–1828) and two members of his Council, Edward Paget, and John Fendall, said it was best to wait and scrutinize future returns to ascertain whether satis, already gradually decreasing in the interior of the country, "exhibit a continued diminution" (Singh 1987: 158-60).

In a Minute of 18th March 1827, Lord Amherst expressed his "bitterest disappointment" at the increase in the number of satis reported in 1825. He, however, still opposed prohibition stating,

> ... I must frankly express ... that I am inclined to recommend our trusting to the progress now making in the diffusion of knowledge amongst the natives, for the gradual suppression of this detestable superstition. I cannot believe it possible that the burning or burying alive of widows will long survive the advancement which every year brings with it in useful and rational learning ... (Singh 1987: 163-64).

The following year, in his Minute of 4th January 1828, Lord Amherst reaffirmed that inaction was the best form of action and the need to rely on "general instructions and the unostentatious exertions of our local officers" for bringing about a substantial reduction in the number of satis, and "at no very distant period, the final extinction of the barbarous rite" (Singh 1987: 164-65).

He consulted eminent Government servants, but they differed considerably on the matter. Courtenay Smith and Alexander Ross urged immediate abolition; Harington was of the view that the custom could be extinguished by a gradual dissemination of moral instruction (Marshman 1874: 53).

The warmest advocate of abolition was Sir William Macnaughten. He said,

Let the Hindoo believe in his three hundred and thirty millions of gods until it may please the Almighty to reclaim him from his idolatry; but let him not immolate thousands of helpless females on the altar of fanaticism, in defiance of the eternal laws of nature and the immutable principles of justice.

Macnaughten ridiculed the specter of Hindu revolt. He pointed out,

Under the Mahomedans, the Hindoos tamely endured all sorts of insults to their religion and violation of their prejudices. Their temples were polluted and destroyed, and many were constrained to become Mussulmans, yet there was no general organized disaffection. The rite was not respected by the hardy and warlike Hindoos of the north-west, but by the sleek and timid inhabitants of Bengal, the fat and greasy citizens of Calcutta, whose very existence depended on the prosperity of the British Government (Marshman 1874: 54-55).

LORD WILLIAM BENTINCK

The appointment of William Bentinck as Governor General, in 1828, gave momentum to the campaign against sati. Bentinck's name had appeared sixth on the list of nominations for the post of Governor General "and few could have foreseen that through the refusals of others it would come to the top" (Philips 1961: 261).

Bentinck ("a practicing and believing Christian," and member of the British and Foreign Bible Society who also professed to be influenced by the Utilitarian doctrine) had decided on abolition even before his arrival in India. In a letter to Lord Combermere from Calcutta, on 12th November 1828, he admitted that the sati question was "very much pressed upon my attention in England" (Rosselli 1974: 63-64; Philips 1977: 94).

Subsequently, corresponding with William Astell Malda on 12th January 1829, Bentinck reiterated his earlier interest in sati. He said,

> I do not believe that among all the most anxious advocates of that measure (abolition of sati) any one of them could feel more deeply than I do, the dreadful responsibility hanging over my happiness in this world and the next, if as the governor-general of India I was to consent to the continuance of this practice for one moment longer, not than our security, but than the real happiness and permanent welfare of the Indian population rendered indispensable. I determined therefore, before I came to India, that I would instantly take up the question ... (Philips 1977: 140).

Bentinck had not been eighteen months in India when he abolished sati. He consulted forty-nine military officers on the effect abolition would have on their men. Twenty-four supported immediate abolition and only five opposed any change. Twelve were for abolition but averse to outright prohibition, eight favoured the indirect intervention of magistrates. Bentinck also consulted H.H. Wilson and Rammohan Roy, both of whom felt an immediate ban was uncalled for (Philips 1977: 335-45; Singh 1987: 216-18; 222-23). Wilson, in fact, defended the petition of the Dharma Sabha protesting the abolition of sati, on the ground that it had been a rash step (Kopf 1969: 175, 266, 270-71; Ahmed 1976: 36; Mitra 1880: 9-10).

In May 1829, the Bengal missionaries sent a long petition to Bentinck urging him to abolish sati (Philips 1977: 191-94). Bentinck addressed the issue in his Minute on Sati, dated 8th November 1829. Therein he stated,

> The first and primary object of my heart is the benefit of the Hindus. I know nothing so important to the improvement of their future conditions, as the establishment of a purer morality, whatever their belief, and a more just conception of the will of God. The first step to this better understanding

will be dissociation of religious belief and practice from blood and murder. They will then, when no longer under this brutalizing excitement, view with more calmness, acknowledged truths...

I disavow in these remarks or in this measure any view whatever to conversion to our own faith. I write and feel as a legislator for the Hindus, and as I believe many enlightened Hindus think and feel (Section B: 403-18).

Sati was abolished in December 1829 (Section B: 419-22).[1] The Regulation banning sati was translated from English to Bengali by William Carey. As sati had never been a commonly observed rite, there was little protest on its official prohibition. "There was neither riot nor disaffection. No sepoy shot at his colonel; nowhere were magistrates or missionaries mobbed, treasuries plundered, or bungalows fired" (Carey 1907: 132-133-134).[2]

Once the ban was announced, Company officials stopped their surveillance of sati, and the allegedly rampant practice seemed to have abruptly ceased. It was a truly unique case of prompt universal compliance of a government diktat.

JESUITS CRITICIZE CAMPAIGN AGAINST HINDUS

The French Jesuit, Abbe Dubois, who lived in Central and South India between 1792 and 1823, severely criticized Baptist attempts to paint Hindus in "the blackest and most odious colours" (Dubois 1997: 77; he was witness to two immolations in Tanjore; one, in 1794, of the widow of a Komatty caste merchant, the second, in 1801, of two of the four wives of the last Tanjore king; Dubois 1906: 361-64).

Dubois was particularly incensed by the endeavours of William Ward to depict "the mild and inoffensive Hindoos, as a people wholly polluted by every kind of wickedness; as a race of barbarians sunk into the deepest abyss of ignorance and immorality ..." (Dubois 1997: 96).

Narrating his own experiences and observations which were strikingly different from those of Ward, Abbe Dubois dwelt at length on the subject of sati. The practice, he said, seldom occurred south of the Peninsula. He calculated that the population this side of the Krishna was not less than thirty million and the instances of sati not more than thirty a year. More people, Dubois claimed, died in France and England every month through suicide and dueling than widows burnt in a year. He said,

> The only difference I can remark, between the one and the other, is, that the deluded Hindoo widow commits suicide from misled religious motives, and from what she considers as an indispensable duty of conjugal devotion; whilst the European suicide puts an end to his existence, in defiance of every religious restraint, and in open violation of his most sacred duties towards God, and towards men ... Are suicide and dueling in Europe less nefarious than suttees in India? (Dubois 1997: 106).

Dubois challenged the accuracy of several statements made by Ward. Polygamy, he pointed out, was strongly discouraged by Hindus of all castes, above all, by Brahmins. Instances of parents marrying "fifty or sixty daughters to a single Brahmin," he said, were entirely unsubstantiated. Further Dubois stated, William Ward derived his knowledge from Hindu informers. He should have known that,

> ...the Hindoo informers in general, before giving information on any subject, begin by studying the character and temper, the disposition and bias of their employers, and give them information accordingly. Those employed by the reverend gentleman, seeing him disposed to blacken and debase the Hindoos by all means, and in all manners, served him according to his taste (Dubois 1997: 108; Section B: 381-89).

SUPPORT FOR ABOLITION AMONG HINDUS

Support for the abolition of sati among Hindus tended to be underplayed in most discussions, which focused on the role of the missionaries and William Bentinck. As early as 1817, Mrityunjaya Vidyalankar, former *pundit* at Fort William and then Chief *Pundit* of the Nizamat Adalat in Calcutta, had prepared a tract in which he argued that the practice had no *Shastric* sanction, and that an ascetic life had greater merit than immolation (Ray 1985: 37-39; Majumdar 1972: 219; Bose 1976: 199; Section B: 399-402). The *Calcutta Journal* reported, "Mrityunjoy, the head Pundit of the Supreme Court, has given it as his opinion that Brahmacharya, or a life of mortification is the law for a widow; and that burning with the husband is merely an alternative. Hence he argues that the alternative can never have the force of law" (Roy 1987: 83-84). Mrityunjaya Vidyalankar (as also Raja Rammohan Roy) argued that the ultimate goal of *all* Hindus was selfless absorption in a divine essence, a union that could not be attained by an act like immolation (Chakravarti 2006: 32-33).

In 1817 or 1818, Bykunthanath Banerjee, Secretary of Unitarian Hindu Community, published a piece in Bengali in which he urged abolition of sati and prescribed an ascetic life for a widow (Roy 1987: 84).

A steadfast opponent of widow immolation was Raja Rammohan Roy (Roy 1987: 81-119). In 1818, he presented his *Conference between an Advocate for, and an Opponent of, the Practice of Burning of Widows Alive*. This was followed in 1820 by the *Second Conference* (Anand 1989: 20-57).[3] Like Mrityunjaya Vidyalankar, Roy, too, argued that sati had no religious approval. A petition, signed in August 1818 by "a great number of the most respectable inhabitants of Calcutta," was apparently authored by him (Majumdar 1941: 115-17). Rammohan Roy succeeded in bringing together members of many castes, though most of his active supporters against sati were Brahmins (Stein 1988: 466).

The next phase of his campaign started with the publication of the weekly newspaper *Sambada Kaumudi* in 1821. In 1822, he wrote a tract, *"Modern Encroachments on the Ancient Rights of Females According to the Hindu Law of Inheritance"* (Robertson 1999: 147-55). In 1829, he produced another work, *Sahamaran Vishaya*, in Bengali, in reply to his orthodox opponents. Rammohan Roy was also active in organizing meetings and debates on this issue (Roy 1987: 97-102).

He was, however, hesitant about the need for legislation to stop the practice. Bentinck, in his Minute on Sati stated, "It is his opinion that the practice might be suppressed quietly and unobservedly by increasing the difficulties ... He apprehended that any public enactment would give rise to general apprehension" (Section B: 403-18).

Among other leading Indians in the forefront of the campaign against sati were Gaurisankar Bhattacharya (editor of *Sambada Bhaskara*), Kalinath Roy Chowdhury, Dwarakanath Tagore and Prasanna Kumar Tagore, Munshi Mathuranath Mullick, Ramakrishna Sinha, and Anandaprasad Bandyopadhyay (Sharma 1988: 53; Roy 1987: 84-87; Kling 1976: 21, 23-24).[4] In a perceptive observation on the Hindu response, the *Calcutta Journal*, on 20th January 1820, stated,

> It is more than gratifying to find, that while the British population in India are generally speaking indifferent to the subject there has arisen among the Hindoos themselves a powerful opposition to the continuation of these barbarous murders, and that great learning, talent, ingenuity and moral courage have been displayed by those who endeavour to prove that even by the Hindoo laws such sacrifices are not binding; and who strenuously labour to effect their abolition (Ray 1985: 37).

Hindu opponents of abolition, led by Radhakant Deb, did not defend the legality of widow burning; rather they took a stand against British interference in Hindu affairs. None of the members of Deb's group encouraged sati in their families. Deb's biographer, Jogesh Chandra Bagal, stated that Deb opposed abolition by the state as he feared that meddling by an alien government could result in the disintegration of Hindu society (Mukhopadhyay 1958: 32).

The *Chandrika,* started in 1822 by Bhawanicharan Banerji, began to defend sati as a reaction to the repeated attacks of the *Darpan* (started by Serampore) and the *Kaumudi* (started by Rammohan Roy). The first article on the subject in the *Chandrika* was essentially an argument against the cultural intrusion of foreigners and Rammohan Roy, who it alleged, did not comprehend the virtuous dimensions of this self-sacrifice.

The *Chandrika,* however, supported every initiative at educational reform. Radhakant Deb was a noted educational reformer and played a prominent role in the administration of Hindu College for over thirty years. He saw no conflict between indigenous and Western learning and sought to integrate both in the Calcutta school system. He also supported efforts at female education (Mittra 1880: 48; Kopf 1969: 180-81, 191-96; Ahmed 1976: 28-32).

HINDU CONTRIBUTION UNDERPLAYED

While British missionaries attempted to "sensationalize" the issue of sati, British historians tended to "monopolize" the credit for its abolition for their countrymen. In a bid to magnify the extent of Hindu opposition, they claimed that the petition against abolition sent to the Privy Council was signed by 18,000 people. In fact, it bore 800 signatures. Edward Thompson concluded that the credit for abolition was almost entirely Lord Bentinck's. P.E. Roberts made no reference to Rammohun Roy while discussing the abolition of sati. Percival Spear mentioned him but added, "Ram Mohun Roy accepted Jesus as one of the religious Masters" (Sharma 1988: 10-11).

1. Sir Edward Ryan, Puisne Judge, Supreme Court of Calcutta, wrote to Lord Bentinck, on 12th August 1829, on the intended abolition Regulation. He said,

   "It seems desirable to view the practice of suttees rather in the light of a usage or custom than as forming any part of the religion of the natives; it is I believe so when commanded as a religious duty, but is considered as a meritorious act for which the husband and wife with their relations will be rewarded by a long period of happiness in a future state. If this view is correct, I think this declaration should appear in the preamble (of the regulation on abolition of sati)...

   "(Hamilton's minute of 3rd December 1824)... also states that the *'highest'* authorities in Hindu law consider the practice as illegal.... To show that this practice is far from being general throughout the provinces subject to this presidency it gives a calculation showing that annually about 250,000 females are widows, of whom, little more than 600 [immolate] themselves ..." (Philips 1977: 268-69).

2. The Utilitarian, James Fitzjames Stephen, who replaced Henry Maine on the Governor General's Council in 1869, expressed the view that the British Empire in India "governs, not indeed on the principle that no religion is true, but distinctly on the principle that no native religion is true." He was clear that the colonial state promoted Western Christian values, as it should (Sturman 2013: 22-23).

3. Rammohan Roy's opposition to sati was attributed to the forcible immolation of his sister-in-law, sometime around 1811, at which he was allegedly present. This incident has, however, been described as "almost certainly a later fabrication" (Majumdar 1972: 218; Collet 1962: 33-34; Mukhopadhyay 1958: 30). Besides sati, Roy also attacked polygamy, which he said made it difficult to implement ancient laws on female inheritance (Collet 1962: 195-98).

   In 1818, Roy failed to dissuade the widows of a physician in Calcutta from immolating themselves. The priests were directed to first light the pyre, Rammohan Roy asserting that this was mandated by the *shastras*. The pyre was left open for the widows to ascend and enter the flames if they chose. Roy clearly expected them not to make the choice. Both, however, entered the pyre. The younger one addressed the onlookers, "You have just seen my husband's first wife perform the duty incumbent on her, and will now see me follow her example" (*Asiatic Journal* March 1818: 290-91).

Rammohan Roy admitted that the practice of forcibly holding the widow on the pyre did not exist outside Bengal and even in Bengal was a recent occurrence (Mukhopadhyay 1957: 114).

4. Several letters and articles published in *The Reformer*, a weekly published and edited by Prosunna Coomar Tagore, in 1833 dealt with the issues of female education, *kulin* marriage, and polygamy (Chattopadhyay 1978: 143-77). While condemning *kulin* marriages, a contributor added,

"... I should not neglect letting you know for the public intimation; that it being now a day of reformation and the people neglect no opportunity in improving these manners, customs and habits and of course whatever they discover, exceptional to justice, morals, and religion, they are in the religious pursuit to rectify it gradually. Should you, giving credit to my assertions, survey with an impartial eye and sound judgment all the quarters wherein the system of polygamy has long been prevalent, you will, I doubt not, find that our Coolin Brahmins who are chief polygamists have now revised their mode of marrying plurally; the number of espouses, they now take is surely less than what one of their situation formerly did ..." (Chattopadhyay 1978: 172).

12

Sati – An Infrequent Occurrence

The strident Evangelical-missionary campaign virtually drowned out other voices on sati. Several near-contemporary and contemporary observers had, however, noted that sati was not a common custom. There was even the interesting case of a traveller who admitted that he had incorporated a fake account of sati in his narrative to enhance the popularity of his work.

The Frenchman, Anquetil-Duperron, described an incident he had supposedly witnessed, in 1758, at the entrance to the city of Ponin (Poona). He wrote,

> It was a young Maratha woman whom the tyranny of custom was forcing to burn herself on her husband's funeral pyre ... I noticed that in these countries, despite their devotion to the senses and to what is most extreme in them, life is given up with greater ease than in our climes.

However, in a note scribbled later in the margin of a printed copy of his work, Anquetil-Duperron confessed,

I was not present at this barbaric if religious ceremony ... I added that line to be freed of the thousand and one questions I was asked on the country's customs; in this I failed to tell the truth (Rose 1990: 124; Section B: 282).

Till the colonial debate commenced, most foreign travellers had declared that sati was not a pervasive practice. Francisco Pelsaert, writing in the time of the Mughal Emperor Jahangir noted that "there are hundreds, or even thousands, who do not do it..." (Pelsaert 2001: 79; Section B: 249). Pietro Della Valle confirmed, ".... This burning of Women upon the death of their Husbands is at their own choice to do it or not, and indeed few practice it ..." (Della Valle 1991: 84-85; Section B: 252). In 1624, Rev. Henry Lord also observed that "... the examples be more rare than in former times" (Neill 1984: 376; Section B: 257). Francois Martin, of the French East India Company, who arrived in India in 1669 and stayed on till his death in 1706, held that the custom was "not very widely practiced now" (Martin Vol. II Part I 1984: 1154-56; Section B: 274).

Even officials of the East India Company, till the closing decades of the eighteenth century, affirmed that sati was not widely prevalent. Alexander Dow, in 1770, stated that the practice had "for the most part, fallen into desuetude in India; nor was it reckoned a religious duty, as has been very erroneously supposed in the West" (Dow I 1973: xxxv; Section B: 390).

George Forster wrote in 1782 that,

The wives of the deceased Hindoos have moderated that spirit of enthusiastic pride, or impulse of affection, which was used to urge them to self destruction on the pile of their husbands. Their grief can now be assuaged, and their religious duties reconciled, by a participation of domestic comforts; and many of the Hindoo widows, especially in the Marhatta country, have acquired by their ability, their wealth, connection, or intrigue, the possession of extensive power and influence (Foster I 1970: 8; Section B: 390).

James Forbes, who joined the English East India Company in 1766 and left India in 1783 after seventeen years of service, recorded that he had never been an eye-witness to the "extraordinary sacrifice" (Forbes I 1988: 279).

William Hodges, a professional painter and member of the Royal Academy who travelled in India during the years 1780–1783, stated that those whom he had met mentioned sati "as taking place among the highest classes of society, whose vanity united with superstitious prejudices might have dictated the circumstance ..." (Hodges 1999: 79).

La De Grandpre, an officer of the French Army, observed towards the end of the eighteenth century, "The inhuman custom of women burning themselves to death on the corpse of their husbands is not yet annihilated in India; but it is confined to the cast of the Bramins" (De Grandpre II 1995: 68; Section B: 297-300).

Eliza Fay, wife of a judge of the Supreme Court at Calcutta, in a letter from that city in September 1781, wrote that though the fact of sati was "indubitable," she had "never had an opportunity of witnessing the various incidental ceremonies, not have I ever seen any European who had been present at them" (Fay 1908: 160-61; Section B: 294-95).

Quintin Craufurd, who's *Sketches Chiefly Relating to the History, Religion, Learning, and Manners of the Hindoos*, was published in 1792, stated that custom prevailed mostly in the territories of the ancient Rajas, particularly in families of "high distinction." But in the territories of the English it "rarely happens ... unless it be done secretly, or before those who may have authority to prevent it can be sufficiently apprized" (Craufurd II 1977: 15; Section B: 312).

H.T. Colebrooke (1765–1837), Judge and later head of the Sadar Diwani Adalat, and Professor of Hindu Law and Sanskrit at Fort William College, who spent over three decades in Bengal, said the practice was rare. In an article titled "On the Duties of a Faithful Hindu Widow," he stated that, "the

martyrs of this superstition have never been numerous."
Further,

> It is certain that the instances of the widow's sacrifices are now rare: on this it is only necessary to appeal to the recollection of every person residing in India, how few instances have actually occurred within his knowledge. And, had they ever been frequent, superstition would hardly have promised its indulgences to spectators (*Asiatick Researches* IV 1795: 205-11).[1]

The French Jesuit, Abbe Dubois wrote, "the country abounds with widows, especially among the Brahmins. Among this caste shorn-heads are to be seen everywhere" (Dubois 1906: 354).

Sir John Malcolm (1769–1833), who administered Central India including Malwa, noted that sati was formerly prevalent in the region as was proved by the numerous sati-stones. The custom, he said, had been most prevalent when Rajputs had power and influence. The Marathas, however, had "rendered this practice very rare."

In the whole of Central India, Malcolm stated, there had not been more than three or four satis annually in the previous twenty years. No widow had immolated herself on the death of any of the last three Rajas of Ragoogurh; the Sesodya family of Pertaubgurh had witnessed no incident for three generations; and the present Raja, Sawut Singh had openly declared against this practice and also female infanticide. On the death of the Raja of Banswarra, in 1819, none of his wives expressed a desire to burn herself. There had been no known instance of sati in Central India for many years, Malcolm affirmed, "in which the parties were not voluntary victims, and acting against the advice and remonstrance of their friends and the public officers of the district where it occurred" (Malcolm 1970a: 206-08; Section B: 393-94).

Mountstuart Elphinstone (1779–1859), who held several important posts including Governor of Bombay, disagreed with missionaries that the practice was due to the degraded condition to which widows, who did not perform the rite, were subjected to. If that were so, he argued, the practice would not have been so rare. He said,

It is more probable that the hopes of immediately entering on the enjoyment of heaven, and, of entitling the husband to the same felicity as well as the glory attending such a voluntary sacrifice, are sufficient to excite the few enthusiastic spirits who go through this awful trial.

He also refuted suggestions that relatives encouraged the practice with a view to obtaining the property of the widow. "It would be judging too harshly human nature," he stated, "to think such conduct frequent even in proportion to the number of cases where the widow has property to leave ..." On the contrary, the relations in most, if not in all, cases, sincerely desired to dissuade the sacrifice,

For this purpose, in addition to their own entreaties, and those of the infant children, when there is such, they procure the intervention of friends of the family, and of persons in authority. If the case be in a family of high rank, the sovereign himself goes to console and dissuade the widow. It is reckoned a bad omen for a government to have many sattis. The common expedient is to engage the widow's attention by such visits while the body is removed and burnt (Elphinstone 1966: 188).

Describing the sight of a widow burning as "a most painful one," Elphinstone observed that "one is humiliated to think that so feeble a being can be elevated by superstition to a self-devotion not surpassed by the noblest examples of patriots or martyrs." Though he had heard of women being dazed with opium in Guzerat, such was not the case in other parts of the country. Widows went through the ceremonies with astonishing composure and presence of mind, "and have been seen seated, unconfined among the flames, apparently praying, and raising their joined hands to their heads with as little agitation as at their ordinary devotions."

Elphinstone declared the practice of sati as "by no means universal in India." It did not occur south of the river Kishna; and in the Bombay Presidency, including the former sovereignty of the Peshwas, amounted to thirty-two a year. In the rest of the Deccan it was probably "more rare" (Elphinstone 1966: 189; Section B: 394-96). Elphinstone's impressions were formed in the early nineteenth century, though he published his work twenty-three years later (Thompson 1928: 68).

William Huggins, an indigo planter in Tirhoot district, wrote in 1824 that sati was not practiced "at a distance from Calcutta ... even in the upper parts of Bengal it is not ..." (Nair 1989: 424; Section B: 391-92).

Bishop Heber, the second Bishop of Calcutta, who toured Upper India in the year 1824–1825, wrote, while passing through the province of Agra, that sati was "by no means common in this part of India; indeed, I have not yet found it common any where except in Bengal, and some parts of Bahar" (Heber II 1993: 325; Section B: 372-74).

Montgomery Martin stated that in the district of Goruckpoor, satis were honoured and "little monuments are raised over the places of the sacrifice. These are much more numerous than one would expect from the number of sacrifices annually to occur, which amount to about thirteen" (Martin Vii 1987: 474-75).

Robert Hamilton, Magistrate of Banaras, in a letter dated 1st March 1829, also stressed the infrequency of the rite. He wrote,

> The city of Benares is one of the most sacred homes of Hinduism in India ... At such a place then it would be expected the performance of this most inhuman rite would be frequent, and that its frequency would be in proportion

to the peculiar sanctity of the spot, a sanctity immemorially acknowledged. How far the practice supports the expectation may be ascertained by the annexed statement shewing the number of suttees that have taken place within the last nine years, during which period seasons of extreme sickness and mortality have prevailed, and from which an average may be fairly deduced. Viewing the average thus taken and bearing in mind the peculiar [holiness] of Benares, it surely cannot be decreed a reasonable testimony in support of the obligatory nature of the rite of suttee. In a population amounting to 500,000 souls at the least calculation the average number of suttees bears no proportion to the number of deaths, indeed I have never met with any satisfactory or reasonable argument on the subject in any of my very frequent conversations with the learned of all ranks and from all parts who have visited me since I have resided at Benares ... (Philips 1977: 171-72).

Frederick John Shore (1818–1837), son of Sir John Shore, was of the view that little credit was due to Lord Bentinck for the abolition of sati. He said that of those he conversed with, "full three out of four were not only convinced that all over Hindostan and Bengal, suttee might be abolished with perfect safety...full five years before the law was actually enacted" (Penner and MacLean 1983: 234-35; Section B: 396-97).

Fanny Parkes, the wife of a Company servant who stayed in India for twenty-four years, commented on hearing of the abolition, "... the rite might have been abolished long before without danger" (Parkes 2003: 88-89; Section B: 392). The reasonable inference would be that as it was rarely practiced, the possibility of large-scale resistance was minimal.

Major Edward C. Archer, aide-de-camp to Lord Combermere, Commander-in-Chief in India (1825–1830), argued in 1830, that while sati had been prohibited in the Company's dominions, it continued in territories not under British rule and this was a cogent reason for the policy of allowing it to grow gradually into disuse. In these territories, as well as in the Company's dominions,

> ...the practice was decreasing fast, and even some of the chiefs of the Bundel Khund States had expressed themselves in decided hostility to its longer prevalence; but they did not seek to put it down by violence. In the British provinces it was of less frequent occurrence; and it might have been more so, had it been left to take its own course. It is the firm persuasion of many, that in the course of a few years the horrible rite of Suttee would have ceased entirely... (Nair 1989: 529-32; Section B: 397).

Even Sir John Kaye, who returned to England in 1845 after serving for several years in India, and, in 1858 succeeded James Stuart Mill as Secretary in the Political and Secret Department at India Office, conceded,

> But for all this, it can hardly be said that widow-burning was ever a national custom. At no time has the practice been so frequent as to constitute more than an exception to the general rule of self-preservation. Still, even in this exceptional state, it was something very horrible and deplorable in Christian eyes, and something to be suppressed, if suppression were possible, by a Christian government established in a heathen land. ... I have said that this practice of Suttee has never been anything more than an exceptional abomination. It never has been universal throughout India — never in any locality has it been general (Kaye 1966: 524; 529).

The entire colonial debate on sati centred on Bengal, though Rajasthan had emerged as a stronghold of the custom.[2] Besides individual satis, mass *jauhars* had taken place at Chittor in 1303, 1535, and 1568 and at Jaisalmer, in 1299, when large numbers of women threw themselves into the fire as their husbands met death on the battlefield (Noble and Sankhyan 2001: 345). Even today, Rajasthan retains its association with sati. The number of sati temples in the Shekhavati region (consisting of the Sikar and Jhunjhunu districts) is unmatched in the rest of the country (Noble and Sankhyan 2001: 364-65). Of the forty-odd cases of sati recorded since independence, some twenty-eight have occurred in Rajasthan, mainly in and around Sikar (Oldenburg 1994: 101).[3]

It is significant that in the area where sati was alleged to have been most prevalent in British times, i.e. West Bengal, no case seems to have been reported for several generations (Chen 2000: 51, 66). While sati temples and *chhatris* (memorials) are found in Rajasthan and other parts of India, not many (or none) seem to have been erected for the thousands who are supposed to have immolated themselves in colonial Bengal. This lends credence to the inference that incidents of widow immolation in Bengal were embellished by Evangelicals and missionaries firstly, to gain the right to proselytization, and subsequently, to justify their presence and British rule in India. The amelioration of the depressed status of Hindu women was held to be a critical component of the civilizing mission of the White Man.

END-NOTES

1. Nathaniel Halhed, in his *A Code of Gentoo Laws*, contested this claim and said "the custom has not for the most part fallen into desuetude" (Halhed 1777: 179).
2. The British response to widow immolation in Rajasthan was markedly different from that in Bengal. James Tod, in his famous work, revived the image of the heroic sati in the warrior tradition that had disappeared in the early nineteenth century colonial discourse in Bengal. In Rajasthan, the widow was "reinvested" with a measure of agency denied to her in Bengal (Major 2012: 72).
3. The Narayani Sati temple in Alwar district, patronized by the barber caste, also enjoys a considerable following.

Some Foreign Accounts of Sati

1

326 BC to AD 1499

1. SATI WITNESSED BY THE GREEKS, DIODORUS – 326 BC (MAJUMDAR 1960: 240-41)

When Eumenes was interring the slain with splendid obsequies, a marvelous thing occurred, of a nature quite contrary to what is customary among the Greeks. For Keteus, the commander of those who had come from India, was killed in the battle when fighting gloriously, and he left two wives who had accompanied him in the expedition, one lately married, while the other had been for a few years his helpmate, but both of them devotedly attached to him. Now, it was an ancient law among the Indians that when young men and maiden were minded to wed, they did not marry according to the judgment of their parents, but by mutual consent. But when in these old times espousals were made between persons of immature age, mistakes of judgment were of frequent occurrence, and when both sides repented their union, many of the women became depraved, and through incontinence fell in love with other men, and when at last they wished to leave the husbands they hand first chosen, but could not in decency do so openly, they got rid of them by poison, a means of destroying life which they could readily procure in the country, which produces in great quantity and variety drugs of fatal potency, some of which cause death if merely introduced as a powder into food or drink. But when this nefarious practice had become quite prevalent, and many lives had been sacrificed, and when it was found that the punishment of the guilty had no effect in deterring other wives from their career of iniquity, they passed a law ordaining that a wife, unless she were pregnant, or had already borne children, should be burned along with her deceased husband, and that if she did not choose to obey the law that she should remain a widow to the end of her life, and be for ever excommunicated from the sacrifices and other solemnities as being an impious person. When these laws had been enacted, it came to pass that the women changed to the very opposite their disposition to violate their duty, for, since each one willingly submitted to the death ordained, rather than endure the excess of infamy which would attend its refusal, they not only provided for the safety and welfare of their husbands in which their own were equally involved, but they contended with each other for this as the highest of all honours, and this happened in the present instance. For although by the law only one was to be burned with the husband, yet at the funeral of Keteus each of his wives strove for the honour of dying with him, as if this were the noblest crown of virtue. When the matter was brought to the generals for decision, the younger wife represented that the other was pregnant and could not therefore take advantage of the law. The elder pleaded that as she was before the other in years, she should be preferred before her in honour also; for in every other case it was the rule that more honour and respect should be accorded to the elder than to the younger. The generals being informed by the midwives that the elder was with child, decided in favour of the younger; whereupon the one who lost her cause went away weeping and wailing, rent the veil from her head, and tore her hair as if some terrible news had been told her. The other, overjoyed at her victory, set forth for the funeral pile, crowned with mitres by the women of her house, and richly attired, as if she were going to some marriage festival, escorted by her kindred setting fort in songs the praises of her virtues. When she came near to the pyre she stripped off her ornaments and distributed them to her servants and friends, bequeathing them, so to speak, as tokens of remembrance to those she loved. Her ornaments consisted of a multitude of finger-rings, set with precious stone of divers colours; upon her head there was no small number of little golden stars, between which were placed sparkling stones of all sorts; about her neck she wore many rows of jewels, some small, others large, and increasing in size gradually as they were placed on the string. At length she took farewell of her domestics, and was assisted by her brother to mount the pyre, and, to the great admiration of the people, who ran together to se the spectacle, she made her exit from life in heroic style. For the whole army under arms marched thrice round the pile before fire was set to it, and the victim, having meanwhile laid herself by her husband's side, scorned to demean herself by uttering shrieks, even when the flames were raging around her – a sight which affected the onlookers variously. Some were filled with pity, others were profuse in their praises, while there were not wanting Greeks who condemned the institution as barbarous and inhuman.

2. EARLY VIEW OF SATI, STRABO – 20 BC (*HOBSON-JOBSON* 1968: 879)

He (Aristobulus) says that he had heard from some persons of wives burning themselves voluntarily with their deceased husbands, and that those women who refused to submit to this custom were disgraced.

3. SATI IN CEYLON, THE *AKHBAR AL –SIN WA'L – HIND*, COMPILED IN AD 851 (AHMAD 1989: 53)

Sometimes when a king is cremated, his wife enters the fire and burns herself along with him, but if they do not wish, they do not do so.

4. SON PROTECTOR OF WIDOWED MOTHER, ALBERUNI – AD 970–1039 (SACHAU II 1989: 155)

If a wife loses her husband by death, she cannot marry another man. She has only to choose between two things — either to remain a widow as long as she lives or to burn herself; and the latter eventuality is considered the preferable, because as a widow she is ill-treated as long as she lives. As regards the wives of the kings, they are in the habit of burning them, whether they wish it or not, by which they desire to prevent any of them by chance committing something unworthy of the illustrious husband. They make an exception only for women of advanced years and for those who have children; for the son is the responsible protector of his mother.

5. SATI IN MALABAR, MARCO POLO ON HIS RETURN JOURNEY FROM CHINA TOWARDS END OF THIRTEENTH CENTURY (POLO 1961: 339-40)

... his relations proceed... to burn the body; and his wife, from motives of pious regard for her husband, throws herself upon the pile, and is consumed with him. Women who display this resolution are much applauded by the community, as, on the other hand, those who shrink from it are despised and reviled.

6. WIDOWS WITH SONS ABIDE WITH THEM, FRIAR ODORIC OF PORDENONE – AD 1325 (YULE AND CORDIER II 1913: 138-40)

But the idolaters of this realm have one detestable custom (that I must mention). For when any man dies, they burn him, and if he leave a wife they burn her alive with him, saying that she ought to go and keep her husband company in the other world. But if the women have sons by her husband she may abide with them, an she will. And, on the other hand, if the wife die there is no law to impose the like on him; but he, if he if likes, can take another wife.

7. SATI IN INDIA THE LESS, FRIAR JORDANUS –
AD 1323–1330 (SASTRI 1972: 203)

In this India, on the death of a noble, or of any people of substance; their bodies are burned: and eke their wives follow them alive to the fire, and, for the sake of worldly glory, and for the love of their husbands, and for eternal life, burn along with them, with as much joy as if they were going to be wedded; and those who do this have the higher repute for virtue and perfection among the rest. Wonderful! I have sometimes seen for one dead man who was burnt, five living women take their places on the fire with him, and die with their dead.

8. SATI WITNESSED, IBN BATTUTA –
AD 1333–1344 (GIBB 1999: 191-93)

Two days later we reached Ajudahan [Pakpattan], a small town belonging to the pious Shaykh Farid ad-Din. As I returned to the camp after visiting this personage, I saw the people hurrying out, and some of our party along with them. I asked them what was happening and they told me that one of the Hindu infidels had died, that a fire had been kindled to burn him, and his wife would burn herself along with him. After the burning my companions came back and told me that she had embraced the dead man until she herself was burned with him. Later on I used often to see a Hindu woman, richly dressed, riding on horseback, followed by both Muslims and infidels and preceded by drums and trumpets; she was accompanied by Brahmans, who are the chiefs of the Hindus. In the sultan's dominions they ask his permission to burn her, which he accords them. The burning of the wife after her husband's death is regarded by them as a commendable act, but is not compulsory; only when a widow burns herself her family acquires a certain prestige by it and gain a reputation for fidelity. A widow who does not burn herself dresses in coarse garments and lives with her own people in misery, despised for her lack of fidelity, but she is not forced to burn herself.

Once in the town of Amjari [Amjhera, near Dhar] I saw three women whose husbands had been killed in battle and who had agreed to burn themselves. Each one had a horse brought to her and mounted it, richly dressed and perfumed. In her right hand she held a coconut, with which she played, and in her left a mirror, in which she looked at her face. They were surrounded by Brahmans and their own relatives, and were preceded by drums, trumpets and bugles. Everyone of the infidels said to them "Take greetings from me to my father, or brother or mother, or friend" and they would say "Yes" and smile at them. I rode out with my companions to see the way in which the burning was carried out.

After three miles we came to a dark place with much water and shady trees, amongst which there were four pavilions, each containing a stone idol. Between the pavilions there was a basin of water over which a dense shade was cast by trees so thickly set that the sun could not penetrate them. The place looked like a spot in hell — God preserve us from it! On reaching these pavilions they descended to the pool, plunged into it and divested themselves of their clothes and ornaments, which they distributed as alms. Each one was then given an unsewn garment of coarse cotton and tied part of it round her waist and part over her head and shoulders. The fires had been lit near this basin in a low lying spot, and oil of sesam poured over them, so that the flames were increased. There were about fifteen men there with faggots of thin wood and about ten others with heavy pieces of wood, and the drummers and trumpeters were standing by waiting for the woman's coming. The fire was screened off by a blanket held by some men, so that she should not be frightened by the sight of it. I saw one of them, on coming to the blanket, pull it violently out of the men's hands, saying to them with a smile "Do you frighten me with the fire? I know that it is a fire, so let me alone." Thereupon she joined her hands above her head in salutation to the fire and cast herself into it. At the same moment the drums, trumpets and bugles were sounded, the men threw their firewood on her and the others put the heavy wood on top of her to prevent her moving, cries were raised and there was a loud clamour. When I saw this I had all but fallen off my horse, if my companions had not quickly brought water to me and laved my face, after which I withdrew.

9. SATI IN CAMBAY, NICOLO CONTI (MID-FOURTEENTH CENTURY) (MAJOR 1992: 6)

It is the custom when husbands die, for one or more of their wives to burn themselves with them, in order to add to the pomp of the funeral. She who was the most dear to the deceased, places herself by his side with her arm round his neck, and burns herself with him; the other wives, when the funeral pile is lighted, cast themselves into the flames.

10. SATI IN CENTRAL INDIA, NICOLO CONTI (MAJOR 1992: 24)

In central India the dead are burned, and the living wives, for the most part, are consumed in the same funeral pyre with their husband, one or more, according to the agreement at the time the marriage was contracted. The first wife is compelled by the law to be burnt, even though she should be the only wife. But others are married under the express agreement that they should add to the splendour of the funeral ceremony by their death, and this is considered a great honour for them. The deceased husband is laid on a couch, dressed in his best garments. A vast funeral pyre is erected over him in the form of a pyramid, constructed of odoriferous woods. The pile being ignited, the wife, habited in her richest garments, walks gaily around it, singing, accompanied by a great concourse of people, and amid the sounds of trumpets, flutes, and songs. In the meantime one of the priests, called Bachali, standing on some elevated spot, exhorts her to a contempt of life and death, promising her all kinds of enjoyment with her husband, much wealth, and abundance of ornaments. When she has walked round the fire several times, she stands near the elevation on which is the priest, and taking off her dress puts on a white linen garment, her body having first been washed according to custom. In obedience to the exhortation of the priest she then springs into the fire. If some show more timidity (for it frequently happens that they become stupified by terror at the sight of the struggles of the others, or of their sufferings in the fire), they are thrown into the fire by the bystanders, whether consenting or not. Their ashes are afterwards collected and placed in urns, which form an ornament for the sepulchres.

11. SATI IN COROMANDAL, HIERONIMO DI SANTO STEFANO (END OF THE FIFTEENTH CENTURY) (MAJOR 1992: 5-6)

.... There is another custom in practice here, that when a man dies and they prepare to burn him, one of his wives burns herself alive with him; and this is their constant habit.

2

AD 1500–1699

1. AN ANONYMOUS NARRATIVE BY SOMEONE WHO WAS PART OF THE PORTUGUESE TRADER, PEDRO ALVARES CABRAL'S, VOYAGE TO BRAZIL AND INDIA AROUND AD 1500 (CABRAL 1938: 82)

... in the mountains of this kingdom [Calicut] there is a very great and powerful king who is called Naremega [Narasimha], and they are idolaters. The king has two or three hundred wives. The day he dies they burn him and all of his wives with him. And this custom prevails for nearly all the others who are married when they die. A ditch is made in which they burn him, and then his wife, dressed as richly as possible, attended by all her relatives, with many instruments and festivity, is led to the trench, and she goes dancing backwards. The trench has a fire burning in it, and into this she lets herself fall. Her relatives are provided and ready with pots of oil and butter, and as soon as she has fallen into it they throw the said pots over her so that she may burn more quickly.

2. SATI CEREMONIES ON THE DEATH OF A KING, LUDOVICO DI VARTHEMA AD – 1502–1507 (VARTHEMA 1997: 77-78)

All the Brahmins and the King are burnt after death and at that time a solemn sacrifice is made to the devil... fifteen or twenty men dressed like devils stand there and make rejoicing. And his wife is always present, making most exceedingly great lamentations, and no other woman ... [Two weeks later the widow came to be burnt] And the said wife, when the feast is prepared, eats a great deal of betel, and eats so much that she loses her wits, and the instruments of the city are constantly sounding...together with the above mentioned men clothed like devils, who carry fire in their mouths, as I have already told you in Calicut. They also offer a sacrifice to Deumo... and she goes many times to the said men clothed like devils, to entreat and tell them to pray to the Deumo that he will be pleased to accept her as his own.

3. SATI IN MALABAR, LEWIS VERTOMANNUS, A GENTLEMAN FROM ROME, WHO VISITED IN AD 1503 (FORBES I 1988: 412-16)

When the king, or any of the priests or gentlemen die, their bodies are burnt in a great fire, made of a pile of wood; then all the while they sacrifice unto the devil. While the bodies are burning, they cast in the fire all manner of sweet savours, as aloes, myrrh, frankincense, storax, sandal, coral, and innumerable other sweet gums, spices, and trees: these make the fire much greater, increasing the flame by reason of their gummosity: the wife also, of the burned king or priest standeth by the fire alone, without the company of any other woman, lamenting and beating her breast. Within fifteen days after, the wife biddeth to a banquet all her husband's kinsfolks; and when they come at a day appointed, they go all to the place where her husband was burnt, and at the same hour of the night: then cometh forth the wife, garnished with all her jewels, and, best apparel: in the same place is made a pit, no deeper than may serve to receive the woman;

this pit is set about with reeds covered with silk, that the pit may not be seen. In the mean time a fire is made in the pit with sundry sorts of sweet woods; and the wife, after that her guests have well banqueted, eateth very much of a certain thing called betel, which troubleth her mind, as though she was half mad, or drunken. After the ceremonies are finished, she taketh her leave of all her kinsfolks, and then with sudden outrage, and a loud cry, lifting up her hands, she hurleth herself into the burning pit; which done, her kinsfolks, standing near unto the fire, cover her with little faggots of sweet wood; hurling also thereon much pitch, that the body may the sooner be consumed: and except the wife should do this after the death of her husband, she should ever after be esteemed an evil woman, be hated of all men, and in fine, in danger to be slain both of her own kinsfolks and her husband's, and therefore she goeth to it the more willingly. The king himself is present at these pompes; which are not commonly used, for all men; but only for kings, priests, and noblemen.

4. SATI IN GOA, TOME PIRES – AD 1511–1516 (PIRES 2005: 59)

It is mostly the custom in this kingdom of Goa for every heathen wife to burn herself alive on the death of her husband. Among themselves they all rate this highly, and if they do not want to burn themselves to death their relatives are dishonoured and they rebuke those who are ill-disposed towards the sacrifice and force them to burn themselves. And those who will not burn themselves on any consideration become public prostitutes and earn money for the upkeep and construction of the temples in their districts, and they die in this way.

5. SATI IN VIJAYANAGAR, DUARTE BARBOSA – AD 1516 (FILLIOZAT 2001: 307-11)

In this kingdom of Narsyngua there are three classes of Heathen, each one of which has a very distinct rule of its own, and also their customs differ much one from the other.

The principal of these is that of the King, the great Lords, the knights and fighting men, who may marry, as I have said, as many women as they wish, and are able to maintain: their sons inherit their estates: the women are bound by very ancient custom, when their husbands die, to burn themselves alive with their corpses which are also burnt. This they do to honour the husband. If such a woman is poor and of low estate, when her husband dies she goes with him to the burning ground "where there is a great pit" in which a pile of wood burns. When the husband's body has been laid therein and begins to burn, she throws herself of her own free will into the midst of the said fire, where both their bodies are reduced to ashes. But if she is a woman of high rank, rich, and with distinguished kindred, whether she be a young maid or an old woman, when her husband dies she accompanies the aforesaid corpse of her husband to the aforesaid burning ground, bewailing him; and there they dig a round pit, very wide and deep, which they fill with wood (and a great quantity of sandal wood therewith), and, when they have kindled it, they lay the man's body herein, and it is burnt while she weeps greatly. Wishing to do all honour to her husband she then causes all his kindred and her own to be called together, that they may come to feast and honour her thereby, all of whom gather together at the said field for this ceremony, where she spends with them and with her kindred and friends all that she has in festivities with music and singing and dancing and banquets. Thereafter she attires herself very richly with all the jewels she possesses, and then distributes to her sons, relatives and friends all the property that remains. Thus arrayed she mounts on a horse, light grey or quite white if possible, that she may be the better seen of all the people. Mounted on this horse they lead her through the whole city with great rejoicings, until they come back to the very spot where the husband has been burnt, where, they cast a great quantity of wood into the pit itself and on its edge they make a great fire. When it has burnt up somewhat they erect a wooden scaffold with four or five steps where they take her up just as she is. When she is on the top she turns herself round thereon three items, worshiping towards the direction of sunrise, and, this done, she calls her sons, kindred and friends, and to each she gives a jewel, whereof she has many with her, and in the same way every piece of her clothing until nothing is left except a small piece of cloth with which she is clothed from the waist down. All this she does and says so firmly, and with such a cheerful countenance, that she seems not about to die. Then she tells the men who are with her on the scaffold to consider what they owe to their wives who, being free to act, yet burn themselves alive for the love of them, and the women she tells to see how much they owe to their husbands, to such a degree as to go with them even to death. Then she ceases speaking, and they place in her hands a pitcher full of oil, and she puts it on her head, and with it she again turns round thrice on the scaffold and again worships towards the rising sun. Then she casts the pitcher of oil into the fire and throws herself after it with as much goodwill as if she were throwing herself on a little cotton, from which she could receive no hurt. The kinsfolk all take part at once and cast into the fire many pitchers of oil and butter which they hold ready for this purpose, and much wood on this, and therewith bursts out such a flame that no more can be seen. The ashes that remain after these ceremonies are thrown into running streams. All this they do in general without any hindrance, as it is the custom of all. Those who do not so, they hold in great dishonour, and their kindred shave their heads and turn them away as disgraced and a shame to their families.

.........This abominable practice of burning is so customary, and is held in such honour among them, that when the King dies four or five hundred women burn themselves in this way...

"Many men who are his intimates are also burnt with him" (it was customary in those days for men in the service of the king to vow to die with him).

6. SATI IN THE DECCAN, SOMMARIO DE GENTI –
AD 1520 (*HOBSON-JOBSON* 1968: 880)

There are in this Kingdom (the Deccan) many heathen, natives of the country, whose custom it is that when they die they are burnt, and their wives along with them; and if these will not do it they remain in disgrace with all their kindred. And as it happens oft times that they are unwilling to do it, their Bramin kinsfolk persuade them thereto, and this in order that such a fine custom should not be broken and fall into oblivion...

In this country of Camboja... when the King dies, the lords voluntarily burn themselves, and so do the King's wives at the same time, and so do other women on the death of their husbands.

7. SATI IN VIJAYANAGAR, FERNAO NUNIZ –
AD 1535 (FILLIOZAT 2001: 243-45)

This kingdom of Bisnaga is all heathen. The women, have the custom of burning themselves when their husbands die, and hold it an honour to do so. When therefore their husbands die they mourn with their relations and those of their husbands, but they hold that the wife who weeps beyond measure has no desire to go in search of her husband; and the mourning finished their relations speak to them, advising them to burn themselves and not to dishonour their generation. After that, it is said, they place the dead man on a bed with a canopy of branches and covered with flowers, and they put the woman on the back of a worthless horse, and she goes after them with many jewels on her, and covered with roses; she carries a mirror in her hand and in the other a branch of flowers, and (she goes accompanied by) many kinds of music, and his relations (go with her) with much pleasure. A man goes also playing on a small drum, and he sings songs to her telling her that she is going to join her husband, and she answers also in singing that so she will do. As soon as she arrives at the place where they are always burned she waits with the musicians till her husband is burned, whose body they place in a very large pit that has been made ready for it, covered with much firewood. Before they light the fire his mother or his nearest relative takes a vessel of water on the head and a firebrand in the hand, and goes three times round the pit, and at each round makes a hole in the pot; and when these three rounds are done breaks the pot, which is small, and throws the torch into the pit. Then they apply the fire, and when the body is burned comes the wife with all the feasters and washes her feet, and then a Brahman performs over her certain ceremonies according to their law; and when he has finished doing this, she draws off with her own hand all the jewels that she wears, and divides them among her female relatives, and if she has sons she commends them to her most honoured relatives. When they have taken off all she has on, even her good clothes, they put on her some common yellow cloths, and her relatives take her hand and she takes a branch in the other, and goes singing and running to the pit where the fire is, and then mounts on some steps which are made high up by the pit. Before they do this they go three times round the fire, and then she mounts the steps and holds in front of her a mat that prevents here from seeing the fire. They throw into the fire a cloth containing rice, and another in which they carry betel leaves, and her comb and mirror with which she adorned herself, saying that all these are needed to adorn herself by her husband's side. Finally she takes leave of all, and puts a pot of oil on her head, and casts herself into the fire with such courage that it is a thing of wonder; and as soon as she throws herself in, the relatives are ready with firewood and quickly cover her with it, and after this is done they all raise loud lamentations. When a captain dies, however many wives he has they all burn themselves, and when the King dies they do the same. This is the custom throughout all the country of the heathen, except with the caste of people called Telugas [mostly Virasaivas], amongst whom the wives are buried alive with their husbands when they die. These go with much pleasure to the pit, inside of which are made two seats of earth, one for him and one for her, and they place each one on his own seat and cover them in little till they are covered up; and so the wife dies with the husband.

8. SATI IN GUJARAT, SEYDI ALI RE'IS, AN OTTOMAN ADMIRAL, WHO WAS IN INDIA IN THE MID-1550s (ALAM AND SUBRAHMANYAM 2008: 119)

We saw the marvels and wonders of Hind. Amongst all the wonders, one is that the people of Gujarat call the *kefer* unbelievers *baniyan*, and those of Hindustan call them *hindu*. They are not People of the Book. They believe in the eternity of the world. When one of them dies, one puts the body back in the clothes that he wore when he was alive, and then burns it on the banks of a river. If it is a man, and if he leaves behind a wife, and she cannot have children, they do not burn her. But if she can remarry, they burn her, willy-nilly. If a certain burns of her own will, her relatives rejoice and play string instruments. If a certain number of Muslims get together, and take her away from the hands of her family when they want to burn her, she becomes their property, and no one can claim her back. For this reason, when someone is ready to be burned, they (the Hindus) recruit some of the Padshah's men so that the (Muslim) population does not stop them.

9. SATI IN VIJAYANAGAR, CAESARO FEDERICI – AD 1565 (FILLIOZAT 2001: 321-24)

I rested in Bezeneger seven moneths ... And in the time I rested there, I saw many strange and beastly deeds done by the Gentiles. First, when there is any Noble man or woman dead, they burne their bodies and if a married man die, his wife must burne herselfe alive, for the love of her husband, and with the body of her husband: so that when any man dyeth, his wife will take a moneths leave, two or three, or as shee will, to burne herselfe in, and that day being come, wherein shee ought to be burnt, that morning she goeth out of her house very early, either on Horsebacke or on an Elephant or else is borne by eight men on a small stage: in one of these orders she goeth, being apparelled like to Bride carried round about the Citie, with her haire downe about her shoulders, garnished with Jewels and Flowers, according to the estate of the partie, and they goe with as great joy as Brides doe in Venice to their Nuptials: she carrieth in her left hand a looking-glasse, and in her right hand an arrow, and singeth through the Citie as passeth, and saith, that she goeth to sleepe with her dear spouse and husband. Shee is accompanied with her kindred and friends untill it be one or two of the clocke in the afternoone, then they go out of the Citie, and going along the Rivers side called Nigondin [Anegondi], which runneth under the walls of the Cities, untill they come unto a place where they use to make this burning of Women, being widdowes, there is prepared in this place a great square Cave, with a little pinnacle hard by it, foure or five steps up: the aforesaid Cave is full of dryed wood. The woman being come thither, accompanied with a great number of people which come to see the thing, then they make ready a great banquet, and she that shee bee burned eateth with as great joy and gladnesse, as though it were her Wedding day: and the feast being ended, then they goe to dancing and singing a certaine time, according as she will. After this, the woman of her owne accord, commandeth them to make the fire in the square Cave where the drie wood is, and when it is kindled, they come and certifie her thereof, then presently she leaveth the feast, and taketh the neerest kinsman of her husband by the hand, and they both goe together to the banke of the foresaid River, where shee putteth off all her jewels and all her clothes, and giveth them to her parents or kinsfolke, and covering herselfe with a cloth, because shee will not bee seene of the people being naked, she throweth herselfe into the River, saying: O wretches, wash away yur sinnes. Comming out of the water, she rowleth herselfe into a yellow cloth of fourteene braces long: and againe she taketh her husbands kinsman by the hand, and they go up to the pinnacle of the square Cave werein the fire is made. When shee is on the pinnacle, she talketh and reasoneth with the people, recommending unto them her children and kindred. Before the pinnacle they use to set a Mat, because they shall not see the fiercenesse of the fire, yet there are many that will have them plucke away, shewing therin an heart not fearfull, and that they are not affraid of that sight. When this silly woman hath reasoned with the people a good while to her content, there is another woman that taketh a pot with oyle, and sprinkleth it over her head, and with the same shee annointeth all her body and afterwards throweth the pot into the fornace, and both the woman and the pot goe together into the fire, and presently the people that are round about the fornace throw after her into the cave great pieces of wood so by this meanes, with the fire and with the blowes that shee hath with the wood throwen after her, she is quickly dead, and after this there groweth such sorrow and such lamentation among the people, that all their mirth is turned into howling and weeping, in such wise, that a man could scarce beare the hearing of it. I have seene many burnt in this manner, because my house was neere to the gate where they goe out to the place of burning [towards NE of Tiruvengalanatha, on the way to Vithala is rocky hill called Pagadanigudda, on the road to which there are many memorial stones]: and when there dyeth any Great man, his Wife with all her Slaves with whom hee hath had carnall copulation, burne themselves together with him.

Also in this Kingdome I have seene amongst the base sort of people this use and order, that the man being dead, hee is carried to the place where they will make his sepulcher, and setting him as it were upright, then cometh his wife before him on his knees, casting her arme about his necke, with imbracing and clasping him, until such time as the Masons have made a wall round about them, and when the wall is as high as their neckes, there cometh a man behind the woman and strangleth her: then when shee is dead the workemen finish the wall over their heads, and so they lie buried both together.

10. SATI AMONG BRAHMINS, JOHN HUYGHEN VAN LINSCHOTEN – AD 1583 (LINSCHOTEN I 1988: 249)

When the Bramenes die, all their friends assemble together, and make a hole in the ground, wherein they throw much wood and other things: and if the man be of any account, [they cast in] sweet Saunders, and other Spices, with Rice, Corne, and such like, and much oyle, because the fire should burne the stronger. Which done, they lay the dead Bramenes in it: then commeth his wife with Musike and [many of] her nearest friends all singing certain praises in commendation of her husbands life, putting her in comfort, and encouraging her to follow her husband, and goe with him, into the other world. Then she taketh [all] her Jewels, and parteth them among her frends, and so with a cheerful countenance, she leapeth into the fire, and is presently covered with wood and oyle: so she is quickly dead and with her husbands bodie burned to ashes...

11. SATI IN MADURAI (CRONIN 1959: 53-54)

We found a pit ten or twelve feet square, and about a man's height deep, full of wood and burning charcoal, as hot as a burning furnace. Thence we were conducted to the widow, in front of whom men were dancing and playing. She ate betel with a cheerful countenance, and we had a few words with her there, trying to dissuade her, but she answered that it would be a great disgrace if she did not accompany in the next world the man who had loved her so much. Then she rose and gave us betel, and went to the river, where she bathed, and put on a cloth dyed with saffron; she distributed her necklace, ear-rings, and arm-rings among her relations, came close to the pit, round which she walked once speaking to each of her acquaintances, and then, raising her hands, jumped with a cheerful face into the fire. Immediately she was covered with some hurdles and large logs, which were ready for the purpose, and some pots of oil were thrown on the fire, so that she should burn more quickly. As soon as she jumped in the fire, the relations and others, both men and women, embraced each other, and raised a great outcry, which lasted for about a quarter of an hour. She looked to be about twenty-four years of age; she left a baby three months old.

12. SATI AT CALICUT AMONG BRAHMINS, FRANCOIS PYRARD OF LAVAL – AD 1607 (PYRARD 2000: 394)

On the death of a Brameny, his wife is bound to show in what affection she holds him, by burning herself alive, leaping into the fire which consumes the corpse of the deceased: this is done with great solemnity in presence of the relatives, and to the sound of music. I have seen the burning of five or six in this sort while I was at Calecut [the custom did not prevail among the Nambudri Brahmins at Calicut, the women may have been from the Konkan or elsewhere]. If they like not to be burned, they may avoid it, but then they are infamous; they have their hair cut, they no longer hold up their heads, and are driven from the society of ladies of honour, without being able to marry again. Yet do most of them prefer to undergo this infamy rather than to be burned. The wives of the Nairs are not required to do this, although 'tis said that one will sometimes cast herself upon the fire out of affection, and of her own free will. But they are not bound to do it, and are even free to marry again without dishonour, provided they are not of the Brameny caste. This rule does not obtain among the common people. I have never seen them to wear mourning for their relations, albeit, when the king dies, all the men of the kingdom shave their beards and hair entirely.

13. SATI AT AGRA, WILLIAM HAWKINS (1608–1613) (FOSTER 1999: 119)

The custome of the Indians is to burne their dead, as you have read in other authors, and at their burning many of their wives will burne with them, because they will bee registred in their bookes for famous and most modest and loving wives, who, leaving all worldly affaires, content themselves to live no longer then their husbands. I have seen many proper women brought before the King, whom (by his commandment) none may burne without his leave and sight of them; I meane those of Agra. When any of these commeth, hee doth perswade them with many promises of gifts and living if they will live, but in my time no perswasion could prevaile, but burne they would. The King, seeing that all would not serve, giveth his leave for her to be carried to the fire, where she burneth herself alive with her dead husband.

14. SATI AT SURAT, NICHOLAS WITHINGTON (1612–1616) (FOSTER 1999: 219-20)

When the Banian dies, his wife, after the burninge of her husband, shaves her head and weres noe more her jewells; in which estate shee continues till shee dye. When the Rasbooche dies, his wife, when his bodye goes to bee burned, accompanieth him, attyred with her beste arrayments and accompanyed with her frends and kyndred, makinge much joye, havinge musicke with them. And cominge to the place of burninge, the fyer beeinge made, sitteth downe, havinge twice or thrice incompassed the place. Firste, shee bewayleth her husband's death, and rejoycinge that shee is nowe reddye to goe and live with him agayne; and then imbraceth her frends and sitteth downe on the toppe of the pile of wood and dry stickes, rockinge her husband's head in her lappe, and soe willeth them to sett fyer on the wood; which beeinge done, her frends throwe oyle and divers other things, with sweete perfumes, uppon her; and shee indures the fyer with such patience that it is to bee admired, beeinge loose and not bounde. Of this manner of burninge I have seen manye. The firste that ever I sawe was in Surratt, with our Agente and the reste of our Englishe. It was verye lamentable. The woman which was burnte was not above ten yeares of age and had never layen with her husband. But this yt was. Hee beeinge a souldier, and goinge uppon service, was slayne in the action, and there burned, but his clothes and turbante were brought home with newes of his death; wheruppon his wife would needes bee burnte, and soe made preparatins for it. And beeinge reddye to sacrefise her selfe with her husband's clothes, which she had with her, order came from the Governor that shee should not dye, in regard she had never layen with her husband; which newes she took wonderfull passionately,desiringe them to sett fyer on the wood presentlye, sayinge her husband was a greate waye before her. But they durste not burne her, till her frends wente to the Governor and intreated him, givinge him a presente for the same; which when they obteyned, they retorned and (with greate joye to her, as she seemed) burnte her to ashes with her husband's clothes and then caste the ashes into the river. This was the firste that ever I sawe; at the sight wherof our Agente was soe greeved and amazed at the undaunted resolution of the younge woman that hee said hee would never see more burnte in that fashion while hee lived. The kyndred of the husband that dies never force the wife to burne her selfe, but her owne kyndred, houldinge it a greate disgrace to theire familie if shee should denye to bee burned; which some have done, but verye fewe. And if they will not burne (yt beeinge in theire choyee), then shee muste shave her hayer and breake her jewells, and is not suffred to eate, drinke, or keepe companye with anye bodye, and soe liveth in this case, miserablye, till her death. Nowe, if any one of them purpose to burne and (after ceremonies done) bee brought to the fyer, and there, feelinge the scorchinge heate, leape out of the fyer, her father and mother will take her and bynde her and throwe her into the fyer and burne her per force; but such weaknesse seldome happeneth amongste them.

15. SATI AT NEGAPATAM, GASPARO BALBI – AD 1583 (*HOBSON-JOBSON* 1968: 880)

Among other sights I saw one I may note as wonderful. When I landed (at Negapatam) from the vessel, I saw a pit full of kindled charcoal; and at that moment a young and beautiful woman was brought by her people on a litter, with a great company of other women, friends of hers, with great festivity, she holding a mirror in her left hand, and a lemon in her right hand...

16. SATI IN CHAUL, RALPH FITCH, WHO VISITED INDIA FROM AD 1583 TO 1591 (LOCKE 1995: 77)

... when the husband dieth (in Chaul) his wife is burned with him, if she be alive; if she will not her head is shaven and then is never any account made of her after.

17. SATI ON THE DEATH OF A NAYAK, PHILLIPP BALDAEUS IN AD 1600 (BANERJEE 2003: 77-78)

I will not enlarge my self in this Place upon that most barbarous Custom of some of these Pagans for the Wives to burn themselves alive with the dead Carcasses of their Husbands, a thing still practis'd in the most populous City of Pandi; for when the Funeral Ceremony of Vinepi Naigne the Prince of the Country, was solemniz'd, with great Pomp, 300 of his Wives did precipitate themselves alive (under the Sound of Drums and Trumpets) into the same Hole fill'd with burning Oil, Butter, and other combustible Matter, which burn'd both his and their Bodies to Ashes.

18. SATI ON THE DEATH OF THE NAYAK OF MADURI, THE JESUIT MISSIONARY, TEIXEIRA, IN 1611 (*HOBSON-JOBSON* 1968: 881)

When I was in India, on the death of the Naique of Madure, a country situated between that of Malabar and that of Choromandel, four hundred wives of his burned themselves along with him.

19. SATI VOLUNTARY, EDWARD TERRY, WHO WAS IN INDIA FROM 1616 TO 1619 (FOSTER 1999: 323)

Their widowes marrie not; but, after the losse of their husbands, cut their haire and spend all their life following as neglected creatures; whence, to bee free from shame, many yong women are ambitious to die with honor (as they esteeme it), when their fiery love brings them to the flames (as they thinke) of martyrdome most willingly; following their dead husbands unto the fire, and there imbracing are burnt with them; but this they doe voluntary, not compelled. The parents and friends of those women will most joyfully accompanie them, and when the wood is fitted for this hellish sacrifice and begins to burne, all the people assembled shoute and make a noyse, that the screeches of this tortured creature may not bee heard. Not much unlike the custome of the Ammonites, who, when they made their children passe through the fire to Moloch, caused certaine tabret or drums to sound, that their cry might not be heard.

20. SATI IN KARNATAKA, MUHAMMAD SHARIF HANAFI – AD 1620 (*HOBSON-JOBSON* 1968: 881)

The author... when in the territory of the Karnatik... arrived in company with his father at the city of Southern Mathura (Madura), where, after a few days, the ruler died and went to hell. The chief had 700 wives, and they all threw themselves at the same time into the fire.

21. SATI AMONG RAJPUTS IN AGRA, FRANCISCO PELSAERT (1620–1627) (PELSAERT 2001: 78-79)

When a Rajput dies, his wives (or rather his wife, for they marry only one if there is genuine love) allow themselves to be burnt alive, as is the practice among the banians or khattris, and in Agra this commonly occurs two or three times a week. It is not a very pleasant spectacle, but I witnessed it out of curiosity, when a woman who lived near our house declared to her friends, immediately on her husband's death, that she would be *sati*, which means that she would accompany him where he had gone, making the announcement with little lamentation, and as if her heart was sealed with grief...

The woman I have mentioned then went, with music and songs, to the Governor to obtain his permission. The Governor urged many sound arguments to show that what she proposed to do was a sin, and merely the inspiration of the devil to secure her voluntary death; and, because she was a handsome young woman of about 18 years of age, he pressed her strongly to dissuade her if possible from her undertaking, and even offered her 500 rupees yearly as long as she should live. He could, however, produce no effect, but she answered with resolute firmness that her motive was not [the fear of] poverty, but love for her husband, and even if she could have all the King's treasures in this world, they would be of no use to her, for she meant to live with her husband. This was her first and last word throughout, she seemed to be out of her senses, and she was taking up far too much time; so the Governor, since governors are not allowed by the King's orders to refuse these requests, gave his consent. Then she hurried off with a light step, as if she might be too late, till she reached the place, a little outside the city, where was a small hut, built of wood, roofed with straw, and decorated with flowers. There she took off all her jewels and distributed them among her friends, and also her clothes, which she disposed of in the same way, keeping only an undergarment. Then she took a handful of rice, and distributed it to all the bystanders; this being done, she embraced her friends and said her last farewells; took her baby, which was only a year old, kissed it, and handed it to her nearest friends; then ran to the hut where her dead husband lay, and kissed and embraced him eagerly. Then she [or they] took the fire and applied the brand, and the friends piled wood before the door; everyone shouted out Ram! Ram! (the name of their god), the shouts continuing till they supposed she was dead. When the burning was over, everyone took a little of the ash of the bones, which they regard as sacred, and preserve. Surely this is as great a love as the women of our country bear to their husbands, for the deed was done not under compulsion but out of sheer love.

At the same time there are hundreds, or even thousands, who do not do it, and there is no such reproach as is asserted by many, who write that those who neglect it incur the reproach of their caste.

22. SATI BY A WEAVER'S WIDOW, WILLIAM METHWOLD, IN THE FIRST QUARTER OF THE SEVENTEENTH CENTURY (MORELAND 1931: 28-30)

...Yet are there some few left, that in pure love to their deceased husbands die voluntarily in solemnizing their funerals, beleeving their soules shall keepe company in their transmigrations. Of the two which I have seene, the first was wife to a weaver, who being dead, and by his profession to be buried [in Telugu country, sati sometimes took the form of burial alive], she, a young woman about 20 yeeres of age, would needs goe with him, and in this order. She was clothed in her best garments, and, accompanied with her neerest kindred and friends, seated on a greene banke by a great ponds side, there enter[t]ayning such as came to looke and take leave on her with bettele (a herbe which they much eat), meerely [absolutely] accommodating her words, actions, and countenance to the musicke, which stood by and plaid no dumps [a mournful melody], but in the same measure and straine they were occasioned at wedding. Newes hereof being brought to our house, three of us took horse, and posted a mile out of towne to be partakers of this spectacle; but comming into her sight before we came at them, they fearing by our speed we had bin sent from the Governour to hinder their proceedings, hastened to her death, and was then covering with earth when wee came in; first sitting downe by her husband, embracing his dead body, and taking leave of all her friends, they, standing round about the grave, with each of them a basket of earth, buried her at once. Yet after we came in, one of them stroke upon the grave, laying his head close unto it, and calling her by her name, and told us she answered and expressed her content in the course she had taken. Over whom there was erected a little thatcht cover, and her kindred not a little glorified in being allied to so resolute and loving a wife.

SATI AMONG KAPU CASTE

The other was a Campowaroes [of the Kapu caste] wife, and she, after the same solemne preparation, retelling her run and crying all the way 'Bama Narina, Bama Narina,' [Rama Narayana?] leapt into the pit where her husband lay burning, upon whom her bystanding friends threw so many logs that she felt not so much fire for the fewell.

Unto whom I adde a third. A gold-smiths wife, whose husband being dead and she willing to accompany him, came attended with her frinds and kindred unto the Cotwall [kotwal, city-governor], who was then with me at the English house, with much importunity desiring his consent, alledging her husbands death and the few friends she had left behind; whereunto the Cotwall replyed that hee himselfe would provide for her at his owne house, diswading her by what other arguments he could use from so desperate a course; but she neglecting them and his offer, he also denied her request, and she departed discontent, uttering these words, that he could not hinder her to dye by some other meanes; and within a short time after I heard she had hanged her self. And this hapned in Musulipatnam, where the officers, being all Mahumetans restraine the Gentiles especially in these cruel and heathenish customes.

23. SATI OF 'CHEERFUL COUNTENANCE,' ANONYMOUS RELATION, IN THE FIRST QUARTER OF THE SEVENTEENTH CENTURY (MORELAND 1931: 74-75)

The strangest and most terrible thing among them seemed to me the fact that some wives jumped alive into the fire beside their dead husbands, though at first I did not believe it. The first time I saw it, I was with Jan van Wesick [chief of the Dutch factory at Nizampatam from 1608 to 1610], and, being informed that it was about to take place, we went there. On arrival we were welcomed by the brother of the deceased, a respectable man, who said we did him great honour. We found a pit 10 or 12 feet square, and about a man's height deep, full of wood and burning charcoal, as hot as a burning furnace would be. Thence we were conducted to the widow, in front of whom men were dancing and playing. She ate betel with a cheerful countenance, and we had a few words with her there, trying to dissuade her, but she answered that it would be a great disgrace if she did not accompany in the next world the man who had loved her so much. Then she rose and gave us betel, and went to the river, where she bathed, and put on a cloth dyed with saffron; she distributed her necklace, earrings, and arm-rings among her relations, came close to the pit, round which she walked once, speaking to each of her acquaintances, and then, raising her hands, jumped with a cheerful face into the fire. Immediately she was covered with some hurdles and large logs, which were ready for the purpose, and some pots of oil were thrown on the fire, so that she should be burnt more quickly. As soon as she jumped into the fire, the relations and others [present], both men and women, embraced each other, and raised a great outcry, which lasted for about a quarter of an hour. She looked to be about 24 years of age; she left a baby three months old.

The second time, things happened as already described, but she was an old woman, about fifty, and, had she not been prevented, she would have come out of the fire after entering it. One of our neighbors, a brahman, having been drowned, was laid on a great heap of wood, and the widow went and lay down beside him, kissing him and embracing him. Some wood was then placed on her body, the fire was kindled by the others, oil was poured over her body, and so she was burnt; but the horror of the two I had seen before made it impossible for me to see this one, or three or four others, being burnt, or, further, that two wives of the brother of the first deceased I have mentioned jumped into the fire beside him.

24. SATI PRACTICED BY FEW, PIETRO DELLA VALLE IN 1623–1624 (DELLA VALLE 1991: 84-85)

....this burning of Women upon the death of their Husbands is at their own choice to do it or not, and indeed few practice it; but she who does it acquires in the Nation a glorious name of Honour and Holiness. 'Tis most usual among great persons, who prize Reputation at a higher rate than others do; and in the death of Personages of great quality, to whom their Wives desire to do Honour by burning themselves quick....

I have likewise heard it said that some Women are burnt against their own will, their Relations resolving to have it so for Honour of the Husband; and that they have been brought to the fire in a manner by force, and made besides themselves with things given them to eat and drink for this purpose, that they might more easily suffer themselves to be cast into the fire; but this the Indians directly deny, saying that force is not us'd to any, and it may be true, at least in Countries where Mahometans command, for there no Woman is suffered to be burnt without leave of the Governour of the place, to whom it belongs first to examine whether the women be willing; and for a Licence there is also paid a good sum of money. Nevertheless 'tis possible too that many Widows, being in the height of their passion taken at their word by their kindred who desire it, go to it afterwards with an ill will, not daring to deny those that exhort them thereunto, especially if oblig'd by their word, nor to discover their own mind freely to the Governour; things which amongst Women, with their natural fearfulness and modesty, easily happen.

SATI BY A DRUMMER'S WIDOW AT IKKERI, PIETRO DELLA VALLE (DELLA VALLE 1991: 266-67; 273-77)

As we return'd home at night we met a Woman in the City of *Ikkeri,* who, her husband being dead, was resolv'd to burn herself, as 'tis the custom with many Indian Women. She rode on Horse-back about the City with face uncovered, holding a Looking-glass in one hand and a Lemon in the other, I know not for what purpose; and beholding herself in the Glass, with a lamentable tone sufficiently pittiful to hear, went along I know not whither, speaking, or singing, certain words, which I understood not; but they told me they were a kind of Farewell to the World and herself; and indeed, being uttered with that passionateness which the Case requir'd and might produce they mov'd pity in all that heard them, even in us who understood not the Language. She was follow'd by many other Women and Men on foot, who, perhaps, were her Relations; they carry'd a great Umbrella over her, as all Persons of quality in *India* are wont to have, thereby to keep off the Sun, whose heat is hurtful and troublesome Before her certain Drums were sounded, whose noise she never ceas'd to accompany with her sad Ditties, or Songs; yet with a calm and constant Countenance, without tears, evidencing more grief for her Husband's death than her own, and more desire to go to him in the other world than regret for her own departure out of this: a Custom, indeed, cruel and barbarous, but, withall, of great generosity and virtue in such Women and therefore worthy of no small praise. They said she was to pass in this manner about the City I know not how many dayes, at the end of which she was to go out of the City and be burnt with more company and solemnity. If I can know when it will be I will not fail to go to see her and by my presence honor her Funeral with that compassionate affection which so great Conjugal Fidelity and Love seem to me to deserve...

November the sixteenth. I was told that the afore-mention'd Woman, who had resolv'd to burrn her self for her Husband's death, was to dye this Evening. But upon further enquiry at the Woman's House I understood that it would not be till after a few dayes more, and there I saw her sitting in a Court, or Yard, and other persons beating Drums about her. She was cloth'd all in white, and deck'd with many Neck-laces, Bracelets and other ornaments of Gold; on her Head she had a Garland of Flowers, spreading forth like the rayes of the Sun; in brief she was wholly in a Nuptial Dress and held a Lemon in her Hand, which is the usual Ceremony. She seem'd to be pleasant enough, talking and laughing in conversation, as a Bride would do in our Countries. She and those with her took notice of my standing there to behold her, and, conjecturing by my foreign Habit who I was, some of them came towards me. I told them by an

Interpreter that I was a Person of a very remote Country, where we had heard by Fame that some Women in *India* love their Husbands so vehemently as when they dye to resolve to dye with them; and that now having intelligence that this Woman was such a one, I was come to see her, that so I might relate in my own Country that I had seen such a thing with my own Eyes. These people were well pleas'd with my coming, and she her self, having heard what I said, rose up from her seat and came to speak to me.

We discours'd together, standing, for a good while. She told me that her name was *Giaccama,* of the Race *Terlenga* [Telinga], that her Husband was a Drummer; whence I wonder'd the more; seeing that Heroical Actions, as this undoubtedly ought to be judg'd, are very rare in people of low quality That it was about nineteen dayes since her Husband's death, that he had left two other Wives elder then she, whom he had married before her, (both which were present at this discourse) yet neither of them was willing to dye, but alledg'd for excuse that they had many Children. This argument gave me occasion to ask *Giaccama,* (who shew'd me a little Son of her own, about six or seven years old, besides a little Daughter she had) how she could perswade her self to leave her own little Children; and I told her, that she ought likewise to live rather than to abandon them at that age. She answer'd me that she left them well recommended to the care of an Uncle of hers there present, who also talk'd with us very cheerfully, as if rejoycing that his Kins-woman should do such an action; and that her Husband's other two remaining Wives would also take care of them. I insisted much upon the tender age of her Children, to avert her from her purpose by moving her to compassion for them, well knowing that no argument is more prevalent with Mothers than their Love and Affection towards their Children. But all my speaking was in vain, and she still answer'd me to all my Reasons, with a Countenance not onely undismay'd and constant, but even cheerful, and spoke in such a manner as shew'd that she had not the least fear of death. She told me also, upon my asking her that she did this of her own accord, was at her own liberty and not forc'd nor perswaded by any one.

Whereupon, I inquiring whether force were at any time us'd in this matter, they told me that ordinarily it was not, but onely sometimes amongst Persons of quality, when some Widow was left young, handsome, and so in danger of marrying again (which amongst them is very ignominious), or committing a worse fault; in such Cases the Friends of the deceas'd Husband, were very strict, and would constrain her to burn her self even against her own will, for preventing the disorders possible to happen in case she should live (a barbarous, indeed, and too cruel Law); but that neither force nor persuasion was used to *Giaccama*, and that she did it of her own free will; in which, as a magnanimous action, (as indeed it was) and amongst them of great honor, both her Relations and herself much glory'd. I ask'd concerning the Ornaments and Flowers she wore, and they told me that such was the Custom, in token of the *Masti's* [maha-sati's] joy (they call the Women, who intends to burn her self for the death of her Husband, *Masti)* in that she, was very shortly, to go to him and therefore had reason to rejoyce; whereas such Widows as will not dye remain in continual sadness and lamentations, shave their Heads and live in perpetual mourning for the death of their Husbands.

At last *Giaccama* caus'd one to tell me that she accounted my coming to see her a great fortune, and held her self much honour'd, as well by my visit and presence as by the Fame which I should Carry of her to my own Country; and that before she dy'd she would come to visit me at my House, and also to ask me, as their custom is, that I would favour her with some thing by way of Alms towards the buying of fewel for the fire wherewith she was to be burnt. I answer'd her that I should esteem her visit and very willingly give her something; not for wood and fire wherein to burn her self, (for her death much displeas'd me, and I would gladly have disswaded her from it, if I could) but to do something else therewith that herself most lik'd; and I promis'd her that, so far as my weak pen could contribute, her Name should remain immortal in the World. Thus I took leave of her, more sad for her death than she was, cursing the custom of *India* which is so unmerciful to Women. *Giaccama* was a Woman of about thirty years of age, of a Complexion very brown for an Indian and almost black, but of a good aspect, tall of stature, well shap'd and proportion'd. My Muse could not forbear from chanting her in a Sonnet which I made upon her death, and reserve among my Poetical Papers.

25. SATI NOT COMMON, REVEREND HENRY LORD IN AD 1624 (NEILL 1984: 376)

...the examples be more rare now than in former times.

26. REV. MADS RASMUSSEN, WHO CAME TO TRANQUEBAR IN 1624, DESCRIBES SATI (OLAFSSON 1932: 136)

In their households all women, who are dwelling in the house of a man as servants, are considered as his wives, but only one of them is the most beloved. And between this most beloved wife and her husband the love is so indissoluble that death cannot separate them, so that when the husband dies, I with my own eyes have seen how a funeral pyre is constructed for the body, whereupon the corpse is laid in the presence of his friends and the heathen priests; and when the corpse has been laid out there, the woman whom he has loved the most when alive jumps into the fire to the corpse, and is burned to ashes together with him. And even if any did wish to protest against this or try to hinder it, she would never consent to live; for any woman who would do so would from that day be considered as one dishonoured, and be despised by all.

27. 'WILLINGLY INCORPORATES HER SELFE WITH FIRE,' SIR THOMAS HERBERT IN AD 1627–28, (BANERJEE 2003: 206)

When Death has cut in two their Union; shee conceits her selfe a loathed carkasse to live after him: she roabs her tender body with a transparent Lawne; her armes, leggs, and thighs, are fettered with wanton chaines of love; her eares, nose, and fingers, adorn'd with Pearles and precious stones; one hand holds choice of flowers; th'other a Ball; Embleams of immortall Paradise. She goes attended with a mighty company; some for love, most for Novelty. The Priest all the way describes the rare joyes she is going to, she grants a modest smile, trips on, and upon sight of the flame, seems transported beyond measure; she sees the carkasse of her Husband layd upon a pyle of pretious wood, and when the fire begins to embrace him, like a mad Lover shee bids Farewell to her Parents, children, and friends, and willingly incorporates her selfe with fire; which quickly makes them one, and nothing: nothing extant save fame, flame, and ashes.

28. SATI IN SURAT, PETER MUNDY IN AD 1628
(MUNDY II 1914: 34-36)

Now before I take leave of Suratt I will relate one accident that happened att my beinge there, whereof I was Eye witnesse, *vizt.* a Banian Woman that voluntarilye burned her selfe alive with the body of here dead husband. The manner of it was as followeth:

A Certaine Banian dieing att Suratt, his wife resolved to burne herselfe alive with the body of her husband, It beinge an ancient Custome used in India, but now not soe much by farr as in former tymes. The Moghull haveinge Conquered their Countrie hath almost abollished that Custome, soe that it may not bee done without speciall lycense from the kinge or Governour of the place where they dwell. This Woman through much importunitie gott leave of the Governour of Suratt to effect her desire.

The Body of her husband was carried to Palparre [Phulpara], which lyes on the River Tapee [Tapti], where are many of their Pagodes or Churches, and great resort thither att severall of their Festivalls. There was it layd att the brink of the river, with his feete and part of his body in the Water. His wife by him, with other women in the said river, stood upp to the middle performinge on themselves certain washinge Ceremonies, for they attribute much holynesse to the great Rivers (especiallie to Ganges) and much of their religion consists in Washinges. In the meane tyme there was readye made the pile or place for the funerall fire, layeing a good quantitie of wood on the floore round about, which were stakes driven in, on which are put a great quantitie of a small kinde drye Thornes and other Combustable stuffe, fashioned like a little lowe house with a doore of the same to it. First the dead body was brought and layd on the said pile, on whome they sett more wood and drye Oxe dung (a great fuell in this Countrie). Then came his wife from the River accompanied with Bramanes (who are their Priests). Then Compassing the Cottage three tymes, shee taketh leave of her Kindred, friends and acquaintance very Cheirefullie, without any shewe of feare or alteration att all, and entreth into it, where sittinge downe, shee taketh her husbands head on her Lapp. The door is presentlie [immediately] shutt upon her, one of her kindred holding a greate pole against it, and others with long poles in their hands to Right the fire if neede bee (or rather I think to knock her downe if shee should chance to gett out). Then shee herselfe with a little torche she carried with her (made of Oyled Lynnen) kindleth it first within, when her friendes without with the like Torches sett it on fire round aboute, which on the suddaine burneth with great violence. The Spectators in the meane tyme makinge all the noyse they can, some with drumms and Countrie Instruments, beateing of brasse platters, Cryeinge or hollwinge, Clapping their hands, all in a Confused manner, while the furie of the flame lasteth. This I conceive is to drowne her voyce if shee should chance to Crye. The sides and upper part of the place was quicklye consumed, yett satt shee upp with life in her, holding upp both her Armes, which might bee occasioned through the scorchinge and shrinckinge of the Sinnewes, for shee held her handes under his head untill the fire was kindled; soe att last not able to sett upp anie Longer, shee fell downe upon her husbands body, when by their friends they were covered with more fuell untill they were both burned to ashes, which presentlie [immediately] is throwne into the river.

29. SATI IN CAMBAY IN 1638, ALBERT DE MANDELSLO (MAJOR 2007: 39-42)

I was soon joined by two of the English merchants at Cambay, who obligingly reproached me with the slur I put on their nation in preferring the house of a Mahometan to their lodge...They proffered me their company to walk and promised to carry me the next morning to a place where an Indian woman was to be burnt of her own consent. The next day the English merchants came to my lodgings, whence we went together to the riverside, outside the city, where this voluntary execution was to be done. The woman's husband was a Rajput and had been killed near Lahore, 200 leagues from Cambay. As soon as she heard of his death, she would needless do his obsequies by causing herself to be burnt alive; but whereas the Mogul and his officers are Mahometans who endeavour by degrees to abolish this heathenish and barbarous custom, the governor had a long time opposed her desires under the pretence of the news of her husband's death being uncertain, he could not consent to doing of the inhuman action, whereof afterwards there would haply be cause to repent. The governor's design was to see whether time would abate anything of her passion, and the earnestness she was in to follow her husband into the other world; but seeing that she was daily more and more insistent to do it, he permitted her to comply with the laws of her religion. She was not above twenty years of age, yet we saw her come to the place of her execution with so much confidence and a cheerfulness so extraordinary to those who go to a present and inevitable death, that I was much inclined to believe that she had dulled her senses with a dose of opium, which is as commonly used in India as in Persia. In front of the procession marched the country music, consisting of haw boys and timdrels. Then followed a great many maids and women, singing and dancing before the widow, who was dressed in her richest clothing, and had her fingers and arms and legs loaded with rings, bracelets, and carkanets. After her came a confused company of men, women, and children, and so concluded the procession. She made a stop at the funeral pile, which had been purposely erected for the ceremony. The woman has washed herself in the river that she might meet her husband in a state of purity, in regard to the body of the deceased being not upon the place she could not accompany it in its passage into the other world. The pile of wood was of apricot trees, among which they had put some sanders and cinnamon. Having looked at it with a certain contempt, she took leave of her kindred and friends, and distributed among them the rings and bracelets about her. I was somewhere near her on horseback with two English merchants, and I think that she perceived in my countenance that I pitied her, whence it came that she cast me one of her bracelets which I had the good hap to catch and still keep in remembrance of so extraordinary an action. As soon as she was got upon the pile, they set fire to it, which she perceiving, poured on her head a vessel of perfumed oil, which the fire immediately taking hold of, she was smothered in an instant, so as she was not perceived to make the least wry face at it. Some that were present caste upon her several cruses of oil, which soon reduced the body to ashes, while the rest of the assembly filled the air with their cries and shouts, such as must needless have hindered those of the widow to be heard, if she had the time to make any in the fire which had made a sudden dispatch of her as if it had been lightning. The ashes were cast into the river...

30. GOVERNOR'S PERMISSION REQUIRED FOR IMMOLATION, JEAN-BAPTISTE TAVERNIER IN AD 1640 (TAVERNIER BOOK III 2000: 163-65)

...it should be remarked that a woman cannot burn herself with the body of her husband without having received permission from the Governor of the place where she dwells, and those Governors who are Musalmans, hold this dreadful custom of self-destruction in horror, and do not readily give permission. On the other hand, it is only childless widows who can be reproached for not having loved their husbands if they have not had courage to burn themselves after their death, and to whom this want of courage will be for the remainder of their lives a cause of reproach. For widows who have children are not permitted under any circumstances to burn themselves with the bodies of their husbands; and so far from custom obliging them, it is ordained that they shall live to watch over the education of their children. Those to whom the Governors peremptorily refuse to grant permission to burn themselves pass the remainder of their lives in severe penances and in doing charitable deeds...

The Governor, seeing that all the remonstrance's with women, who are urged to burn themselves even by their relatives and by the Brahmans, fail to turn them from the damnable resolution which they have taken to die in so cruel a fashion, when his secretary indicates by a sign that he has received a bribe, at length allows them to do what they wish, and in a rage tells all the idolaters who accompany them that they may 'go to the devil.'...

SATI BY THE WIDOWS OF RAMA RAYA OF VIJAYANAGAR, TAVERNIER (TAVERNIER BOOK III 2000: 170)

The Raja of Vellore [Rama Raja of Vijayanagar], of whom I have spoken in the first book of this account of India, having at the same time lost both this town and his life by the victory which the General of the King of Bijapur gained over him, there was great mourning in all his Court. Eleven of the women of his household were keenly affected by his death, and all resolved to burn themselves when his body was burnt. The General of the Bijapur army having heard of this resolve, thought that he would be able to dissuade these desperate women by flattering them, and promising them all kinds of good treatment. But seeing that this was of no effect, and that they were absolutely determined to be burnt with the body of the deceased, he directed that they should be kept shut up in a room. He who received this order, on going to execute it, was told by the infuriated women that it was in vain, that he might do his best, but that it was useless to keep them prisoners, and that if they were not allowed to do what they wished, they had resolved that in three hours there would not be one of them left alive. He jeered at this threat, and would not believe that it could be carried into effect. But the officer in charge of the women, on opening the door at the end of three hours, found the eleven all dead and stretched on the ground, without any apparent indications that they had hastened their deaths, either by steel, rope, or poison, nor could anyone see how they had been able to make away with themselves. On this occasion it was assuredly the case that the evil spirit had played his game....

31. CREMATION AND SATI AMONG BRAHMINS, NICCOLAO MANUCCI (1656–1717), (MANUCCI III 1990: 57-58)

... After a husband's (a Brahman) death, a widow adopts one of four courses. Those most sprightly and vigorous burn alive with the corpse of the defunct husband. This is carried out as follows:

Wood is heaped up to a height of eight or nine feet, and about the same length and breadth. Upon the top the corpse of the dead Brahman is laid, dressed as when alive, the head to the south and the feet to the north. After he has been laid thus on the bonfire, there comes the wise man of the village and pronounces certain magic words at the five organs of sense, and anoints them with butter. The anointing done, the parents and the nearest relations throw four or five grains of uncooked rice into his mouth.

When these ceremonies are finished they turn the body over on *its* side. As they do so the widow without tears – nay, on the contrary, all radiant and joyous—mounts to the top of the pyre, and lying down on her side, closely embraces her dead husband. At once the relations bind her feet strongly by two ropes to two posts driven into the ground for the purpose. Next they throw some more wood and dried cow dung on the two bodies; the quantity is almost as much as that beneath them. The woman is then spoken to by her name, and three times distinctly she is called on to say whether she consents to go to heaven. To this she replies in the affirmative. Her answers having been received, they apply a light, and when the bodies have been consumed, each man returns home envying the firmness and constancy which the woman has been granted the felicity of displaying... in the Brahman caste, where there ought doubtless to be something good, one meets with nothing that is not entirely evil.

SATI AMONG RAJAHS FOR HONOUR, MANUCCI (MANUCCI III 1990: 62-65)

Among the caste of Rajahs it is imperative that on the husband's death the wife be burnt alive with his body, for should regard for her own honour even not force her to this act, the relations will force her to it, it being an inviolate custom of their caste. It is so whether the husband die at home of disease or of wounds upon the field of battle...

Be this as it may, no sooner has news of a Rajah's death arrived in his country, and the wife is satisfied that he no longer lives, than she is accorded three days of grace. During those days she is permitted to adorn herself as magnificently as she can; and thus arrayed she goes about the streets with lemons tied round her head like a crown; her body is uncovered from the waist upwards, and rubbed over with saffron, as also is her face. In this state she takes leave of all those she meets in the streets with a smiling face and free manners, and speeches repugnant to her sex and her claim to nobility.

When the three days have passed, they prepare in an open field a circular pit, deep and wide, which is filled with wood and cow dung. Fire is then applied. On beholding this pyre, she who is to be the victim of her honour, issues, clad in new attire, covered with divers coloured flowers, some arranged like crowns, others like necklaces. Escorted by all her friend, male and female, she approaches the fire. Before it stand a small screen about five feet high. Over its top they throw into the fire a little saffron and some butter and other spices. After prayers have been recited the heroine withdraws about forty paces and returns two times, one after the other, to the place she started from, and each time performs the same ceremonial. At length she retires for the third time some forty paces farther than before; at that moment the screen before the fire is withdrawn. Then, with a rush, she bounds into the pit, and in a short time there is nothing left her ashes to furnish an epitaph on her constancy.

The Hindus think so highly of those who are burnt in this way that they assert their reincarnation as goddesses in the heaven of Vishnu; and in that quality there are erected to them statues as soon as they are dead. This is done equally for the husband (the man's cenotaph is called *chhatri*). They assume that men blessed with wives of such great virtue as to sacrifice life for their honour, must without fail be placed among the gods.

But if any wife is found to have greater love of life than of honour, her relations do not leave her to enjoy it for very long, for they throw her into the fire by force, where she ends by undergoing the same suffering without acquiring the same laudations. Thus it is much better for them to endure this hard penalty with firmness and equanimity than to be subjected to it by the violence of others.

SATI OBSERVED AT VIZAGAPATAM (MANUCCI I 1990: 147-49)

It is wonderful to see what is done when any Hindu rajas or prince expires. Before he is taken away to be burnt they shave his head, his beard, and his whole body, anointing it with essence of roses, binding it up in fine cloth all smeared with different jasmine oils mixed with saffron. The body is laid upon laths of sandal and aloes wood, bound together in the shape of an open bier. The women who are to be burnt with him follow; they are women with whom the rajah had lived. The principal wife who has sons is preserved, with the idea of maintaining the family line. The women sacrificed are commonly fifteen, twenty, or even thirty in number, as I have seen at various times.

It is a memorable thing to see these women on horseback surrounding the corpse, and calling out thousands of praises of their husband, the good life he led, and the pleasures he enjoyed here below. Feeling under an obligation for so many favours received, they look forward in the next life to receive still greater delight in his society there. All this is carried out with much joy and animation, they being richly clad, oiled, and perfumed.

Reaching the place of death, they descend gracefully from their steeds, and assist in lifting the bier on to the heap of wood. This stands in a pit. The principal wife among them places herself on one side, embracing the corpse and uttering innumerable praises; the others range themselves round the body in the same way. The burners set fire to the wood all round, and dexterously empty on it pots of oil and butter to increase the rapidity of the cremation. When the fire has taken they throw on more oil, and when the heat reaches them the women naturally move and begin to shriek. They are soon choked by the smoke, while the men surrounding the pyre raise a great noise with drums and gongs and loud shouts, while the burners skilfully force them to lie down by thrusting at them with poles. Thus are they burnt both for this life and the next.

The next day the Brahman and many relations go to the spot and collect the bones, and send them to be thrown into the Ganges river, whatever the distance may be. Some people out of piety send them to be thrown in the river at the *Tirth* (place of pilgrimage), of which I have spoken (II. 58), flowing below the fortress of Allahabad. If such princes die in battle, the women immolate themselves with still greater alacrity on receiving the turban sent them as a sign of their husband's death. With it in their hands they are cremated. I have seen some die with their husband's body in their arms without making a sign of movement. The reason is that the Brahmans provide them with certain beverages — *bhang* (hemp), opium, and such like, which entirely stupefy them.

Others, by use of sorcery, become eager, ardent, mad, demanding that the authorities put no hindrance in their way when in search of their beloved, alleging as a reason that they are suffering acutely from deprivation of their loved one. This happened at Vizagapatao (*visakha+ patanam* so named from a temple to Visakha, the sage, which once stood there) at the time when Mestre Olca (Mr. Holcombe, Deputy – Governor of Vizagapatam) governed it. He refused permission for the burning of some woman of this sort. She appeared in his presence, and with great anxiety prayed to him to set no impediment to what was her desire. Mr. Holcombe and the rest of those present noticed that she seemed to have abandoned her feminine nature. He entreated her in the cause of humanity, and offered her the good advice not to give herself up to die by burning. He undertook to support her for the rest of her life. This talk caused her pain, and she persisted in demanding permission. Mr. Holcombe, seeing he could not stop her, spoke secretly to a Brahman who was with her, promising him a sum of money if he removed the apprehensions that possessed the woman. If he did not effect this he would have to burn alongside of her, and also the rest of the Brahmans who had come with her. Saying this, he sent orders to close the factory gates as if quite ready to act. The Brahmans, not to lose the money, and not to put their own lives in danger, went behind the woman without her being aware of it, and gently touched her clothes at the back with their fingers. She totally changed colour, and. raising her hands to her face, and drooping her head in a shamefaced way, went back to her house.

32. SOME INSTANCES OF SATI WITNESSED, FRANCOIS BERNIER (1658–1667), (BERNIER 1994: 309-15)

In regard to the women who actually burn themselves, I was present at so many of those shocking exhibitions that I could not persuade myself to attend any more, nor is it without a feeling of horror that I revert to the subject. I shall endeavour, nevertheless, to describe what passed before my eyes; but I cannot hope to give you an adequate conception of the fortitude displayed by these infatuated victims during the whole of the frightful tragedy: it must be seen to be believed.

a. When travelling from *Ahmed-abad* to *Agra,* through the territories of *Rajas,* and while the caravan halted under the shade of a banyan-tree until the cool of the evening, news reached us that a widow was then on the point of burning herself with the body of her husband. I ran at once to the spot, and going to the edge of a large and nearly dry reservoir, observed at the bottom a deep pit filled with wood: the body of a dead man extended thereon; a woman seated upon the same pile; four or five *Brahmens* setting fire to it in every part; five middle-aged women, tolerably well dressed, holding one another by the hand, singing and dancing round the pit; and a great number of spectators of both sexes.

The pile, whereon large quantities of butter [ghee] and oil had been thrown, was soon enveloped in flames, and I saw the fire catch the woman's garments, which were impregnated with scented oil, mixed with sandalwood powder and saffron; but I could not perceive the slightest indication of pain or even uneasiness in the victim, and it was said that she pronounced with emphasis the words *five, two,* to signify that this being the fifth time she had burned herself with the same husband, there were wanted only two more similar sacrifices to render her perfect, according to the doctrine of the transmigration of souls: as if a certain reminiscence, or prophetic spirit, had been imparted to her at that moment of her dissolution.

But this was only the commencement of the infernal tragedy. I thought that the singing and dancing of the five women were nothing more than some unmeaning ceremony; great therefore was my astonishment when I saw that the flames having ignited the clothes of one of these females, she cast herself head-foremost into the pit. The horrid example was followed by another woman, as soon as the flames caught her person: the three women who remained then took hold of each other by the hand, resuming the dance with perfect composure; and after a short lapse of time, they also precipitated themselves, one after the other, into the fire.

I soon learnt the meaning of these multiplied sacrifices. The five women were slaves, and having witnessed the deep affliction of their mistress in consequence of the illness of her husband, whom she promised not to survive, they were so moved with compassion that they entered into an engagement to perish by the same flames that consumed their beloved mistress...

b. As I was leaving *Sourate* for *Persia,* I witnessed the devotion and burning of another widow: several Englishmen and Dutchmen and Monsieur *Chardin* of *Paris* [the celebrated traveler] were present. She was of the middle age, and by no means uncomely. I do not expect, with my limited powers of expression, to convey a full idea of the brutish boldness, or ferocious gaiety depicted on this woman's countenance; of her undaunted step; of the freedom from all perturbation with which she conversed, and permitted herself to be washed; of the look of confidence, or rather of insensibility which she cast upon us; of her easy air, free from dejection; of her lofty carriage, void of embarrassment, when she was examining her little cabin, composed of dry and thick millet straw, with an intermixture of small wood; when she entered into that cabin, sat down upon the funeral pile, placed her deceased husband's head in her lap, took up a torch, and with her own hand lighted the fire within, while I know not how many *Brahmens* were busily engaged in kindling it without...

c. It is true, however, that I have known some of these unhappy widows shrink at the sight of the piled wood; so as to leave no doubt on my mind that they would willingly have recanted, if recantation had been permitted by the merciless *Brahmens;* but those demons excite or astound the affrighted victims, and even thrust them into the fire. I was present when a poor young woman, who had fallen back five or six paces from the pit, was thus driven forward; and I saw another of these wretched beings struggling to leave the funeral pile when the fire increased around her person, but she was prevented from escaping by the long poles of the diabolical executioners...

d. At *Lahor* I saw a most beautiful young widow sacrificed, who could not, I think, have been more than twelve years of age. The poor little creature appeared more dead than alive when she approached the dreadful pit: the agony of her mind cannot be described; she trembled and wept bitterly; but three or four of the *Brahmens,* assisted by an old woman who held her under the arm, forced the unwilling victim toward the fatal spot, seated her on the wood, tied her hands and feet, lest she should run away, and in that situation the innocent creature was burnt alive. I found it difficult to repress my feelings and to prevent their bursting forth into clamorous and unavailing rage; but restrained by prudential considerations...

33. SATI IN SOUTH INDIA, JON OLAFSSON, THE ICELANDER, WHO CAME IN THE MID-SEVENTEENTH CENTURY (OLAFFSON 1932: 135-36)

...During our sojourn one such woman allowed herself to be burned alive with her husband. She went with great joy and much music and laid herself in the arms of her dead husband, embracing him, and a multitude of married women bore her company to the beating of drums and the sound of trumpets. The wife of one merchant in the town was with difficulty hindered from being burned by the firm intervention of our officers, for all cases which occurred in the town were brought up before the court in the fortress, where they had to be dealt with, adjudged and decided upon, according to the royal command. The other kind of woman, who received leave to be burned, if she so desired, was the woman who had no children. Otherwise it was not permitted that any should burn.

34. SATI, JEAN DE THEVENOT IN AD 1666–1667 (THEVENOT 1949: 79; 119-20)

IN KANDHAR

The King of *Persia* suffers not the Gentiles Wives there to burn themselves when their Husbands are dead.

WIDOWHOOD

The *Indian* Wives have a far different fate from that of their Husbands, for they cannot provide themselves of a second, when their first Husband is dead; they dare not Marry again, they have their Hair cut off for ever after; and though they be but five or six years old (they are obliged) if they will not burn themselves, to live in perpetual Widowhood, which happens very often... it is rare (though they be young and beautiful), that they ever find another Husband; not but that some of them transgress the Law of Widowhood, but they are turned out of the Tribe when it comes to be known; and such of them as are resolved to Marry again, have recourse to the Christians or Mahometans, and then they forsake Gentilisme. In fine, the Gentiles make the glory of Widowhood, to consist in being burnt with the Bodies of their Husbands (sati); when one asks them the cause of it, they say it is the custom; they pretend it was always so in the Indies, and so they hide their cruel Jealousie under the vail of Antiquity...

35. THE SPANISH MISSIONARY, DOMIMGO NAVARRETE, IN 1670 (NAVARRETE 1960: 335)

Not many Years since, as they were carrying a Woman at Rogiapuy [Rajapur] near Goa to be burnt with her Husband, it hapned that some Portugueses who came to that part seeing the Train, had the Curiosity to draw near; the Woman seeing them left her People, and running embraced one of them, begging they would protect her. They did it very handsomely, defended themselves against the Infidels, and carry'd her off. She went to Goa, was instructed, baptiz'd, and marry'd to him she had fled to. She was living in the Year 1670, when I was at Goa. A most fortunate Woman!

36. THE ENGLISHMAN, THOMAS BOWREY, SAW A WIDOW BURNING IN SOUTH INDIA IN 1672 (BANERJEE 2003: 190; 205)

... I could discerne the body of a man on a light fire neare to which lay much combustible matter piled round, hollow in the middle, which they Soon Set fire to, and then most of the crowde did separate themselves, standinge round it at 2 or 3 yards diatance...

I rode close up to the younge woman, who was Seemingly Extraordinary chearefull. I asked her the reason why she was soe deluded by the Brachmans, who overhearinge me Seemed to be angry, but She e're they had time to Speake, Smiled and Said it was the happiest houre that Ever She Saw. She Spake something quick, which Shewd great desperateness in her, and without all controversie these Satyrical Priests give them something to intoxicate...

This Silly Creature, with a most chearefull Smilelinge countenance, lift up her hands, and accordinge to the country compliments, Salam'd to all her friends, especially to the Brachmans, and lookeinge earnestly upon me, gave me some white and yellow flowers she tooke from her haire of her head that was beautifully adorned after the Gentue fashion, and with Strange nimblenesse Sprange into the fire.

37. SATI, JOHN FRYER, SURGEON OF THE EAST INDIA COMPANY (1672–1681) (FRYER I 1992: 95-96)

[From Fort St. George] ... the *Gentues* burn them [the dead]; and in the Husband's Flames the Wife offers her self a Sacrifice to his *Manes*, or else she shaves and turns Whore for a Livelihood, none of her Friends looking upon her; hers, not her Husband's Acquaintance, thrusting her upon it; to which end they give her *Dutry*; when half mad she throws her self into the Fire, and they ready with great Logs keep her in his Funeral Pile.

SATI AT SURAT (FRYER I 1992: 256)

Here are many Monuments of their misled Zeal; the most dreadful to remember, is an extraordinary one erected by the River side, where they Burn their Dead in Honour of a Woman who Burnt her self with her dead Husband. Several Corps were Flaming in their Funeral Piles; which after the Fire has satisfied its self with, they cast the Ashes up into the Air, and some upon the Water; that every Element mat have a share.

SATI IN THE CANATICK-COUNTRY (FRYER II 1992: 18)

We went next day to the Governor, who Complimented us highly; he is under the Tyrannical Government of *Seva Gi*, where all Barbarous Customs are exercised; and here it is permitted the Women not only to burn with their dead Husbands, but here are many Monuments raised in honour of them.

SATIS IN EAST INDIA (FRYER II 1992: 117)

Those that have Buried their Husbands (or rather Burnt them) are rifled of all their Jewels, and Shaved, always wearing a Red *Lungy* [among the Sravak Vanyas of Gujarat], whereby to be known that they have not undergone the Conflagration; for which cause they are despised, and live more Uncomfortably than the meanest Servant.

38. SATI AT MADRAS, ABBE CARRE (1672–1674) (ABBE CARRE 1990: 592-93)

The Hindus celebrated the funeral of one of their principal men with great ceremonies and a profusion of different kinds of exquisite liquors [? liquors are not mentioned by other observers]; which were poured on the pyre. The wretched corpse was accompanied by one of his wives to a cruel death. She threw herself into the middle of the blazing flames, and while the two were being burnt, all the caste mourners gave vent to howls and an appalling uproar round the fire, with strange ceremonies and superstitions...On the death of one of their caste, his principal wife is not obliged to die by burning herself alive with him, if she has had children or had passed the age of thirty-five years.

39. SATI IN GUJARAT, FATHER VINCENZO IN 1678 (WEINBERGER-THOMAS 2000: 50)

In the States governed by Mohametans, it is rare that the permission [to burn oneself] be accorded: nevertheless, some women, in order to conform to sacred law and show themselves more faithful to their spouses, still purchase for a certain price the authorization to do so from the Governors. When I was in Suratte [in Gujarat], one of them requested this and when it was denied her, the woman let it be known to the Divan that she would burn herself in her own house, since she could not bear to live with such a reputation for infidelity. Others, condemned to perpetual widowhood, wear fiery red clothing for the rest of their days, as a sign of the debt they have incurred.

In the States in which Gentile [Hindu] Princes reign, above all in the Canara country [in Karnataka], it is common practice to burn widows...

40. WIDOW IMMOLATION NOT WIDELY PRACTICED; SATI AT PONDICHERRY, FRANCOIS MARTIN IN 1680s (MARTIN 1984 VOL. II PART I: 1154–56)

Those who have read works on India must be well aware of the fact that among some Hindu communities it is customary for the widow to immolate herself with the body of her dead husband. This custom, more social than religious, which at one time had the force of law, is not very widely practiced now. With the exception of the wives of important people who are forced to comply with custom, other women are allowed a choice. It is true that those who refuse to burn themselves live out the rest of their lives like slaves in misery.

They have to live in the homes of their defunct husbands, serving the kinspeople of the latter with shaven heads and arms forever bereft of all jewelry. If a woman refuses to burn herself, her refusal is regarded as a stain on family honour and she is abhorred thereafter. A Brahmin who at one time had enjoyed an important position in the army but who had since been reduced to a lowly state as a result of the recent wars had taken up residence at Pondicherry. He was seventy years old and died very suddenly. His wife, aged forty-five, a woman who was greatly respected by the community, got ready to burn herself along with her husband. When I heard of this, I sent some messengers to her to dissuade her from engaging on such a step. I even offered to provide her with everything she needed for the rest of her life so that she would not want for anything. She thanked me but told me very plainly that she had nothing to live for after the death of her husband, and to remain among the living was itself a punishment for her. I tried again to dissuade her and after several attempts she informed me that if I persisted she would first cut out her tongue with her teeth and send it to me and then plunge herself head first into a tank. We left her alone as it seemed impossible to sway her from her purpose. The resolution of this woman was really astonishing. While they prepared the pyre before her, she told her friends how happy she would be to rejoin her husband. After the pyre had been erected according to their custom, she went around it three times never once faltering in her movement or changing in her demeanour. She then took leave of all the people who had come for the ceremony and gave away her few possessions to those who were the dearest to her. She mounted the pyre unassisted and lay down beside her dead husband. The fire was then lit against the wind and since the wood was green and wet (it was the rainy season) there was more smoke than flame. The woman with a courage which defies imagination, knew that they were not lighting the pyre in the proper way. She asked the Brahmins to light the flame on the other side so that it would spread quickly because of the wind. Her advice was followed and the entire pyre rose up in flames with the addition of combustible materials which were thrown on it. The two bodies were reduced to cinders without a single cry having been heard from this woman. I cannot explain this resolution and can only attribute it to force of custom. This practice, however, is not as rigidly adhered to now as it used to be in previous times. The Emperor has abolished this practice in his territory but sometimes those who wish to perform it manage to get their way by giving presents. The more avaricious officials even tolerate this custom. Many historians and others are of the opinion that the women who wish to perform this action are given some beverage or drug which disturbs their equilibrium and so stimulates their imagination that they are no longer aware of the horror and pain of such a terrible death. Under ordinary circumstances even the thought of such a death which is reserved as a punishment only for the most horrendous of crimes, is enough to make one shudder. I can say quite truthfully that with regard to the woman who burnt herself now and of one other whom I prevented from so doing several years ago, the reason advanced by them for taking this supreme step were extremely worthy. The calm and unfettered spirit, the serenity of expression and the complete sense of dedication with which these women go to their death can only be condemned by tenets of a religion such as ours.

41. SATI IN SURAT, J. OVINGTON IN AD 1689 (OVINGTON 1994: 201)

... the loving Husband inamour'd with his kind or beautiful Wife, would sometimes burn himself with her in the Funeral Pile, in expectation of a happy future Enjoyment of her. But this was seldom. For it generally fell to the Wives lot to be committed to the Flames with the dead Husband. And this Heathenish Custom was introduc'd, because of the libidinous disposition of the Women, who thro' their inordinate Lust would often poison their Husbands, to make way for a new Lover. This was so far incouraged by the

Politick *Bramin*, who was always a Gainer by her Death; that if any Woman refus'd to burn, her Head was order'd presently to be shav'd, that she might appear Contemptible and Infamous for ever after. For all the Jewels she put on, who deckt her Body for the Flames, when she was resolv'd to die, were carefully lookt after by the Priest, and made his Propriety after her Death; because he only had power to touch the Ashes, and rake therein for Gold and Silver.

Since the *Mahometans* became Masters of the *Indies*, this execrable Custom is much abated, and almost laid aside, by the Orders which the *Nabobs* receive for suppressing and extinguishing it in all their Provinces. And now it is very rare, except it be some *Rajahs* Wives, that the *Indian* Women burn at all; and those that do, obtain the liberty by costly Presents and powerful Applications to the Governours; by which Women who are forc'd to survive their Husbands by a superiour Authority, evade that Ignominy and Contempt which would otherwise be cast upon them.

42. ALEXANDER HAMILTON, A FREE-TRADER WHO TOURED THE EAST INDIES FROM 1688 TO 1723, DESCRIBED AN INCIDENT INVOLVING JOB CHARNOCK, FOUNDER OF CALCUTTA (WHO DIED IN 1693), (HAMILTON II 1744: 8-9)

Mr. Channoch went one Time ... to see a young widow act that tragic catastrophe, but he was so smitten with the widow's beauty, that he sent his Guards to take her by force from the Executioners, and conducted her to his own lodgings. They lived lovingly many years, and had several children, at length she died, after he had settled in Calcutta, but instead of converting her to Christianity, she made him a Proselyte to Paganism, and the only Part of Christianity that was remarkable in him, was burying her decently, and he built a Tomb over her, where all his Life after her Death, he kept the anniversary Day of her Death by sacrificing a Cock on her Tomb, after the Pagan manner.

43. SATI, GIOVANNI CARERI IN AD 1695
(THEVENOT AND CARERI 1949: 211-12)

Monday 7th, I saw the dismal Spectacle of a wretched *Pagan* Woman, the Kindred of her dead Husband had obtain'd at the Price of great Presents from the *Suba,* to be Burn'd with the dead Body, according to their wicked unmerciful Custom. In the Afternoon the Woman came out well Clad, and adorn'd with Jewels, as if she had gone to be Marry'd, with Musick Playing, and Singing. She was attended by the Kindred of both Sexes, Friends, and *Brachman* Priests. Being come to the Place appointed, she went about undaunted, taking Leave of them all; after which she was laid all along, with her Head on a Block, in a Cottage twelve Spans square, made of small Wood wet with Oil, but bound to a Stake, that she might not run away with the fright of the Fire. Lying in this Posture, chewing *Betelle,* she asked of the Standers by, whether they had any Business by her to the other World; and having received several Gifts, and Letters from those Ignorant People, to carry to their dead Friends, she wrapp'd them up in a Cloth. This done, the *Brachman,* who had been Encouraging of her, came out of the Hut, and caus'd it to be Fir'd; the Friends pouring Vessels of Oil on her, that she might be the sooner reduc'd to Ashes, and out of Pain. *Francis de Miranda* told me, That as soon, as the Fire was out, the *Brachmans* would go gather all the melted Gold, Silver, and Copper. This Barbarous Action was perform'd a Mile from *Ponda*.

3

AD 1700–1799

1.FRENCH EDITOR, BERNARD PICART, IN 1733, ARGUED THAT THE DESIRE FOR FAME WAS THE MOTIVATING FACTOR (MAJOR 2006: 83; 88)

... the Indies afford us a thousand instances of the like nature in favour of the weaker sex, who are so fickle and inconstant that in one and the same moment almost, they'll be all fondness and all disdain? 'Tis not therefore a sincere and unaffected conjugal love; for were that the case the women of other countries would in that respect by far excel them. 'Tis ambition, a thirst after glory, that prompts them to this compliance. Their law has inseparably connected these two irresistible inducements with this inhuman sacrifice...

2. JOHN MACDONALD, A FOOTMAN WHO TRAVELLED FROM 1745 TO 1779, STATED THAT THE WIDOW IMMOLATED 'TO OBTAIN HEAVEN AND GOD'S FAVOUR' (MAJOR 2006: 42)

... why should I think this woman has done wrong? She has done this to obtain heaven and God's favour; and have not the greatest and most learned men in England and other

Christian countries done the same, who had the Bible to
direct them?

3. ABBE DE GUYON, IN 1757, ON THE INDIFFERENCE TO DEATH (DE GUYON 1757: 57-58)

Among all these customs there are few which do not resound
to the praise of the Indians; but the sentiments some of them
entertained to death cannot be excused. They look upon it
with such indifference as must be a shock to nature ... This
practice is founded on their notions of the metempsychosis,
which passes among them as an undoubted truth...

If we believe the ancients, they themselves had given
occasion to this cruel alternative. It had been found, that
many were so cruel as to poison their husbands in the hope
of espousing others. The necessity there was to put a stop to
an abuse, which began to grow as common as it was
enormous, occasioned the magistrates to make an order that
every woman who survived her husband should be obliged
to follow him to the pile. Thus what in its original was only
a testimony of friendship or greatness of soul, became
afterwards an inviolable law; and is at this day an article of
religion.

4. JOHN HENRY GROSE, IN 1757, REFUTED ALLEGATIONS AGAINST HINDU WOMEN (GROSE 1757: 144-45, 308)

... an over refinement of conjecture, as false as it is injurious
to the women of this country, no such practice [of poisoning
their husbands] being either attested by creditable tradition,
or warranted by the behaviour of the other Indian women
not subject to this custom, who are generally of a mould of
mind too soft and tender to incur even the suspicion of such
a detestable barbarity.

... Another reason too for their prodigious affection and
veneration for their husbands, is their early marriage... After
which, the parties, in the tenderness of that ductile age, are
bought up until that of consummation, in the constant
inculcation to them of mutual dearness, as a sacred point of

religion. And the women especially entertain such a strong impression of this doctrine, that, notwithstanding the influence of a climate far from favourable to chastity, instances of infidelity are at least as rare among them as in any people of the world besides.

5. LUKE SCRAFTON EXPRESSED HIGH OPINION ON THE CHARACTER OF HINDU WOMEN (SCRAFTON 1763: 9)

... no women are more remarkable for their conjugal fidelity, in which they are distinguished beyond the rest of their sex, by that remarkable custom of burning with their husband.

...Let it be considered, they are brought up together from their infancy; the woman has no opportunity of ever conversing with any other man; her affections are centred solely on this one object of her love; she is firmly persuaded that by being burnt with him, she shall be happy with him in another world; that if she neglects this last token of affection, he may take another wife, and she be separated from him forever. However false these principles, yet, if those poor women are persuaded that they are true, you must allow that they are powerful motives.

6. 'EXTREME LOVE OF SOME WOMEN FOR THEIR HUSBAND,' FRENCH ORIENTALIST, PIERRE SONNERAT (MAJOR 2006: 87; 94; 79; 98)

... The Brahmins encourage her to sacrifice herself with assurances that she is going to enjoy eternal felicity in paradise, where she will become the wife of some god, who will espouse her as a reward for her virtue. They further promise her that her name shall be celebrated throughout the earth, and sung in all their sacrifices, which is still a further inducement for some women to burn themselves; as there is no legal obligation.

To dispose them for this heroic, or rather insane, action, the Brahmins make use of beverages mixed with opium; and it is thus they animate and inflame the unhappy victim of conjugal fidelity...

...however extravagant and atrocious this custom may appear, it is easy to give a reason for it. The extreme love of some women for their husband, the despair at their loss, and the desire to follow them, was the first cause of this sacrifice, which custom authorized and time made universal...

7. SATI, IN 1758, AT ENTRANCE TO THE CITY OF PONIN [PUNE], ANQUETIL-DUPERRON WHO VISITED INDIA FROM 1755 TO 1761 (ROSE 1990: 24)

The next day, at the entrance to the city, opposite Vagholi village, Anquetil saw the strangest sight of his life: "It was a young Maratha woman," he writes, "whom the tyranny of custom was forcing to burn herself on her husband's funeral pyre...But (I don't know whether what I have to state will be believed) I noticed that in these countries, despite their devotion to the senses and to what is most extreme in them, life is given up with greater ease than in our climes." What is amazing about this story is not that it was a figment of Anquetil's imagination but that, in a note scribbled much later in the margin of the printed copy of his work, he acknowledged his lie. "I was not present at this barbaric if religious ceremony...I added that line to be freed of the thousand and one questions I was asked on the country's customs; in this I failed to tell the truth." In those times, a traveller returning from India had to narrate at least one incident of sati to prove his credibility!

8. SATI MAINLY AMONG BANIAS, *A VOYAGE TO CALCUTTA IN 1761,* AUTHOR UNKNOWN (NAIR 1984: 134-35)

... this custom is observed by the better sort only: it prevails most among the Banyans, who are commonly merchants. I have often discoursed with the Banyans, on this subject; and they told me, as it was an injunction of their Bramenies or priests from time immemorial, they thought themselves obliged to follow the example of their father in this as well as everything else.

9. JOHN ZEPHANIAH HOLWELL, BRIEFLY GOVERNOR OF BENGAL, IN 1767 ON THE REASONS FOR WIDOW IMMOLATION (MARSHALL 1970: 91-96)

Although we have already shewn that the bloody sacrifices of the ancients was no part of the Gentoo tenets, yet there subsists amongst them at this day, a voluntary sacrifice, of too singular a nature, to pass by us unnoticed; the rather as it has been frequently mentioned of various authors, without we conceive that knowledge and perspicuity which the matter calls for; the sacrifice we allude to, is the Gentoo wives burning with the bodies of their deceased husbands. We have taken no small pains to investigate this seeming cruel custom, and hope we shall be able to throw same satisfactory lights on this very extraordinary subject, which has hitherto been hid in obscurity; in order to which we will first remove one or two obstructions that lie in our way, and hinder our nearer and more perfect view of it.

The cause commonly assigned for the origin of this sacrifice (peculiar to the wives of this nation) is, that it was a law constituted to put a period to a wicked practice that the Gentoos' wives had of poisoning their husbands; for this assertion we cannot trace the smallest semblance of truth, and indeed the known fact, that the sacrifice must be voluntary, of its self refutes that common mistake. It also has been a received opinion, that if the wife refuses to burn, she loses her cast (or tribe) and is stamped with disgrace and infamy, an opinion equally void of foundation in fact as the other. The real state of this case is thus circumstanced. The first wife (for the Gentoo laws allow bigamy, although they frequently do not benefit themselves of the indulgence, if they have issue of the first) has it in her choice to burn, but is not permitted to declare her resolution before twenty-four hours after the decease of her husband; if she refuses, the right devolves to the second, if either, after the expiration of twenty-four hours, publicly declare, before the Bramins and witnesses, their resolution to burn, they cannot then retract. If they both refuse at the expiration of that term, the worst consequence that attends their refusal, is lying under the imputation of being wanting to their own honor, purification, and the prosperity of their family, for from their infancy, they are instructed of the household Bramin to look upon this catastrophe, as most glorious to themselves, and beneficial to their children: the truth is, that the children of the wife who burns, become thereof, illustrious, and are sought after in marriage of the most opulent and honourable of their cast, and sometimes received into a cast superiour to their own.

That the Bramins take unwearied pains to encourage, promote, and confirm in the minds of the Gentoo wives, this spirit of burning, is certain (their motives for it, the penetration of our readers may by and by probably discover) and although they seldom lose their labor, yet instances happen, where fear, or love of life, sets at nought all their preaching; for it sometimes falls out that the first wife refuses, and the second burns; at others, they both refuse; and as but one can burn, it so happens, that when the second wife has issue by the deceased, and the first none, there commonly ensues a violent contention between them, which of the two shall make the sacrifice; but this dispute is generally determined by the Bramins, in favor of the first, unless she is prevailed on by perswasion, or other motives to wave her right, in favor of the second. Having elucidated these matters, we will proceed to give our readers the best account, we have been able to obtain of the origin of this remarkable custom ...

When people have lived together to an advanced age, in mutual acts of confidence, friendship and affection; the sacrifice a Gentoo widow makes of her person (under such an affecting circumstance as the loss of friend and husband) seems less an object of wonder; but when we see women in the bloom of youth, and beauty, in the calm possession of their reason and understanding, with astonishing fortitude, set at nought, the tender considerations of parents, children, friends, and the horror and torments of the death they court, we cannot resist viewing such an act, and such a victim, with tears of commiseration, awe and reverence.

We have been present at many of these sacrifices: in some of the victims, we have observed a pitiable dread, tremor, and reluctance, that strongly spoke repentance for their declared resolution; but it was now too late to retract, or retreat; Bistnoo was waiting for the spirit. If the self doomed victim discovers want of courage and fortitude, she is with gentle force obliged to ascend the pile, where she is held down with long poles, held by men on each side of the pile, until the flames reach her; her screams and cries, in the mean time, being drowned amidst the deafening noise of loud musick, and the acclamations of the multitude. Others we have seen go through this fiery trial, with most amazing steady, calm, resolution, and joyous fortitude. It will not we hope be unacceptable, if we present our readers with an instance of the latter, which happened some years past at the East India Company's factory at Cossimbuzaar in the time of Sir Francis Russell's chiefship, the author, and several other gentlemen of the factory were present, some of whom are now living: from a narrative, which the author then transmitted to England he is now enabled to give the particulars of this most remarkable proof of female fortitude, and constancy.

SATI IN KASIMBAZAR

"At five of the clock on the morning of the 4th of February, 1742–3, died Rhaam Chund Pundit of the Mahahrattor [presumably Maratha] tribe, aged twenty-eight years; his widow (for he had but one wife) aged between seventeen and eighteen, as soon as he expired, disdaining to wait the term allowed her for reflection, immediately declared to the Bramins and witnesses present her resolution to burn; as the family was of no small consideration, all the merchants of Cossimbuzaar, and her relations, left no arguments unessayed to dissuade her from it — Lady Russell, with the tenderest humanity, sent her several messages to the same purpose; the infant state of her children (two girls and a boy, the eldest not four years of age) and the terrors and pain of the death she sought, were painted to her in the strongest and most lively colouring — she was deaf to all, she gratefully thanked Lady Russell, and sent her word she had now nothing to live for, but recommended her children to her protection. When the torments of burning were urged in terrorem to her, she with a resolved and calm countenance, put her finger into the fire, and held it there a considerable time; she then with one hand put fire in the palm of the other, sprinkled incense on it, and fumigated the Bramins. The consideration of her children left destitute of a parent was again urged to her. She replied, he that made them, would take care of them. She was at last given to understand, she should not be permitted to burn; this for a short space seemed to give her deep affliction, but soon recollecting herself, she told them, death was in her power, and that if she was not allowed to burn, according to the principles of her cast, she would starve herself. Her friends, finding her thus peremptory and resolved, were obliged at last to assent.

The body of the deceased was carried down to the water side, early the following morning, the widow followed about ten o'clock, accompanied by three very principal Bramins, her children, parents, and relations, and a numerous concourse of people. The order of leave for her burning did not arrive from Hosseyn Khan, Fouzdaar of Morshadabad, until after one, and it was then brought by one of the Soubah's own officers, who had orders to see that she burnt voluntarily. The time they waited for the order was employed in praying with the Bramins, and washing in the Ganges; as soon as it arrived, she retired and stayed for the space of half an hour in the midst of her female relations, amongst whom was her mother; she then divested herself of her bracelets, and other ornaments, and tyed them in a cloth, which hung like an apron before her, and was conducted by her female relations to one corner of the pile; on the pile was an arched arbor formed of dry sticks, boughs and leaves, open only at one end to admit her entrance; in this the body of the deceased was deposited, his head at the end opposite to the opening. At the corner of the pile, to which she had been conducted, the Bramin had made a small fire, round which she and the three Bramins sat for some minutes, one of them gave into her hand a leaf of the bale tree (the wood commonly consecrated to form part of the funeral pile) with sundry things on it, which she threw into the fire; one of the others gave her a second leaf, which she held over the flame, whilst he dropped three times some ghee on it, which melted, and fell into the fire (these two operations, were preparatory symbols of her approaching dissolution by fire) and whilst they were performing this, the third Bramih read to her some portions of the Aughtorrah Bhade, and asked her some questions, to which she answered with a steady, and serene countenance; but the noise was so great, we could not understand what she said, although we were within a yard of her. These over, she was led with great solemnity three times round the pile, the Bramins reading before her; when she came the third time to the small fire, she stopped, took her rings off her toes and fingers, and put them to her other ornaments; here she took a solemn majestic leave of her children, parents, and relations; after which, one of the Bramins dip'd a large wick of cotton in some ghee, and gave it ready lighted into her hand, and led her to the open side of the arbor; there, all the Bramins fell at her feet; after she had blessed them, they retired weeping; by two steps, she ascending the pile and entered the arbor; on her entrance, she made a profound reverence at the feet of the deceased, and advanced and seated herself of his head; she looked, in silent meditation on his face, for the space of a minute, then set fire to the arbor, in three places; observing that she had set fire to leeward, and that the flames blew from her, instantly seeing her error she rose, and set fire to windward, and resumed her station; ensign Daniel with his cane, separated the grass and leaves on the windward side, by which means we had a distinct view of her as she sat. With what dignity, and undaunted a countenance, she set fire to the pile the last time, and assumed her seat, can only be conceived, for words cannot convey a just idea of her. The pile being of combustible matter, the supporters of the roof were presently consumed, and it tumbled upon her."

10. A SATI ON THE SHORES OF THE GANGES, DUTCH TRAVELLER, J.S. STAVORINUS, AROUND AD 1770 (WEINBERGER-THOMAS 2000: 97-100)

On the 25th of November, having received intimation that the solemnity would take place about noon, I went betimes, with some of my friends, to the place which had been pointed out to us; it was a few paces out of *Chinsurah*, upon the banks of the *Ganges*.

We here found the body of the deceased upon a *kadel*, or couch, covered with a piece of white cotton, and strewed with *siri*, or betel-leaves.

The woman, who was to be the victim, sat upon the couch, at the foot-end, with her legs crossed under her [in the lotus posture], and her face turned towards that of the deceased, which was uncovered. The husband seemed to me, to have been a person of almost fifty years of age, and his widow was full thirty. She had a yellow cotton cloth wrapped around her, and her arms and hands were adorned with rings of chancos [*sankhas*: shells used as conches in rituals or for bracelets]. Her hair, which hung loose all around her head, was plentifully strewed with ground sandalwood. She had a little green branch in her right hand, with which she drove away the flies from the body.

Round her, upon the ground, sat ten or twelve women, who kept supplying her with fresh betel, a portion of which she had continually in her mouth; and when she had half masticated it, she gave it to one of her female friends, or to others of the bystanders, who begged it of her, wrapped it up in pieces of cloth, and preserved it as a relic.

She sat, for the greatest part of the time, like one buried in deepest meditation; yet with a countenance that betrayed not the least signs of fear. The other women, her relations and friends, spoke to her continually of the happiness she was about to enjoy, with her husband, in a future life. One of these women, who sat behind her, upon the couch, frequently embraced her and seemed to talk the most, and very earnestly with her.

Besides the women, several men, as well her relations, as brahmins, were present, who at intervals struck their cymbals and beat their drums, accompanied by the songs, or cries of the women, making a most deafening noise. At half past ten, they began to prepare the funeral pile, at the distance of a little more than eight feet from the spot, where the unfortunate woman was sitting, but which she beheld with the most stoic indifference, as if it in no way concerned her.

The pile was made by driving four green bamboo stakes into the earth, leaving about five feet above the ground, and being about six feet from each other, forming a square, in which was first laid a layer of large firewood, which was very dry, and easily combustible; upon this was put a quantity of dry straw, or reeds, which hung beyond the wood, and was plentifully besmeared with ghee [clarified butter] ... This was done alternately, till the pile was almost five feet in height; and the whole was then strewed with fine powdered rosin. Finally, a white cotton sheet, which was first washed in the *Ganges*, was spread over the pile, thus completely prepared for consuming the devoted victim.

The widow was then admonished by a brahmin, that it was time to begin the rites. She was then taken up by two women, from the couch, carried a little further, and put down upon the ground, while the others made a circle round her, and continued to offer her fresh betel, accompanied by entreaties that, as she would, in so short a time, appear with her husband in the presence of *Ram*, or their highest god, she would supplicate for various favors for them; and above all, that she would salute their deceased friends whom she might meet in the celestial abodes, in their names.

In the meantime, the body was taken up from the couch by four men, and carried to the river, where it was washed clean, and rubbed with turmeric, but which was afterwards washed off again. Upon this, one of the brahmins took a little clay out of the river, and marked the forehead of the deceased with it, wrapping the body up in white linen; which, when this had been done, was carried to the pile, and laid upon it.

The woman, who had beheld all these preparations, was then led by two of her female relations to the *Ganges*, in order to wash in the river. When she came again upon the bank, her clothes were pulled off, and a piece of red silk and cotton gingham was wrapped round her body. One of her male relatives took out her gold nose-jewel [*nath*: one of the symbols of marriage], while she sat down, and gave it to her, but she returned it to him for a memorial of her. Thereupon she again went to the river, and taking up some water in her hands, muttered some prayers, and offered it to the sun. All her ornaments were taken from her, and her amulets were broken, and chaplets of white flowers were put upon her neck and hands. Her hair was tucked up with five combs, and her forehead was marked with clay in the same manner as that of her husband. Her head was covered with a piece of silk and a cloth was tied round her body, in which the brahmins put some parched rice.

She then took her last farewell of her friends, both men and women who had assisted her in the preparation, and she was conducted by two of her female relations to the pile. When she came to it, she scattered from that side, where the head of the deceased lay, flowers and parched rice upon the spectators. She then took some boiled rice, rolled in a ball, and put it into the mouth of the deceased, laying several other similar balls of rice under the pile. Two brahmins next led her three times round it, while she threw parched rice among the bystanders, who gathered it up with eagerness. The last time that she went round, she set a little earthen burning lamp at each of the four corners. The whole of this was done during an incessant clamor of cymbals and drums, and amidst the shouts of the brahmins, and of her relations. After having thus walked three times round the pile, she mounted courageously upon it, laid herself down upon the right side next to the body, which she embraced with both her arms; a piece of white cotton was spread over them both, they were bound together over the arms, and middle, with two easy bandages, and a quantity of firewood, straw, *ghee*, and rosin, was laid upon them. In the last place, her nearest relation, to whom she had given her nose-jewel, came with a burning torch, and set the straw on fire, and in a moment the whole was in flame. The noise of the drums was redoubled, and the shouts of the spectators were more loud and incessant than ever, so that the shrieks of the unfortunate woman, had she uttered any, could not possibly have been heard.

What most surprised me, at this horrid and barbarous rite, was the tranquility of the woman, and the joy expressed by her relations, and the spectators. The wretched victim, who beheld these preparations making for her cruel death, seemed to be much less affected by it than we Europeans who were present. She underwent everything with the greatest intrepidity, and her countenance seemed, at times, to be animated with pleasure, even at the moment when she was ascending the fatal pile.

Her feet appeared from between the firewood on the side where I stood; and I had an opportunity of observing them, because a little breeze, playing upon that side, cleared it of the flame and smoke; I paid particular attention to her, in order to discover whether any convulsive motions agitated her feet, but they remained immovable, in the midst of the conflagration.

11. COMTE DE MODAVE ON HIS EXPERIENCE ON 31ST DECEMBER 1774, IN FAIZABAD [PRESENT DAY UTTAR PRADESH] (WEINBERGER-THOMAS 2000: 94-96)

That horrible spectacle so preoccupied me that for two days I could think of nothing else. The image of that woman is so deeply etched in my memory that it will never be erased. She displayed neither confusion nor agitation and complied with each of those ghastly ceremonies as though it were the most unimportant thing in the world.

12. NATHANIEL HALHED OF THE EAST INDIA COMPANY IN A LETTER TO REV. GEORGE COSTARD IN 1779 (ROCHER 1983: 296)

... I must be excused if I presume to differ a little with you on the subject of the burning of women at the death of their husbands. You allow the antiquity of the custom from the authority of Strabo; but wonder "that the Bramins should not have put a stop to a practice so contrary to all sentiments of reason and humanity, as *human nature is every where the same.*" Of this latter opinion I really have learned to doubt more and more every day. Arrian informs us that the Brachmans thought it unbecoming the dignity of their character and the rigour of their philosophy to wait for the approaches of death thro' all the horrid gradations of debilitating infirmities. That they voluntarily put an end to their lives when they thought old age began to impair their intellectual faculties; and if I mistake not, he adds that one of that sect actually burnt himself alive in Alexander's presence. Death has by no means the same effect on an Asiatic as on an European mind. The former meets it with a placid and silent resignation that almost disarms it of all terror. Not that the Indians court it with the military ardour and head long ferocity of the ancient Danes, as described by Mallet, for they are very timid, and tremblingly alive to the apprehensions of danger. But death, when it comes on gradually and by the necessary decays of nature, never seems to shock their imaginations, or alarm their consciences. You know how very widely in this respect Europeans differ from them. But it would have been better, if I had allowed your argument of the sameness of human nature, and had placed my own doctrine on what I conceive to be its proper foundation, the difference of education. Indeed, I was a convert in some degree to Helvetius, before I read his work, and I cannot but think that the mere diversity of education only in different parts of the world removes men as wide from each other, as if they were not of the same species. An Englishman has nothing in common with a Gentoo but his form and his senses. The configuration (may I say so?) of the soul, the whole texture of the interior man is as unlike as to a horse. I have myself seen a Gentoo, who thinking himself upon the point of death, had ordered his bed to be carried down to the side of the Ganges, that he might have the satisfaction of dying in sight of the holy river. The man did not die so soon as was expected, and his relations erected a small shed of mats to fence him from the wind. He had continued there already two or three years when I saw him, and said if he did into die within a short period, he was afraid he should be obliged to build himself a new shed. Others are frequently carried down and laid on the sand below high water mark before they are dead, and are taken away even while living, by the tide. Nor are they at all shocked by the idea of thus anticipating a funeral. I have said perhaps more than enough to make you doubt whether human nature (considered I mean relatively as it exists in adult persons, and not with respect to its original source and stamen) be really so much the same as is commonly asserted. And you must at least believe the concurrent testimony of all the Gentoos who have ever been taxed with cruelty for admitting wives to burn themselves with their deceased husbands, that it does by no means strike their ideas as shocking and repugnant to humanity. Most assuredly the act is generally voluntary on the part of the women; and it is equally certain that should they refuse, and persist in their refusal, their relations could not force them to submit. The recusants might be sure of protection from government, and even from individuals. We are also sure that no temptations whatever and no specious pretences of religion could persuade our European wives to give us so convincing a proof of their conjugal affection; and yet under the mild administration of an English legislature in Bengal, where it is morally impossible that an universal force could be exerted against the Gentoo women by their relations, we find the practice continue in its genuine vigour, and examples of the sacrifice occurring every week in some parts or other of the provinces.

13. ELIZA FAY, IN A LETTER FROM CALCUTTA IN SEPTEMBER 1781 (FAY 1908: 160-61)

I now propose, having full leisure, to give you some account of the East Indian customs and ceremonies, such as I have been able to collect, but it must be considered as a mere sketch to point your further researches. And first for that horrible custom of widows burning themselves with the dead bodies of their husbands. The fact is indubitable, but I have never had an opportunity of witnessing the various incidental ceremonies, not have I ever seen any European who had been present at them. I cannot suppose that the usages originates in the superior tenderness and ardent attachment of Indian wives towards their spouses, since the same tenderness and ardour would doubtless extend to his offspring, and prevent them from exposing the innocent survivors to the miseries attendant on an orphan state, and they would see clearly that to live and cherish these pledges of affection would be the most rational and natural way of shewing their regard for both husband and children. I apprehend that as personal fondness can have no part here at all, – since all matches are made between the parents of the parties, who are betrothed to each other at too early a period for choice to be consulted, – this practice is entirely a political scheme intended to insure the care and good offices of wives to their husbands, who have not failed in most countries to invent a sufficient number of rules to render the weaker sex totally subservient to their authority. I cannot avoid smiling when I hear gentlemen bring forward the conduct of Hindoo women as a test of superior character, since I am well aware that, so much are we the slaves of habit *everywhere*, that were it necessary for a woman's reputation to burn herself in England, many a one who has *accepted* a husband merely for the sake of an establishment, who has lived him without affection, perhaps thwarted his views, dissipated his fortune, and rendered his life uncomfortable to its close, would yet mount the funeral pile with all imaginable decency, and die with heroic fortitude. The most specious sacrifices are not always the greatest. She who wages war with a naturally petulant temper, who practices a rigid self-denial, endures without complaining the unkindness, infidelity, extravagance, meanness, or scorn of the man to whom she has given a tender and confiding heart, and for whose happiness and well-being in life all the powers of her mind are engaged — is ten times more of a heroine than the salve of bigotry and superstition, who affects to scorn the life demanded of her by the laws of her country or at least that country's custom. Many such we have in England, and I doubt not in India likewise: so indeed we ought: have we not a religion more pure than that of India?

14. SATI IN BANARAS, WILLIAM HODGES, FAMOUS PAINTER WHO TRAVELLED IN INDIA FROM 1780 TO 1783 (HODGES 1999: 79-83)

WHILE I was pursuing my professional labours in Benares, I received information of a ceremony which was to take place on the banks of the river, and which greatly excited my curiosity. I had often read and repeatedly heard of that most horrid custom amongst, perhaps, the most mild and gentle of the human race, the Hindoos; the sacrifice of the wife on the death of the husband, and that by a means from which nature seems to shrink with the utmost abhorrence, by burning. Many instances of this practice have been given by travelers; those whom I have met with only mention it as taking place among the highest classes of society, whose vanity united with superstitious prejudices might have dictated the circumstance; and I confess I could not entertain any other ideas, when I observed the theatrical parade that seemed to attend it...

The person whom I saw was of the Bhyse (merchant) tribe or cast; a class of people we should naturally suppose exempt from the high and impetuous pride of rank, and in whom the natural desire to preserve life should in general predominate, undiverted from its proper course by a prospect of posthumous fame. I may add, that these motives are greatly strengthened by the exemption of this class from that infamy with which the refusal is inevitably branded in their superiors. Upon my repairing to the spot, on the banks of the river, where the ceremony was to take place, I found the body of the man on a bier, and covered with linen, already brought down and laid at the edge of the river. At this time, about ten in the morning, only a few people were assembled, who appeared destitute of feeling at the catastrophe that was to take place; I may even say that they displayed the most perfect apathy and indifference. After waiting a considerable time the wife appeared, attended by the Bramins, and music, with some few relations. The procession was slow and solemn; the victim moved with a steady and firm step; and, apparently with a perfect composure of countenance, approached close to the body of her husband, where for some time they halted. She then addressed those who were near her with composure, and without the least trepidation of voice or change of countenance. She held in her left hand a cocoa nut, in which was a read colour mixed up, and dipping in it the fore-finger of her right hand, she marked those near her, to whom the whished to shew the last act of attention. As at this time I stood close to her, she observed me attentively, and with the colour marked me on the forehead. She might be about twenty-four or five years of age, a time of life when the bloom of beauty has generally fled the cheek in India; but still she preserved a sufficient share to prove that she must have been handsome: her figure was small, but elegantly turned; and the form of her hands and arms was particularly beautiful. Her dress was a loose robe of white flowing drapery, that extended from her head to the feet. The place of sacrifice was higher up on the bank of the river, a hundred yards or more from the spot where we now stood. The pile was composed of dried branches, leaves, and rushes, with a door on one side, and arched and covered on the top: by the side of the door stood a man with a lighted brand. From the time the woman appeared to the taking up of the body to convey it into the pile, might occupy a space of half an hour, which was employed in prayer with the Bramins, in attentions to those who stood near her, and conversation with her relations. When the body was taken up she followed close to it, attended by the chief Bramin; and when it was deposited in the pile, she bowed to all round her, and entered without speaking. The moment she entered, the door was closed; the fire was put to the combustibles, which instantly flamed, and immense quantities of dried wood and other matters were thrown upon it. This last part of the ceremony was accompanied with the shouts of the multitude, who now became numerous, and the whole seemed a mass of confused rejoicing. For my part I felt myself actuated by very different sentiments: the event that I had been witness to was such, that the minutest circumstance attending it could not be erased from my memory; and when the melancholy which had overwhelmed me was somewhat abated, I made a drawing of the subject, and from a picture since painted the annexed plate was engraved.

15. PLAN TO RESCUE A WIDOW ABORTED, LA DE GRANDPRE, AN OFFICER OF THE FRENCH ARMY WHO VISITED INDIA IN 1789 (DE GRANDPRE II 1995: 68-74)

The inhuman custom of women burning themselves to death on the corpse of their husbands is not yet annihilated in India; but it is confined to the cast of the Bramins. When an individual of their cast dies, one of his wives is bound to exhibit this dreadful proof of her affection. This lamentable sacrifice is not imposed upon them by law, for they may refuse to make it; but in that case they lose their character, are held in dishonour, and are deprived of their cast, a misfortune so intolerable, that they prefer to it the alternative of being burnt alive. Nature however revolts in some of these widows, and it is probable, if left to themselves, that they would never consent to so cruel a sacrifice; but the old women and priests are incessantly importuning them, and representing, that after death the most exquisite happiness is their lot: as they are commonly young, it is no difficult matter to triumph over their weakness and irresolution; they accordingly submit to the custom, and the prejudice which ordains it keeps its ground ...

My servant, a very brave fellow, who had been discharged from the military service for the loss of a finger, and who disliked the Bramins, informed me one day, that a woman was going to be burnt at a place which he pointed out to me, on the left side of the river, between Fulta and Mayapoor. Having enquired into the circumstance, I learned, that she was both young and handsome, that she had already twice put off the ceremony, but that the day being a third time fixed, nothing could longer defer it. I conceived, that a woman who had twice hesitated, would find at least no great pleasure in submitting, and conjecturing, that she might not be sorry to escape altogether, I formed the resolution of endeavouring to save her. I asked my man if he would assist me, which he readily agreed to, adding, that he had told it me with the hope of engaging me in the enterprise. He requested that one of his comrades might be of the party, who was a bold fellow and would be of great use to me; I commended his zeal, and accepted the proffered services of his friend.

I took with me twenty good European sailors, whom I put on board my sloop, in the bow of which I mounted a swivel: I provided also a dozen musquets, eight pistols, and a score of sabers. Two officers accompanied me, who were resolved to aid me to the utmost of their power. I encouraged the sailors by promising them the sixth part of the value of whatever jewels the woman should have about her, intending to leave the remainder for herself, if she did not choose to stay with me. My servant and his companion were without arms, as it was not my intention to employ them in fighting. I disposed my forces into three bodies, in the following manner. One of the officers and eight men were to guard the boat. The other officer and six men were to follow me at a short distance with pistols, but to reserve their fire till I gave orders. Six of the most resolute I selected to attend me in the business; four of them armed with musquets, and two, who were to keep themselves close at my side, with pistols. The party who were left to guard the boat had musquets, and were to be in readiness to cover my retreat: besides his fire arms, every man had a sabre, and no one was to fire without express leave. Such was the arrangement of my force, and I had no doubt from the valour of my people, that my intentions would be admirably seconded. They had all seen some service, and would bravely stand before a veteran and experienced enemy, much more before men like the natives of this country. It was planned by my servant and his companion, that I should go up to the widow and touch her: this was a violation that would deprive her of her cast, and she would then have no right to burn herself: at the same time they were to tell her in the Moorish language, not to be frightened, but resign herself wholly to their direction, for that they came to rescue her. They were then to carry her off as expeditiously as possible, under the escort of the officer and party following me, while I and my six chosen sailors were to bear the burnt of the contest, that they might have time to reach the boat, to which I was to retreat, when I supposed them safely arrived here.

I hoped, that men, unarmed and thus taken by surprise, seeing a body of Europeans with sabres and pistols, would not have the courage to attack us; but being prepared to receive them if they did, I resolved to run the risk.

My intention was to leave the woman afterwards to her own disposal, that is to say, to give her the choice of either going with me, or of settling at Calcutta upon the produce of her jewels, which I should of course have the precaution to bring away with her.

My whole plan was prepared and ready, and I set out to execute it. I arrived at the place, and alertly jumped ashore. The arrangements agreed upon were made with precision. I advanced, and was astonished at the stillness and silence that prevailed. I came to the spot. Alas! the dreadful sacrifice has been completed the preceding evening. I had been misinformed of the day. The wall was still warm, and the ashes were smoking, I retuned with an oppression of heart that I can hardly express and as much affected as if I had been a witness to the barbarous execution. My regret for this woman was as great as the pleasure I should have felt in saving her, and the idea I had formed of her youth and beauty.

16. AN ACCOUNT FROM THE *CALCUTTA GAZETTE* OF 10TH FEBRUARY 1785 (BLECHYNDEN 2003: 229-32)

An Account of a Woman Burning Herself. (By an Officer) – A few days since, going in a budgerow from Ghyretty to dine at Chinsurah, I perceived near Chandernagore a vast crowd assembled on the shore; upon inquiry, I found this large concourse of people were gathered to see a Gentoo woman burn herself with her husband. As I had read many accounts of this strange and barbarous ceremony, but had never seen it performed, I was resolved upon the present occasion to be an eye-witness. I went ashore, and walked up close to the girl; she seemed about twenty-one years of age, and was standing up, decorated with flowers; pieces of silk were tied upon her wrists. Two of her children were near her; the eldest, about eight or nine years of age, was mixing up rice in a large pan, some of which, with many ceremonies, he put into his deceased father's mouth, who was laid upon his back on the pile: this was composed of straw and dry wood, and about four feet high; close round it were six bamboo stakes drove into the ground, about seven feet in height, to keep the pile from giving way too soon after the fire was communicated to it. The girl to me appeared stupid, and so very weak, that two Brahmins were obliged to support her. I asked some persons present whether bhang or opium had not been give to her; they declared not, but that the loss of her husband was the sole cause of her dejection. I however perceived, from the redness of her eyes, that narcotics had been administered; she seemed not in the least ruffled, but surveyed the crowd with great composure, nor did the dreadful preparations appear in the smallest degree to disconcert her. The Brahmins took her down to the Ganges; she sat on the edge of the water and was bathed, while prayers were repeated. Her clothes were then taken off, and a red silk covering (a *saurry*) put upon her. When she returned from the river, fresh flowers were again put around her neck and arms. At this time, the Brahmins alone asked her, whether the sacrifice she was about to make of herself was her own free choice; and whether any force had been used to compel her to devote herself to death contrary to her inclination. She bowed her head, but I could not hear anything she said, or perceive that she spoke at all. She afterwards sat down, and threw several handfuls of cowries among the crowd, which were scrambled for with great avidity. She then took leave of her children and relations in a very affecting manner. The Brahmins afterwards fixed several combs in her hair, and led her six or seven times round her husband's corpse. I perceived, as often as she came to his head she bowed, and some words were repeated by those who attended her which I could not understand; she then was lifted upon the pile, and laid herself down by her deceased husband, with her arms about his neck. Two people immediately passed a rope twice across the bodies, and fastened it so tight to the stakes that it would have effectually prevented her from rising had she attempted. I could not refrain, at this moment, from asking a person who had been near me all the time, and who had been very ready in explaining every circumstance I had wished to be informed of, the reason of their binding down with cords a willing victim; he hold me that, however great her resolution might be, it was very possible, when the fire was first kindled, she might attempt to rise, which the ropes would hinder her from doing. A great quantity of straw and dry wood was now laid upon her, and several pots of ghee thrown over it. The preparations, after the unhappy creature was laid upon the pile, took up some time, and this dreadful interval must have appeared to her more terrible than the worst of deaths. She distinctly heard the people around her ordering more fuel, and the fatal brand called for which was to consume her to ashes. When everything was ready, her eldest son came and set fire to the under part of the straw: in a moment all was in a blaze. Two men kept a very long bamboo closely pressed upon the bodies, but the heat was so great that people were constantly employed for some time pouring pots of water upon their heads. Vast quantities of straw, wood, etc. were thrown upon the pile for several minutes after it was lighted, and the heat was so great, that a termination must have been very soon put to the torments of the miserable devoted woman.

17. SIR WILLIAM JONES, EMINENT ORIENTALIST, ON BEING INFORMED OF A SATI
(*HOBSON-JOBSON* 1968: 882)

My father, said he (Pundit Rhadacaunt), died at the age of one hundred years, and my mother, who was eighty years old, became a sati, and burned herself to expiate sins.

18. NARRATIVE OF AN EYEWITNESS FROM POONAH, 24TH JULY 1786 (*ASIATIC ANNUAL REGISTER FOR 1800:* 336-38)

... Soon after I and my conductor had quitted the house, we were informed the *Suttee* (for that is the name given to the person who so devotes herself) has passed, and her track was marked by the *goolal* and beetle leaf, which she had scattered as she went along. She had reached the *mootah* which runs close under the tower before we arrived, and having performed her last ablutions, was sitting at the water's edge: over her head was held a punkar, an attendant fanned her with a handkerchief, and she was surrounded by her relations, a few friends and some chosen Brahmans, the populace being kept aloof by a guard from government. In this situation, I learn from good authority, she distributed among the Brahmans two thousand rupees and the jewels with which she came decorated; reserving only, as is usual on these occasions, a small ornament on her nose, called *motee* (perhaps from a pearl or two on it,) and a bracelet of plain gold on each wrist. From her posture, I could see only her hands, which, with the palms joined, rose above her head in an attitude of invocation. Quitting therefore, this post, I removed to an eminence that gave me an opportunity of observing the construction of the funeral pile, and commanded the pathway by which I understood she would approach it.

The spot chosen for its erection was about forty paces from the river, and directly fronting the suttee. When I came up, the frame only was fixed; it consisted of four uprights, each of about ten feet high; they stood rather more than nine feet asunder lengthwise, and under six in breadth; soon after by ropes fastened near the top of the uprights, was suspended a roof of rafters, and on it again heaped as many billets as it would bear; beneath arose a pile of more substantial timbers, to the height of four feet, which was covered over with dry straw, and bushes of a fragrant and sacred shrub called *toolsee*. The sides and one end being then filled up with the same materials, the other extremity was left open as an entrance. After this ceremony the lady got up and walked forward, supported in the midst by her friends: she approached the door-way, and there having paid certain devotions, retired a few yards aside, and was encircled as before. The dead body now brought from the bank (whence it had hitherto remained close to the place the suttee lately sat on) was laid upon the pile, and with it several sweetmeats and a paper bag, containing either flour or dust of sandal. The widow got up, and walked three times slowly round the pile; then seating herself opposite to the entrance, on a small square stone, constantly used on such occasions, and on which two feet were rudely sketched, she received and returned the melancholy compliments of her companions with great serenity; she then stood up a second time, and, having stroked her right hand over the heads of a favoured few in a very fervid manner, gently inclining her person towards them, she let her arm fall round their necks in a faint embrace, and turned from them.

Then, with her hands upheld to heaven, but with her eyes cast on the ground, she continued for sometime fixed and immoveable; at length, without altering a feature, or betraying the smallest symptom of agitation, she ascended the door way unassisted, and, laying down beside her husband's corpse, gave herself, in the meridian of health and beauty, a victim to the flames. As soon as she entered, she was hid from our view by bundles of straw, with which the aperture was closed up, and all the actors in this tragic scene seemed to vie with each other who should be most forward in hurrying it to a conclusion. At once, some darkened air with a cloud of *goolal*; some darting their hatchets at the suspending cords, broke the laden roof from her; and others rushed eagerly forward to apply the fatal torch; at this moment of agony, when the mind must have lost its influence, the trumpets broke forth from every quarter.

When the conflagration took place, and not till then, the pile was fed for a time with large quantities of ghee thrown by the nearest of kin, but except the *toolsee* and straw before mentioned, no combustible whatever, that I either saw or could learn, was used in preparing the pile. It is said to be the custom that as the suttee ascends the pile, she is furnished with a lighted taper to set fire to it herself; and my companion, who was a Brahman, asserted that in this instance it was the case, but I traced the whole progress of the ceremonies with so close and eager an attention, that I think I may safely contradict him.

As curiosity may be excited to know something of the subject of this terrible, though here not uncommon immolation, I have collected the following particulars: The lady's name was Toolseboy; her husband's Ragaboy Tauntea; he was about thirty years old, and nephew to Junaboy Daddah, a person of distinction in this place; a little girl of about four years of age, the fruit of their unison, survives them. Toolseboy was nineteen, her stature above the middle standard, her form elegant, and her features interesting and expressive; her eyes, in particular, animated and commanding: at the solemn moment in which I saw her, these beauties were eminently conspicuous.

19. SATI, IN 1792, BY MUKTABAI (ONLY SURVIVING CHILD OF RANI AHALYA BAI HOLKAR OF INDORE) (MARTIN 1983A: 390)

The battle-field had widowed Ahalya Bye at twenty; yet — despite the modern heresy of the Hindoos, that the voluntary sacrifice of life, on the part of the bereaved survivor, ensures immediate reunion between those whom death has divided, and their mutual entrance into the highest heaven, she had not been tempted by this lying doctrine to commit suicide, but had lived to protect her children and establish the independence of the Holkar principality. Now, flinging herself at the feet of Muchta Bye, she besought her child, by every argument a false creed could sanction, to renounce her purpose. The reply of the daughter was affectionate but decided. "You are old, mother," she said, "and a few years will end your pious life. My only child and husband are gone, and when you follow, life I feel will be insupportable; but the opportunity of terminating it with honour will then have passed." Every effort, short of coercion, was vainly practiced to prevent the intended "*suttee*;" but the unfaltering resolve of the devoted widow remained unshaken, and her wretched parent accompanied the procession, with forced composure, to the funeral pyre: but when the first vivid burst of flame told the actual consummation of the sacrifice, self-command was lost in anguish; the agonizing shrieks of their beloved ruler mingled with the exulting shouts of the immense multitude; and excited almost to madness, the aged princess gnawed the hands she could not liberate from the two Brahmins, who with difficulty held her back from rushing to die with her child. After three days spent in fasting and speechless grief, Ahalya Bye recovered her equanimity so far as to resume her laborious round of daily occupations, including four hours spent in receiving ambassadors, hearing petitions or complaints, and transacting other business in full durbar or court; and she seemed to find solace in erecting a beautiful monument to the memory of those she lamented, and in increasing the already large proportion of the revenues devoted to religious purposes and public works.

20. SIR CHARLES MALET, RESIDENT AT POONA, ON AN INCIDENT IN THE CITY ON 5TH SEPTEMBER 1792, AS RELATED IN HIS DIARY (FORBES II 1988: 394-96)

An extraordinary incident happened this day. A sepoy of my guard, of the *Mharatta*, or *Columbee* tribe, died; his wife immediately declared herself a suttee; that is, resolved to devote herself to the flames with his body: she accordingly assumed the yellow garment, the turban, the mirror, and all other insignia usual on such occasions. When informed of her resolution, I desired the officer of the guard, captain H—, to endeavour to divert the suttee from her intention, and in case of failure to acquaint me with the result. He soon communicated his despair of success, and I desired her to be brought to me.

I found her a healthy young woman, about twenty-two years of age, in a state of mind firmly resolved on sacrificing herself with her dead husband, whom she incessantly and passionately invoked, with every endearing expression. The scene was singular and affecting: I scarce knew how to commence the difficult task of soothing grief so poignant, or of diverting a resolution founded on despair. IN the course of my endeavours I found the poor suttee had no relations at Poonah; her father and mother lived in her native village, at some distance. I discovered like-wise that her husband's death had exposed her to the dread of absolute distress. The first subject furnished a strong counteracting power to the passionate grief that possessed her mind, and by proper application awakened a new sensation: which, followed up, produced a flood of tears, the first symptom of relaxation from determined grief; such as must have been the despairing sorrow of Niobe! A counteracting passion being thus excited, the dread of distress was soothed by assurances, properly introduced, of maintenance in the means of devoting her future life to the discharge of religious ceremonies at the shrine of her household gods, in honour of her husband's memory; which would be more grateful to the gods, and acceptable to him, than sacrificing on his pyreal pile.

After these and a variety of other arguments, which occupied nearly three hours, in the course whereof gentle restraint was sometimes imposed on occasional fits of passion and anguish, she was at length persuaded to suspend her fatal purpose, until the arrival of her parents; to whom a messenger was dispatched in her presence, with a letter, and money for the expenses of their journey to the capital. The Hindoos attach the merit of the most sublime and holy heroism to this self-devotion; but the resolution once suspended, is seldom resumed, and was not in the present instance.

21. SATI AT SANTIPORE IN 1792, THOMAS TWINING OF THE EAST INDIA COMPANY (TWINING 1893: 463-67)

Having hired a small covered boat, rowed by four men and steered by a fifth; I left Calcutta on a visit to my friend Mr. Fletcher at Santipore, sixty miles higher up the Ganges ... Soon after dark I crept under the low flat roof of my little boat and went asleep on a mattress my servants had spread for me.

I got up soon after daybreak and went upon the forepart of the boat between the roof and the rowers, to enjoy the coolness of the morning air. When I had been here about half an hour I observed on the shore to our left several persons coming from the interior to the river, and others standing together near it, a sight so usual at this time of the day that it did not strike me as at all singular. As, however, we came nearer, some singularity was observable, for the people did not enter the river to bathe. I therefore noticed them more attentively, when the discovery of a *pile*, which I could perceive amongst the crowd at once suggested a painful solution of what was passing, and the opinion of my boatmen removed all doubt. It was certainly a suttee, or burning of a Hindoo widow that was about to take place. Though feeling a great repugnance for painful sights, I determined to avail myself of an opportunity which so seldom offers itself to a native of Europe of *seeing* one of the most remarkable customs of the East. I accordingly directed the boat to be steered towards the people, and soon landed amongst them, close to the body of the deceased Hindoo, which had apparently just been placed at the edge of the water, with which some Bramins, or persons of the family, were then washing it. The deceased appeared to have been about thirty-five years of age, and to have been rather a tall man. I did not learn what his illness had been, but he was reduced almost to a skeleton. He was lying on his back on a small bedstead, with his knees up, and was quite uncovered, excepting a cloth about his middle. I looked about for his widow, but could see no one distinguishable by anything particular from the rest of the females. Walking a few yards up the shore I saw the pile. It was about 4 'feet high, something less in width, and about 5 'feet in length. The bottom part was composed of dried faggots, upon which was a thick layer of dried palm leaves, rushes, and stalks of sugar-canes. While I was standing here the circle of people who surrounded the pile, looking at the preparations, opened towards the river, and the dead body was brought through on the bedstead, and after having been put down for a minute near the pile, was lifted up and placed upon it, the head towards the south, the face turned towards the Ganges.

During these proceedings I was standing about ten feet from the north-west angle of the pile, in the inner line of the circle formed by the people. Looking now to my right I perceived the unfortunate woman. She was sitting between two young children, a little within the circle and immediately opposite the middle of the western side of the pile. A white cloth fell from the top of her head over each check, but her face was partly visible where I stood.

As she sat, her elbows rested upon her knees, her hands supporting her head. Her eyes, half closed, were fixed upon the ground but without taking notice of anything. Several women, whom I supposed to be her relations and friends, were sitting or standing behind her, but there was no communication of any kind between them and the widow, nor between the latter and her children; not a tear was shed nor a word spoken.

After a few minutes the woman rose, and some Bramins stepping forward, put into her hand a cloth containing something, and then ranged themselves partly behind her, partly by her side, some of the women doing the same. In this movement I lost sight of the children, and supposed that they had been secretly withdrawn by some one of the family or of the attendants. Followed by the Bramins and women, she now began to walk gently within the circle to the left, distributing as she went the contents of her cloth. She would necessarily pass close to me and this circumstance seemed to favour the little chance there was saving her life. I determined to attract her attention as she passed me, and to be guided by the result as to any further interference. When, therefore, she came to where I was standing, I stepped forward and held my hand towards her as expressive of a desire to share the farewell offering she was giving away. The unexpected appearance of an European, whom she now saw for the first time in all probability in her life, undoubtedly surprised her, although her feelings seemed too deadened by the circumstances of her situation to be susceptible of much impression. She had not raised her eyes from the ground to look at the persons she had passed, but my advancing, together with my dress, caused her to look at me while she put a small quantity of burnt rice into my hand. She appeared to be about twenty years of age, and had the regular delicate features so usual among the native women of India. Having received her rice as graciously as I could, I allowed her to pass on. I considered, however, what had occurred as so favaourable that I resolved to speak to her when she came to me again, for I understood that she was to walk round three times.

Having proceeded slowly round the pile she came to the part where she had been seated with her children, and a few steps more brought her near to me a second time. I again advanced as she approached, and having again received a few grains of rice, which she seemed quite prepared to give me, I expressed my grief at her intention, and entreated her to relinquish it for the sake of her children, for whom as well as for herself I promised provision and protection. Although she said nothing, I thought her look seemed to express thankfulness for the proposition she had heard. I had not time to say more, the pressure of the Bramins, watchful lest their victim should escape, obliging her to move on.

Having once more completed her round and come to where I stood, she herself turned to put some rice into my hand. I eagerly seized the last opportunity I should have of renewing my exhortation, promising her a pension for life and provision for her children. Though her head remained inclined towards the ground, she looked at me while I spoke, and her countenance impressed me with the assurance that if she had been free from the fatal influence which surrounded her it would not have been difficult to turn her from her resolution. Pressed on as before, she turned her eyes from me and moved forwards.

The last scene of this shocking tragedy was now approaching. The procession did not quite complete the third round, for having reached the head of the pile the widow advanced to the side of it next the river, when two men, laying hold of her, raised her in their arms and laid her upon it, with her face towards the face of her dead husband. It was, however, found that the bent knees of the latter prevented her being placed sufficiently near the corpse to be tied to it. As soon as the bystanders perceived this difficulty there was a considerable rumour amongst them. Some called out that the woman had better be placed behind the man, others observing that she was now in her proper place. After some discussion the former arrangement was decided on, and the miserable woman was again lifted up and carried round to the opposite side, where she was placed close to the back of the deceased, her face towards him. A rope which had been put under the dead body being passed also under and then over her's, the two — the living and the dead — were tied firmly together. Dry combustible materials, similar to those on which the bodies rested, were now heaped over them, and I entirely lost sight of the woman.

When the pile had been thus raised about eighteen inches more, two long bamboos were fastened to pegs in the ground on one side, and being passed over it were depressed till their ends reached the other pegs, to which also they were secured. The pressure upon the pile by these means was very considerable, and would effectually prevent the woman from rising. Indeed, it seemed to me doubtful whether the quantity of stuff piled upon her and closely pressed down would not smother her, and happily rescue her from a more painful death. There was, however, scarcely time allowed for this; for as soon as the bamboos were fastened down, fire was brought from a small burning heap that was ready for the purpose, and applied amidst the shouts of the people, first to the head of the pile, then at the bottom, and afterwards to different parts of it. The ignition was immediate, and to increase its action and direct the flames through the middle, ghee, a sort of liquid butter was poured upon the top. There was no shouting after the first exclamation on lighting, but the noise was still considerable, seeming, however, to be accidentally occasioned by the talking and observations of the people rather than studiously produced to conceal the shrieks of the woman. Indeed, the way in which she was covered up and pressed down would render her cries very feeble; nor, if they did reach the ears of the bystanders, would they be likely to excite either horror or pity, for I saw not a single countenance that testified either of these feelings. The flames were so excited as the ghee flowed down upon them that they quickly pierced through the crackling faggots, and must, as far as I could judge, have reached the poor woman in less than two minutes after the pile was lighted; and though their rapidly-increasing progress would soon put an end to her sufferings, these for some seconds must have been dreadful. At length they made their way through the top of the pile, and the whole was one general blaze. There could be little doubt that the agonies of the wretched widow were now over, but this desirable fact was rendered unquestionable by a circumstance which occurred shortly after. It was an explosion in the pile, like the discharge of a pistol. Had this happened sooner I should have concluded that gunpowder had been put amongst the materials to accelerate their combustion. The noise was followed by clamorous expressions of satisfaction amongst the spectators. Upon my asking a Hindoo near me what all this meant, he said that the skull of one of the dead had burst, and that the people had shouted because this occurrence was a favourable omen. In a few moments more there was a similar explosion, followed by a similar burst of satisfaction round the whole circle.

22. SATI, QUENTIN CRAUFURD IN 1792 (CRAUFURD II 1977: 14-32)

The practice of burning the dead ... at present prevails most in the Mahratta dominions, and in the countries of the ancient Rajahs, where instances of the kind are frequently to be met with, particularly in families of high distinction. In the territories belonging to the English, it has everywhere been opposed, and rarely happens there unless it be done secretly, or before those who may have authority to prevent it can be sufficiently apprized. ...

I never was present at such a ceremony, but a person of my acquaintance, who happened to see one, gave me the following description of it:

A funeral pile being erected on a piece of ground that was consecrated to the purpose, the body of the Rajah was brought from the fort, accompanied by many Brahmans, and others, and followed by the widow, attended by relations of both sexes. Being arrived at the funeral pile, the body was placed on it, and certain ceremonies being performed, the widow took leave of her relations. She embraced those of her own sex; took off some jewels that she wore, and distributed them among them, as the last tokens of her affection. The women appeared to be greatly afflicted, some silently weeping, and others making excessive lamentations. But she was perfectly composed, smiled, and endeavoured to comfort them. She then advanced to the pile, and in a solemn manner walked round it. She stopped; and after contemplating the corpse, touched the feet with her hand, raising it to her forehead, inclining her body forwards. She then saluted the spectators in the same manner; and with the assistance of the Brahmans mounted the pile, and seated herself by the side of the corpse. Some who stood near her, with torches in their hands, set fire to it, and, as it was composed of dry wood, straw, and other such combustible materials, it was instantly in a flame. The smoke was at first so great, that I imagine this unfortunate young victim must have been immediately suffocated, which, I own, afforded me a sort of melancholy comfort, from the idea that her sufferings would soon be ended. ...

Two English officers, who were in the service of the Nabob of Arcot, being present at one of these ceremonies in the province of Tanjour, were so affected by it, that they drew their swords and rescued the woman. But although she was immediately restored to her relations, and it clearly appeared that they had not used any kind of liberty with her, nor had any other motive for what they did but the sudden impulse of humanity; the Brahmans positively rejected her solicitations for permission to burn herself afterwards; saying she was polluted and had lost the virtues of her cast. To satisfy them for the insult, the officers were put under arrest, and afterwards sent to serve in a different part of the country.

A Rajah, in one of those provinces that are under the dominion of the English, being dangerously ill, it was privately communicated to the person who commanded in the province, that his wife, in case of his death, intended to burn herself with his body. The Rajah had an only child, a boy of about five years of age. The European commandant dispatched a native of distinction, in whom he had confidence, with instructions, if the Rajah died, to represent to his widow the danger to which her son must be exposed, if left to the doubtful care of ambitious relations, who had often attempted to disturb even the peace of his father: that to live for his sake, would be yielding an unnatural and imaginary duty to one natural and important; and that by discharging the office of a tender and prudent mother, she would best prove her affection and respect for the memory of her deceased husband. He was likewise desired to signify to the Brahmans, that should they attempt to proceed to the ceremony, an officer, who commanded a neighbouring garrison, had orders to prevent it. The fear of some public act of violence prevailed with the priests, and not the arguments; with which, on the contrary, they were highly offended, and even affected to treat them with much contempt. The Rajah died, and the widow, being a woman of sense and merit, was afterwards of infinite use to her son. Having thus a claim to the protection and good offices of the person who, it may be said, had forced her to live, she, through his means, enjoyed a degree of respect and consideration, which, according to the custom of the country, she must otherwise have lost. She obtained from him several marks of indulgence for her son ...

23. SATI AT NURPUR, RAFAIL DANIBEGOV, A GEORGIAN, WHO ARRIVED IN INDIA IN 1795 (KEMP 1959: 117-18)

Setting out from here [Lahore], in forty days I arrived at the town of Norpor or Far [Nurpur] standing on a hill. The first sight that met my eyes on entering the town was a most melancholy and affecting one. An idol worshipper had died — it was necessary to burn him. This is what happens at this ceremony. Having placed the dead body on a richly decorated bier, they carried it to the place assigned for burning according to their custom. The deceased had two wives, who, dressed in magnificent and costly clothes, followed their husband's bier. As soon as they came to the appointed place the people made a huge pyre of wood over which they laid some planks and placed the body of the dead man on top. As according to the cruel custom the wives out of love for their husband have to sacrifice themselves voluntarily to the fire together with him, these two richly dressed women seated themselves on the pyre on either side of their husband. The priests having poured plenty of oil and other combustible materials over all three, suddenly set light to the pile from all sides and these two innocent together with their husband's corps were devoured by the flames. The people standing around the burning pyre began to play various instruments, and they continued to play until all had turned to ashes, including these unfortunate women. Nevertheless women may chose not to perform this inhuman rite; their relatives and friends even try to persuade them to remain alive, either for the sake of their children or the inheritance left by the husband. But if they once decide, if they once approach the flames with the intention of throwing themselves into them, and then suddenly feeling fear want to turn back, the watchers around the pyre threaten them with a different death — by the sword, in which case the wretched women would not escape, being regarded as unworthy to live.

4

AD 1800–1845

1. *THE ASIATIC ANNUAL REGISTER FOR THE YEAR 1802* UNDER CORRESPONDENCE WITH THE EDITOR, DATED 16 OCTOBER 1802 SUTTEE AT TANJORE, 19 APRIL 1802 (*THE ASIATIC ANNUAL REGISTER FOR THE YEAR 1802*: 122-24)

Sometime ago I communicated to you an account of a Hindu woman burning herself at the funeral pile of her husband at Poonah, in 1786; which, though attended with circumstances sufficiently horrid, has been exceeded by an instance of a more recent date, in the self-immolation of the two widows of Ameer Jung, the late Regent of Tanjore: of which the following is an authentic and circumstantial narrative.

The Regent died on the 19th April 1802, about 10 o'clock a.m. The moment he expired, two of his wives adorned themselves with their jewels and richest cloaths, entered the apartment in which the body was laid, and, after three prostrations, sat down by it, and announced to the whole court, which had assembled around it, their determination to devote themselves to the flames.

The youngest of the women was the regular wife and about twenty years of age, and without children; the other was a wife of inferior rank, aged twenty-six, having one child, a daughter four years old. The fathers and brothers of both were present in the assembly; they made use of the most pressing and affecting entreaties to avert them from their purpose, but without success.

The British Resident at Tanjore, having been apprised of the intention of these ladies, and not being able to be personally present at the residence of the late regent, had sent his hircarrah to the spot, with orders to use every possible effort, short of absolute force, to prevent the horrid sacrifice. When the relations of the ladies found their entreaties of no avail to induce them to relinquish their purpose, the hircarrah was sent for; but his threats of the displeasure of government had only a temporary and feeble effect. The Mahratta chiefs observed that the Company had never interfered in their religious institutions and ceremonies; that the sacrifice in question was by no means uncommon in Tanjore; that it was highly proper to use every art of persuasion and entreaty to induce the women to relinquish their resolution; but, if they persisted in it, force ought not to be used to restrain them.

The women laughed at the menaces of the hircarrah, when he told them that their fathers and brothers would be exposed to the displeasure of government. The younger widow observed that it was not the custom of the English government to punish one person for the act of another; and pointing to her father, who had actually thrown himself at her feet in an agony of grief, asked the hircarrah if he thought any other inducement could alter her resolution, when the affliction of her father failed to move it. The young brother of the other widow went into the women's apartments, and returned with his sister's child in his arms, which he laid at her feet; but such was the resolution of those astonishing women, that not a single expression of regret, not a sigh or tear could be drawn from them.

Any one of these weaknesses would have disqualified them from burning with the body; and the efforts of the relations were strenuously and constantly directed to excite them, but in vain. In an answer to an observation of the hircarrah, that if the late regent had been aware of their intention he would have forbidden it, they said they had formed their resolution a year before, and communicated it to him; who, after several ineffectual attempts to dissuade them, had consented to it.

The hircarrah, however, determined to protract the performance of the obsequies, if possible, until the arrival of the Resident. The women waited with patience until seven in the evening, taking no other refreshment than a little betel occasionally. They then sent for the hircarrah, and told him that they suspected the cause of delay, and were resolved, if the procession did not immediately set out, to kill themselves before him. Their relatives now gave up the point in despair. The other chiefs who had taken no part hitherto now interfered, and said they had a right to be indulged, and should not be restrained. The hircarrah retired, and the procession set out.

The younger and regular wife mounted the pile on which the body of the deceased regent had been placed, and they were consumed together. The fate of the other, who was not entitled to this distinction, was, in appearance, more dreadful. A pit eight feet deep, and six in diameter, had been dug a few yards distant from the pile; it was filled with combustible matter, and fire set to it. When the flames were at the fiercest, fire was applied to the pile in which the young widow and the body of the regent had been enclosed. The other, unsupported, walked thrice round the pit, and, after making obescience to the pile, threw herself in the midst of the flames, and was no more heard or seen.

2. SATI NEAR CALCUTTA," LT. R.G. WALLACE (NAIR 1989: 320-21)

... On the 12th of September 1807, near Barnagore, three miles from Calcutta, the body of a Koolin Brahmin named Kristo Deb Mookergee, who died at the age of ninety-two, was burned. He had left twelve wives, three of who were burned with him. One was a venerable lady, having white locks. Being unable to walk from age, she was placed upon the pile by the Brahmins. The two others were young, and one of them was very beautiful. The old lady was placed on one side of the body, and the two others on the opposite side, when an old Brahmin, the eldest son of the deceased, set the pile on fire, which was instantly in a blaze, amidst the shout of Brahmins, and din of tom toms and tooteries, which drowned the dying cries of the victims. "The Koolin Brahmins," says Dr. Buchanan, "are the purest and marry as many wives as they please. Hindoos think it an honour to have a Koolin Brahmin for a son-in-law. They sometimes have great numbers of wives. Rajeb Bonnerjee, of Calcutta, has forty, Raj Chunder Bonnerjee forty-two, Ramrajee Bonnerjee fifty, and Birjod Mookerjee, of Bisrampore, now dead, had ninety."

3. ANNE DEANE, WHO TOURED INDIA BETWEEN 1804 AND 1814, ON AN INCIDENT AT ALLAHABAD (DEANE 1823: 86-87)

During our stay at *Allahabad*, it was understood that a Hindoo woman had signified her intention to end her existence on the funeral pile of her husband. The Judge, with whom we were on a visit, sent for her father, and endeavoured to prevail on him to dissuade her. He said he had done all he could; but she was firmly determined upon it. The Judge then sent for her, but talked with as little success; she was bent upon immortalizing her name, and, as she said, of showing her family the way to heaven. In short, the day was fixed, and a gentleman who was present gave me a description of this horrid ceremony. An immense concourse of people having assembled, her approach was announced by the blowing of horns and beating of drums: next came a number of *Brahmins*, bearing lighted torches, and singing some appropriate stanzas to inspire this victim of credulity, who followed, attended by her relations and friends, all bearing torches but herself. She was richly dressed, having her hands, neck, and feet, covered with ornaments. The dead body of her husband was carried on a bier immediately before her. It was then placed upon the funeral pile, the priests forming a circle round. The father and mother having led the young woman within the circle, left her there, and retired among the crowd. Music, or rather discordant sounds, struck up, and the *Brahmins* again sung, while she marched slowly round the pile; when, divesting herself of her ornaments, with wonderful presence of mind, she distributed them to her weeping friends; then, exchanging her veil of white muslin for one of crimson, she was presented with a lighted torch, (the *Brahmins* meantime exhorting her by songs and gestures to be firm,) and again marched round the pile. She stopped a few moments, *salaamed* to all she knew, then putting the torch into the hand of her father, she calmly ascended the funeral pile, and seated herself by the side of her husband, amid the shouts and plaudits of the multitude. Her father, he believed, set fire to the pile; but a number of torches were instantly applied, drums beating, trumpets sounding, horns blowing, and guns firing, so that all was at once a scene of confusion and noise, sufficient to have drowned her cries if she had uttered any. Among other things, he observed that they threw a quantity of oil, salt, and dry straw, to increase the fury of the flame; and in less than ten minutes, nothing remained but ashes. What rendered this sacrifice the more unnatural, was, his being an old man, and she a young woman; but then he was a Brahmin! and it is considered incumbent on the widow of a Brahmin to pay this respect to his remains, or become an outcast from her family for ever...

4. SATI IN THE TEHRI REGION, WILLIAM MOORCROFT WHO TOURED THE REGION FROM 1819 TO 1825 AND WAS THE FIRST EUROPEAN TO CROSS THE HIMALAYAS (MOORCROFT 1 1989: 145-46)

The practice of the horrible rite of Sati is frequent in these mountains: two widows were burnt during my stay, the elder of whom was not more than fourteen. The wives of

Fateh Chand [brother of Sansar Chand] were in readiness to accompany his body to the pile, when the success of my endeavours rescued them, for a while at least, from so fearful a consummation.

5. PREVENTION OF A SATI, *CALCUTTA JOURNAL*, 19 MARCH 1823 (RAY 1985: 123-29)

To the Editor of the Journal
Sir,

Among the many instances of the immolation of Hindoo Widows, with the bodies of their deceased Husbands, brought to public notice through the medium of the *Calcutta Journal*, I believe, very few, indeed, have been prevented from taking place by the presence and exertions of Europeans, who are for humanity's sake so much interested in the entire abolition of this cruel and dreadful roasting system, at which human nature shudders. I shall therefore, take the liberty, through the same useful channel, of giving a plain statement of facts, regarding the prevention of a Suttee, which was to have taken place, on the 10th instant, at the small village of Buja, about three and a half miles distant from the post of Kotgurh; but for the timely presence of a single European (the writer of this) who was the means of obviating it.

On the evening of the 9th instant, a report was circulated in this neighbourhood that the widow of a Zumeendar of Kunait cast [caste] in consequence of the demise of her husband the preceding day, had come to the resolution of sacrificing herself on the funeral pile, the day following about noon, which she was deterred from carrying into effect earlier, owing to the badness of the weather. By mere accident, the circumstances came to my knowledge, and as occurrences of this nature are rare to the best of my information, though they do occasionally come to pass in this quarter; and having never had an opportunity of being present at one of these inhuman offerings, of a deluded, degraded, and a religiously immoral people, I was firmly resolved on being an eye witness of the ceremony, in the faint though uncertain hope that an European spectator might prove serviceable to the devoted victim when the dreadful moment arrived.

With this view, early after breakfast on the 10th, I repaired to the spot on foot as quickly as possible, lest the sacrifice should take place earlier than was given out, accompanied by some of my servants and a good many other people, some of whom were of the Rajpoot cast. On my arrival at the village, which I found to be half a mile and upwards, beyond the spot where the funeral pile was to be erected, I saw several hundred people — men, women and children, who had assembled from the surrounding villages; far and near, to witness the Tumashee, as they called it, of a human being burnt to ashes; and I immediately sent a person to inform the intended victim of a superstitious and barbarous religion, that I wished to see and speak with her. Soon after moving forward a little, I observed her dancing, apparently in tolerable though assumed spirits to the music of drums and trumpets, in the midst of a crowded circle of women, close to which the corpse of her husband was lying on a pall covered, and wrapped up with various silks. On my approaching her, the music ceased, and I addressed her and the assembled multitude, in the following terms: - I asked her, if she intended to ascend the flaming pile of her deceased partner in life; she unhesitatingly replied, that she did; and that the time for the ceremony had arrived. I then explained to her, that self-destruction was the worst of acts, and a heinous crime in the sight of the Supreme Ruler of the universe; that if she did not at once retract her vow, she would in a very short time rashly force herself into the presence of her Maker. To all which she answered with composure, that it was her own free will, having no family or near relations, she could not survive her husband and would follow him; and having bathed the corpse according to custom, she could not now return to her dwelling; but must destroy herself as other females of her family had done before her, or be considered in the light of an outcast the remainder of her life. She then inquired over and over again if she did not burn herself, how she could, deprived as she was of her husband, alone manage to earn a subsistence for her future support? To this, I immediately replied, that I would willingly provide her during life with every necessary she might stand in need of. I spoke to several of the people near me, regarding her fate, and they told me they could not take upon themselves to interfere in the matter.

I left her for a few minutes, but before doing so, thinking, I perceived from her manners and actions, some symptoms of wavering; arising, as I supposed, from what she often repeated, about a provision for her future life, in the event of retracting the rash step she was on the point of committing. I again readily and more anxiously approached her, reiterating my entreaties with more force, using every argument in my power, and offering over and over again to support her for life. After a considerable time had been spent in this manner, I plainly saw, she began to listen more attentively, to what I urged in dissuading her from the dreadful crime of self-immolation, and being ably seconded in this good work by several of the Hindoos who accompanied me, and by others who, (to their honor let it be said), to my joy and surprise, instantly stepped forward, supported my arguments, unsolicited, in a manner I little expected, and reasoned with the woman to comply with my wishes. Upon which soon after she gave a tacit assent: the corpse was conveyed forthwith to the pile, the assembled multitude dispersed, disappointed at the result of my humble endeavours, and I had the inexpressible satisfaction of beholding at a distance (for I was determined not to leave the spot where I had taken my stand till the ceremony of burning the body of the deceased had terminated, lest the widow who had taken her seat near me, should again consent and follow the procession, which was preceded by drums and trumpets) the flaming pile which consumed to ashes the remains of her late husband.

At the period of my arrival, the woman was decked out in her best attire for the occasion of her exit from this world, dancing and singing a doleful and melancholy song to rude noisy and discordant instruments, in which last, many others of the women present joined. She appeared perfectly sensible and composed. She is between 40 and 50 years of age and now appears happy and contented at having been timely rescued from the worst of deaths through the humble exertions and persuasive means adopted by a single European.

In sending these particulars for publication, instrumental as I have been in preserving the life of a poor and destitute Hindoo Widow, I take no credit to myself; I do so more in the hope that others of our nation, similarly situated and prompted by humanity will never allow of an occurrence of this nature to happen without using their best and every endeavour for its prevention. On leaving this place, I did so with the firm determination of rendering the intended victim every assistance in my power; but I little expected that persuasive arguments alone would have terminated so favourably as they have done in this instance and first attempt of a single individual.

Some of the people assembled were much disappointed, especially the Brahmans, who assist on all such occasions; an interested, discontented and vile set of wretches, who though they live on the fat of the land, are always dissatisfied, and one or two others who expected to benefit by her untimely destruction; however the majority expressed themselves in a very different manner; in a manner that surprized me not a little, considering that the population of these hills with the exception of a few scattered Mohumedan families, consists entirely of Hindoos.

It is worthy of remark in this instance, that the deceased husband died two days previous to that on which the performance of this horrible sacrifice was to have taken place; and this being the case, is it not contrary to the customs observed by the Hindoos? As far as my knowledge extends, it is a gross violation of Hindooism; for on the demise of any of them, whether of a high or low cast, no food should be eaten or water drunk by any of the family of relations of the deceased person till his body has either been consumed by the flames, buried or thrown into a river.

I am perfectly convinced from what I know of the character of the mountaineers, after a few years residence among them, (many of whom even of the better sort express their detestation and deprecate this inhuman custom) that a single word from our enlightened Government would put a final stop to the practice throughout the whole of the hill dependencies. Why I should like to know, cannot the Burning of Widows be prevented by an order equally as well as the atrocious crime of Female Infanticide, once so prevalent in these mountains and at Sagur? And it still continues in its full vigour in the protected Seikh States, where it is as notorious as that of the Immolation of Widows in various parts near the seat of the Supreme Government. This species of crime is also common among all Rajpoots, who assign as a reason for burying their infant female children as soon as born, the great expense and difficulty attending a suitable marriage of that high, proud and warlike people. The thoughts of future dishonour to any of their females, drives them to despair and to commit the most cruel and unheard of acts on that portion of the human species, which it is incumbent on and the duty of man to rear with that care and attention which the frailty of the sex requires.

Let it be here mentioned to the honour of an individual that he was the means of preventing a similar sacrifice at Soohathoo some months ago. I am not sufficiently acquainted with the circumstances to state them, but I understand that after the woman had actually set out for the pile, he induced her to return.

In conclusion, I may further add for the information of others, that of three instances of Suttees which were about to take place to my knowledge, in these mountains, and at which Europeans were present, at all events aware of, two of them have been obviated; which is an example to many interested in the abolition of the custom that should not be passed over in silence.

Your obedient servant, P-G-.

Kotgurh, December 12, 1822

P.S. - Since the above was written, two other Sutees were about to take place at Kotgurh; both Widows, who were in an advanced state of pregnancy, wished to destroy themselves with their deceased husbands; but I rejoice to say, that the Natives, for the sake of their infant families, considering their intentions nothing less then murder, overruled their wishes, and in one of them absolutely used force for its prevention. This being the case, may I ask any of your numerous Correspondents whether compulsory measures would not be justifiable on like occasions! for had these deluded women been allowed to follow their own inclinations, four instead of two human beings would have suffered the cruelest of deaths.

6. THE SATI, FANNY PARKES, WHO TRAVELLED IN INDIA FROM 1822 TO 1846 (PARKES 2003: 58-61)

A rich *baniya,* a corn chandler, whose house was near the gate of our grounds, departed this life; he was an Hindu. On the 7th of November, the natives in the bazaar were making a great noise with their tom-toms, drums, and other discordant musical instruments, rejoicing that his widow had determined to perform *sati,* i.e. to burn on his funeral-pile.

The magistrate sent for the woman, used every argument to dissuade her, and offered her money. Her only answer was dashing her head on the floor, and saying, 'If you will not let me burn with my husband, I will hang myself in your court of justice.' The *shastras* say, 'The prayers and imprecations of a *sati* are never uttered in vain; the great gods themselves cannot listen to them unmoved.'

If a widow touch either food or water from the time her husband expires until she ascends the pile, she cannot, by

Hindu law, be burned with the body; therefore the magistrate kept the corpse *forty-eight* hours, in the hope that hunger would compel the woman to eat. Guards were set over her, but she never touched anything. My husband accompanied the magistrate to see the *sati:* about five thousand people were collected together on the banks of the Ganges: the pile was then built, and the putrid body placed upon it; the magistrate stationed guards to prevent the people from approaching it. After having bathed in the river, the widow lighted a brand, walked round the pile, set it on fire, and then mounted cheerfully: the flame caught and blazed up instantly; she sat down, placing the head of the corpse on her lap, and repeated several times the usual form, *'Ram, Ram, sati; Ram, Ram, sati;* i.e. 'God, God, I am chaste.'

As the wind drove the fierce fire upon her, she shook her arms and limbs as if in agony; at length she started up and approached the side to escape. An Hindu, one of the police who had been placed near the pile to see she had fair play, and should not be burned by force, raised his sword to strike her, and the poor wretch shrank back into the flames. The magistrate seized and committed him to prison. The woman again approached the side of the blazing pile, sprang fairly out, and ran into the Ganges, which was within a few yards. When the crowd and the brothers of the dead man saw this, they called out, 'Cut her down, knock her on the head with a bamboo; tie her hands and feet, and throw her in again' and rushed down to execute their murderous intentions, when the gentlemen and the police drove them back.

The woman drank some water, and having extinguished the fire on her red garment, said she would mount the pile again and be burned.

The magistrate placed his hand on her shoulder (which rendered her impure), and said, 'By your own law, having once quitted the pile you cannot ascend again; I forbid it. You are now an outcast from the Hindus, but I will take charge of you, the Company will protect you, and you shall never want food or clothing.'

He then sent her, in a palanquin, under a guard, to the hospital. The crowd made way, shrinking from her with signs of horror, but returned peaceably to their homes: the Hindus annoyed at her escape, and the Musulmans saying, 'It was better that she should escape, but it was a pity we should have lost the *tamasha* (amusement) of seeing her burnt to death.'...

While we were in Calcutta, many satis took place; but as they were generally on the other side of the river, we only heard of them after they had occurred. Here the people passed in procession, flags flying, and drums beating, close by our door. I saw them from the verandah; the widow, dressed in a red garment, was walking in the midst. My servants all ran to me, begging to be allowed to go and see the *tamasha* (fun, sport), and having obtained permission, they all started off; except one man, who was pulling the *pankha,* and he looked greatly vexed at being obliged to remain...

The *sati* took place on the banks of the Ganges, under the Bund between the Fort and Raj Ghat, a spot reckoned very holy and fortunate for the performance of the rite.

Several of our friends requested me, in case another *sati* occurred, to send them timely notice. Five days afterwards, I was informed that a *ranee* (Hindu Queen or Princess) was to be burned. Accordingly I sent word to all my friends. Eight thousand people were assembled on the *sati-mound,* who waited from midday to sunset: then a cry arose —The memsahib sent us here! The memsahib said it was to take place today! See, the sun has set, there can now be no *sati!'* The people dispersed. My informant told me what he him self believed, and I mystified some eight thousand people most unintentionally.

TEMPLE OF BHAWANI AND SATIS, ALOPEE BAGH

In Alopee Bagh, in the centre of a large plantation of mango trees, is a small temple dedicated to Bhawani; there is no image in it, merely a raised altar, on which victims were, I suppose, formerly sacrificed. Each of the small buildings on the right contains the ashes of a *sati;* there are seven *sati-graves* of masonry on this, and six of earth on the other side, near the temple, in the mango tope. The largest *sati-tomb* contains the ashes of a woman who was burnt in 1825, i.e. six years ago. The ashes are always buried near a temple sacred to Bhawani, and *never* by any other. Families too poor to raise a tomb of masonry in memory of the burnt-sacrifice are contented to raise a mound of earth, and place a *kulsa* of red earthenware to mark the spot...

7. A SATI ON THE NARMADA IN 1829, W.H. SLEEMAN WHO SERVED IN THE SAGAR AND NARMADA REGION, (SLEEMAN 2003: 17-22)

On Tuesday, November 24, 1829, I had an application from the heads of the most respectable and most extensive family of Brahmans in this district to suffer this old woman to burn herself with the remains of her husband, Ummed Singh Upadhya, who had that morning died upon the banks of the Nerbudda. I threatened to enforce my order and punish severely any man who assisted; and placed a police guard for the purpose of seeing that no one did so. She remained sitting by the edge of the water without eating or drinking. The next day, the body of her husband was burned to ashes in a small pit of about eight feet square, and three or four feet deep, before several thousand spectators who had assembled to see the suttee. All strangers dispersed before evening, as there seemed to be no prospect of my yielding to the urgent solicitations of her family, who dared not touch food till she had burned herself, or declared herself willing to return to them. Her sons, grandsons, and some other relations remained with her, while the rest surrounded my house, the one urging me to allow her to burn, and the other urging her to desist. She remained sitting on a bare rock in the bed of the Nerbudda, refusing every kind of sustenance, and exposed to the intense heat of the sun by day, and the severe cold of the night, with only a thin sheet thrown over her shoulders. On Thursday, to cut-off all hope of her being moved from her purpose, she put on the *dhaja*, or coarse red turban, and broke her bracelets in pieces, by which she became dead in law, and forever excluded from castes. Should she choose to live after this, she could never return to her family. Her children and grandchildren were still with her, but all their entreaties were unavailing; and I became satisfied that she would starve herself to death, if not allowed to burn, by which the family would be disgraced, her miseries prolonged, and I myself rendered liable to be charged with a wanton abuse of authority, for no prohibition of the kind I had issued had as yet received the formal sanction of the Government.

On Saturday, the 28th, in the morning, I rode out ten miles to the spot, and found the poor old widow sitting with the *dhaja* round her head, a brass plate before her with undressed rice and flowers, and a coconut in each hand. She talked very collectedly, telling me that she had determined to mix her ashes with those of her departed husband, and should patently wait my permission to do so, assured that God would enable her to sustain life till that was given, though she dared not eat or drink. Looking at the sun, then rising before her over a long and beautiful reach of the Nerbudda river, she said calmly, 'My soul has been for five days with my husband's near that sun, nothing but my earthly frame is left; and this I know you will in time suffer to be mixed with the ashes of his in yonder pit, became it is not in your nature or usage wantonly to prolong the miseries of a poor old woman.'

'Indeed, it is not, — My object and duty is to save and preserve them; and I am come to dissuade you from this idle purpose, to urge you to live, and to keep your family from the disgrace of being thought your murderers.'

'I am not afraid of their ever being so thought: they have all, like good children, done everything in their power to induce me to live among them, and, if I had done so, I know they would have loved and honoured me. But my duties to them have now ended. I commit them all to your care, and I go to attend my husband, *Ummed Singh Upadhya*, with whose ashes on the funeral pile mine have been already three times mixed.'

This was the first time in her long life that she had ever pronounced the name of her husband, for in India no woman, high or low, ever pronounces the name of her husband — she would consider it disrespectful towards him to do so; and it is often amusing to see their embarrassment when asked the question by any European gentleman. ... When the old lady named her husband, as she did with strong emphasis, and in a very deliberate manner, everyone present was satisfied that she had resolved to die. 'I have,' she continued, 'tasted largely of the bounty of Government, having been maintained by it with all my large family in ease and comfort upon our rent-free lands; and I feel assured that my children will not be suffered to want; but with them I have nothing more to do, our intercourse and communion here end. My soul *(pran}* is with *Ummed Singh Upadhya*, and my ashes must here mix with his.'

Again looking to the sun — 'I see them together,' said she, with a tone and countenance that affected me a good deal, 'under the bridal canopy!' — alluding to the ceremonies of marriage; and I am satisfied that she at that moment really believed that she saw her own spirit and that of her husband under the bridal canopy in paradise.

I tried to work upon her pride and her fears, I told her that it was probable that the rent-free lands by which her family had been so long supported might be resumed by the Government as a mark of its displeasure against the children for not dissuading her from this sacrifice; that the temples over her ancestors upon the bank might be levelled with the ground, in order to prevent their operating to induce others to make similar sacrifices; and lastly, that not one single brick or stone should ever mark the place where she died if she persisted in her resolution But, it she consented to live, a splendid habitation should be built for her among these temples, a handsome provision assigned for her support out of these rent-free lands, her children should come daily to visit her, and I should frequently do the same She smiled, but held out her arm and said: 'My pulse has long ceased to beat, my spirit has departed, and I have nothing left but a little *earth*, that I wish to mix with the ashes of my husband. I shall suffer nothing in burning, and, if you wish proof, order some fire, and you shall see this arm consumed without giving me any pain.' I did not attempt to feel her pulse, but some of my people did, and declared that it had ceased to be perceptible. At this time every native present believed that she was incapable of suffering pain, and her end confirmed them in their opinion.

Satisfied myself that it would be unavailing to attempt to save her life, 1 sent for all the principal members of the family, and consented that she should be suffered to burn herself if they would enter into engagements that no other member of their family should ever do the same. This they all agreed to, and the papers having been drawn out in due form about midday, I sent down notice to the old lady, who seemed extremely pleased and thankful. The ceremonies of bathing were gone through before three, while the wood and other combustible materials for a strong fire were collected and put into the pit. After bathing, she called for a 'pan' (betel leaf) and ate it, then rose up and with one arm on the shoulder of her eldest son and the other on that of her nephew, approached the fire. I had sentries placed all round, and no other person was allowed to approach within five paces. As she rose up fire was set to the pile and it was instantly in a blaze. The distance was about 150 yards. She came on with a calm and cheerful countenance, stopped once, and, casting her eyes upward, said, 'Why have they kept me five days from thee, my husband?' On coming to the sentries her supporters stopped; she walked once round the pit, paused a moment, and, while muttering a prayer, threw some flowers into the fire. She then walked up deliberately and steadily to the brink, stepped into the centre of the flame, sat down, and leaning back in the midst as if reposing upon a couch, was consumed without uttering a shriek or betraying one sign of agony.

A few instruments of music had been provided, and they played as usual, as she approached the fire, not, as is commonly supposed, in order to drown screams, but to prevent the last words of the victim from being heard, as these are supposed to be prophetic and might become sources of pain or strife to the living. It was not expected that I should yield, and but few people had assembled to witness the sacrifice, so that there was little or nothing in the circumstances immediately around to stimulate her to any extraordinary exertions; and I am persuaded that it was the desire of again being united to her husband in the next world and the entire confidence that she would be so if she now burned herself that alone sustained her. From the morning he died (Tuesday) till Wednesday evening she ate *'pans,'* or betel leaves, but nothing else; and from Wednesday evening she ceased eating them. She drank no water from Tuesday. She went into the fire with the same cloth about her that she had worn in the bed of the river; but it was made wet from a persuasion that even the shadow of any impure thing falling upon her from going to the pile contaminates the woman unless counteracted by the sheet moistened in the holy stream.

I must do the family the justice to say that they all exerted themselves to dissuade the widow from her purpose, and had she lived she would assuredly have been cherished and honoured as the finest member of the whole house. There is no people in the world among whom parents are more loved, honoured, and obeyed than among the Hindoos; and the grandmother is always more honoured than the mother. No queen upon her throne could ever have been approached with more reverence by her subjects than was this old lady by all the members of her family as she sat upon a naked rock in the bed of the river, with only a red rag upon her head and a single white sheet over her shoulders.

8. A SATI AS NARRATED BY SIR FREDERICK HALLIDAY, THE FIRST LIEUTENANT-GOVERNOR OF BENGAL, 1854–1859 (BUCKLAND 1976: 160-61)

Suttee was prohibited by law in 1829. At and before that time I was acting as Magistrate of the district of Hooghly. Before the new law came into operation notice was one day brought to me that a *Suttee* was about to occur a few miles from my residence. Such things were frequent in Hooghly as the banks of that side of the river were considered particularly propitious for such sacrifices. When the message reached me, Dr. Wise of the Medical Service and a clergyman (whose name I forget) who was Chaplain to the Governor General, were visiting me and expressed a wish to witness the ceremony. Accordingly we drove to the appointed place where a large crowd of natives was assembled on the river bank and the funeral pile already prepared, the intended victim seated on the ground in front of it. Chairs were brought for us and we sat down near the woman. My companions, who did not speak the language, then began to press the widow with all the reasons they could urge to dissuade her from the purpose, all of which at their request I made the woman understand in her own language. To this she listened with grave and respectful attention but without being at all moved by it; the priests and many of the spectators also listening to what was said.

At length she showed some impatience and asked to be allowed to proceed to the pile. Seeing that nothing further could be done, I gave her the permission, but before she had moved, the clergyman begged me to put to her one more question, — "Did she know what pain she was about to suffer?" She, seated on the ground close to my feet, looked up at me with a scornful expression in her intelligent face and said for answer, "Bring a lamp": the lamp was brought, of the small sauce-boat fashion used by peasants, and also some *ghi* or melted butter and a large cotton wick. These she herself arranged in the most effective form and then said, "Light it;" which was done and the lamp placed on the ground before her. Then steadfastly looking at me with an air of grave defiance she rested her right elbow on the ground and put her finger into the flame of the lamp. The finger scorched, blistered, and blackened and finally twisted up in a way which I can only compare to what I have seen happen to a quill pen in the flame of a candle. This lasted for some time, during which she never moved her hand, uttered a sound or altered the expression of her countenance. She then said: "Are you satisfied?" To which I answered hastily, "Quite satisfied," upon which with great deliberation she removed her finger from the flame saying: "Now may I go?" To this I assented and she moved down the slope to the pile. This was placed on the edge of the stream. It was about 4 feet high, about the same length, and perhaps 3 feet broad, composed of alternate layers of small billets of wood and light dry brushwood between 4 upright stakes. Round this she was marched in a noisy procession 2 or 3 times and then ascended it, laying herself down on her side with her face in her hands like one composing herself to sleep, after which she was covered up with light brushwood for several inches, but not so as to prevent her rising had she been so minded. The attendants then began to fasten her down with long bamboos. This I immediately prohibited and they desisted unwillingly but without any show of anger. Her son, a man of about 30, was now called upon to light the pile.

It was one of those frequent cases in which the husband's death had occurred too far off for the body to be brought to the pile, and instead of it a part of his clothing had been laid thereon by the widow's side. A great deal of powdered resin and, I thing, some *ghi* had been thrown upon the wood which first gave a dense smoke and then burst into flame. Until the flames drove me back I stood near enough to touch the pile, but I heard no sound and saw no motion, except one gentle upheaving of the brushwood over the body, after which all was still. The son who had lighted the pile remained near it until was in full combustion, and then rushing up the bank threw himself on the ground in a paroxysm of grief. So ended the last *Suttee* that was lawfully celebrated in the district of Hooghly and perhaps in Bengal.

The prohibition of this horrible custom which had been a subject of grave apprehension to which the Government, until the time of Lord William Bentinck, had always feared to apply itself was affected without the smallest opposition or difficulty. At first applications for leave to perform it were not unfrequent but being in every case sternly forbidden were at once abandoned, the Brahmins merely remarking that if the widow was not permitted to burn she would infallibly be struck dead. This never occurred in my district or anywhere else so far as I know.

9. SATI IN GUJERAT, A.K. FORBES (FORBES II 1997: 201)

RAJA GUMBHEER SINGH, RAJA OF EDUR

In the year AD 1833, Raja Gumbheer Singh became a Dev. Fourteen Ranees became suttees with his corpse, but the mother of the present raja, Jowan Singh, remained alive to rear her infant son...

On the events following the death of Raja Gumbheer Singh from a dispatch of the Bombay Government to the Court of Directors, dated 8 October, 1833 (Forbes II 1997: 206-07)

We have the honour to communicate to your honorable Court the death of Gumbheer Singh, the Raja of Eedur, which took place on the 12th August last, on which occasion the political commissioner for Goozerat deputed his first assistant, Mr. Erskine, to Eedur, with a view to prevent any disturbances arising in consequence of this event, and at the same time to signify to the several chiefs the desire of the British government to continue the succession in the person of the only son of the late raja; and it is now our painful duty to report to your honorable Court the deplorable tragedy which occurred in the performance of the funeral rites of the deceased.

The death of the raja, who had been for several days in a state of stupor, was for some time concealed, and remained unknown to the mother of the young raja until after the funeral ceremony; but the other seven ranees or wives took the resolution of burning with their husband, and, accordingly, early on the morning of the 13th August, these infatuated women, two concubines of different caste from the raja, one principal personal servant, and four domestic slave women, were taken down with the corpse, and burnt with it before the whole assembled population of Eedur, the ministers and every person of authority aiding in the horrid ceremony. Nor was any effort made by a single person connected with the raja's family, or having any influence at Eedur, to dissuade any of the parties from taking this fatal step. It is stated by Mr. Erskine that one of the ranees was several months advanced in pregnancy, and another, who throughout showed a disinclination to the sacrifice, had never cohabited with the raja. The eldest in years, who was the second in rank, was aged sixty, and the youngest, to whom the raja had only been married nineteen months, was only twenty years of age. Notwithstanding the religious prejudices of the people, an universal feeling of horror and disgust is said to prevail against the principal actors in this atrocity, and it is the general belief that if proper means had been taken, there would not have been more than three lives sacrificed. It is related by an eye witness, that just before the lighting of the pile, the eldest ranee addressed the ministers saying that she herself had all along resolved upon immolating herself, and that no expostulations would have any effect upon her, but that it was strange that she had not heard a word of dissuasion or compassion expressed by any one and the concluded by desiring them to go and live on the plunder they were securing to themselves by the destruction of their chief's whole family. The ministers were influenced by personal interest in sparing the life of the surviving ranee, she being the mother of the raja's only son, and her loss might have been prejudicial to their views.

In the year AD 1835, Raja Kurun Singh of Ahmednugger
died. Mr. Erskine, the British agent, was then at Wuktapoor,
a few miles from that capital. When he heard the news, he
went to Ahmednugger, to prevent the Ranees becoming
suttees. The corpse lay for three days, the belly having been
opened, and filled with spices. On the third day, some
Rajpoot chiefs were sent to Mr. Erskine to urge that the
women would not be burned by force, but at their own desire,
and that it was their custom from the time of their ancestors.
Mr. Erskine detained the ambassadors, but sent no reply.
The Rajpoots in the town, therefore called in Bheels from
the surrounding country, and sent word to Soorujmul to
advance with the troops, determining that they would burn
the women secretly if they could, or otherwise resist the
British agent if he came to prevent them by force. Soorujmul,
however, did not come up until it was too late. The Bheels
secretly erected a funeral pile on the side of the town furthest
removed from the British encampment; they placed within
it much cotton, clarified butter, cocoa nut shells, and other
inflammable substances. Mr. Erskine had set guards at all
the gates of the town, and the Rajpoots, therefore opened a
new one, and, in the middle of the night, armed themselves
and carried the suttees out by it. There were three Ranees
upon whom the desire of accompanying their lord came;
they were daughters of a Deora chief of the house of Seerohee,
of the Chowra of Wursora, and of the Rehwur of Runasun.
The Rajpoots had taken the precaution of placing Bheels to
watch Mr. Erskine's camp, and, when the suttees were
burned, the flame of the pile rising high into the air, attracted
the attention of the British agent, who sent to ascertain the
cause. The Bheels opposed this advanced party, and let fly
arrows at them. The agent then mounted, and moved on
with his force, but the affair was over, and the Rajpoots
retired; however one British officer was shot by the Bheels.

MR. ERSKINE TO THE RESIDENT AT BARODA, 9th FEBRUARY, 1835 (FORBES II 1997: 212)

The camp was removed about eight o'clock, and all was quiet till an alarm was given about half-past two o'clock in the morning, that the pile was on fire. The Guikowar horse were encamped between the ground we formerly occupied and the river, on the banks of which the pile had been erected, and I have been informed this morning that the cries and supplications of the women were so vociferous, that every man who was asleep started from his bed. Enough people to perpetrate the violence were taken, but no more, and the women were dragged over a broken part of the wall, on the river side, by these ruffians, attended by Kurun Singh's two sons, and, with the utmost haste, hurried into the pile, which, saturated with oil and clarified butter, was set fire to, and the abomination completed. Any attempt to prevent the sutee must have been too late, as, when I was informed of the fire, I beheld the extensive blaze, and knew that all was over.

SATI NOW RARE, A.K. FORBES, (FORBES II 1997: 427-28)

.... These spectacles, so full of horror, are now, it is true, but rarely witnessed: they still, occur sometimes. The rite was compulsory only in the case of Rajpoots; by some castes of Hindoos, — as, for instance, by the Nagur Brahmins, — it was never practiced at all.

10. MARIANNE POSTANS (YOUNG), WHO VISITED CUTCH IN 1834, DESCRIBES AN IMMOLATION (*CUTCH; OR RANDOM SKETCHES* 1839; REPRODUCED IN PEARCE II 1989: 304-07

News of the widow's intentions having spread, a great concourse of people of both sexes, the women clad in their gala costumes, assembled round the pyre. In a short time after their arrival the fated victim appeared, accompanied by the Brahmins, her relations, and the body of the deceased. The spectators showered chaplets of mogree upon her head, and greeted her appearance with laudatory exclamations at her constancy and virtue. The women specially pressed forward to touch her garments — an act which is considered meritorious, and highly desirable for absolution and protection from the 'evil eye.' The widow was a remarkably handsome woman, apparently about thirty, and most superbly attired. Her manner was marked by great apathy to all around her, and by a complete indifference to the preparations which for the first time met her eye. From this circumstance an impression was given that she might be under the influence of opium; and in conformity with the declared intention of the European officers present to interfere should any coercive measures be adopted by the Brahmins or relatives, two medical officers were requested to give their opinion on the subject. They both agreed that she was quite free from any influence calculated to induce torper or intoxication.

Captain Burnes then addressed the woman, desiring to know whether the act she was about to perform, were voluntary or enforced, and assuring her that, should she entertain the slightest reluctance to the fulfillment of her vow, he, on the part of the British Government, would guarantee the protection of her life and property. Her answer was calm, heroic and constant to her purpose: 'I die of my own free will; give me back my husband, and I will consent to live; if I die not with him, the souls of seven husbands will condemn me.'

Ere the renewal of the horrid ceremonies of death were permitted again, the voice of mercy, of expostulation, and even of entreaty, was heard; but the trail was vain, and the cool and collected manner with which the woman still declared her determination unalterable, chilled and startled the most courageous. Physical pangs evidently excited no fears in her; her singular creed, the customs of her country, and her sense of conjugal duty, excluded from her mind the natural emotions of personal dread; and never did martyr to a true cause go to the stake with more constancy and firmness, than did this delicate and gentle woman prepare to become the victim of a deliberate sacrifice to the demonical tenets of her heathen creed.

Accompanied by the officiating Brahmin, the widow walked seven times round the pyre, repeating the usual mantras, or prayers, strewing rice and cowries on the ground, and sprinkling water from her hand over the bystanders, who believe this to be efficacious in preventing disease, and in expiating committed sins. She then removed her jewels and presented them to her relations, saying a few words to each with a calm soft smile of encouragement and hope.

The Brahmins then presented her with a lighted torch, bearing which —

Fresh as a flower just blown,
And warm with life her youthful pulses playing,

she stepped through the fatal door, and sat within the pile. The body of her husband, wrapped in rich kinkaub, was then carried seven times round the pile, and finally laid across her knees. Thorns and grass were piled over the door; and again it was insisted that free space should be left, as it was hoped the poor victim might yet relent, and rush from her fiery prison to the protection so freely offered. The command was readily obeyed; the strength of a child would have sufficed to burst the frail barrier which confined her, and a breathless pause succeeded; but the woman's constancy was faithful to the last. Not a sigh broke the death-like silence of the crowd, until a light smoke curling from the summit of the pyre, and then a tongue of flame darting with bright and lightning-like rapidity into the clear blue sky, told us that the sacrifice was completed.

Fearlessly had this courageous woman fired the pile, and not a groan had betrayed to us the moment when her spirit fled. At sight of the flame a fiendish shout of exultation rent the air; the tom-toms sounded, the people clapped their hands with delight as the evidence of their murderous work burst on their view, whilst the English spectators of this sad scene withdrew, bearing deep compassion in their hearts, to philosophize, as best they might, on a custom so fraught with horror, so incompatible with reason, and so revolting to human sympathy.

11. EXTRACT OF A LETTER FROM THE HON. W. OSBORNE ON THE FUNERAL OF MAHARAJA RANJIT SINGH (OSBORNE 1973: 223-26)

Simla, July 12th, 1839.

Runjeet Sing in dead, poor fellow! And died as like the old Lion as he had lived...His four wives, all very handsome, burnt themselves with his body, as did five of his Cachmerian slave girls, one of whom, who was called the Lotus, or Lily, I often saw last year in my first visit to Lahore. Everything was done to prevent it, but in vain. They were guaranteed in their rank and in all their possessions, but they insisted upon it; and the account from the European officers who were present describes it as the most horrible sight. The four wives seated themselves on the pile with Runjeet Sing's head upon their laps; and his principal wife desired Kurruck Sing, Runjeet's son and heir, and Dheean Sing, the late prime minister, to come to her upon the pile, and made the former take the Maharajah's dead hand in his own, and swear to protect and favour Dheean Sing as Runjeet Sing had done; and she made the latter swear to bear the same true allegiance to the son which he had faithfully borne to his father.

She then set fire to the pile with her own hands, and they are dead — nine living being having perished together without a shriek or a groan. Dheean Sing threw himself twice on the pile, and said he could not survive his master, but was dragged away by main force...

12. SATI BY THE WIVES OF RANJIT SINGH, HENRY STEINBACH (STEINBACH 1982: 17-19)

The funeral obsequies of this extraordinary man were too remarkable not to be mentioned here. Upon his death being made public, the whole of the Sikh Sirdars at Lahore, assembled to do honour to his suttee, and four of his favorite queens, together with seven female slaves, having, in conformity with the horrible practice of the country, expressed their intention of burning themselves upon his funeral pile, preparations were immediately made for the solemnity. It s said that much dissuasion is exercised in cases of suttee; ostensibly such may be the case; but in private, every argument to the contrary is made use of by the relatives of the wretched victim, and the promise once given cannot be retracted. A street of a double line of infantry having been formed, the procession proceeded at a slow pace to its destination, only a quarter of a mile distant, and within the precincts of the palace. The corpse of the late Maharajah, placed upon a splendidly gilt car, constructed in the form of a ship, with sails of gilt cloth to waft him (according to native superstition) into paradise, was borne upon the shoulders of soldiers, preceded by a body of native musicians, playing their wild and melancholy airs. His four queens, dressed in their most sumptuous apparel, then followed, each in a separate gilt chair, borne upon the shoulders of their attendants; the female slaves following on foot. Before each of the queens was carried a large mirror, and gilt parasol, the emblems of their rank. After them came the successor to the throne, the Maharajah Kurruck Singh, attended by the whole of the Sikh Sirdars, barefooted, and clothed in white; none but persons of noble rank being permitted to join the procession. To the last moment of this terrible sacrifice, the queens exhibited the most perfect equanimity; far from evincing any dread of the terrible death which awaited them, they appeared in a high state of excitement, and ascended the funeral pile with alacrity. The slaves also appeared perfectly resigned, but less enthusiastic. The body of the Maharajah having been placed upon the pile, his queens seated themselves around it, when the whole were covered over with a canopy of the most costly Kashmir shawls. The Maharajah Kurruck Singh then taking a lighted torch in his hand, pronounced a short prayer, set fire to the pile, and in an instant the whole mass, being composed of very ignitable material, was in flames.

The noise from the *tom toms* (drums) and shouts of the spectators immediately drowned any exclamation from the wretched victims. It was with some difficulty that the Rajah Dhyan Singh (Runjeet's minister), under strong excitement, was prevented from throwing himself into the flames...

13. SATI AT RANJIT SINGH'S DEATH, S.S. THORBURN, (THORBURN 1970: 20-21)

The end came in the evening. Next morning the corpse was washed with Ganges water and conveyed in state to the place of cremation. Behind the bier, surrounded by priests chanting funeral hymns, were conveyed in gorgeous carriages Runjit Singh's four queens in rich clothing sparkling with jewels, and behind the queens walked five slave-girls plainly clad. Arrived, Rani Kundan, the chief wife, placed the hands of her lord's son, grandson, and prime minister on the breast of the corpse, and caused each to swear to be true to the other two and the Khalsa, otherwise a suttee's curse would bring upon them the torments incurred by the slaughter of a thousand cows. Then mounting the pyre, the brave woman sat down beside the body, and placed the head upon her lap, whilst the other wives and slave-girls — some recent purchases and hardly women yet — grouped themselves around. At the appointed moment the pile was lighted. As the flames shot up, the faces of the devoted women, still calm and transfigured, were visible for the last time: a moment so — then smoke and fire enveloped them. In a little while the sacrifice was consummated; the great Maharaja, his wives, and his slave-girls were ashes.

14. SATI BY THE WIDOW OF RAJA DHYAN SINGH IN 1843, ALEXANDER GARDNER, COLONEL OF ARTILLERY IN THE SERVICE OF MAHARAJA RANJIT SINGH (GARDNER 1970: 245-50)

...Thus perished the wise and brave Dhyan Singh, whose fall was deplored by the whole army: but it was avenged, and that quickly...

The excitement was wound up to frenzy by the conduct of the young and exquisitely lovely wife of Dhyan Singh, the daughter of the Rajput chief of Pathankot. This lady vowed that she would not become *sati* until she had the heads of Lehna Singh and Ajit Singh. I myself laid their heads at the feet of Dhyan Singh's corpse that evening.

The Sindhanwalias attempted to defend the fort, but in a feeble manner at first. Forty thousand men attacked them, and they saw that all was lost. When, however, the wall was breached, and death became imminent, they fought with desperation and inflicted heavy loss on the army. Ajit Singh and Lehna Singh were killed with no more mercy than they had shown, and Raja Dhyan Singh was avenged.

The *sati* of his widow then took place, and seldom, if ever, have I been so powerfully affected as at the self-immolation of the gentle and lovely girl, whose love for her husband passed all bounds. During the day, while inciting the army to avenge her husband's murder, she had appeared in public before the soldiers, discarding the seclusion of a lifetime. When his murderers had been slain she gave directions as to the disposition of his property with a stoicism and self-possession to which no one beside her could lay claim: she thanked her brave avengers, and declared that she would tell of their good deeds to her husband when in heaven. There was nothing left for her, she said, but to join him.

Great efforts were made among the assembly to prevent the sacrifice of a sweet little maiden of nine or ten years of age who had been passionately attached to the murdered Raja. When not allowed to get upon the pyre, she vowed she would not live, slipped from the hands of those who would hold her, rushed to the battlements of the city, and threw herself from them. We picked her up more dead than alive, and the beautiful devotee seated on the pyre at last consented to take the child in her lap to share her doom.

They placed her husband's diamond *kalgi* (aigrette) in her turban, and she then fastened it with her own hands in the turban of her stepson, Hira Singh. Then, smiling on those around, she lit the pyre, the flames of which glistened on the arms and accoutrements, and eve, it seemed to me, on the swimming eyes of the soldiery. So perished the widow of Dhyan Singh, with thirteen of her female slaves.

15. SATI WITNESSED BY SIR HENRY LAWRENCE IN NEPAL (EDWARDES AND MERIVALE II 1872: 36-37)

November 5, 1845. I have just returned from a suttee; after twenty years' residence in India this is the first I have seen. A terrible sight, but less so than I expected. The woman was cool and collected, and evidently under no sort of coercion. The corpse was that of a Goorkha commandant; it was laid on a small platform, raised on six or eight stakes driven into an island, eight or nine feet square, in the bed of the Bagmutty. The platform had a double bottom; between the two was laid wood, resin, and ghee; the corner stakes met above, forming a rude canopy. About a hundred spectators, chiefly beggars and old women, were collected to view the spectacle. Ten or twelve Sepoys and as many Brahmins were assisting around the pile. When Dr. Christie and I arrived the woman was inside a small (open) rattee close to the river, apparently dressing; we could just see her tinsel head-dress. In about five minutes she came out mounted on the back of a man. At the edge of the rattee her carrier stopped, and she, dipping her finger in a platter, took red dye stuff and made *teekas* on the foreheads of some of the assistants. He then carried her to the pile, and round it four or five times, during which time she took rice and spices from a platter and threw it to the people around, who held out their hands, and many their sheets, to catch it; other begged for alms and her ornaments. Two or three tomtoms were all the time being beat. After finishing the circuits, she dismounted, stooped, and washed her hands in the river, and then uncovered her husband's feet, placed her head to them, and kissed them. She then ascended the pile, made more distributions of rice, etc. and some pice, and commenced disrobing herself, taking off her tiara and upper coloured silks, and gave them to persons around. She then sat down and took off her armlets and bracelets and gave them. All this took at least a quarter of an hour, during which time she was as composed as at a festival. She then lay down close behind the corpse, her head close to her husband's. The platform was so narrow that she had to be squeezed between the corpse and the stakes on her side. Her hair throughout was loose, hanging over her shoulder. She was a Goorkha, about thirty-five or forty years old. When laid down, the coloured sheet over her husband was drawn so as to cover her too, and then three strong bamboos were placed across the pair, and each held at either end by a man so as to prevent her rising. They did not press on her, but would have effectually kept her down had she struggled. Over these bamboos some loose faggots were thrown, and then two lighted lamp-wicks were placed on the head of the corpse; and a minute after a torch was applied under the platform close to the heads, when a strong flame broke out. The crowd shouted and the tom-toms beat more loudly so as to have drowned any cry that may have been uttered by the victim; but whatever were her pains, they could not have lasted a minute. The fire was fed with ghee and sulphur, and a strong flame kept up so as in five minutes to have quite consumed all the head of the platform. I have seen the sad spectacle, and shall not willingly witness another...

16. SATI AT MANDI, A MOUNTAIN STATE, G.T. VIGNE (VIGNE I 1981: 82-86)

One morning my munshi came to me, and told me that a Sati (Suttee), or widow, who was going to burn herself on the funeral pile of her husband, was about to pass by the garden gate. I hastened to obtain a sight of her. She was dressed in her gayest attire; a large crowd of persons followed her, as she walked forward with a hurried and faltering step, like that of a person about to faint. A brahmin supported her on either side, and these, as well as many around, were calling loudly and almost fiercely upon the different Hindu deities; and the name which was most repeatedly and most earnestly called upon was that of Jaganath; but I do not know whether they alluded to the great idol of Bengal, or to some local divinity. *Jugu* signifies a place, and *nath* is a Sanscrit word for lord, or master, applied to Vishnu, or Krishna. Her countenance had assumed a sickly and ghastly appearance, which was partly owing to internal agitation, and partly, so I was informed, to the effects of opium and bang [a preparation from the outer bark of hemp], and other narcotics, with which she had been previously drugged, in order to render her less awake to the misery of her situation. She was not, however, so insensible to what was passing as to be inattentive to two persons in particular, amongst several others who were stooping before her, and were evidently imploring her blessing: they were probably near relations. She was presented at intervals with a plate of moist red colour, in which saffron was no doubt an ingredient, and into this she dipped the ends of her fingers, and then impressed them on the shoulders of the persons who stooped before her in order to be thus marked.

In about half an hour the preparations were completed. She was regularly thatched in, upon the top of the pile, whilst her husband's body yet lay outside. It was finally lifted up to her; the head, as usual, and which is the most interesting part of the ceremony, was received upon her lap; the fire was applied in different parts; and all was so quickly enveloped in a shroud of mingled flame and smoke, that I believe her sufferings to have been of very short duration, as she must almost immediately have been suffocated.

At Lahore I once, taking a Sepahi with me, threaded my way up to the pile, and offered the unhappy victim a sum of money if she would not burn. I should perhaps rather say that I mentioned it to the bystanders; for I am not certain that she was told of it, or that she would quite have comprehended my meaning. She was the widow of one of the last of the rightful family of the Jumu Rajahs, who had been dispossessed of their country and possessions by its present Rajah, Gulab Singh.

In this present instance I sent to the Rajah, requesting his interference. He returned me a very civil message, to the purport that he was very sorry for it, but could not interfere, and called upon me shortly afterwards, but not until it was too late. I represented to him that there was nothing he could do which would be so likely to secure to himself the good wishes and considerations of the British community in India, for which he was so anxious, as the suppression of such horrible ceremonies as that which had just taken place. He assured me that it would be impossible to stop them, and that every entreaty was always used to persuade the woman not to burn herself; that presents to a large amount were always offered with the same intention, but were never of any use. It is, I believe, usual to do so, but it has not effect, — at Mundi at least, but that of enhancing the merit of the Sati, who generally turns a deaf ear to all promises and expostulations. The woman became a Sati When she crossed the threshold of her door, and would, most probably (so I was told), have been put to death by her relations had she afterwards retreated. So long as she remained in the house she had the power of refusal; but had she, being the wife of a Rajput, persevered in her determination not to be burnt with her husband, she would have lost her caste, have lived, at least in Mundi, despised and miserable, and would not have been permitted to marry again.

The Rajah also told me that omission of the ceremony would be looked upon as an act of disrespect to the memory of a deceased Rajah; and of the truth of this assertion, there could be no doubt. I had seen the tombs of the Rajahs of Mundi by the roadside, a few hundred yards from the entrance to the town: the place of their ashes is marked by a long narrow stone slab, standing upright in the ground, and on each of them is sculptured, in relief, a small sitting figure of the deceased, attended by other figures in the same attitude, purporting to represent the Satis who were burnt with him. The number of female figures varied, but none of the later Rajahs had fewer than twenty disposed in regular order in rows, above and below him. The late Rajah had been dead but three months, and the puppet representations of no less than twenty-five women, who had been burnt with him, were evidently freshly produced by the rude chisel of the Mundi sculptor...

5

Some Missionary Accounts

1.DESCRIPTION OF A SUTTEE IN 1789 AT BALI, MIDWAY BETWEEN CALCUTTA AND SERAMPORE BY THE BAPTIST DOCTOR, JOHN THOMAS (LEWIS 1873: 142-44)

Lord's-day, August 30th, 1789. — I was called up this morning upon the bank, to see a woman who was going to be burnt alive with her dead husband. I found a great concourse of people gathered together, and the pile preparing. The dead body was close by; and the unhappy woman was a little on one side, being daubed over with turmeric, which is used in their superstitions. The Brahmans, being all around her, I asked for the chief; who seemed excessively confident that he was doing right. I talked with him of the crime of murder, and of self murder; and of the great wrath of Almighty God revealed against all murder. He and others pleaded, first the shastras, then their custom, and, last of all, caste. I argued that, if there were, it must be a shastra of men, or devils, and not of God. And, as to custom, I said, it was the custom of thieves to steal, and of murderers to kill, and it was the custom of many men to ruin themselves in soul and body for ever; but was that any just reason why we should do so too? These and other arguments they assented to, and said that my words were very good. But, last of all, they came to the miserable motive which was chief with them, and that was, they said, if she did not burn, the family would lose caste. All her relations seemed to me influenced by this: and rather than they should suffer disgrace, they were glad that she should suffer a cruel and untimely death.

Moreover I told them that inasmuch as it was the Brahmans' duty, according to the shastras, to forbid all evil among the common people, and they were present, aiding and assisting the murder, they must be obnoxious to punishment, — everyone of them for neglect, and how much more such of them as were active in such a horrid cause.

They had now been hindered for some time in their ceremony, and they entreated me to depart. I was determined to stay, and be at least an eye witness of the whole, so I refused. They became clamorous, and some of them violent; but I told them I knew I was among murderers, and they might murder me if they pleased; but I would rather lose my life than go away. And so I was determined to do; but I really had no apprehension of their doing more than lift me out of their way. Then others persuaded them to be quiet, and begged me to remove a few cubits from the pile. To this I yielded, and, after repeated and gentle entreaties, removed further and further by degrees.

Before this, I should say, the woman had gone off to a little distance. I insisted on speaking with her; but this was strongly objected to. I told them I certainly would, if I died for it. They said that she could not speak to me; and I replied, I only wanted to speak to her, and would not require her to give any answer to what I should say. At length they yielded, and the Brahmans themselves made a path through the multitude, down to the river, where the poor woman was. She was an elderly person, at least fifty years old. Her attendants withdrew, and left her standing in the water, about two feet deep. I asked her, whether or not it was of her own will, or by persuasion of the Brahmans, that she was going to do this violence to herself. She answered, it was of her own will. I endeavoured to prove to her, that no law of God ever required any such thing. I told her that she and I were both sinners against God already; —that we were in this world for a short time, and that there was another state prepared for us. I added, 'You are going to die; or rather, to kill yourself. This is a great sin. God will be very angry with you. Have pity — have mercy on yourself and your children. — Consider what you are about. Your pains of body will soon be over; but your soul will fall into hell-fire and suffer the punishment of self-murderers.'

She seemed to be ready enough to converse. She pointed up to the heavens, and, with seeming composure, said something that I could not hear; but this I understood plainly, pointing to her forehead, she said it was all written there. The bystanders also told me, that she said she had died six times before with this same husband. She was not only infatuated with the dreams and superstitions of the country, but was evidently intoxicated, either with opium, bhang, or spirits. Her speech was thick, and her tongue and eyes heavy, while there was a merry cast upon her countenance. In fact, had I seen her in the field, and on any other occasion, I should have said, That is a drunken woman.

I found all I said of no avail, and returned to the pile, with my soul in uproar. I alternately looked and tormented my own spirit, and then cried out, and told them their hands were imbrued in innocent blood; and that in the account of God they were murderers. Some said my words were very true. The dead body was then laid on the pile, and a little rice and curry set before its mouth. Then, after being washed, the woman was brought from the river, with a basket of *koey*, or parched rice, in her hand. This she scattered about; and, seeing the people scramble for it, she, looking down beside her basket, actually laughed, as though she had not been the victim. I do not think she was suffered to walk alone. I am sure it would have been very crookedly had she done so. She was now immediately laid on the pile; in their doing which she showed some reluctance, by objecting to the placing of the wood, or some other trifle, which they overruled with a great deal of noise. Her right arm being placed under the head of the body, and she lying by its left side, dry *tal* or *toddy-tree* leaves were thrown over them both, and upon these a quantity of oil or *ghi* was poured. On the side where the woman lay, two long bamboos were fastened by ropes to a stake, driven into the earth at the edge of the pile; and the leaves having been laid over the bodies, these bamboos were bent over the pile, and, a man taking hold of each, they were pulled down, so that they must have compressed the bodies like a lemon-squeezer: only the slender bamboos were too flexible to crush her, being intended only to secure her, and to restrain her dying struggles. The nearest relative then set fire to the pile beneath her head, and, with a great shout, they drowned all her expiring shrieks. The flames began slowly to consume, and so ended this horrid scene. I would have made yet more strenuous attempts to save the unhappy victim, but I was well assured that all would be in vain.

I wonder that the Government has never done any thing to put a stop to this most inhuman practice...

2. REV. WILLIAM CAREY ON A SATI HE WITNESSED IN APRIL 1799 AT NOASERAI, THIRTY MILES FROM CALCUTTA (CAREY 1934: 170-71)

We saw a number of people assembled on the river-side. I asked for what they were met, and they told me to burn the body of a dead man. I inquired if his wife would die with him; they answered yes, and pointed to her. She was standing by the pile of large billets of wood, on the top of which lay her husband's dead body. Her nearest relative stood by her; and near her was a basket of sweetmeats. I asked if this was her choice, or if she were brought to it by any improper influence. They answered that it was perfectly voluntary. I talked till reasoning was of no use, and then began to exclaim with all my might against what they were doing, telling them it was it was shocking murder. They told me it was a great act of holiness, and added in a very surly manner, that, if I did not like to see it, I might go further off, and desired me to do so. I said I would not go, that I was determined to stay and see the murder, against which I should certainly bear witness at the tribunal of God.

I exhorted the widow not to throw away her life; to fear nothing, for no evil would follow her refusal to be burned. But in the most calm manner she mounted the pile, and danced on it with her hands extended, as if in the utmost tranquility of spirit. Previous to this, the relative, whose office it was to set fire to the pile, led her six times round it — thrice at a time. As she went round, she scattered the sweetmeats amongst the people, who ate them as a very holy thing. This being ended, she lay down beside the corpse, and put one arm under its neck and the other over it, when a quantity of dry cocoa-leaves and other substances were heaped over them to a considerable height and then *ghi* was poured on the top. Two bamboos were then put over them, and held fast down, and fire put to the pile, which immediately blazed very fiercely, owing to the dry and combustible materials of which it was composed.

No sooner was the fire kindled than all the people set up a great shout of joy, invoking Siva. It was impossible to have heard the woman, had she groaned, or even cried aloud, on account of the shoutings of the people, and again it was impossible for her to stir or struggle, by reason of the bamboos held down on her, like the levers of a press. We made much objection to their use of these, insisting that it was undue force, to prevent her getting up when the fire burned. But they declared it was only done to keep the fire from falling down. We could not bear to see more, but left them, exclaiming loudly against the murder, and filled with horror at what we had seen.

3. TWO IMMOLATIONS WITNESSED BY REV. WILLIAM WARD (WARD IV 1990: 101)

Soon after my arrival in Bengal, I was an eye-witness to two instances of the burning of widows to death: — on the latter occasion two women were burnt together; one of them appeared to possess great resolution, but the other was almost dead with fear. In the year 1812, I saw another widow burnt to death at Soonduru-pooru, a distance of about three miles from Serampore; and in the month of November, 1812, the wife of Ramu-nidhee, a banker, of Serampore, was burnt alive with the dead body of her husband, not half a mile from the Mission-house. These facts respecting the murder of the helpless widow as a religious ceremony are indeed so notorious, that the most careless traveler may convince himself, if he takes the least notice of what is doing on the banks of the river. The natives do not attempt to hide these murders, but rather glory in them as proofs of the divine nature of their religion...

4. SOME ACCOUNTS OF WIDOW IMMOLATION RELATED TO REV. WILLIAM WARD (WARD IV 1990: 101-110)

ACCOUNT I

Several years ago Ram-Nathu the second Sungskritu pundit in the college of Fort William, saw thirteen women burn themselves with one Mooktua-ramu of Oola, near Shantee-pooru. After the pile, which was very large, had been set on fire, a quantity of pitch being previously thrown into it to make it burn the fiercer, another of this man's wives came, and insisted on burning: while she was repeating the formulas, however, her resolution failed, and she wished to escape, but her son, perceiving this pushed her into the fire, which had been kindled on the sloping bank of the river, and the poor woman, to save herself, caught hold of another woman, a wife also of the deceased, and pulled her into the fire where they both perished.

ACCOUNT II

About the year 1789, Ubhuyu-churunu, a bramhun, saw four women burnt with Ramu-kantu, a kooleenu bramhun, at Vasu-duroonee, near Kalee-ghatu. Three of these women were already surrounded by the flames when the fourth arrived. She insisted on being burnt with them; accordingly, after going rapidly through the preparatory ceremonies, (the bramhuns in the mean time bringing a large quantity of combustible materials,) some fresh wood was laid near the fire already kindled, upon which this infatuated female threw herself. In a moment faggots, oil, pitch, &c. were thrown upon her, and, amidst the shouts of the mob, she expired.

ACCOUNT III

Ramu-Huree, a bramhun, had three wives living at Khuruduh, near Calcutta, at the time of his death, about the year 1802. One of them was deranged; with another he had never cohabited, and by the other he had one son. The latter had agreed with her husband, that, whenever he should die, she would burn with him; and he promised her, that if he died at Patna, where his employer lived, the body should be sent down to Khuruduh. This woman touched her husband's body at the time of this agreement, as a solemn ratification of what she said. After some time this man died at Patna, and a friend fastened the body in a box, and sent it down on a boat. As soon as it arrived at Khuruduh, the news was sent to his relations. The wife who had made the agreement failed in her resolution, and sat in the house weeping. Her son, who was grown to manhood, ordered her repeatedly, in the most brutal manner, to proceed to the funeral pile; and reminded her, that, it was through her that his father's body had been brought so far: but she refused and still remained weeping. While this was going forward, the deranged wife, hearing that her husband was dead, and that his body had arrived at the landing-place, instantly declared that she would burn with him. The people endeavoured to terrify her, and divert her from her purpose;

but she persisted in affirming that she would positively burn. She came to the house and poured the most bitter reproaches on the wife who was unwilling to die. This poor deranged wretch had a chain on her leg: a spectator proposed to take it off, and lead her to the funeral pile; and the third wife arriving, she was led with this deranged woman to the body: the wood, and other articles for the funeral pile were prepared, and a large crowd had assembled by the river side. As soon as the deranged wife saw the dead body, which was very much disfigured, and exceedingly offensive, she declared it was not her husband; that in fact they were going to burn her with a dead cow. She poured curses on them all, and protested she would not burn with a dead cow. The other female, who had never touched her husband, except at the marriage ceremony, was then bound to this putrid carcase, and devoured by the flames.

ACCOUNT IV

About the year 1796, the following most shocking and atrocious murder under the name of suhu-murunu, was perpetrated at Mujil-pooru, about a day's journey south from Calcutta. Bancha-ramu, a bramhun of the above place, dying, his wife at a late hour went to be burnt, with the body: all the previous ceremonies were performed; she was fastened on the pile, and the fire was kindled; but the night was dark and rainy. When the fire began to scorch this poor woman, she contrived to disentangle herself from the dead body, and creeping from under the pile, hid herself among some brush-wood. In a little time it was discovered that there was only one body on the pile. The relations immediately took the alarm, and searched for the poor wretch; the son soon dragged her forth, and insisted that she should throw herself on the pile again, or drown or hang herself. She pleaded for her life at the hands of her own son, and declared that she could not embrace so horrid a death — but she pleaded in vain: the son urged, that he should lose his cast, and that therefore he would die, or she should. Unable to persuade her to hang or drown herself, the son and the others present then tied her hands and feet, and threw her on the funeral pile where she quickly perished.

ACCOUNT V

Gopee-nathu, a bramhun employed in the Serampore printing-office, was informed by his nephew, that in the year 1799, he saw thirty seven females burnt alive with the remains of Unutu-ramu, a bramhun of Bagna-para, near Nudeeya. This kooleenu bramhun had more than a hundred wives. At the first kindling of the firer only three of them were present; *but the fire was kept burning three days!* When one or more arrived, the ceremonies were performed, and *they threw themselves on the blazing fire!* On the first day, three were burnt; on the second fifteen; and on the third nineteen! Among these, some were forty-years old, and others as young as sixteen. The three first had lived with this bramhun; the others had seldom seen him. From one family he had married four sisters; two of these were among the slaughtered victims.

ACCOUNT VI

In the year 1812, a kooleenu bramhun, who had married twenty-five women, died at Choona-khalee. Thirteen died during his life-time; the remaining twelve perished with him on the funeral pile, leaving thirty children to deplore the fatal effects of this horrid system.

ACCOUNT VII

Some years ago, a kooleenu bramhun, of considerable property, died at Sookhuchuru, three miles east of Serampore: He had married more than forty women, eighteen of whom perished on the funeral pile. On this occasion a fire extending ten or twelve yards in length was prepared into which they threw themselves, leaving more than forty children.

About the year 1802, the wife of a man of property of the writer cast was burnt at Kashee-pooru, in the suburbs of Calcutta. The bramhun who witnessed this scene informed me, that when he went to the spot, he saw a vast crowd of people assembled; and amongst the rest the above female, a girl about fourteen years old, and another female, of a different cast who had cohabited with the deceased. The girl addressed herself to the mistress of her husband, and asked her what she did there: it was true, her husband had never loved her, nor had he for one day since their marriage lived with her; yet she was now resolved to enjoy his company after death. She added, (continuing her address to the mistress of her husband.) 'If, however, you will accompany him, come, let us burn together; if not, arise and depart.' She then asked the woman what her husband had bequeathed to her, and was answered that he had given her twenty-five roopees, and some clothes. To this the wife of the deceased added twenty-five more. After this conversation, the bramhuns hastened the ceremonies; her friends entreated her to eat some sweetmeats, but she declined it, and declared that she would eat nothing but that which she came to eat, (fire.) At this time the clouds gathered thick, and there was the appearance of heavy rain: some persons urged delay till the rain was over but she requested them to hasten the business, for she was ready. A bramhun now arrived, and entreated the favour of this woman to forgive a debt due to her husband, for which his brother was in confinement. She forgave it, leaving a written order behind her, to which she affixed her mark. After the ceremonies by the side of the river, and near the pile, were concluded, she laid herself down on the pile, placing one arm under the head of the deceased, and the other over his breast, and they were thus tied together. At the time of lighting the pile, the rain fell in torrents, and the fire was so partially lighted, that during half an hour it only singed her clothes and her hair. This devoted female, however, remained in the same posture on the pile till the rain ceased, when, in a few seconds, the fire devoured her. It was reported that she had cohabited with others, but she denied it before she ascended the pile.

ACCOUNT IX

An English clergyman, now deceased, once related to me, two scenes to which he had been an eye-witness: — one was that of a young woman, who appeared to possess the most perfect serenity of mind during every part of the preparatory ceremonies: calm and placid, she acted as though unconscious of the least danger; she smiled at some, gave presents to others, and walked round the funeral pile, and laid herself down by the dead body, with as much composure as though she had been about to take rest at night. The other scene was very different: the woman, middle aged and corpulent, appeared to go through the business with extreme reluctance and agitation; the bramhuns watched her, followed her closely, held her up, and led her round the funeral pile, and seemed to feel uneasy till they had tied her fast to the dead body, and had brought the faggots and bamboo levers over. This clergyman added, that he saw one of this woman's arms move, as in convulsive motions, for some time after the pile was lighted. The Hindoos say, that it is a proof the woman was a great sinner, if any part of her body is seen to move after the pile has been lighted; and, on the contrary, if she is not seen to move, they exclaim, 'Ah ! what a perfect creature she was! What a blessed suhumurunu was her's!' A respectable native once told me, that he had heard of a woman shrieking dreadfully after she was laid on the pile, which, however, did not save her life.

ACCOUNT X

Instances of children of eight or ten years of age thus devoting themselves are not uncommon. About the year 1804, a child eight years old was burnt with the dead body of Hureenathu, a bramhun of Elo, near Calcutta. At the time the news arrived of the death of this child's husband, she was playing with other children at a neighbour's house. Having just before been severely chastised by her aunt, and having formerly suffered much from her, she resolved to burn with the dead body, in order to avoid similar treatment in future; nor could her relations induce her to alter her resolution. She said she would enter the fire, but would not go back to her aunt. As soon as she was laid on the pile, she appeared to die, (no doubt from fear,) even before the fire touched her. The Hindoos say, it is often the case, that the female who is really Sadhwee, is united to her husband immediately on hearing the news of his death, without the delay of the fire. Another instance of the same kind occurred in the year 1802, at Vurisha, near Calcutta; a child eight years old, was burnt with her husband. Before she went to the funeral pile, she was compelled to put her hand upon some burning coals, and hold it there for some time, to convince her friends that she should not shrink at the sight of the fire. About the 1794, a girl, fifteen years old, who had been delivered of her first child about three weeks, was burnt with her husband, Deveee-churunu, a bramhun of Muniramu-pooru near Barrack-pooru. Her friends remonstrated with her and did all except (what they ought to have done) use force. When they urged the situation of the infant she would leave, she begged they would not disturb her mind with such things: it was only a female child, and therefore the leaving it was of less consequence. After she had mounted the pile, she sat up, and assured the officiating bramhun she then recollected, that in a former birth he was her father.

Account XI

Women eighty years old and upwards sometimes burn with their husbands. About the year 1791, Gopalu-naya-lunkara, a very learned bramhun, died at Nudeeya. He was supposed to have been one hundred years old at the time of his death; his wife about eighty. She was almost in a state of second childhood, yet her gray hairs availed nothing against this most abominable custom. A similar instance occurred about the year 1809, at Shantee-pooru when the wife of Rama-chundru-vusoo, a kayusthu, at the age of eighty or eighty-five was burnt with the corpse of her husband.

Account XII

Mrityoonjuyu, the first Sungskritu pundit in the College of Fort-William, once saw a bramhunee at Rungu-pooru, who had escaped from the pile. She was carried away by a mat-maker, from whom she eloped, and afterwards lived with a Musulman groom. About the year 1804, a woman who had lived with a man as his wife, burnt herself with his body at Kalee-ghatu, near Calcutta. Some years ago, a sepoy from the upper provinces died at Khiddiru-pooru, near Calcutta. The woman who had cohabited with him went to the head land-owner, and requested him to provide the materials for burning her with the dead body. He did so, and this adulteress entered, entered the flames, and was consumed with the dead body of her paramour.

Account XIII

In Qrissa, the defenceless widow is compelled to cast herself into a pit of fire. If, on the death of a raja, his wife burn herself with him, his concubines are seized, and by beating, dragging, binding, and other forcible methods, are compelled to throw themselves into the pit, where they are all destroyed together. On this subject I beg leave to insert a letter drawn up by Purushoo-ramu, a learned bramhum – 'Shree Purushoo-ramu writes: I have myself seen the wives of one of the rajas of Oorisya burn with their husband. These are the particulars: after the death of raja Gopee-nat'hu-devu, the head-queen, of her own accord, being prepared to be burnt with the body, a pit was dug, and quantities of wood piled up in it, upon which the corpse was laid, and upon this more faggots: when the fire blazed with the greatest fury, the head-queen cast herself into the flames and perished. The two other wives of the raja were unwilling to follow this example; but they were seized by force, and thrown into the pit, and consumed. This happened about the year 1793.'

5. ACCOUNT OF A SATI BY THE MISSIONARY J. MARSHMAN, INCLUDED BY WILLIAM WILBERFORCE IN THE PUBLISHED EDITION OF HIS SPEECH IN PARLIAMENT IN 1813 (*PARLIAMENTARY DEBATES,* 1ST SERIES, XXVI, 860-62)

A person informing us that a woman was about to be burnt with the corpse of her husband, near our house, I, with several of our brethren, hastened to the place: but before we could arrive, the pile was in flames. It was a horrible sight. The most shocking indifference and levity appeared among those who were present. I never saw any thing more brutal than their behaviour. The dreadful scene had not the least appearance of a religious ceremony. It resembled rabble of boys in England, collected for the purpose of worrying to death a cat or a dog. A bamboo, perhaps twenty feet long, had been fastened at one end to a stake driven into the ground, and held down over the fire by men at the other. Such were the confusion, the levity, the bursts of brutal laughter, while the poor woman was burning alive before their eyes, that it seemed as if every spark of humanity was extinguished by this accursed superstition. That which added to the cruelty was the smallness of the fire. It did not consist of so much wood as we consume in dressing a dinner: no, not this fire that was to consume the living and the dead! I saw the legs of the poor creature hanging out of the fire while her body was in flames. After a while, they took a bamboo ten or twelve feet long and stirred it, pushing and beating the half consumed corpses, as you would repair a fire of green wood, by throwing the unconsumed pieces into the middle. Perceiving the legs hanging out, they beat them with the bamboo for some time, in order to break the ligatures which fastened them at the knees, (for they would not have come near to touch them for the world). At length they succeeded in bending them upwards into the fire, the skin and muscles giving way, and discovering the knee sockets bare, with the balls of the leg bones: a sight this which, I need not say, made me thrill with horror, especially when I recollected that this hapless victim of superstition was alive but a few minutes before. To have seen savage wolves thus tearing a human body, limb from limb, would have been shocking; but to see relations and neighbours do this to one with whom they had familiarly conversed not an hour before, and to do it with an air of levity, was almost too much for me to bear.

You expect, perhaps, to hear, that this unhappy victim was the wife of some Brahmin of high cast. She was the wife of a barber who dwelt in Serampore, and had died that morning, leaving the son I have mentioned, and a daughter of about eleven years of age. Thus has this infernal superstition aggravated the common miseries of life, and left these children stripped of both their parents in one day. Nor is this an uncommon case. It often happens to children far more helpless than these; sometimes to children possessed of property, which is then left, as well as themselves, to the mercy of those who have decoyed their mother to their father's funeral pile!

6. REV. WILLIAM TENNANT IN 1803 (MAJOR 2006: 81, 88, 96, 97)

Human nature is not always consistent; nor are the efforts of the mind always proportioned to our opportunities for exertion. Bred in scenes of the most voluptuous sensuality, these Indian ladies exhibit on occasion the most magnanimous exertion of fortitude of which history records any example... There is hardly an instance of any individual of these ladies, nursed in the lap of pleasure, having shrunk from this horrid trial of their fortitude, after it was undertaken; and incredible as it may seem, hardly any instance of their betraying symptoms of fear, hesitation or pain...

This resolution is formed with deliberation, and is declared to be voluntary and fixed, three several times [sic] in the presence of relations. This is done that no advantage may seem to have been taken of the transient ebullition of frantic grief, and that the person devoting herself might have full time to reflect on the important sacrifice she is about to make to her affections, or to the customs of her country...

Various causes have been assigned for this unexampled fortitude, which perhaps is owing to the all-powerful effect of custom in this country, and the immediate hope of entering on a state of exquisite enjoyment. An Hindoo no more thinks of evading the customary rites of religion, than an European thinks of evading the unerring stroke of death.

7. REV. CLAUDIUS BUCHANAN IN A LETTER TO THE ARCHBISHOP OF CANTERBURY IN 1805 ON INCIDENTS OF SATI WITNESSED BY REV. DAVID BROWN IN THE SUBURBS OF CALCUTTA (PEARSON I 1819: 376)

In the course of the last two months, the Rev. Mr. Brown, the senior of the English clergy now in India, has witnessed the burning alive of eight women at the place of sacrifice, in the suburbs of Calcutta, as he passed casually on his way from his country-house to the church in town. How can the minister of the alter approach without trembling to his holy office, when he reflects on such scenes, and on their connexion with the sin of his country.

8. REV. CLAUDIUS BUCHANAN WRITING FROM CALCUTTA ON 30TH SEPTEMBER 1807 (BUCHANAN 1849: 22)

A horrid tragedy was acted, on the 12th instant, near Barnagore (a place about three miles above Calcutta). A Koolin Brahmin of Cammar-hattie, by name Kristo Deb Mookerjee, died at the advanced age of ninety-two. He had twelve wives: and three of them were burned alive with his dead body. Of these three, one was a venerable lady, having white locks, who had been long known in the neighbourhood. Not being able to walk, she was carried in a palanquin to the place of burning; and was then placed by the Brahmins on the funeral pile. The other two ladies were younger; one of them of a very pleasing and interesting countenance. The old lady was placed on one side of the dead husband, and the two other wives laid themselves down on the other side; and then an old Brahmin, the eldest son of the deceased, applied his torch to the pile, with unaverted face. The pile suddenly blazed, for it was covered with combustibles; and this human sacrifice was completed amidst the din of drums and symbals, and the shouts of Brahmins.

9. REV. CLAUDIUS BUCHANAN ON AN INCIDENT OF SATI NARRATED TO HIM (BUCHANAN 1814; THE INCIDENT IS ALSO QUOTED BY WARD IV 1990: 105)

Goopeenaut, a Brahmun employed in the Serampore printing office in 1799, saw twenty-two females burnt alive with the remains of Ununtu, a Brahmun of Bagnapore, near Nuddeya. This Kooleen Brahmun had more than a hundred wives. At the first kindling of the fire only three of these wives had arrived. The fire was kept kindled three days! On the first day three were burnt, on the second and third days nineteen more. Some of these women were as much as forty years old, and others as young as sixteen. The first three had lived with the Brahmun, the others had seldom seen him. He married in one house four sisters; two of these were burnt.

10. THE BAPTIST MISSIONARY JOURNAL, *FRIEND OF INDIA,* IN SEPTEMBER 1824, CONTAINED THE FOLLOWING ACCOUNT OF A SUTTEE AT CUTTACK IN ORISSA (IT WAS INCLUDED BY J. PEGGS, IN HIS *CRIES OF AGONY*; PEGGS 1984: 3-5)

On Aug.19, 1824, this place was defiled with innocent blood. About twelve o'clock the Judge sent a note to the Mission House, informing us of the intended Suttee. The woman was a Telinga, the wife of a Brahmun who died that morning about daybreak. Her reply to the several questions proposed to her through the Telinga interpreter was, "What have I any more to do with the world? I must go to my husband." Support for life, and a conveyance to her own home, were offered, but they were rejected. From my pundit I have gathered particulars which cast light upon this dreadful rite. He stated, that it is customary to lament the dead with crying and noise, but she did not; sating she was going to her husband. She said, she was a stranger and had nothing, and therefore desired the neighbours to provide what was necessary for a Suttee. She said also, that she had been a Suttee in *three former births*, and must be so *four times more*, and then she should attain endless felicity. Those who should dare to prevent her by confining her in a house or jail, their seed should die and they should descend into hell. Some approved of this, others said, that as she had no son nor daughter therefore she wished to die. To this she replied, she had a brother and sister, and in her own country many friends, but she wished to go to her husband. From joog to joog (age to age), in this manner, with the same husband, she was to be born and die.

"About half-past three o'clock she proceeded to the pile. I was then too unwell to venture out. Mrs. P. saw her on the way and talked with her. About six o'clock in the evening I went to the spot, expecting the tragical business to be closed. I was, however, surprised to find nothing more done than the pile partly prepared. The Judge and three other gentlemen, with some of our English congregation, were present, and a great number of Natives. Frequent and persevering efforts were made by the above gentlemen to dissuade her from her purpose, assisted by the members of the Mission who were present. She was sitting near the pile with the corpse of her husband covered with a cloth lying near her. I knew two Telinga Brahmuns present, and taking them endeavoured to speak to the woman. I told her I was a Padree; that God had sent me and others to teach the people the true Incarnation, Jesus Christ, who died for our sins: that if she would go with me to my house she would be able to learn this knowledge; and that I would send her in a palkee to her own country: but if she ate fire and died now, how could she gain this knowledge without which she could not be saved. I told her, thus to destroy herself was not God's will. I fear my translators were not faithful; but all the poor woman said was, 'Narayun, Narayun.' This she repeated with a stupidity of mind truly indescribable. Mr. B., one of the gentlemen present, was desirous to convince her, by some ordeal, that she could not burn; but the infatuated woman; played with a piece of fire like a child, though when her hand was pressed upon a coal she showed no resolution. He lifted up one of her eye-lids, and affirmed that she was *intoxicated*. This was stated to the Judge, and urged as a sufficient reason to forbid the horrid murder; but he thought it wanted evidence, and hesitated to use his authority to save her. The pile, which was slowly preparing, was about eight feet long, four feet wide, and about two feet high. At each corner was a piece of wood which supported the roof; three sides of the pile were blocked up. Raw flax was laid on the wood, upon which the corpse was placed. Ghee was forbidden to be put on pile by the Judge, that the woman might have the opportunity to escape, by feeling the effects of the fire gradually: a practice which, if the Suttee were always, according to ancient custom, to ascend the funeral pile while burning, or if, previous to if being lighted, she were left unbound and unincumbered, might prevent the shedding of much innocent blood. As she had been touched by several persons after her first bathing, she went to the river and bathed again. I saw her enter the pile as a person would get into bed, and lay herself down by the left side of her husband and farthest from the entrance of the pile. The wood under the corpse, after a short time burned fiercely; and it was horrible to see it consuming; the head and elevated stiffened hand of the deceased, while the poor woman was scarcely touched by the devouring element. I stopped about a quarter of an hour, hoping the unhappy sufferer might labour to escape; but, alas! no signs of it appeared; and, after viewing the burning of the dead; and the living, till my feelings and concern for my health determined me to go away, I left the horrid circle and hastened home. All such outrages upon the principles of society are unnatural and inhuman, and, when said to be from religious motives, a species of insanity; and hence may properly be suppressed by the powerful voice of reason and authority. When shall these murders cease? Where does the salutary godlike power lie, or from what quarter will it originate to abolish them?

11. THE FOLLOWING ACCOUNT WAS COMMUNICATED FROM THE TEMPLE OF JUGGERNAUT IN ORISSA, IN JULY L824, TO J. PEGGS BY HIS COLLEAGUE, THE REV. W BAMPTON (PEGGS 1984: 5-6)

The infatuated woman, whose death I witnessed, was the widow of a Brahmun who had died in the morning. The man's age seems to have been about forty and the woman's thirty-five. The place where the Suttee took place was called Swurgu Dwar, which signifies the gate of heaven; and when I reached it I found the coolies employed in digging the hole, which was circular, about six feet deep, its diameter at bottom perhaps a little less than its depth, and at top twice as much. Soon after my arrival, about twelve persons came, each bringing a load of wood on his or her head, for several of them were women. I charged the labourers with being accessary to the crime about to be committed, and the general reply was, that they worked for money, and did this work as they did other work, because they were paid for it. Carelessness or cheerfulness characterised all the Hindoos near or on the spot. The pit being finished, a quantity of water was mixed with cow-dung and sprinkled on the margin about one-third of the way down; two ropes were also well wetted with the same mixture. Inquiring the use of two bamboos which lay near, I was told that they were *to stir the fire and turn about the bodies*! The bits of wood prepared for the occasion were between twelve and eighteen inches long, and on an average five or six in circumference; a quantity of them were thrown into the pit, and a man at the bottom proceeded to set them up on their ends two or three thick round the sides; upon this he placed a second tier; and on the second, a third; he also covered the bottom perhaps five or six inches thick, so that the pit was now two-thirds lined with wood. Soon after all was finished, the dead man was brought on a rough bier, which I suppose might have been made in less than a quarter of an hour. I soon saw the procession (if it may be called one), halting a few hundred yards before me: the crowd was kept off the woman by a square made of four pieces of wood, five or six feet long. The rabble were preceded by some of their rude music. Unwilling to see her burn herself, my worthy companions, Lieut. W. and T.B. Esq., tried several times to I prevent the horrid deed, and I lent my feeble assistance, but all to no purpose. They halted twenty or thirty yards from the flaming pit, where the last effort was made, and, that failing, her infamous coadjutors gave her a lighted lamp, which I think she put into an earthen pot under her arm. In a little time all was confusion; and a scene, the most perfectly hellish that we ever saw, was presented; a way was made for the woman to the pit, and its margin was left clear; she advanced to the edge facing her husband, and two or three times waved her right hand; she then hastily walked round the pit, and in one place I thought the flames caught her legs; having completed the circle, she again waved her hand as before, and then jumped into the fire...

At this moment I believe the drums beat, and an infernal shout rent the air, but I can scarcely say I know, — all was confusion. A dense smoke issued from the pit, intermixed at intervals with partial bursts of flame, occasioned by quantities of powdered resin thrown into the pit by handfuls. In a little time they allowed the fire to clear itself, and we then saw the wretched woman in the midst of it: I think her posture was that of sitting on her heels; she sometimes moved gently backward and forward, as if she bowed. The poor creature still kept an erect posture; but at length seemed partially to rise, and pitched forward with her head against the side of the pit, about two feet from her husband's left hand. The motion of her head in this position indicated pain, and she continued to live two or three minutes longer. The gentlemen then went home, but I staid a little longer and saw the bodies taken out: for, though the women are burnt in these pits, the bodies are taken out while they are distinguishable, and consumed in two different fires (at least that is the case here), and we are told it is done that *the son may make sure of some fragments of both his parents to be thrown into the Ganges.* Now the ropes came into use; one was doubled and the middle thrown down to catch the man's chin, one or two bamboo levers were put under his head to raise it and get the rope round his neck; the rope was then twisted, in order to fasten it, and they began to draw, but they failed, for the rope slipped off. Another man then attempted to fasten the rope; he succeeded, and they drew up the body, with the exception, I think, of the legs; but it was quite dark, and nothing could be seen but by the light of the fire. They then tried to raise the woman, but could not easily get the rope round her neck, so they put it on her arm, which projected in such a way as to favour their doing so; and, after twisting it well, they drew her nearly to the top of the pit: but they seemed afraid that they should lose her again if they trusted entirely to her arm, so she was held just below the edge of the pit till another man put the other rope under her chin, and she was then drawn quite up. Some of the people employed themselves in arranging the wood for the fires to consume the bodies, and I staid perhaps ten minutes longer, finally leaving the bodies on the brink of the pit. Such are the facts, and I leave them to produce their proper effect.

12. BISHOP HEBER, THE SECOND PROTESTANT BISHOP OF CALCUTTA, ON AN INCIDENT IN 1824 (HEBER I 1993: 70-72)

Returning one day form Calcutta [January 1824], I passed by two funeral piles, the one preparing for a single person, the other nearly consumed, on which a Suttee had just taken place. For this latter purpose a stage had been constructed of bamboos about eighteen inches or two feet above the ground, *on* which the dead body had been laid, and *under* which, as my native servants told me, the unhappy widow had been stretched out, surrounded with combustibles. Only a heap of glowing embers was now seen here, besides two long bamboos, which seemed intended to keep down any struggles which nature might force from her. *On* the stage was what seemed a large bundle of coarse cotton cloth, smoking, and partially blackened, emitting a very offensive smell. This my servants said was the husband's body. The woman they expressly affirmed had been laid *below* it, and ghee poured over her to hasten her end, and they also said the bamboos had been laid *across* her. I notice these particulars, because they differ from the account of a similar and recent ceremony, given by the Baptist Missionaries, in which it is said that the widow is laid by the side of her husband, on the platform, with her arm embracing him, and her face turned to him. Here I asked repeatedly, and received a different account. Yet the Missionaries have had every possible opportunity of learning, if not of actually witnessing, all the particulars of the ceremony which they describe. Perhaps these particulars vary in different instances. At all events it is a proof how hard it is to gain, in this country, accurate information as to facts which seem most obvious to the senses. I felt very sick at heart, and regretted I had not been half an hour sooner, though probably my attempts at persuasion would have had no chance of success. I would at least have tried to reconcile her to life. There were perhaps twenty or thirty people present, with about the same degree of interest, though certainly not the same merriment, as would have been called forth by a bonfire in England. I saw no weeping, and heard no lamentations. But when the boat drew near a sort of shout was raised, I believe in honour of Brahma, which was met by a similar outcry from my boatmen.

SATI IN GHAZIPUR, BISHOP HEBER (HEBER I 1993: 350-52)

... Suttees are more abundant here than even in the neighbourhood of Calcutta, but chiefly confined to the lower ranks. The last yearly returns amounted to above forty, and there were several of which no account was given to the magistrate. It has been, indeed, a singular omission on the part of Government, that, though an ordinance has been passed, commanding all persons celebrating a suttee to send in notice of their intention to the nearest police officer, no punishment has been prescribed for neglect of this order, nor has it ever been embodied in the standing regulations, so as to make it law, or authorize a magistrate to commit to prison for contempt of it...

... the person of whom I was told was no Brahmin; he was a labourer, who had left his family in a time of scarcity, and gone to live (as was believed,) in the neighbourhood of Moorshedabad, whence he had once, in the course of several years, sent his wife a small sum of money from his savings, by a friend who was going up the country. Such remittances, to the honour of the labouring class in India are usual, and equally to their honour, when entrusted to any one to convey, are very seldom embezzled. Some years after, however, when the son of the absentee was grown up, he returned one day from a fair at a little distance, saying he had heard bad news, and that *a man unknown* had told him his father was dead. On this authority the widow determined to burn herself, and it was judged sufficient that an old garment of the supposed dead man should be burned with her. Now, it is very plain how easily, if the son wanted to get rid of his mother, he might have brought home such a story to induce her to burn, and it is also very plain, that whether she was willing or not, he might carry her to the stake, and (if the police are to take no cognizance of the matter) might burn her under pretence of a suttee.

NOT COMMON IN AGRA REGION, BISHOP HEBER (HEBER II 1993: 325)

At Horal [near Dhotana in the province of Agra] ... a small temple is raised in the neighbourhood. Within I saw the representation of four human feet, one pair larger than the other, on a little altar against the wall, and was told that it was the customary way of commemorating that the favourite wife had burnt herself with her husband. This horrible custom, I am glad to find, is by no means common in this part of India; indeed, I have not yet found it common any where except in Bengal, and some parts of Bahar.

13. REV. J. ENGLAND IN THE MADRAS PRESIDENCY, IN A LETTER, DATED JUNE, 1826 (PEGGS 1984: 6-8)

I received a note from a gentleman that a *Suttee* was about to take place near his house. On hastening to the spot, I found the preparations considerably advanced, and a large concourse of spectators assembled. On my left, stood the horrid pile; it was an oblong bed of dry cow-dung cakes, about ten feet long, and seven wide, and three high. At each corner of it, a rough stake about eight feet in length was driven into the ground; and at about a foot from the top of these supporters was fastened, by cords, a frame of the same dimensions as the bed, and forming a flat canopy. This name must have been of considerable weight; it was covered with very dry small faggots, which the officiating Brahmuns continued to throw upon it, till they rose two feet above the framework. On my right, sat the poor deluded widow, who was to be the victim of this heart-rending display of Hindoo *purity* and *gentleness*; she was attended by a dozen or more Brahmuns; her mother, sister, and son (an interesting boy about three years of age), and other relatives were also with her. *Her own infant, not twelve months old, was crafty kept from her by the Brahmuns.* She had already performed a number of preparatory ceremonies; one of which was washing herself in a strong decoction of saffron, which is supposed to have a purifying effect. It imparted to her a horrid ghastliness; - her eyes indicated a degree of melancholy wildness; a forced and unnatural smile now and then played on her countenance: and every thing about her person and her conduct indicated that *narcotics* had been administered in no small quantities. Close by me stood the *Fausdar*, a native officer, who, besides regulating the police, is the chief military officer at the station. So heartily did he engage in this murderous work, that he gave the poor widow twenty pagodas (between six and seven pounds sterling), *to confirm her resolution to be burned*! The Rev. Mr. Campbell addressed her in the Carnatic language, but the effect of his address was counteracted by the influence of the Brahmuns. The pile being completed, a quantity of straw was spread on the top. An increase of activity was soon visible among the men whose *"feet are swift to shed blood."* Muntrams (prayers or incantations) having been repeated over the pile, and the woman and every thing being in readiness, the hurdle to which the corpse of the husband lad been fastened was now raised by six of the officiating Brahmuns; the end of a cord about two yards long, attached at the other end to the head of the bier, was taken by the widow, and the whole moved slowly towards the pile. The corpse was laid on the right side, and four men furnished with sharp swords, one stationed at each corner, now drew them from their scabbards. The trembling, ghastly offering to the Moloch of Hindooism, then began her seven circuits round the fatal pile, and finally halted opposite to her husband's corpse, at the left side of it, where she was evidently greatly agitated. Five or six Brahmuns began to talk to her with much vehemence, till, in a paroxysm of desperation, *assisted by the Brahmuns*, the hapless widow ascended the bed of destruction. *Her mother and her sister*, too, stood by, weeping and agonized; but all was in vain — the blood-thirsty men prevailed. The devoted woman then proceeded to disengage the rings from her fingers, wrists, and ears; her murderers stretching out their greedy hands to receive them: afterwards all her trinkets, &c., were produced and distributed among the same relentless and rapacious priests. While in the act of taking a ring from her ear, *her mother and sister*, unable any longer to sustain the extremity of their anguish, went up to the side of the pile, and *entreated that the horrid purpose might be abandoned*, but the woman fearing the encounter, and the strength of her resolution, without uttering a word, or even casting a *parting glance* at her supplicating parent and sister, threw herself down on the pile, and clasped the half-putrid corpse in her arms. Straw in abundance was heaped on the dead and the *living*, gums, resins, and other inflammable substances were thrown upon the straw which covered the bodies, while muntrams were repeated at their heads: six or eight pieces of kindled cow-dune cake were introduced among the straw, at different parts of the pile;

ghee and inflammable materials were applied, and the whole blazed in as many places. The men with swords at each corner then hacked the cords which supported the canopy of faggots — it fell and covered the lifeless corpse and the living woman! A piercing sound caught my ear; I listened a few seconds, and, notwithstanding the noise of the multitude, heard the shrieks of misery which issued from the burning pile. In an agony of feeling, we directed the attention of the Brahmuns to this; and, *while so doing*, again — still louder and more piercing than before — the burning woman rent the air with her shrieks! Several of the Brahmuns called out to the *half-consumed, still conscious and imploring widow*, TO COMFORT HER. The pile was now enveloped in flames, and so intense was the heat, that, as by one consent, the Brahmuns and spectators retreated several paces: they then sang a Sanscrit hymn; the hymn ended but not the shrieks and groans of the agonized sufferer; *they* still pierced our ears, and almost rent our hearts! Scarcely conscious of what I did, in the midst of these vain repetitions, I left this scene of fiendish barbarity.

14. SATI IN THE KARNATAK COUNTRY, FROM *MISSIONARY NOTICES*, NO. XXVIII (THOMPSON 1928: 148-52)

June 9, 1826 – About five o'clock in the evening of the 9th instant I received a note from a gentleman that a suttee was about to take place near his house. On hastening to this spot, I found the preparations considerably advanced, and a large concourse of spectators assembled, and continually increasing, till they amounted to six or eight thousand. On my left stood a horrid pile. It was an oblong bed of dry cow-dung cakes about ten feet long and seven wide and three high. At each end of it a rough stake about eight feet in length was driven into the ground, and at about a foot from the top of these supporters was fastened, by cords, a frame of the same dimensions as the bed below, and forming a flat canopy to the couch of death. This frame must have been of considerable weight, as it was covered with very dry small faggots, which the officiating Brahmuns continued to throw upon it till they rose two feet above the framework. On the right sat the poor deluded widow, who was to be the victim of this heart-rending display of Hindoo purity and gentleness. She was attended by a dozen or more Brahmuns; her mother, sister, and son, an interesting boy about three years of age, and other relatives were also with her. Her own infant, not twelve months old, was craftily kept from her by the Brahmuns. She had already performed a number of preparatory ceremonies, one of which was washing herself in a strong decoction of saffron, which is supposed to have a purifying effect. One effect it certainly produced: it imparted to her a horrid ghastliness; her eyes indicated a degree of melancholy wildness; a forced and unnatural smile now and then played on her countenance; and, indeed, everything about her person and her conduct indicated that narcotics had been administered in no small quantities. She was clad in her best apparel, which had been tinted by the same decoction with which her body – alas! so soon to be fuel for the flames – had been washed. Her jewels for the last time were employed to ornament her person; in her fine long black hair at the back of her head, as in a bag of network, were enclosed so large a quantity of small white odoriferous flowers as almost to prevent her head from being turned; and about two yards from where the unfortunate woman sat, immediately in her view, was the corpse of her husband, tied by a cord to a kind of hurdle made of bamboos. Her attention, however, so far as I could observe, was never, even for a moment, directed towards it. To divert her thoughts from dwelling on the scene around her, and in which she was shortly to became so conspicuous an object and doubtless to prevent her resolution from failing her at the approaching crisis, the Brahmuns continued plying her with betel-leaf, plantains, cocoa-nuts, etc. to distribute among her friends as presents; and the manner in which these presents were received sufficiently evinced the almost divine regard with which the giver was contemplated. Besides these different kinds of fruits, several small brass pans filled with parched rice, sandal-wood powder, etc. were before her.

From these she occasionally distributed to the Brahmuns or distinguished individuals by pinches of their contents; and the receivers of these presents appeared to consider them as peculiarly precious. When, however, an interval, though but momentary, occurred amidst these employments, her countenance assumed an expression that indicated indescribable apprehension and horror.

Close by me stood the Fouzdar, a native officer, who, besides regulating the police, is the chief military officer at the station. Under his authority and personal superintendence this inhuman business was carrying on. So heartily did he engage in the murderous work that he gave the poor widow twenty pagodas – between six and seven pounds sterling – to confirm her resolution to be burned!

All my hopes of prevailing on the widow to retract her rash vow and openly to declare her determination not to burn were precluded, as she was a Gentoo woman, of whose language I had no knowledge. Happily, however, Mr. Campbell, of the London Missionary Society, was present and with the hope that she would understand him he advanced to address her in the Carnatica language. His attempt in this respect was successful, for, notwithstanding the prohibition of the Fouzdar, he succeeded in getting near enough for her to hear his address; and from the attention she paid to what he said and the fact of her answering it was evident that she understood him. The effect of Mr. Campbell's solemn and feeling address was counteracted by the influence and exhortations of the Brahmuns, who surrounded their victim like so many beasts of prey, fearful of its escaping their grasp; and he was obliged to retire, without having effected anything more than to exhibit the striking contrast which exists between the spirit of the Gospel of Our Blessed Lord and that of what has often been termed 'mild and amicable' Hindooism.

By this time the pile was completed, and a quantity of straw was now spread on the top of the bed of cow-dung cakes. An increase of activity was soon visible among the men whose 'feet are so swift to shed blood.' Muntrams (prayers or incantations) having been repeated over the pile and the woman, and everything being in readiness, the hurdle to which the corpse of the husband had been fastened was now raised by six of the officiating Brahmuns; the end of a cord about two yards long, attached at the other end to the head of the bier, was taken by the widow, and the whole moved slowly towards the pile. The corpse was then laid on the right side upon the straw, with which it was covered, and four men furnished with sharp swords, one stationed at each corner, now drew them from their scabbards. The trembling, ghastly offering to the Moloch of Hindooism then began her seven circuits round the fatal pile, and finally halted opposite to her husband's corpse at the left side of it, where she was evidently greatly agitated. Here five or six Brahmuns began to talk to her with much vehemence, till, in a paroxysm of desperation, assisted by the Brahmuns, the hopeless widow ascended the bed of destruction. Her mother and her sister, unable any longer to sustain the extremity of their anguish, went up to the side of the pile and entreated that the horrid purpose might be abandoned; but the woman, fearing the encounter and the strength of her resolution, without uttering a word or even casting a part glance at her supplicating parent and sister, threw herself down on the pile and clasped the half-putrid corpse in her arms. Straw in abundance was then heaped on the dead and the living; gums, resins and other inflammable materials were thrown upon the straw which covered the bodies by one party of the Brahmuns, while muntrams were repeated at their heads by the other. Six or eight pieces of kindled cow-dung cakes were introduced among the straw at different parts of the pile, ghee and inflammable materials were applied, and the whole blazed in at many places. The men with swords at each corner then hacked the cords which supported the flat canopy of faggots – it fell and covered the lifeless corpse and the living woman!!!

The flames now began to ascend, and comparative silence was restored. The active agents in this work of destruction were fearlessly and explicitly charged with murder and warned of the future awful account which they would have to render. The Fouzdar, in a haughty, irritated tone of voice, inquired, 'To whom shall I have to give an account?' He was informed, 'To Jehovah, the true and living God.' To the charge of murdering the widow and hurrying her soul and perdition, the chief Brahmun, in a frenzy of enthusiastic triumph, exclaimed, accompanying what he said with the most extravagant gesticulations: 'She is now in heaven — she is already in glory!' At this moment a piercing sound caught my ear; I listened a few seconds, and, notwithstanding the noise of the multitude, heard the shrieks of misery which issued from the burning pile!! In an agony of feeling we directed the attention of the Brahmuns to this, and while doing so, again, still louder and more piercing than before, the burning woman rent the air with her shrieks!! Several of the Brahmuns called out to the half consumed, still conscious and imploring widow to comfort her. What the real effect on the mind of this wretched victim to Hindoo infatuation would be in easily conceived. They then sang in chorus a Sanscrita hymn declaring that her soul would be wafted to heaven on the zephyrs of their holy praise. The pile was now enveloped in flames, and so intense was the heat that, as by one consent, the Brahmuns and the spectators retreated several paces; and the hymn ended, but not the shrieks and groans of the agonized sufferer: they still pierced our ears and almost rent our hearts! Effectually to overpower them, the Brahmuns in a body began calling aloud, Rayana! Rayana! (one of the thousand names of Vishnu). Scarcely conscious of what I did, in the midst of these vain repetitions I left these scene of fiendish barbarity (At Bangalore, Mysore.)

15. ABBE J.A. DUBOIS' RESPONSE TO REV. WILLIAM WARD'S ATTACK ON THE HINDUS IN A SPEECH HE DELIVERED AT LIVERPOOL (DUBOIS 1997: 95-110)

We had, until these latter times, been almost uniformly taught by both ancient and modern historians, who have written on India and its inhabitants, to look on the Hindoos as a mild, sober, industrious, forbearing, patient, and submissive people, who although possessing a system of political government quite original, and having no parallel in any other nation on earth, had, nevertheless, reached a reasonable height on the scale of civilization, cultivated the arts with some success, made tolerable progress in some branches of the highest sciences, such as astronomy, philosophy, ethics, &c., established among themselves, through the division of castes, a system of subordination and order, which, by assigning in the most precise manner to each individual his rank and duties in the great community, allowed nobody to remain idle, and provided in the most efficacious manner for the wants of the whole; as a people living under a form of government founded on so solid a basis that no human effort, no kind of opposition or oppression had been able to subvert, or even to shake it.

The enquiries of many enlightened and judicious authors of several nations, who in more modern times had visited the country, and made an attentive study of the character, manners and customs of these people, as well as of the system of civilization established among them, had generally served to strengthen the favourable opinion already entertained of them; and I am happy to have it my power to declare, that close and impartial researches on the subject, during a period of thirty years of free and unrestrained intercourse among the natives of all ranks and classes, have had the effect of producing the same favourable impressions on my own mind.

It was reserved for a few enthusiasts, who have of late years made their appearance in the country, under the imposing title of reformers, to reverse this pleasing picture, by giving us the most shocking accounts on the subject, and by holding out to our view, the mild and inoffensive Hindoos, as a people wholly polluted by every kind of wickedness; as a race of barbarians sunk into the deepest abyss of ignorance and immorality; as a people far below the most savage nations, and approaching nearer, by their beastly habits and unnatural vices, to the brute than the human creation.

If you have perused the pamphlets published of late at home, by the Rev.-, and above all, his address to the ladies of Liverpool, you will have observed, that all these and many other no less degrading, odious, and false notions are fully upheld, and boldly professed by that gentleman.

.... The Rev. Gentleman begins his attacks on the Hindoo fair sex, by stating that "women in India are in a state of ignorance and degradation, which has no parallel in the history of tribes the most savage and barbarous;" and some lines farther he says, that "a Hindoo female is, in fact, a mere animal kept for burthen or slaughter in the house of her husband....

On the other hand, it may be said, with truth, that so far are the Hindoo females from being held in that low state of contempt and degradation in which the Rev. – repeatedly describes them in his letter, that on the contrary, they lie under much less restraint, enjoy more real freedom, and are in possession of more enviable privileges than the persons of their sex in any other Asiatic country. In fact, to them belong the entire management of their household, the care of their children, the superintendence of the menial servants, the distribution of alms and charities. To their charge are generally intrusted the money, jewels, and other valuables. To them belongs the care of procuring provisions, and providing for all expenses. It is they also who are charged, almost to the exclusion of their husbands, with the most important affair of procuring wives for their sons, and husbands for their daughters, and, in doing this, they evince a niceness, an attention, and foresight which are not certainly surpassed in any country; while in the management of their domestic business, they in general show a shrewdness, a saving-ness, and an intelligence which would do honour to the best housewives in Europe.

In the mean while, the austerity and roughness with which they are outwardly treated in public, by their husbands, is rather a matter of form, and entirely ceases when the husband and his wife are in private. It is then that the Hindoo females assume all that empire which is everywhere exercised in civilized countries, by the persons of their sex over the male part of creation; find means to bring them under their subjection, and rule over them, in several instances, with a despotic sway. In short, although outwardly exposed in public to the forbidding and repulsive frowns of an austere husband, they can be considered in no other light than as perfectly the mistresses within the house.

The influence of the Hindoo females on the welfare of families is so well known, that the successes or misfortunes of the Hindoos are almost entirely attributed to their good or bad management. When a person prospers in the world, it is customary to say that he has the happiness to possess an intelligent wife, to whom he is indebted for his welfare; and when any one runs to ruin, it is the custom to say that he has for his partner a bad wife, to whom his misfortunes must chiefly be attributed. In short, a good-natured and intelligent wife is considered by all castes of natives, as the most valuable of all the blessings which could be bestowed on a family and a bad one as the most dreaded of all curses; so great is their influence on the fate of the Hindoo households.

The authority of married women within their houses is chiefly exerted in preserving good order and peace among the persons who compose their families; and a great many among them discharge this important duty with a prudence and a discretion which have scarcely a parallel in Europe. I have known families composed of between thirty and forty persons, or more, consisting of grown sons and daughters, all married and all having children, living together under the superintendence of an old matron — their mother or mother-in-law. The latter, by good management, and by accommodating herself to the temper of her daughters-in-law; by using, according to circumstances, firmness or forbearance, succeeded in preserving peace and harmony during many years amongst so many females, who had all jarring interests, and still more jarring tempers. I ask you whether it would be possible to attain the same end, in the same circumstances, in our countries; where it is scarcely possibly to make two women living under the same roof to agree together...

Parents, chiefly mothers, foster their children, both males and females, with an equal tenderness. So far from females being despised while living under the paternal roof, their parents and brothers are often seen submitting themselves to severe privations for the purpose of procuring trinkets and jewels for their daughters or sisters, in order that they may be able to appear in public with decency and advantage, while the males are seen in rags or half naked, and live forgotten at home.

The principal care of parents is to procure suitable establishments for their daughters, over whom mothers continue to exercise a kind of paramount authority, even after their marriage, being particularly attentive to check that despotic sway which so many mothers-in-law are but too well disposed to exercise over their daughters-in-law...

In fact, among the Hindoos the person of a woman is sacred. She cannot be touched in public by a man, even with the end of the fingers. How abject so ever may be her condition, she is never addressed by any body, not excepting the persons of the highest rank, but under the respectful name of *mother* (umma). A dwelling in which only females are to be found, even the hut of the most helpless widow, is an inviolable asylum into which the most determined libertine would never dare to penetrate; or, should he do it, his audacity would not remain unpunished. A woman can frequent the most crowded places without being exposed to the least insult. A male who would stop merely to gaze on a female who is passing by, as our loungers in Europe are accustomed to do, would be considered by all as an insolent and uneducated person. Even a mere look designed to insult a woman would be resented and avenged. In short, the least insult by words or otherwise, the least mark of disrespect offered in public to a female, is instantly resented and avenged by her husband, her sons, or her brothers, who would expose themselves to all dangers rather than overlook an offence offered to their wives, their mothers, or sisters, or see them treated in public with disregard...

To be sure, they will not dance *waltzes*, or deliver in any other way their persons into the arms of another man. They are too well aware of what they owe to their husbands, and to the modesty of their sex, to allow themselves such gross violations of decorum; but what I have already stated, and what I am still about to state, will prove that although "without a knowledge of the alphabet," they are dutiful daughters, faithful wives, tender mothers, and intelligent housewives; and they are not in fact, as shamelessly asserted by the Rev. Gentleman, "mere animals kept for slaughter or for burden in the houses of their husbands."

In fact, there is perhaps no kind of honest employment in a civilized country in which the Hindoo females have not a due share. Besides the management of the household, and the care of the family, which are (as already noticed) under their control, the wives and daughters of husbandmen attend, and assist their husbands and fathers in the labours of agriculture. Those of tradesmen assist theirs in carrying on their trade. Merchants are attended and assisted by theirs in their shops. Many females are shopkeepers on their own account; and *without a knowledge of the alphabet*, or of the decimal scale, they keep by other means their accounts in excellent order, and are considered as still shrewder than the males themselves in their commercial dealings. Several shops entirely kept by females, without the help of males, may be seen in large towns in every bazar street. I have sometimes observed female shopkeepers sitting down cross-legged in their shops, and serving their customers with the greatest ease and affability. A greater number are seen selling fish, betel, flowers, vegetables, fruits, and sundry articles of subsistence or furniture. The poor classes, which unfortunately form the majority of the population, let themselves as servants or journey-women, or earn otherwise a scanty subsistence by selling grass, fuel, straw, &c. &c. In short, there is no kind of work, no kind of trade, in a civilized society, in which the Hindoo females are not seen actively engaged, and occupying a conspicuous place. I am acquainted with industrious widows, who, having undertaken a small trade with a trifling capital of forty or fifty rupees, have, by their economy, their labours, and industry, increased it, within these past ten years, to the amount of five or six hundred. ...

..... I believe that it may be said without giving offence, that the Europeans are not qualified to form a fair judgment on the subject, on account of the difficulty, not to say impossibility, of holding a free and confidential intercourse with the respectable part of the Hindoo females. All their knowledge in this respect is derived from their criminal connections with concubines, ordinarily of the lowest tribes, or other females of the most dissolute dispositions. Hence arise the false notions of the Europeans. The knowledge I have attained on the subject is not hearsay, but from personal observations. My profession has afforded me repeated opportunities to become acquainted with the character of the Hindoo females, and by living with them on a footing of paternal familiarity I have had numberless opportunities of conversing with them without restraint. Their conversation on subjects connected with their internal economy and domestic concerns was not certainly destitute of interest, and on all other subjects within their reach I have generally found them communicative, gay, and lively....

The Rev.- returns again to the stale subject of the burning of the Hindoo widows, on the pile of their deceased husbands, and quotes the lamentable fact of seven hundred and six victims having devoted themselves to that barbarous superstition, in the course of the year 1817, in the presidency of Bengal. It is a well-known fact, (as I observed in a former letter,) that these nefarious sacrifices have increased of late years; but the reverend gentleman is not perhaps apprized, that many persons of good sense, who have made enquiries about the causes of this increasing evil, have been of opinion, that its aggravation was in a great measure owing to his intemperate zeal, and that of many of his associates in the work of reform. He is not, perhaps aware, that owing to their abrupt attacks on the most deep-laid prejudices of the country, the zeal of the Hindoos had been roused to a determined spirit of opposition and resistance, when they saw their most sacred customs and practices publicly reviled, laughed at, and turned into ridicule, by words, and in writing, in numberless religious tracts, circulated with profusion, in every direction, all over the country.

Those horrid suicides, called *Suttees*, have unfortunately prevailed from the earliest times to the present in the country, chiefly in. the north of India, and the putting a stop to them altogether, by coercion, appears a measure too pregnant with danger to be attempted. In the moral order, as well as the physical, we are often reduced to the sad necessity of tolerating great evils not to be exposed to greater ones.

Those execrable sacrifices occur but seldom in the south of the Peninsula. I suppose that the population of the country on this side of the Krishna, does not fall short of thirty millions, and I am persuaded, that the number of *suttees* does not amount to thirty in a year. But thirty suttees in a year, in a population of thirty millions, are certainly by far too many; and nobody deplores, more bitterly than I do, those horrid excesses of superstition and fanaticism.

But, after all, is suicide confined to the Hindoo widows; and are our countries free from such detestable excesses? So far from this being the case, I am persuaded that more persons perish in France and England, in a month, through suicide and duelling, than during a whole year in India, through *suttees*. The only difference I can remark, between the one and the other, is, that the deluded Hindoo widow commits suicide from misled religious motives, and from what she considers as an indispensable duty of conjugal devotion; whilst the European suicide puts an end to his existence, in defiance of every religious restraint, and in open violation of his most sacred duties towards God, and towards men.

Shall, therefore, our whole compassion be engrossed by the Hindoo widow, and shall we not reserve a tear, or a sigh, for our still more guilty and more unfortunate countrymen?

Are suicide and duelling in Europe less nefarious than suttees in India? Why, then, is the deluded Hindoo widow arraigned with so much severity, while the laws against duellists are dormant, and the tribunals of justice generally under the necessity of overlooking those deliberate and malicious murders?

The Rev.- in order to render the Hindoo females more and more abject and despicable, quotes two or three shocking stories, which, if they are not altogether false, are at least misrepresented and exaggerated to such a degree as to render his accounts entirely unworthy of credit. He says, for instance, that "parents, in some cases, marry fifty or sixty daughters to a single Brahmin." I question whether a single case of such turpitude might be cited among the thirty millions of inhabitants, who people this side of the Peninsula; and I am persuaded, that if such instances occur in Bengal, they are rare, and that the few Brahmins who may allow themselves such open transgression of the usages of their caste, are spurned and shunned by the individuals of their tribe who preserve any sense of honour; for polygamy is strongly discouraged by the Hindoo customs among all castes, and above all, in that of the Brahmins, among whom marriage is generally confined to the pair...

6

Sati – A Rare Phenomenon

1. ALEXANDER DOW IN 1770 (DOW I 1973: XXXV)

The extraordinary custom of the women burning themselves with their deceased husbands, has, for the most part, fallen into desuetude in India; nor was it reckoned a religious duty, as has been very erroneously supposed in the West.

2. GEORGE FORSTER WRITING FROM BANARAS IN 1782 (FORSTER I 1970: 68)

The wives of the deceased Hindoos have moderated that spirit of enthusiastic pride, or impulse of affection, which was used to urge them to self destruction on the pile of their husbands. Their grief can now be assuaged, and their religious duties reconciled, by a participation of domestic comforts; and many of the Hindoo widows, especially in the Marhatta country, have acquired by their ability, their wealth, connection, or intrigue, the possession of extensive power and influence.

3. SATI RARE IN PUNJAB AND ELSEWHERE EXCEPT JAMMU, *"TOUR TO LAHORE,"* THE MANUSCRIPT NOTES OF AN OFFICER OF THE BENGAL ARMY, *THE ASIATIC ANNUAL REGISTER*, VOL. X1, FOR THE YEAR 1809 (MADRA AND SINGH 2004: 229)

Both the Sik'hs and Singhs marry one wife, and in the event of her death may marry again; but if the husband die, the widow cannot again enter the nuptial state, but the widow of a Jaut is allowed to marry a second or third husband. Widows rarely declare themselves Suttees in any part of the Punjab; but in the city of Jumoo, a contrary practice prevails. There it is generally practiced, and is indeed considered as an indispensable sacrifice to the names of the deceased husband, and if the widow does not voluntarily attend the corpse of her husband, and consign herself with it to the flames, the rajeepoots consider it their duty, in such cases, to put the widows to death, and to cast their bodies into the fire, to be burnt with her husband's. So horrible a custom as this, does, I believe, no where else prevail. However frequent the instances of widows devoting themselves to death on the pile with their deceased husbands, yet in all these cases, excepting in the city of Jumoo, if it be not in every instance voluntary, there is no where else, that it is ever urged or enforced by any measure of compulsion.

4. "CALCUTTA IN 1824," WILLIAM HUGGINS, INDIGO PLANTER IN TIRHOOT DISTRICT (NAIR 1989: 424)

In Bengal, and, curious to relate, in the immediate vicinity of Calcutta, the culpable points of Hindoo superstition are carried in greater excess than in any other part of India. ... It is here that the widow sacrifices herself upon the burning pile of her deceased husband, and by this self-devotion affords us an example that superstition is often stronger than the love of life or fear of death. This practice is confined principally to certain families of high caste, who consider the adherence to it as a point of honour, which confers lustre on their name, and is carefully inculcated in their daughter's minds, so that it is not the result of a momentary impulse, but of a long resolved determination, and, therefore, the victims do not conduct themselves like mad enthusiasts, but collected martyrs. No drugs are administered, no intoxicating spices to inspire her with false courage; but with calm and collected fortitude, this child of error and victim of family pride, embraces her husband's corpse, and clasps the faggot of death. Music drowns her cries, bamboos are thrown across to prevent her convulsive struggles, or escape; and her form is quickly changed to a heap of ashes.

At a distance from Calcutta it is not practiced, even in the upper parts of Bengal it is not; however, our government has so far interfered with it as to oblige persons, on an occasion of this kind, to obtain permission from a magistrate.

5. NO SATI IN TWENTY YEARS, FANNY PARKES WRITING IN 1826 (PARKES 2003: 39)

December 23rd- We arrived at Nobutpoor, a very pretty place. The bungalow is on a high bank, just above the Curamnassa river. To the right you have a view of a suspension-bridge, built of bamboo and rope; on the left is a sati ground, to me a most interesting sight. I had heard a great deal regarding *satis* in Calcutta, but had never seen one [Parkes had arrived in India in 1822]; here was a spot to which it was customary to bring the widows to be burned alive, on the banks of the Curamnassa, a river considered holy by the Hindus.

In the sketch I took of the place are seven *sati* mounds, raised of earth, one of which is kept in good repair, and there are several more in the mango tope to the left. The people said no *sati* had taken place there for twenty years, but that the family who owned the large mound kept it in repair, and were very proud of the glory reflected on their house by one of the females having become *sati*.

6. JOHN MALCOLM, WHO ADMINISTERED CENTRAL INDIA, INCLUDING MALWA, ON DECLINE IN INCIDENTS OF SATI (MALCOLM 1970a: 206-08).

The practice of Suttee, or self-immolation of widows, was formerly very common in Central India, as is proved by the numerous grave-stones, on which the figures of the husband and the wife who burnt herself after his death are both engraven. This usage prevailed most when the Rajpoots had power and influence... the Mahrattas, since they acquired paramount power in this country, have, by a wise neglect and indifference, which neither encouraged by approval, nor provoked by prohibition, rendered this practice very rare. In the whole of Central India there have not been, as far as can be learnt, above three or four Suttees annually for the last twenty years.... There has not been a Suttee with any of the last three Rajas of Ragoogurh; the Sesodya family of Pertaubgurh have had none for three generations; and the present Raja, Sawut Singh (an excellent man) is not only adverse to this shocking usage, but the open and declared enemy of female infanticide. When the Raja of Banswarra died (in 1819), not one of his wives desired to burn ... in Central India ... no Suttee has been known to take place for many years, in which the parties were not voluntary victims, and acting against the advice and remonstrance of their friends, and the public officers of the district where it occurred.

JOHN MALCOLM (MALCOLM II 1970b: 154-55; 446)

We may and ought to be grateful that superior knowledge has removed us far from the ignorance and errors of our Hindu subjects, but we should be humbled to think in how many points, in how many duties of life, great classes of this sober, honest, kind, and inoffensive people excel us. That they have some usages revolting to reason and to nature is certain. At the sacrifice of life in the shocking practice of sati and infanticide, all must shudder, except those whom habit has reconciled to such acts of inhumanity; but while we feel and express abhorrence at them, we must not forget that they are comparatively local and limited, and that one of them, infanticide, is held in as great horror by all but a few families of Hindus as by us. While all agree in sentiment regarding the sinfulness of the voluntary sacrifice of widows, a great difference of opinion exists as to the mode of terminating the practice. The diffusion of knowledge, the force of example, the mild and conciliating but strong remonstrances of superiors, with the undisguised feelings of shocked humanity, will, we may hope, gradually eradicate a barbarous rite which has already fallen into disusage in many parts of India, from ceasing to excite that sympathy in the people, and, consequently, to meet with that encouragement from their priests and superiors, which it formerly did...

Satis have decreased, and, indeed, are almost unknown in many of the southern parts of India; and in the countries of the Deccan, Malwa, and Hindustan, they are of rare occurrence. In Bengal Proper this shocking usage is more prevalent than in any part of India...

7. HON. MOUNTSTUART ELPHINSTONE, (1779–1859), WHO HELD SEVERAL IMPORTANT POSTS INCLUDING GOVERNOR OF BOMBAY (ELPHINSTONE 1966: 187-89)

It is well-known that Indian widows sometimes sacrifice themselves on the funeral pile of their husbands, and that such victims are called Sattis...The practice is ascribed by Diodorus, as it still is by our missionaries, to the degraded condition to which a woman who outlives her husband is condemned. If the motive were one of so general an influence, the practice would scarcely be so rare. It is most probable that the hopes of immediately entering on the enjoyment of heaven, and, of entitling the husband to the same felicity, as well as the glory attending such a voluntary sacrifice, are sufficient to excite the few enthusiastic spirits who go through this awful trial.

It has been said that the relations encourage self-immolation for the purpose of obtaining the property of the widow. It would be judging too harshly human nature to think such conduct frequent even in proportion to the number of cases where the widow has property to leave; and in fact, it may be confidently relied on, that the relations are almost in all, if not in all cases, sincerely desirous of dissuading the sacrifice. For this purpose, in addition to their own entreaties, and those of the infant children, when there is such, they procure the intervention of friends of the family, and of persons in authority. If the case be in a family of high rank, the sovereign himself goes to console and dissuade the widow. It is reckoned a bad omen for a government to have many sattis. The common expedient is, to engage the widow's attention by such visits while the body is removed and burnt.

The mode of concremation is various: in Bengal, the living and dead bodies are stretched on a pile where strong ropes and bamboos are thrown across them so as to prevent ant attempt to rise In Orissa, the woman throws herself into the pyre, which is below the level of the ground. In the Deckan, the woman sits down on the pyre with her husband's head in her lap, and remains there till suffocated, or crushed by the fall of a heavy roof of logs of wood, which is fixed by cords to posts at the corners of the pile.

The sight of a widow burning is a most painful one; but it is hard to say whether the spectator is most affected by pity or admiration. The more than human serenity of the victim, and the respect which she receives from those around her, are heightened by her gentle demeanour, and her care to omit nothing in distributing her last presents, and paying the usual marks of courtesy to the bystanders; while the cruel death that awaits her is doubly felt from her own apparent insensibility to its terrors. The reflections which succeed are of a different character, and one is humiliated to think that so feeble a being can be elevated by superstition to a self-devotion not surpassed by the noblest examples of patriots or martyrs.

I have heard that, in Guzerat, women about to burn are often stupefied with opium. In most other parts this is certainly not the case. Women go through all the ceremonies with astonishing composure and presence of mind, and have been seen seated, unconfined among the flames, apparently praying, and raising their joined hands to their heads with as little agitation as at their ordinary devotions. On the other hand, frightful instances have occurred of women bursting from amidst the flames, and being thrust back by the assistants. One of these diabolical attempts was made in Bengal, when an English gentleman happened to be among the spectators, and succeeded in preventing the accomplishment of the tragedy; but, next day, he was surprised to encounter the bitterest reproaches from the woman, for having been the occasion of her disgrace, and the obstacle to her being then in heaven enjoying the company of her husband, and the blessings of those she had left behind.

The practice is by no means universal in India. It never occurs in the south of the river Kishna; and under the Bombay presidency, including the former sovereignty of the Bramin Peshwas, it amounts to thirty-two a year. In the rest of the Deckan it is probably more rare. In Hindostan and Bengal it is so common, that some hundreds are officially reported as burning annually within the British dominions alone.

8. FREDERICK JOHN SHORE, SON OF SIR JOHN SHORE (PENNER AND MACLEAN 1983: 184-85; 234-35)

When we consider the prospects of the widow if she resolved to live, and, on the other hand, the fame and glory which she believed she should reap by burning herself with the corpse of the husband, the wonder is, not that so many, but that so few, suttees occurred...

Every friend to humanity will rejoice at this [abolition of sati]; but every little credit is due to Lord William for the measure... I can only say, that of all whom I conversed with, whether of the civil, military, mercantile, or miscellaneous classes, full three out of four were not only convinced, that all over Hindostan and Bengal, suttee might be abolished with perfect safety, but were anxious to see the promulgation of a law to this effect — and this full five years before the law was actually enacted. It is obvious, that when such were the sentiments of the majority of the English in India, i.e. of the rulers of the country, the abolition would have been effected a little sooner or later, whoever might have been appointed to the situation of Governor-General.

9. "CALCUTTA IN 1830," MAJOR EDWARD C. ARCHER, AIDE-DE-CAMP TO LORD COMBERMERE (NAIR 1989: 529-32)

...... But while the custom is by law prohibited in the Company's dominions, it continues in the neighbouring countries not under British rule; and this is a cogent reason for the policy of allowing it to grow gradually into disuse. In these countries, as well as in the Company's territories, the practice was decreasing fast, and even some of the chiefs of the Bundel Khund States had expressed themselves in decided hostility to its longer prevalence; but they did not seek to put it down by violence. In the British provinces it was of less frequent occurrence; and it might have been more so, had it been left to take its own course.

It is the firm persuasion of many, that in the course of a few years the horrible rite of Suttee would have ceased entirely, and in its natural death we never should have apprehended its resuscitation, as we may have cause to fear its spirit being raised from the judicial condemnation to which we have consigned it. It is the means, which have been objectionable...

10. THE SUTTEE, CAPTAIN LEOPOLD VON ORLICH WRITING ON JAN. 12, 1843 (ORLICH I 1985: 169)

.... according to the assurances which I have received from well-informed persons, it appears that as far as control is possible, no Suttee has taken place within the last ten years in Bengal and in the Presidency of Bombay; this cruel custom does not prevail to the south of the river Kishna. Even the relations themselves, now often endeavour to prevent the burning of the widows; and in families of high rank, the prince of the country, in person, undertakes to offer consolation, and, while he is endeavouring to dissuade the widow from her purpose, the corpse is hastily carried away and consumed.

Appendix I

TRANSLATION OF A BEWASTA RECEIVED FROM
MUTOONJOY, PUNDIT OF THE SUPREME COURT,
RESPECTING THE BURNING OF WIDOWS, AND OTHER
SACRIFICES PREVALENT AMONG THE HINDOOS.
(GREAT BRITAIN. HOUSE OF COMMONS PAPERS. 1821)
VOL. 18—PAPERS RELATING TO EAST INDIA AFFAIRS,
VIZ. HINDOO WIDOWS AND VOLUNTARY IMMOLATIONS,
PP. 124-25).

...In the texts of Yogeeshwur, treating of the duties of women, there is no mention made of the practices of sahamarna and anoomarana.

The commentator Vijnianeahnur, in making his remarks on that part which treats of the duties of women, takes an opportunity of mentioning the acts of anoomarana and sahamarana, by introducing the instance related in the Muha Barut, of the restlessly amorous dove who sacrificed herself on the death of her mate. He next declares it to be established from the authorities of Shunka, Angiras and Harita, that both these acts are rewarded with paradise. With a view of proving the legality of the act of anoogumun, he cities an argument against it which he subsequently reconciles to his own opinion. His adversary alleges that the Srute prohibits any one from willfully curtailing life through desire; and that consequently the act of anoogumun must be unjustifiable. He replies, while life remains there remains also an opportunity for the attainment of absorption, with the eternal incomparable happiness of the divine essence, by the acquisition of holy knowledge. On this account it has been forbidden willfully to shorten existence. But in a person who is careless about absorption, and who is desirous to attain a paradise of temporary and inconsiderable bliss, the act of anoogumun is justifiable as is the performance of any other voluntary act: but from this reasoning it appears evident, that leading a life of austerity is preferred as the superior alternative, and that the act of anoogumun is held to be of inferior merit.

In conformity with this mode of considering the question, some have asserted that the injunction to perform the act of anoogumun extends to such women only as are impelled to commit suicide, in defiance of the prohibition of the Shasters, from the violence of their desires to attain paradise; in the same manner as the particular incantation used for the destruction of an enemy, is enjoined to such men only as are impelled to destroy a fellow-creature, in defiance of the prohibition, through implacability of their anger.

On the subject of anoogumun, the Shasters exhibit a great variety of opinions; but no difference prevails with regard to the priority of leading a life of austerity. The difference of opinion may be traced to this source: The followers of Mimangsuk's philosophy assert, that killing, although (abstractedly considered it is a sinful act), yet ceases to be sinful if enjoined by any particular Shaster. The adherents to the Sankhya system, on the other hand, are of opinion, that wanton killing is sinful and superinduces punishment; but if sanctioned by the law is productive both of reward and punishment. In the opinion of the former therefore, as each mode of conduct is attended with the same reward, to die by anoogumun or to live as a brahmachari is optional.

In the opinion of the latter, to live as a brahmachari only is allowable, and not to die by anoogumun, as that the act involves the crime of suicide.

According to the doctrine inculcated by the Vedasta, Kamya acts, that is to say, those which are voluntary and performed with a view of reward, are to be avoided in as great a degree as those which are forbidden.

The species of suicide therefore, termed anoogumun, being voluntary, ought, according to that doctrine, also to be avoided. Moreover, the following tale has been extracted from the Poorawnas by Calidasa: -"when Kundurpu was reduced to ashes by the fire of the anger of Shwu, the virtuous Rutee, his wife, formed the resolution of accompanying him. With this view, she prevailed on Mudhoo, a friend of her deceased husband, to prepare the pile and apply the fire; but just as she was about to perform the sacrifice, she was prevailed upon to desist by the gods, who in a voice from heaven, held out hopes to her of a reunion with her departed lord."

From the above it would appear, that not the slightest offence attaches either to the women who depart from their resolution, or to those who persuade them to relinquish their intention.

In the Bhagaruta also it is recorded, that Kripee (the widow of Dronacharya) did not accompany her deceased husband on account of the extreme affection she bore her infant son; and yet she was never considered culpable. It is therefore, perfectly legal, and in every respect unexceptionable in others, to endeavour by the allurements of worldly pleasures, or by means of any other inducements, to dissuade a widow from the intention of sacrificing herself which she may have formed; nor is she at all culpable should she be attracted by affection for her children, or any other worldly tie, from the fulfillment of her resolution.

As the act of anoomarana is purely voluntary, it cannot be an ordinance of the Shasters. A thousand Shasters are not capable of inducing death; for that is an event universally readed by the human species.

The directions of the Shasters on this head apply only to such as are afflicted with pain arising from disease or separation, as consider death preferable to the sufferings they endure; and come forward, voluntarily, with a firm resolution, of putting a period to their existence. The act of dying is not enjoined; but merely the mode of it, as entering the fire, falling from a mountain, &c. The Shasters say, if you are obstinately bent on death, at all events, put an end to yourself by such and such means; as a father, after all his admonitions to the contrary, had failed of producing the desired effect, would point out to a son, who was obstinately bent on visiting a distant country, the proper path he should pursue. These observations apply equally to the suicide, (effected by falling from a mountain, drowning, &c.) in the case of persons afflicted with incurable diseases.

(A true translation.) (signed) W.H. Macnaghten act dep reg. (A.K. Ray 1985: 86-87).

Appendix II

LORD WILLIAM BENTINCK'S MINUTE ON SATI, 8th NOVEMBER 1829

Whether the question be to continue or to discontinue the practice of suttee, the decision is equally surrounded by an awful responsibility. To consent to the consignment, year after year, of hundreds of innocent victims to a cruel and untimely end, when the power exists of preventing it, is a predicament which no conscience can contemplate without horror. But on the other hand, if heretofore received opinions are to be considered of any value, to put to hazard, by a contrary course, the very safety of the British empire in India, and to extinguish at once all hopes of those great improvements affecting the condition, not of hundreds and thousands, but of millions, which can only be expected from the continuance of our supremacy, is an alternative which, even in the light of humanity itself, may be considered as a still greater evil. It is upon this first and highest consideration alone, the good of mankind, that the tolerance of this inhuman and impious rite can, in my opinion, be justified on the part of the government of a civilized nation. While the solution of this question is appalling from the unparalleled magnitude of its possible results, the consideration belonging to it are such as to make even the stoutest mind distrust its decision. On the one side, religion, humanity under the most appalling form, as well as vanity and ambition, in short all the most powerful influences over the human heart, are arrayed to bias and mislead the judgment. On the other side, the sanction of countless ages, the example of all the Mussulman conquerors, the unanimous concurrence in the same policy of our own most able rulers, together with the universal veneration of the people, seem authoritatively to forbid, both to feeling and to reason, any interference on the exercise of their natural prerogative. In venturing to be the first to deviate from this practice, it becomes me to shew that nothing has been yielded to feeling, but that reason, and reason alone, has governed the decision. So far indeed from presuming to condemn the conduct of my predecessors, I am ready to say, that in the same circumstances, I should have acted as they have done. So far from being chargeable with political rashness, as this departure from an established policy might infer, I hope to be able so completely to prove the safety of the measure, as even to render necessary any calculation of the degree of risk, which for the attainment of so great a benefit, might wisely and justly be incurred. So far also from being the sole champion of a great and dangerous innovation, I shall be able to prove that the vast preponderance of present authority has long been in favour of abolition. Past experience indeed ought to prevent me, above all men, from coming lightly to so positive a conclusion. When governor of Madras, I saw, in the mutiny of Vellore, the dreadful consequences of a supposed violation of religious customs upon the minds of the native population and soldiery: I cannot forget that I was then the innocent victim of that unfortunate catastrophe, and I might reasonably dread, when the responsibility would justly attach to *me* in the event of failure, a recurrence of the same fate. Prudence and self-interest would counsel me to tread in the footsteps of my predecessors. But in a case of such momentous importance to humanity and civilization, that man must be reckless of all his present or future happiness who could listen to the dictates of so wicked and selfish a policy. With the firm undoubting conviction entertained upon this question, I should be guilty of little short of the crime of multiplied murder, if I could hesitate in the performance of this solemn obligation. I have been already stung with this feeling. Every day's delay adds a victim to the dreadful list, which might perhaps have been prevented by a more early submission of the preset question. But during the whole of the present year, much public agitation has been excited, and when discontent is broad, when exaggerations of all kinds are busily circulated, and when the native army have been under a degree of alarm, lest their allowances should suffer with that of their European officers, it would have been unwise to have given a handle to artful and designing enemies to disturb the public peace. The recent measures of government for protecting the interest of the sepoys against the late reduction of companies, will have removed all apprehension of the intentions of government; and the consideration of this circumstance having been the sole cause of hesitation on my part, I will now proceed, praying the blessing of God upon our counsels, to state the grounds upon which my opinion has been formed.

We have now before us two reports of the nizamat adalat with statements of suttees in 1827 and 1828, exhibiting a decrease of 54 in the latter year as compared with 1827, and a still greater proportion as compared with former years. If this diminution could be ascribed to any change of opinion upon the question, produced by the progress of education or civilization, the fact would be most satisfactory; and to disturb this sure though slow process of self correction would be most impolite and unwise. But I think it may be safely affirmed, that though in Calcutta truth may be said to have made a considerable advance among the higher orders; yet in respect to the population at large, no change whatever has taken place, and that form these causes at least no hope of the abandonment of the rite can be rationally entertained.

The decrease, if it be real, may be the result of less sickly seasons, as the increase in 1824 and 1825 was of the greater prevalence of cholera. But it is probably in a greater measure due to the more open discouragement of the practice given by the greater part of the European functionaries in latter years; the effect of which would be to produce corresponding activity in the police officers, by which either the number would be really diminished, or would be made to appear so in the returns.

It seems to be the very general opinion that our interference has hitherto done more harm than good, by lending a sort of sanction to the ceremony, while it has undoubtedly tended to cripple the efforts of magistrates and others to prevent the practice.

I think it will clearly appear, from a perusal of the documents annexed to this minute, and from the facts which I shall have to adduce, that the passive submission of the people to the influence and power beyond the law, which in fact and practically may be and is often exercised without opposition by every public officer, is so great, that the suppression of the rite would be completely effected by a tacit sanction alone on the part of government. This mode of extinguishing it has been recommended by many of those whose advice has been asked, and no doubt this, in several respects might be a preferable course, as being equally effectual, while more silent, not exciting the alarm which might possibly come from a public enactment, and from which, in case of failure, it would be easy to retreat with less inconvenience and without any compromise of character. But this course is clearly not open to government, bound by parliament to rule by law, and not by their good pleasure. Under the present position of the British empire moreover, it may be fairly doubted, if any such underhand proceeding would be really good policy. When we had powerful neighbors and had greater reason to doubt our own security, expediency might recommend an indirect and more cautious proceeding, but now that we are supreme, my opinion is decidedly in favour of an open, avowed and general prohibition, resting altogether upon the moral goodness of the act, and our power to enforce it, and so decided is my feeling against any half measure, that were I not convinced of the safety of total abolition, I certainly should have advised the cessation of all interference.

Of all those who have given their advice against the abolition of the rite, and have described the ill effects likely to ensue from it, there is no one to whom I am disposed to pay greater deference than Mr. Horace Wilson. I purposely select his opinion, because, independently of his vast knowledge of oriental literature, it has fallen to his lot, as secretary to the Hindu College, and possessing the general esteem both of the parents and of the youths, to have more confidential intercourse with natives of all classes, than any man in India. While his opportunity of obtaining information has been great beyond all others, his talents and judgment enable him to form a just estimate of its value. I shall state the most forcible of his reasons, and how far I do and do not agree with him.

Ist. Mr. Wilson considered it to be a dangerous evasion of the real difficulties, to attempt to prove that suttees are not 'essentially a part of the Hindu religion' – I entirely agree in this opinion. The question is, not what the rite is, but what it is supposed to be; and I have no doubt that the conscientious belief of every order of Hindus, with few exceptions, regard it as sacred.

2nd. Mr. Wilson thinks that the attempt to put down the practice will inspire extensive dissatisfaction. I agree also in this opinion. He thinks that success will only be partial, which I doubt. He does not imagine that the promulgated prohibition will lead to any immediate and overt act of insubordination, but that affrays and much agitation of the pubic mind must ensue. But he conceives, that, if once they suspect that it is the intention of the British government to abandon this hitherto inviolate principle of allowing the most complete toleration in matters of religion, that there will arise, in the minds of all, so deep a distrust of our ulterior designs, that they will no longer be tractable to any arrangement intended for their improvement and that the principles of morality as well as of a more virtuous and exalted rule of action, now actively inculcated by European education and knowledge, will receive a fatal check. I must acknowledge that a similar opinion as to the probable excitation of a deep distrust of our future intentions was mentioned to me in conversation by that enlightened native, Ram Mohan Roy, a warm advocate for the abolition of suttees, and of all other superstitions and corruptions, engrafted on the Hindu religion, which he considers originally to have been a pure deism. It was his opinion that the practice might be suppressed, quietly and unobservedly, by increasing the difficulties, and by the indirect agency of the police. He apprehended that any public enactment would give rise to general apprehension, that the reasoning would be, 'While the English were contending for power, they deemed it politic to allow universal toleration, and to respect our religion; but having obtained the supremacy, their first act is a violation of their professions, and the next will probably be, like the Mahomedan conquerors, to force upon us their own religion.

Admitting, as I am always disposed to do, that much truth is contained in these remarks, but not at all assenting to the conclusions which though not described, bear the most unfavourable import, I shall now enquire into the evil and the extent of danger which may practically result from this measure.

It must be first observed, that of the 463 suttees occurring in the whole of the presidency of Fort William, 420 took place in Bengal, Bihar and Orissa, or what are termed the lower provinces, and of these latter, 287 in the Calcutta division alone.

It might be very difficult to make a stranger to India understand, much less believe, that in a population of so many millions of people, as the Calcutta division includes, and the same may be said of all the lower provinces, so great is the want of courage and of vigour of character, and such the habitual submission of centuries, that insurrection or hostile opposition to the will of the ruling power may be affirmed to be an impossible danger. I speak of the population taken separately from the army, and I may add for the information of the stranger, and also in support of my assertion, that few of the natives of the lower provinces are to be found in our military ranks. I therefore at once deny the danger in toto, in reference to this part of our territories, where the practice principally obtains. If, however, security were wanting against extensive popular tumult or revolution, I should say that the permanent settlement, which though a failure in many other respects and in its most important essentials, has this great advantage at least, of having created a vast body of rich landed proprietors, deeply interested in the continuance of the British dominion, and having complete command over the mass of the people, and, in respect to the apprehension of ulterior views, I cannot believe that it could last but for the moment. The same large proprietary body, connected for the most part with Calcutta, can have no fears of the kind, and through their interpretation of our intentions, and that of their numerous dependants, and agents, the public mind could not long remain in a state of deception.

Were the scene of this sad destruction of human life laid in the upper instead of the lower provinces, in the midst of a bold and manly people, I might speak with less confidence upon the question of safety. In these provinces the suttees amount to 43 only — upon a population of nearly twenty millions. It cannot be expected that any general feeling, where combination of any kind is so unusual, could be excited in defence of a rite, in which so few participate, a rite also, notoriously made too often subservient to views of personal interest on the part of the other members of the family.

It is stated by Mr. Wilson that interference with infanticide and the capital punishment of Brahmins offer a fallacious analogy with the prohibition now proposed. The distinction is not perceptible to my judgment. The former practice, though confined to particular families, is probably viewed as a religious custom; and as for the latter, the necessity of the enactment proves the general existence of the exception, and it is impossible to conceive a more direct and open violation of the shastras, or one more at variance with the general feelings of the Hindu population. To this day, in all Hindu states, the life of Brahmins is, I believe, still held scared.

But I have taken up too much time in giving my own opinions, when those of the greatest experience and the highest official authority are upon our records. In the report of the nizamat adalat for 1828, four out of five of the judges recommended to the governor-general in council the immediate abolition of the practice, and attest its safety. The fifth judge, though not opposed to the opinions of the rest of the bench, did not feel then prepared to give his entire assent. In the report of this year, the measure has come up with the unanimous recommendation of the court. The two superintendents of police for the upper and lower provinces, Mr. Walter Ewer, and Mr. Charles Barwell, have in the strongest terms expressed their opinion that the suppression might be effected without the least danger. The former officer has urged the measure upon the attention of government in the most forcible manner. No documents exist to shew the opinions of the public functionaries in the interior, but I am informed that nine-tenths are in favour of the abolition.

How again are these opinions supported by practical experience?

Within the limits of the Supreme Court at Calcutta, not a suttee has taken place since the time of Sir John Anstruther.

In the Delhi territory, Sir Charles Metcalfe never permitted a suttee to be performed.

In Jessore, one of the districts of the Calcutta division, in 1824 there were 30 suttees, in 1825 – 16, in 1826 – 3, in 1827 and 1828 there were none. To no other cause can this be assigned, than to a power beyond the law, exercised by the acting magistrate, against which, however, no public remonstrance was made. Mr. Pigou has been since appointed to Cuttack, and has pursued the same strong interference as in Jessore, but his course, although most humane, was properly arrested, as being illegal, by the commissioners. Though the case of Jessore is perhaps one of the strongest examples of efficacious and un-opposed interposition, I really believe that there are few districts in which the same arbitrary power is not exercised to prevent the practice. In the last week, in the report of the acting commission, Mr. Smith, he states that in Ghazipur in the last year 16, and in the preceding years 7 suttees had been prevented by the persuasions, or rather it should be said by the *threats* of the police.

Innumerable cases of the same kind might be obtained from the public records.

It is stated in the letter of the collector of Gaya, Mr. Trotter, but upon what authority I have omitted to enquire, that the peishwa (I presume he means the ex-peishwa Baji Rao) would not allow the rite to be performed, and that in Tanjore it is equally interdicted. These facts, if true, would be positive proofs at least that no unanimity exists among the Hindus upon the point of religious obligations.

Having made enquiries also how far suttees are permitted in the European foreign settlements, I find, from Dr. Carey, that at Chinsurah no such sacrifices had ever been permitted by the Dutch government; that within the limits of Chandernagore itself they were also prevented, but allowed to be performed in the British territories. The Danish government of Serampore has not forbidden the rite in conformity to the example of the British government.

It is a very important fact, that though representations have been made by the disappointed party to superior authority, it does not appear that a single instance of direct opposition to the execution of the prohibitory orders of our civil functionaries has ever occurred. How then can it be reasonably feared that to the government itself, from whom all authority is derived, and whose power is now universally considered to be irresistible, anything bearing the semblance of resistance can be manifest. Mr. Wilson also is of opinion that no immediate overt act of insubordination would follow the publication of the edict. The regulations of government may be evaded, the police may be corrupted, but even here the price paid as hush money will operate as a penalty indirectly forwarding the object of government.

I venture then to think it completely proved that, from the native population, nothing of extensive combination or even of partial opposition may be expected from the abolition.

It is however a very different and much more important question, how far the feelings of the native army might take alarm, how far the rite may be in general observance by them, and whether as in the case of Vellore, designing persons might not make use of the circumstance either for the purpose of immediate revolt, or of sowing the seeds of permanent disaffection. Reflecting upon the vast disproportion of numbers between our native and European troops, it was obvious that there might be, in any general combination of the former, the greatest danger to the state, and it became necessary therefore to use every precaution to ascertain the impression likely to be made upon the minds of the native soldiery.

Before I detail to council the means l have taken to satisfy my mind upon this very important branch of the enquiry, I shall beg leave to advert to the name of Lord Hastings. It is impossible but that to his most humane, benevolent, and enlightened mind, this practice must have been often the subject of deep and anxious meditation. It was consequently a circumstance of ill omen and severe disappointment not to have found, upon the records, the valuable advice and direction of his long experience and wisdom. It is true that during the greater part of his administration, he was engaged in war, when the introduction of such a measure would have been highly injudicious. To his successor, Lord Amherst, also the same obstacle was opposed. I am however fortunate in possessing a letter from Lord Hastings to a friend in England upon suttees, and from the following extract, dated 21st November 1825, I am induced to believe that, had he remained in India, this practice would long since have been suppressed. 'The subject which you wish to discuss is one which must interest one's feeling most deeply; but it is also one of extreme nicety. When I mention that in one of the years during my administration of government in India, above eight hundred widows sacrificed themselves within the provinces comprised in the presidency of Bengal, to which number I very much suspect, that very many not notified to the magistrates should be added, I will hope to have credit for being acutely sensible to such an outrage against humanity. At the same time, I was aware how much danger might attend the endeavouring to suppress, forcibly, a practice so rooted in the religious belief of the natives. No men of low caste are admitted into the ranks of the Bengal army. Therefore the whole of that formidable body must be regarded as blindly partial to a custom which they consider equally referable to family honour and to points of faith. To attempt the extinction of the horrid superstition, without being supported in the procedure by a real concurrence on the part of the army, would be distinctly perilous. I have no scruple to say, that I did believe, I could have carried with me the assent of the army towards such an object. That persuasion, however, arose from circumstances which gave me peculiar influence over the native troops.'

Lord Hastings left India in 1823. It is quite certain that the government of that time were much more strongly impressed with the risk of the undertaking, than is now very generally felt. It would have been fortunate could this measure have proceeded under the auspices of that distinguished nobleman, and that the state might have had the benefit of the influence which undoubtedly he possessed, in a peculiar degree, over the native troops. Since that period, however, six years have elapsed. Within the territories all has been peaceful and prosperous, while without, Ava and Bharatpur, to whom alone a strange sort of consequence was ascribed by public opinions, have been made to acknowledge our supremacy. In this interval, experience has enlarged our knowledge, and has given us surer data upon which to distinguish truth from illusion, and to ascertain the real circumstances of our position and power. It is upon these that the concurring opinion of the officers of the civil and military services at large having been founded is entitled to our utmost confidence.

I have the honour to lay before council the copy of a circular addressed to forty-nine officers, pointed out to me by the secretary to government in the military department, as being from their judgment and experience the best enabled to appreciate the effect of the proposed measure upon the native army, together with their answers. For more easy reference, an abstract of each answer is annexed in a separate paper and classed with those to the same purport.

It appears — first, that of those whose opinions are directly adverse to all interference, whatever, with the practice, the number is only *five*. Secondly, of those who are favourable to abolition, but averse to absolute and direct prohibition under the authority of the government, the number is *twelve*. Thirdly, of those who are favourable to abolition, to be effected by the indirect interference of magistrates and other public officers, the number is *eight*. Fourthly, of those who advocate the total, immediate and public suppression of the practice, the number is *twenty-eight*.

It will be observed also, of those who are against an open and direct prohibition, few entertain any fear of immediate danger. They refer to a distinct and undefined evil. I can conceive the possibility of the expression of dissatisfaction and anger being immediately manifested upon this supposed attack on their religious usages; but the distant danger seems to me altogether groundless, provided that perfect respect continues to be paid to all their innocent rites and ceremonies, and provided also, that a kind and considerate regard be continued to their worldly interests and comforts.

I trust therefore that the council will agree with me in the satisfactory nature of this statement, and that they will partake in the perfect confidence which it has given me of the expediency and safety of the abolition.

In the answer of one of the military officers, Lieutenant-Colonel Todd, he has recommended that the tax on pilgrims should be simultaneously given up, for the purpose of affording an undoubted proof of our disinterestedness and of our desire to remove every obnoxious obstacle to the gratification of their religious duties. A very considerable revenue is raised from this head; but if it were to be the price of satisfaction and confidence to the Hindus, and of the removal of all distrust of our present and future intentions, the sacrifice might be a measure of good policy. The objections that must be entertained by all to the principle of the tax, which in England has latterly excited very great reprobation, formed an additional motive for the enquiry. I enclose the copy of a circular letter addressed to different individuals at present in charge of the districts where the tax is collected, or who have had opportunities from their local knowledge of forming a judgment upon this question. It will be seen that opinions vary, but upon a review of the whole, my conviction is that, in connection with the present measure, it is inexpedient to repeal the tax. It is a subject upon which I shall not neglect to bestow more attention than I have been able to do. An abstract of these opinions is annexed to this minute.

I have now to submit for the consideration of council the draft of a regulation enacting the abolition of suttees. It is accompanied by a paper containing the remarks and suggestions of the judges of the nizamat adalat. In this paper is repeated the unanimous opinion of the court in favour of the proposed measure. The suggestions of the nizamat adalat are, in some measure, at variance with a principal object I had in view of preventing collision between the parties to the suttee and the officers of police. It is only in the previous processes or during the actual performance of the rite, when the feelings of all may be more or less roused to a high degree of excitement, that I apprehend the possibility of affray, or of acts of violence, through an indiscreet and injudicious exercise of authority. It seemed to me prudent, therefore, that the police in the first instance should warn and advise, but not forcibly prohibit, and if the suttee, in defiance of this notice, were performed, that a report should be made to the magistrate, who would summon the parties and proceed as in any other case of crime. The sadar court appear to think these precautions unnecessary and I hope they may be so, but, in the beginning, we cannot, I think, proceed with too much circumspection. Upon the same principle, in order to guard against a too hasty or severe a sentence, emanating from extreme zeal on the part of the local judge, I have proposed that the case should only be cognizable by the commissioner of circuit. These are, however, questions which I should wish to see discussed in council. The other recommendations of the court are well worthy of our adoption.

I have now brought this paper to a close, and I trust I have redeemed my pledge of not allowing, in the consideration of this question, passion or feeling to have any part. I trust it will appear that due weight has been given to all difficulties and objections; that facts have been stated with truth and impartiality; that the conclusion to which I have come is completely borne out, both by reason and authority. It may be justly asserted that the government, in this act, will only be following, not preceding the tide of public opinion, long flowing in this direction: and when we have taken into consideration the experience and wisdom of that highest public tribunal, the nizamat adalat, who in unison with our wisest and ablest public functionaries have been, year after year, almost soliciting the government to pass this act, the moral and political responsibility of not abolishing this practice far surpasses in my judgment that of the opposite course.

But discarding, as I have done, every inviting appeal from sympathy and humanity, and having given my verdict, I may now be permitted to express the anxious feelings with which I desire the success of this measure.

The first and primary object of my heart is the benefit of the Hindus. I know nothing so important to the improvement of their future conditions, as the establishment of a purer morality, whatever their belief, and a more just conception of the will of God. The first step to this better understanding will be dissociation of religious belief and practice from blood and murder. They will then, when no longer under this brutalizing excitement, view with more calmness, acknowledged truths. They will see that there can be no inconsistency in the ways of providence, that to the command received as divine by all races of men, 'No innocent blood shall be spilt,' there can be no exception, and when they shall have been convinced of the error of this first and most criminal of their customs, may it not be hoped, that others which stand in the way of their improvement may likewise pass away, and that [with] this emancipation from those chains and shackles upon their minds and actions, they may no longer continue as they have done, the slaves of every foreign conqueror, but that they may assume their just places among the great families of mankind. I disavow in these remarks or in this measure any view whatever to conversion to our own faith. I write and feel as a legislator for the Hindus, and as I believe many enlightened Hindus think and feel.

Descending from these higher considerations, it cannot be a dishonest ambition that the government of which I form a part, should have the credit of an act, which is to wash out a foul stain upon British rule, and to stay the sacrifice of humanity and justice to a doubtful expediency; and finally, as a branch of the general administration of .the empire, I may be permitted to feel deeply anxious, that our course shall be in accordance with the noble example set to us by the British government at home and that the adaptation, where practicable, to the circumstances of this vast Indian population, of the same enlightened principles, may promote here as well as there, the general prosperity, and may exalt the character of our nation (Philips 1977: 335-345).

Appendix III

SATI: REGULATION XVII, AD 1829 OF
THE BENGAL CODE

4 December 1829

A regulation for declaring the practice of suttee, or of burning or burying alive the widows of Hindus, illegal, and punishable by the criminal courts. Passed by the governor-general in council on the 4th December 1829, corresponding with the 20th Aughun 1236 Bengal era; the 23rd Aughun 1237 Fasli; the 21st Aughun 1237 Vilayati; the 8th Aughun 1886 Samvat; and the 6th Jamadi-us-Sani 1245 Hegira.

The practice of suttee, or of burning or burying alive the widows of Hindus, is revolting to the feelings of human nature; it is nowhere enjoined by the religion of the Hindus as an imperative duty; on the contrary a life of purity and retirement on the part of the widow is more especially and preferably inculcated, and by a vast majority of that people throughout India the practice is not kept up, nor observed: in some extensive districts it does not exist: in those in which it has been most frequent it is notorious that in many instances acts of atrocity have been perpetrated which have been shocking to the Hindus themselves, and in their eyes unlawful and wicked. The measures hitherto adopted to discourage and prevent such acts have failed of success, and the governor-general in council is deeply impressed with the conviction that the abuses in question cannot be effectually put an end to without abolishing the practice altogether. Actuated by these considerations the governor-general in council, without intending to depart from one of the first and most important principles of the system of British government in India, that all classes of the people be secure in the observance of their religious usages, so long as that system can be adhered to without violation of the paramount dictates of justice and humanity, has deemed it right to establish the following rules, which are hereby enacted to be in force from the time of their promulgation throughout the territories immediately subject to the presidency of Fort William.

II. The practice of suttee, or of burning or burying alive the widows of Hindus, is hereby declared illegal, and punishable by the criminal courts.

III. First. All zamindars, taluqdars, or other proprietors of land, whether malguzari or lakhiraj; all sadar farmers and under-renters of land of every description; all dependent taluqdars; all naibs and other local agents; all native officers employed in the collection of the revenue and rents of land on the part of government, or the court of wards; and all munduls or other head men of villages are hereby declared especially accountable for the immediate communication to the officers of the nearest police station of any intended sacrifice of the nature described in the foregoing section; and any zamindar, or other description of persons above noticed, to whom such responsibility is declared to attach, who may be convicted of willfully neglecting or delaying to furnish the information above required, shall be liable to be fined by the magistrate or joint magistrate in any sum not exceeding two hundred rupees, and in default of payment to be confined for any period of imprisonment not exceeding six months.

Secondly. Immediately on receiving intelligence that the sacrifice declared illegal by this regulation is likely to occur, the police darogha shall either repair in person to the spot, or depute his mohurrir or jamadar, accompanied by one or more burkundazes of the Hindu religion, and it shall be the duty of the police-officers to announce to the persons assembled for the performance of the ceremony, that it is illegal; and to endeavour to prevail on them to disperse, explaining to them that in the event of their persisting in it they will involve themselves in a crime, and become subject to punishment by the criminal courts. Should the parties assembled proceed in defiance of these remonstrances to carry the ceremony into effect, it shall be the duty of the police-officers to use all lawful means in their power to prevent the sacrifice from taking place, and to apprehend the principal persons aiding and abetting in the performance of it, and in the event of the police-officers being unable to apprehend them, they shall endeavour to ascertain their names and places of abode, and shall immediately communicate the whole of the particulars to the magistrate or joint magistrate for his orders:

Thirdly. Should intelligence of a sacrifice have been carried into effect before their arrival at the spot, they will nevertheless institute a full enquiry into the circumstances of the case, in like manner as on all other occasions of unnatural death, and report them for the information and orders of the magistrate or joint magistrate, to whom they may be subordinate.

IV. First. On the receipt of the reports required to be made by the police daroghas, under the provisions of the foregoing section, the magistrate or joint magistrate of the jurisdiction in which the sacrifice may have taken place, shall enquire into the circumstances of the case, and shall adopt the necessary measures for bringing the parties concerned in promoting it to trial before the court of circuit.

Secondly. It is hereby declared, that after the promulgation of this regulation all persons convicted of aiding and abetting in the sacrifice of a Hindu widow, by burning or burying her alive, whether the sacrifice be voluntary on her part or not, shall be deemed guilty of culpable homicide, and shall be liable to punishment by fine or by both fine and imprisonment, at the discretion of the court of circuit, according to the nature and circumstances of the case, and the degree of guilt established against the offender; nor shall it be held to be any plea of justification that he or she was desired by the party sacrificed to assist in putting her to death.

Thirdly. Persons committed to take their trial before the court of circuit for the offence above mentioned shall be admitted to bail or not, at the discretion of the magistrate or joint magistrate, subject to the general rules in force in regard to the admission of bail.

V. It is further deemed necessary to declare, that nothing contained in this regulation shall be construed to preclude the court of nizamat adalat from passing sentence of death on persons convicted of using violence or compulsion, or of having assisted in burning or burying alive a Hindu widow while labouring under a state of intoxication, or stupefaction, or other cause impeding the exercise of her free will, when, from the aggravated nature of the offence, proved against the prisoner, the court may see no circumstances to render him or her a proper object of mercy (Philips 1977: 360-362).

Appendix IV

THE COMMISSION OF SATI (PREVENTION) ACT, 1987
NO. 3 OF 1988

[3rd January. 1988]

An Act to provide for the more effective prevention of the commission of sati and its glorification and for matters connected therewith or incidental thereto.

Whereas sati or the burning or buying alive of widows or women is revolting to the feelings of human nature and is nowhere enjoined by any of the religions of India as an imperative duty;

And whereas it is necessary to take more effective measures to prevent the commission of sati and its glorification;

Be it enacted by Parliament in the Thirty-eighth Year of the Republic of India as follows: -

PART I

Preliminary

1. (1) This Act may be called the Commission of Sati (Prevention) Act, 1987.

(2) It extends to the whole of India except the State of Jammu and Kashmir.

(3) It shall come into force in a State on such date as the Central Government may, by notification in the Official Gazette, appoint, and different dates may be appointed for different States.

2. (1) In this Act, unless the context otherwise requires, -

(a) "Code" means the Code of Criminal Procedure, 1973;

(b) "glorification", in relation to sati, whether such sati was committed before or after the commencement of this Act, includes, among other things, -

(i) the observance of any ceremony or the taking out of a procession in connection with the commission of sati; or

(ii) the supporting, justifying or propagating the practice of sati in any manner; or

(iii) the arranging of any function to eulogise the person who has committed sati; or

(iv) the creation of a trust, or the collection of funds, or the construction of a temple or other structure or the carrying on of any form of worship or the performance of any ceremony thereat, with a view to perpetuate the honour of, or to preserve the memory of, a person who has committed sati;

(c) "sati" means the act of burning or burying alive of -

(i) any widow along with the body of her deceased husband or any other relative or with any article, object or thing associated with the husband or such relative; or

(ii) any woman along with the body of her relatives, irrespective of whether such burning or burying is claimed to be voluntary on the part of the widow or the woman or otherwise;

(d) "Special Court" means a Special Court constituted under section 9;

(e) "temple" includes any building or other structure, whether roofed or not, constructed or made to preserve the memory of a person in respect of whom sati has been committed or used or intended to be used for the carrying on of any form of worship or for the observance of any ceremony in connection with such commission. (2) Words and expressions used but not defined in this Act and defined in the Indian Penal Code or in the Code shall have the same meaning as are respectively assigned to them in the Indian Penal Code or the Code.

Part II

Punishments For Offences Relating To Sati

3. Notwithstanding anything contained in the Indian Penal Code, whoever attempts to commit sati and does any act towards such commission shall be punishable with imprisonment for a term which may extend to six months or with fine or with both:
Provided that the Special Court trying an offence under this section shall, before convicting any person, take into consideration the circumstances leading to the commission of the offence, the act committed, the state of mind of the person charged of the offence at the time of the commission of the act and all other relevant factors.

4. (l) Notwithstanding anything contained in the Indian Penal Code, if any person commits sati, whoever abets the commission of such sati, either directly or indirectly, shall be punishable with death or imprisonment for life and shall also be liable to fine.
(2) If any person attempts to commit sati, whoever abets such attempt, either directly or indirectly, shall be punishable with imprisonment for life and shall also be liable to fine.
Explanation - For the purposes of this section, any of the following acts or the like shall also be deemed to be an abetment, namely: -
(a) any inducement to a widow or woman to get her burnt or buried alive along with the body of her deceased husband or with any other relative or with any article, object or thing associated with the husband or such relative, irrespective of whether she is in a fit state of

mind or is labouring under a state of intoxication or stupefaction or other cause impeding the exercise of her free will;

(b) making a widow or woman believe that the commission of sati would result in some spiritual benefit to her or her deceased husband or relative or the general well being of the family;

(c) encouraging a widow or woman to remain fixed in her resolve to commit sati and thus instigating her to commit sati;

(d) participating in any procession in connection with the commission of sati or aiding the widow or woman in her decision to commit sati by taking her along with the body of her deceased husband or relative to the cremation or burial ground;

(e) being present at the place where sati is committed as an active participant to such commission or to any ceremony connected with it;

(f) preventing or obstructing the widow or woman from saving herself from being burnt or buried alive;

(g) obstructing or interfering with the police in discharge of its duties of taking any steps to prevent the commission of sati.

5. Whoever does any act for the glorification of sati shall be punishable with imprisonment for a term which shall not be less than one year but which may extend to seven years and with fine which shall not be less man five thousand rupees but which may extend to thirty thousand rupees.

PART III

Powers of Collector or District Magistrate to Prevent Offences Relating to Sati

6. (1) Where the Collector or the District Magistrate is of the opinion that sati or any abetment thereof is being, or is about to be commission of sati by any person in any area or areas specified in the commission of sati by any person in any area or areas specified in the order.

(2) The Collector or the District Magistrate may also, by order, prohibit the glorification in any manner of sati by any person in any areas or areas specified in the order.

(3) Whoever contravenes any order made under sub-section (1) or sub-section (2) shall, if such contravention is not punishable under any other provision of this Act, be punishable with imprisonment for a term which shall not be less than one year but which may extend to seven years and with fine which shall not be less than five thousand rupees but which may extend to thirty thousand rupees.

7. (l) The State Government may, if it is satisfied that in any temple or other structure which has been in existence for not less than twenty years, any form of worship or the performance of any ceremony is carried on with a view to perpetuate the honour of, or to preserve the memory of, any person in respect of whom sati has been committed, by order, direct the removal of such temple or other structure.

(2) The Collector or the District Magistrate may, if satisfied that in any temple or other structure, other than that referred to in sub-section (1), any form of worship or the performance of any ceremony is carried on with a view to perpetuate the honour of, or to preserve the memory of, any person in respect of whom sati has been committed, by order, direct the removal of such temple or other structure.

(3) Where any order under sub-section (1) or sub-section (2) is not complied with, the State Government or the Collector or the District Magistrate, as the case may be, shall cause the temple or other structure to be removed through a police officer not below the rank of a Sub-inspector at the cost of the defaulter.

8. (1) Where the Collector or the District Magistrate has reason to believe that any funds or property have been collected or acquired for the purpose of glorification or the commission of sati or which may be found under

circumstances which create suspicion of the commission of any offence under this Act, he may seize such funds or property.

(2) Every Collector or District Magistrate acting under sub-section (1) shall report the seizure to the Special Court, if any, constituted to try any offence in relation to which such funds or property were collected or acquired and shall await the orders of such Special Court as to the disposal of the same.

PART IV

Special Courts

9. (1) Notwithstanding anything contained in the Code, all offences under this Act shall be triable only by a Special Court constituted under this section.

(2) The State Government shall, by notification in the Official Gazette, constitute one or more Special Courts for the trial of offences under this Act and every Special Court shall exercise jurisdiction in respect of the whole or such part of the State as may be specified in the notification.

(3) A Special Court shall be presided over by a Judge to be appointed by the State Government with the concurrence of the Chief Justice of the High Court.

(4) A person shall not be qualified for appointment as a Judge of a Special Court unless he is, immediately before such appointment, a Sessions Judge or an Additional Sessions Judge in any State.

10. (l) For every Special Court, the State Government shall appoint a person to be a Special Public Prosecutor.

(2) A person shall be eligible to be appointed as a Special Public Prosecutor under this section only if he had been in practice as an advocate for not less than seven years or has held any post for a period of not less than seven years under the State requiring special knowledge of law.

(3) Every person appointed as a Special Public Prosecutor under this section shall be deemed to be a

Public Prosecutor within the meaning of clause (u) of section 2 of the Code and the provisions of the Code shall have effect accordingly.

11. (1) A Special Court may take cognizance of any offence, without the accused being committed to it for trial, upon receiving a complaint of facts which constitute such offence, or upon a police report on such facts.

(2) Subject to the other provisions of this Act, a Special Court shall, for the trial of any offence, have all the powers of a Court of Session and shall try such offence as if it were a Court of Session, so far as may be, in accordance with the procedure prescribed in the Code for trial before a Court of Session.

12. (1) When trying any offence under this Act, a Special Court may also try any other offence with which the accused may, under the Code, be charged at the same trial if the offence is connected with such other offence.

(2) If, in the course of any trial of any offence under this Act it is found that the accused person has committed any other offence under this Act or under any other law, a other Special Court may convict such person also of such other offence and pass any sentence authorized by this Act or such other law for the punishment thereof.

(3) In every inquiry or trial, the proceedings shall be held as expeditiously as possible and, in particular, where the examination of witnesses has begun, the same shall be continued from day to day until all the witnesses in attendance have been examined, and if any Special Court finds the adjournment of the same beyond the following date to be necessary, it shall record for doing so.

13. Where a person has been convicted of an offence under this Act, the Special Court trying such offence may, if it is considered necessary so to do, declare that any funds or property seized under section 8 shall stand forfeited to the State.

14. (1) Notwithstanding anything contained in the Code, an appeal shall lie as a matter of right from any judgment, sentence or order, not being an interlocutory order, of a Special Court to the High Court both on facts and on law.

(2) Every appeal under this section shall be preferred within a period of thirty days from the date of the judgment, sentence or order appealed from:

Provided that the High Court may entertain an appeal after the expiry of the same period of thirty days if it is satisfied that the appellant had sufficient cause for not preferring the appeal within the period of thirty days.

PART V

Miscellaneous

15. No suit, prosecution or other legal proceeding shall lie against the State Government or any officer or authority of the State Government for anything which is in good faith done or intended to be done in pursuance of this Act or any rules or orders made under this Act.

16. Where any person is prosecuted of an offence under section 4, the burden of proving that he had not committed the offence under the said section shall be on him.

17. (1) All officers of Government are hereby required and empowered to assist the police in the execution of the provisions of this Act or any rule or order made there under.
(2) All village officers and such other officers as may be specified by the Collector or the District Magistrate in relation to any area and the inhabitants of such area shall, if they have reason to believe or have the knowledge that sati is about to be, or has been, committed in the area shall forthwith report such fact to the nearest police station.

(3) Whoever contravenes the provisions of sub-section (I) or sub-section (2) shall be punishable with imprisonment of either description for a term which may extend to two years and shall also be liable to fine.

18. A person convicted of an offence under sub-section (1) or section 4 in relation to the commission of sati shall be disqualified from inheriting the property of the person in respect of whom sati has been committed or the property of any other person which he would have been entitled to inherit on the death of the person in respect of whom such sati has been committed.

19. In the Representation of the People Act, 1951,-
(a) in section 8, in sub-section (2) after the proviso, the following proviso shall be inserted, namely: -
"Provided further that a person convicted by a Special Court for the contravention of any of the provisions of the Commission of Sati (Prevention) Act, 1987 shall be disqualified from the date of such conviction and shall continue to be disqualified for a further period of five years since his release;"
(b) in section 123, after clause (3A), the following clause shall be inserted, namely: -
(3B) The propagation of the practice or the commission of sati or its glorification by a candidate or his agent or any other person with the consent of the candidate or his election agent for the furtherance of the prospects of the election of that candidate or for prejudicially affecting the election of any candidate.
Explanation - For the purposes of this clause, "sati" and "glorification" in relation to sati shall have the meanings respectively assigned to them in the Commission of Sati (Prevention) Act, 1987.'

20. The provisions of this Act or any rule or order made there under shall have effect notwithstanding anything inconsistent therewith contained in any enactment other than this Act or in any instrument having effect by virtue of any enactment other than this Act.

21. (1) The Central Government may, by notification in the Official Gazette, make rules for carrying out the provisions of this Act.

(2) Every rule made under this section shall be laid, as soon as may be after it is made, before each House of Parliament, while it is in session, for a total period of thirty days which may be comprised in one session or in two or more successive sessions, and if, before the expiry of the session immediately following the session or the successive sessions aforesaid, both Houses agree in making any modification in the rule or both Houses agree that the rule should not be made, the rule shall thereafter have effect only in such modified form or be of no effect, as the case may be; so, however, that any such modification or annulment shall be without prejudice to the validity of anything previously done under that rule.

22. (1) All laws in force in any State immediately before the commencement of this Act in that State which provide for the prevention or the glorification of sati shall, on such commencement, stand repealed.

(2) Notwithstanding such repeal, anything done or any action taken under the law repealed under sub-section (1) shall be deemed to have been done or taken under the corresponding provisions of this Act, and, in particular, any case taken cognizance of by a Special Court under the provisions of any law so repealed and pending before it immediately before the commencement of this Act in that State shall continue to be dealt with by the Special Court after such commencement as if such Special Court had been constituted under section 9 of this Act (Narasimha 1990: 175-183).

Select Bibliography

PRIMARY SOURCES

Books and Tracts by Foreign Travellers

Barbosa, Duarte. 2002. *The Book of Duarte Barbosa,* edited by Mansel Longworth Dames, Asian Educational Services, first published in 1918–1921.

Bernier, Francois. 1994. *Travels in the Mogul Empire AD 1656–1668,* second edition revised by Vincent A. Smith, Low Price Publications, first published in 1934.

Bowrey, Thomas. 1905. *A Geographical Account of Countries Round the Bay of Bengal, 1669 to 1679,* edited by Richard C. Temple, The Hakluyt Society.

Burnell, John. 1933. *Bombay in the Days of Queen Anne,* The Hakluyt Society.

Cabral, Pedro. 1938. *The Voyage of Pedro Alvares Cabral to Brazil and India from Contemporary Documents and Narratives,* The Hakluyt Society.

Carre, Abbe. 1990. *The Travels of the Abbe Carre in India and the Near East 1672 to 1674,* 3 vols., edited by Charles Fawcett, Asian Educational Services.

Craufurd, Q. 1977. From the 2nd edition. *Sketches Chiefly Relating to the History, Religion, Learning and Manners of the Hindoos*, 2 vols., Researchco Publications, first published in 1792.

Deane, A. 1823. *A Tour Through the Upper Provinces of Hindostan Comprising a Period Between the Years 1804 and 1814*, C&J Rivington.

De Grandpre, La. 1995. *Voyage in the Indian Ocean*, Asian Educational Services, first published in 1803.

Della Valle, Pietro. 1991. *The Travels of Pietro Della Valle in India*, edited by Edward Gray, Asian Educational Services, first published in 1892.

Fay, Eliza. 1908. *The Original Letters from India of Mrs. Eliza Fay*, Messrs Thacker, Spink & Co.

Filliozat, Vasundhara. 2001. Edited, *Vijayanagar*, National Book Trust.

Foster, William. 1999. Edited. *Early Travels in India 1583–1619*, Low Price Publications, first published in 1921.

Fryer, John. 1992. *A New Account of East India and Persia Being Nine Years' Travels 1672–1681*, 3 vols., edited by William Crooke, Asian Educational Services, first published in 1909.

Guyon, Abbe de. 1757. *A New History of the East Indies, Ancient and Modern*, R. and J. Dodsley.

Hamilton, Alexander. 1744. *A New Account of the East Indies*, 2 vols., C. Hitch and A. Millar.

Hodges, William. 1999. *Travels in India During the Years 1780, 1781, 1782, and 1783*, Munshiram Manoharlal.

Ibn Battuta. 1999. *Travels in Asia and Africa 1325–1354*, translated by H.A.R. Gibb, Low Price Publications, first published in 1929.

Kemp, P.M. 1959. Translated and edited, *Russian Travellers to India and Persia [1624–1798]*, Jiwan Prakashan.

Linschoten, John Huyghen Van. 1988. *The Voyage of John Huyghen Van Linschoten to the East Indies*, 2 vols., Asian Educational Services, first published in 1885.

Locke, J. Courtenay. 1995. *The First Englishmen in India*, Asian Educational Services, first published in 1930.

Major, R.H. 1992. *India in the Fifteenth Century: Being a Collection of Narratives of Voyages to India*, Asian Educational Services, first published in 1858.

Majumdar, R.C. 1960. *The Classical Accounts of India,* Firma K.L. Mukhopdhyay.

Mandelslo, Albert de. 1969. "The Voyages and Travels of J. Albert de Mandelslo into the East Indies 1638–40," in Adam Olearius, *Voyages and Travels of the Ambassadors,* translated by John Davies, John Starkey and Thomas Basset.

Manucci, Niccolao. 1990. *Mogul India or Storia Do Mogor,* Vols. I-IV, translated by William Irvine, Low Price Publications, first published in 1907–1908.

Martin, Francois. 1984. *India in the 17th Century (Social, Economic, and Political). Memoirs of Francois Martin,* Vol. II, Part I, 1681–1688, translated and annotated by Lotika Varadarajan, Manohar.

Masson, Charles. 1997. *Narrative of Various Journeys in Balochistan, Afghanistan and the Panjab. Including a Residence in those Countries from 1826 to 1838,* 3 vols., Munshiram Manoharlal, first published in 1842.

Moorcroft, William and George Trebeck. 1989. *Travels in India. Himalayan Provinces of Hindustan and the Punjab in Ladakh and Kashmir in Peshawar, Kabul, Kunduz and Bokhara from 1819 to 1825,* 2 vols., Asian Educational Services, first published in 1841.

Moreland, W.H. 1931. Edited. *Relations of Golconda in the Early Seventeenth Century,* The Hakluyt Society.

Mundy, Peter. 1914. *The Travels of Peter Mundy in Europe and Asia* Vol. II, edited by R.C. Temple, The Hakluyt Society.

Navarrete. 1960. *The Travels and Controversies of Friar Domingo Navarrette 1618–1686,* Vol. II, The Hakluyt Society.

Olafsson, Jon. 1932. *The Life of the Icelander Jon Olafsson Traveller to India,* edited by Sir Richard Temple, The Hakluyt Society.

Orlich, Captain Leopold Von. 1985. *Travels in India Including Sinde and the Punjab,* 2 vols., Usha, first published in 1845.

Ovington, J. 1994. *A Voyage to Surat in the Year 1689,* edited by H.G. Rawlinson, Asian Educational Services, first published in 1929.

Parkes, Fanny. 2003. *Begums, Thugs & Englishmen,* Penguin, first published in 1850.

Pelsaert, Francisco. 2001. *Jahangir's India. The Remonstrantie of Francisco Pelsaert,* translated from the Dutch by W.H. Moreland and P. Geyl, Low Price Publications, first published in 1925.

Pires, Tome. 2005. *Suma Oriental of Tome Pires*, edited by Armando Cortesao, Asian Educational Services.

Polo, Marco. 1961. *The Travels of Marco Polo*, introduction by F.W. Mote, Dell Publishing Company.

Pyrard, Francois. 2000. *The Voyage of Francois Pyrard of Laval to the East Indies, the Maldives the Moluccas and Brazil*, edited by Albert Gray, Asian Educational Services, first published in 1887.

Sachau, Edward. 1989. *Alberuni's India,* Atlantic Publishers and Distributors.

Sastri, Nilakanta K.A. 1972. *Foreign Notices of South India. From Megasthenes to Ma Huan*, University of Madras.

Tavernier, Jean-Baptiste. 2000. *Travels in India,* edited by William Crooke, Low Price Publications.

Thevenot and Careri. 1949. *Indian Travels of Thevenot and Careri,* edited by Surendranath Sen, National Archives of India.

Varthema, Ludovico di. 1997. *The Itinerary of Ludovico di Varthema of Bologna from 1502 to 1508*, translated by John W. Jones, Asian Educational Services, first published in 1863.

Vigne, G.T. 1981. *Travels in Kashmir, Ladakh, Iskardo, the Countries Adjoining the Mountain-Course of the Indus and the Himalaya, North of the Punjab,* Vol. I, Sagar Publications.

Wheeler, Talboys, J. 1975. Edited. *Early Travels in India,* Deep Publication.

Wheeler, J. Talboys and Michael Macmillan. 1956. Edited. *European Travellers in India,* Susil Gupta Ltd.

Yule, Henry and Henri Cordier. 1913–1916. Edited. *Cathy and the Way Thither*, 4 vols., The Hakluyt Society.

Yule, Henry. 1863. Edited. *The Wonders of the East, by Friar Jordanus of the Order of Preachers and Bishops of Columbum in India the Greater (circa 1330),* The Hakluyt Society.

PRIMARY TEXTS

Banabhatta. 1896. *Kadambari.* Translated by C.M. Ridding, Royal Asiatic Society.

Harsa-carita. 1897. Translated by E.B. Cowell and F.W. Thomas, Motilal Banarsidass, reprint.

Jimutavahana's Dayabhaga. The Hindu Law of Inheritance in Bengal. 2002. Edited and Translated with an Introduction and Notes by Ludo Rocher, Oxford University Press.

Kalhana. 1900. *Rajatarangani. A Chronicle of the Kings of Kashmir*. Edited and translated by M.A. Stein, Motilal Banarsidass, reprint.

The Hymns of the Rgveda. 1986. Translated by Ralph T.H. Griffith, Motilal Banarsidass, first published in 1889.

The Laws of Manu. 1970. Translated by G. Buhler, Motilal Banarsidass, first published in 1886.

The Institutes of Vishnu. 1990. Translated by Julius Jolly, Charles Scribner's Sons, reprint.

A Critical Edited and Annotated Translation of the Vaisnava-Dharmasastra. 2010. By Patrick Olivelle, Harvard University Press.

Yajnavalkya Smriti with the commentary of Vijnanesvara called Mitaksara. 1918. Translated by Rai Bahadur Srisa Chandra Vidyarnava, The Indian Press.

EVANGELICAL AND MISSIONARY WRITINGS ON INDIA

An account of the proceedings at a public meeting held at the City of York, on the 19th January 1827, to take into consideration the expediency of petitioning Parliament on the subject of Hindoo widows in British India, York, 1827.

Buchanan, Claudius. 1805. *Memoir of the Expediency of an Ecclesiastical Establishment for British India*, T. Cadell and W. Davies.

——. 1812. *The works of the Reverend Claudius Buchanan, LL.D: comprising his Eras of light, Light of the World, and, Star in the East...*, Samuel T. Armstrong.

——. 1814. *An Apology for Christianity in India*, Cadell and Davies.

——. 1849. *Christian Researches in Asia*, Ward & Co., first published in 1811.

Carey, Eustace. 1836. *Memoir of William Carey, D.D.*, Jackson and Walford.

Carey, Mrs. Eustace. 1857. *Eustace Carey. A Missionary in India*, J. Heaton & Son.

Carey, William. 1792. *An Enquiry into the Obligations of Christians, to Use Means for the Conversion of the Heathens*, Leicester.

Dubois, Abbe J.A. 1906. *Hindu Manners, Customs and Ceremonies*, ed., by Henry K. Beauchamp, Clarendon Press.

——. 1997. *Letters on the State of Christianity in India*, Associated Publishing House, first published in 1823.

Essays Relative to the Habits, Character and Moral Improvement of the Hindoos, 1823, England.

Grant, Charles. 1832. *Observations on the State of Society among the Asiatic Subjects of Great Britain, particularly with respect to Morals; and on the means of improving it. Written chiefly in the Year 1792,* Select Committee of the House of Commons, 16 August 1832.

Grimshawe, T.S. 1825. *An earnest appeal to British humanity on behalf of Hindoo widows; in which the abolition of the barbarous rite of burning alive is proved to be both safe and practicable,* London.

Heber, Reginald. 1993. *Narrative of a Journey Through the Upper Provinces of India from Calcutta to Bombay, 1824–1825 (With Notes Upon Ceylon), An Account of a Journey to Madras and the Southern Provinces, 1826, and Letters Written in India,* 3 vols., Low Price Publications, first published in 1827.

Hole, Charles. 1896. *The Early History of the CMS, for Africa and the East to the End of Anno Domini 1814,* London.

Hough, Rev. James. 1845. *The History of Christianity in India,* Vols. IV and V, Church Missionary House.

Hyde, Henry, B. 1901. *Parochial Annals of Bengal: Being a history of the Bengal Ecclesiastical Establishment of the Honourable East India Company in the 17th and 18th Centuries Compiled From Original Sources,* Bengal Secretariat Book Depot.

Johns, William. 1816. *A collection of facts and opinions relative to the burning of widows, and other destructive customs in British India: Respectfully submitted to the consideration of Government, as soliciting a further extension of their humane interference,* W.H. Pearce.

Long, J. 1848. *Handbook of Bengal Missions,* J.F. Shaw.

——. 1974. reprint. *Calcutta in the Olden Time,* Sanskrit Pustak Bhandar.

Lushington, C. 1824. *The History, Design and Present State, of the Religious, Benevolent and Charitable Institutions, founded by the British in Calcutta and Its Vicinity,* The Hindostanee Press.

Marshman, John Clark. 1859. *The Life and Times of Carey, Marshman and Ward,* Longman and Co.

——. 1874. *The History of India,* Vol. III, Longmans, Green, Reader & Dyer.

Peggs, J. 1984. Reprint. *Cries of Agony. An Historical Account of Suttee, Infanticide, Ghat Murders & Slavery in India,* Discovery Publishing House.

Poynder, John. 1827. *Human Sacrifices in India: A Speech to the Court of Proprietors of East India Company*, J. Hatchard and Son.

Robertson, William. 1981. *An Historical Disquisition Concerning Ancient India*, Rare Reprints, first published 1818.

Sherring, Rev. M.A. 1875. *The History of Protestant Missions in India*, Trubner & Co.

Teignmouth, Lord. 1808. *Considerations of the practicability, policy, and obligation of communicating Christianity to India*, London.

Tennant, Rev. William. 1802. *Indian Recreations: Consisting chiefly of strictures on the domestic and rural economy of the Mahometans and Hindoos*, C. Stewart.

Ward, William. 1822. *Farewell Letters to a Few Friends in Britain and America, on Returning to Bengal in 1821*, Lexington, Kentucky.

———. 1990. *History, Literature, and Mythology of the Hindoos*, Low Price Publications, from third edition published in 1817–1820.

Williams, L. and M. 1892. Edited. *Serampore Letters: Being the unpublished correspondence of William Carey and others with John Williams, 1800–1816*, G.P. Putnam's Sons.

BRITISH MEMOIRS, DISPATCHES, CORRESPONDENCE

Campbell, George. 1893. *Memoirs of My Indian Career*, 2 vols., Macmillan and Co.

Edwardes, Sir Herbert B. and Herman Merivale. 1872. *Life of Sir Henry Lawrence*, Vol. II, Smith, Elder & Co.

Gardner, Alexander. 1970. *Memories of Alexander Gardner*, edited by Major Hugh Pearse, 2nd Batt. The East Sorvey Regiment, Languages Department, Punjab, first published in 1898.

Gleig, Rev. G.R. 1830. *The Life of Major-General Sir Thomas Munro*, 3 vols., Henry Colburn and Richard Bentley.

———. 1841. *Memoirs of the Life of the Right Hon. Warren Hastings*, 3 vols., Richard Bentley.

Kaye, John W. 1856. *Life and Correspondence of Major-General Sir John Malcolm, G.C.B.*, Vol. II, Smith, Elder & Co.

Malcolm, Sir John. 1836. *The Life of Robert, Lord Clive: Collected From the Family Papers*, John Murray.

Martin, Montgomery R. 1984. *The Despatches, Minutes and Correspondence of the Marquess Wellesley During his Administration in India*, Inter-India Publications, first published in 1837.

Pearce, Robert R. 1989. *Memoirs and Correspondence of the Most Noble Richard Marquess Wellesley,* 3 vols., S.S. Publishers, first published in 1846.

Pearson, Rev. Hugh. 1819. *Memoirs of the Life and Writings of the Rev. Claudius Buchanan, D.D.,* 2 vols., T. Cadell & W. Davies.

Philips, C.H. 1977. Edited. *The Correspondence of Lord William Cavendish Bentinck Governor-General of India 1828–1835,* 2 vols., Oxford University Press.

Teignmouth, Lord. 1976. *The Works of Sir William Jones with the Life of the Author,* Agam Kala Prakashan, first published in 1799.

Teignmouth, Lord. 1843. *Memoir of the Life and Correspondence of John, Lord Teignmouth, by His Son, Lord Teignmouth,* 2 vols., Hatchard and Son.

COLONIAL WRITINGS ON INDIA

Beveridge, H. 1978. *Warren Hastings in Bengal,* edited with introduction by Shri Ramakanta Chakravarti, Sanskrit Pustak Bhandar, first published in 1798.

Buckland, C.E. 1976. *Bengal Under the Lieutenant-Governors: Being a Narrative of the Principle Events and Public Measures during Their Periods of Office, from 1854 to 1898,* Vol. I, Deep Publications, first published in 1901.

Bushby, Henry Jeffreys. 1832. *Widow-Burning: A Narrative,* Parbury, Allen & Co.

Carey, W.H. 1907. *Good Old Days of Honorable John Company,* Vol. II, R. Cambray & Co., earlier edition in 1882.

Chaplin, William. 1803–1804. "The Suicide of Hindu Widows By Burning Themselves with the Bodies of Their Deceased Husbands is A Practice Revolting to Natural Feeling and Inconsistent with Moral Duty," *Primitiae Orientalis,* Calcutta.

Colebrooke, H.T. 1795. "On the Duties of a Faithful Hindu Widow," in *Asiatic Researches,* Vol. IV, reprinted in H.T. Colebrooke, *Essays on the Religion and Philosophy of the Hindus,* Vol. II, Indological Book House, 1972.

——. 1984. *Dayabhaga and Mitaksara. Two Treatises On the Hindu Law of Inheritance,* Translated into English with annotations, Parimal Publications, first published in 1810.

——. 1873. *Miscellaneous Essays,* edited by E.B. Cowell, Vol. II, Trubner.

Colebrooke, T.E. 1873a. *Life of H.T. Colebrooke,* prefatory volume to *Essays on the Religion and Philosophy,* Trubner and Co.

Dow, Alexander. 1973. *The History of Hindostan,* Vol. I, Today & Tomorrow's Printers & Publishers, first published in 1770.

Elphinstone, Mountstuart. 1966. *The History of India. The Hindu and Mahometan Periods,* Kitab Mahal, first published in 1841.

Forbes, A.K. 1997. *Ras Mala. Hindoo Annals of the Province of Goozerat in Western India,* Vol. II, Low Price Publications, first published in 1924.

Forbes, James. 1988. *Oriental Memoirs,* 4 vols., Gian Publishing House, first published in 1813.

Forster, George. 1970. *A Journey From Bengal to England,* 2 vols., Languages Department, Punjab, first published in 1808.

Graham, Maria. 1814. *Letters on India,* Longman, Hurst, etc.

Grose, John Henry. 1772. *A Voyage to the East Indies with Observations on the Several Parts There,* 2 vols., S. Hooper, first published in 1757.

Halhed, Nathaniel. 1776. *A Code of Gentoo Laws, or, Ordinations of the Pundits, from a Persian Translation Made From the Original Written in the Shanscrit Language,* London.

———. 1778. *A Grammar of the Bengali Language,* Printed at Hooghly in Bengal.

Hunter, W.W. 1868. *The Annals of Rural Bengal,* Vol. I, Smith, Elder, and Co.

Jones, William. 1796. *Institutes of Hindu Law: or, the Ordinances of Menu,* J. Sewell, Cornhill, and J. Debrett.

Kaye, John W. 1966. *The Administration of the East India Company,* Kitab Mahal, first published in 1853.

———. 1859. *Christianity in India,* Smith, Elder & Co.

Malcolm, Sir John. 1970a. *A Memoir of Central India Including Malwa,* Vol. II, Sagar Publications, first published in 1823.

———. 1970b. *The Political History of India (1784 to 1823),* Vol. II, Associated Publishing House, first published in 1826.

Martin, Montgomery R. 1983a. *The History of the Indian Empire,* Vol. I, Mayur Publications.

———. 1983b. *British India. Its History, Topography, Government, Military, Defence, Finance, Commerce, and Staple Products,* Mayur Publications, first published in 1855.

———. 1987. *Eastern India. The History, Antiquities, Topography and Statistics,* Cosmo Publications, first published in 1838.

Mill, James. 1848. *The History of British India*, fifth edition, edited by H.H. Wilson, Piper, Stephenson and Spence.

Muir, Ramsay. 1971. *The Making of British India*, Capital Book House, first published in 1915.

Orme, Robert. 1978. *Historical Fragments of the Mogul Empire, of the Morattoes, and of the English Concerns in Indostan*, Associated Publishing House, first published in 1782.

Osborne, The Hon. W.G. 1973. *The Court and Camp of Runjeet Sing*, Oxford University Press, first published in 1840.

Scrafton, Luke. 1763. *Reflections on the Government of Indostan*, W. Richardson and S. Clark, first published in 1761.

Sleeman, W.H. 2003. *Rambles & Recollections of an Indian Official*, revised and annotated by Vincent Smith, Rupa.

Steinbach, Henry. 1982. *Punjab. History, Commerce, Production, Government, Manufactures, Laws and Religion*, Sumit Publications, first published in 1845.

Tennant, Rev. William. 1802. *Indian Recreations*, C. Stewart.

Thorburn, S.S. 1970. *The Punjab in Peace and War*, Languages Department, Punjab, first published in 1883.

Tod, James. 2010. *Annals and Antiquities of Rajasthan*, Vol. II, Low Price Publications, first published in 1920.

Twining, Thomas. 1893. *Travels in India: A Hundred Years Ago* (preserved by his son T.T. Twining and edited by Rev. William Twining), James R. Osgood, McILvaine & Co.

Vansittart, H. 1976. *Narrative of Transactions in Bengal*, K.P. Bagchi & Co., first published in 1766.

Verelst, H. 1772. *A View of the Rise, Progress and Present State of the English Government in Bengal*, J. Nourse, Brotherton and Sewell.

Wheeler, Talboys, J. 1972. *Early Records of British India: A History of the English Settlements in India*, Vishal Publishers.

Wilkins, Charles. 1808. *A Grammar of the Sanscrit Language*, W. Blumer and Co. 1808.

Wilson, C.R. 1895. *The Early Annals of the English in Bengal: Being the Bengal Public Consultations for the First Half of the Eighteenth Century*, W. Thacker & Company.

Wilson, C.R., and W.H. Wilson. 1968. *Glimpses of the Olden Times, India Under East India Company*, Eastlight Book House.

Wilson, H.H. 1854. "On the supposed Vaidik authority for the burning of Hindu widows and on the Funeral ceremonies of the Hindus," *Journal of the Royal Asiatic Society*, Vol. XVI, Part I.

BRITISH OFFICIAL DOCUMENTS

Carter, Mia and Barbara Harlow. 2003. *Archives of Empire, Vol. I, from the East India Company to the Suez Canal*, Duke University Press.

Sharp, H. 1920. *Selections From Educational Records, Part I, 1781–1839*, Superintendent Government Printing.

Zastoupil, Lynn and Martin Moir. 1999. Edited. *The Great Education Debate. Documents Relating to the Orientalist-Anglicist Controversy, 1781–1843*, Curzon.

EPIGRAPHIC SOURCES

Corpus Inscriptionum Indicarum
Epigraphia Indica

PARLIAMENTARY PAPERS

Parliamentary Debates
Parliamentary Papers

JOURNALS, MAGAZINES, PERIODICALS

Asiatic Annual Register
Asiatic Journal
Asiatic Researches
Bengal Past and Present
Calcutta Gazette
Calcutta Journal
Calcutta Review
Economic and Political Weekly
Feminist Review
Friend of India
History
Journal of Asian History
Journal of the Asiatic Society of Bengal
Journal of the Asiatic Society of Pakistan
Journal of the Royal Asiatic Society

Journal of the Royal Asiatic Society of Great Britain & Ireland
Manushi
Missionary Register
Modern Asian Studies
Modern Review
New Quest
Oriental Herald and the Journal of General Literature
Pacific Affairs
Seminar
Signs
South Asian Review
The Journal of Commonwealth and Comparative Politics
The Indian Antiquary
The Sociological Review

NEWSPAPERS

Bhaskar
Hindustan Times
Mail Today
The Pioneer
Times of India

OTHER WORKS

Acharya, Jayaraj. 1996. "Sati Was Not Enforced in Ancient Nepal," in *Journal of South Asian Women Studies*, Vol. 2, No. 2.

Agrawal, Ashvini. 2004. "Widow Burning and the Madri Episode. An Analysis of the Evidence of the *Mahabharata*," in Ajay Mitra Shastri ed., *Mahabharata; The End of an Era (Yuganta),* Indian Institute of Advanced Study and Aryan Books International.

Ahmad, S. Maqbul. 1989. *Arabic Classical Accounts of India and China*, Indian Institute of Advanced Study.

Ahmad, Zakiuddin. 1968. "Sati in Eighteenth Century Bengal," in *Journal of the Asiatic Society of Pakistan,* Vol. XIII, No. 2.

Ahmed, Salahuddin 1976. *Social Ideas and Social Change in Bengal 1818–1835*, RDDHI.

Aiyangar, S.K. 1906. "Self-immolation which is not sati," *The Indian Antiquary*, Vol. 35.

Alam, Muzaffar and Sanjay Subrahmanyam. 2008. *Indo-Persian Travels in the Age of Discoveries 1400–1800*, Cambridge University Press.

Altekar, A.S. 1978. *The Position of Women in Hindu Society*, Motilal Banarsidass, first published in 1938.

Anand, Mulkraj. 1989. *Sati*, B.R. Publishing Corporation.

Annett, E.A. *William Carey, Pioneer Missionary to India*, The Sunday School Union, year of publication not stated.

Arberry, A.J. 1960. *Oriental Essays*, George Allen & Unwin.

Archer, Mildred. 1979. *India and British Portraiture, 1770–1825*, Sotheby Parke Bernet, Oxford University Press.

Arnold, David. 2007. *Science, Technology and Medicine in Colonial India*, Cambridge University Press.

Ballantyne, Tony. 2002. *Orientalism and Race. Aryanism in the British Empire*, Palgrave.

Balleine, G.R. 1951. *A History of the Evangelical Party in the Church of England*, Church Book Room.

Ballhatchet, K.A. 1957. *Social Policy and Change in Western India, 1817–1830*, Oxford University Press.

———. 1980. *Race, Sex and Class Under the Raj*, Weidenfeld and Nicolson.

Banerjee, Pompa. 2003. *Burning Women*, Palgrave.

Bayly, C.A. 1991. Ed. *An Illustrated History of Modern India 1600–1947*, Oxford University Press.

———. 2001. "From Ritual to Ceremony: Death Ritual and Society in Hindu North India since 1600," in *Origins of Nationality in South Asia*, Oxford University Press.

———. 2010. "Rammohan Roy and the Advent of Constitutional Liberalism in India, 1800–30," in Shruti Kapila edited, *An Intellectual History for India*, Cambridge University Press.

Bearce, G.D. 1961. *British Attitudes Towards India, 1784–1858*, Oxford University Press.

Beauchamp, Joan. 1934. *British Imperialism in India*, Martin Lawrence.

Blechynden, Kathleen. 2003. *Calcutta, Past and Present*, Sundeep Prakashan, first published in 1905.

Blunt, Sir Edward. 1938. *The I.C.S.*, Faber and Faber.

Bose, Mandakranta. 2000. Edited. *Faces of the Feminine in Ancient, Medieval, and Modern India*, Oxford University Press.

Bose, N.S. 1976. *Indian Awakening and Bengal,* Firma K.L. Mukhopadhyay.

Briggs, Asa. 1967. *The Age of Improvement 1783–1867,* Longmans.

Bryant, Edwin. 2002. *The Quest for the Origins of Vedic Culture,* Oxford University Press.

Buckland, C.E. 1971. *Dictionary of Indian Biography,* Indological Book House, first published in 1906.

Busteed, H.E. 1972. *Echoes from Old Calcutta,* Irish University Press, first published in 1882.

Cannon, Garland. 1970. *The Letters of Sir William Jones,* 2 vols., Clarendon Press.

———. 1990. *The Life and Mind of Oriental Jones,* Cambridge University Press.

———. 1993. Edited. *Collected Works of Sir William Jones,* New York University Press.

Carey, S.P. 1934. *William Carey,* The Wakeman Trust, first published in 1924.

Carson, Penelope. 2012. *The East India Company and Religion 1698–1858,* The Boydell Press.

Cassels, Nancy G. 2010. *Social Legislation of the East India Company,* Sage.

Chakraborti, Haripada. 1974. *Early Brahmi Records in India,* Sanskrit Pustak Bhandar.

Chakravarti, Uma. 2006. "Whatever Happened to the Vedic Dasi?", in Kumkum Sangari and Sudesh Vaid edited, *Recasting Women: Essays in Colonial History,* Zubaan.

Chandrababu, B.S. and M.L. Thilagavathi. 2009. *Woman: Her History and Her Struggle for Emancipation,* Bharathi Puthakalayam.

Chattopadhyay, Gautam. 1978. Edited. *Bengal: Early Nineteenth Century (Selected Documents),* Research India Publications.

Chen, Martha Alter. 2000. *Perpetual Mourning. Widowhood in Rural India,* Oxford University Press.

Cohn, Bernard. 1966. "Recruitment and Training of British Civil Servants in India, 1600–1860," in Ralph Braibanti edited, *Asian Bureaucratic Systems Emergent from the British Imperial Tradition,* Duke University Press.

Collet, S.D. 1962. *The Life and Letters of Raja Rammohan Roy,* edited by D.K. Biswas and P.C. Ganguli, Sadharan Brahmo Samaj, first published in 1900.

Coomaraswamy, A.K. 1913. "Sati: A Defence of the Indian Woman," in *The Sociological Review*, 6.

———. 1948. *The Dance of Shiva: Fourteen Indian Essays*, Asia Publishing House.

Coupland, Reginald. 1945. *Wilberforce*, Oxford University Press.

Courtright, Paul B. 1994. "The Iconography of Sati," in John S. Hawley edited, *Sati, the Blessing and the Curse*, Oxford University Press.

———. 1995. "Sati, Sacrifice, and Marriage: The Modernity of Tradition," in Lindsey Harlan and Paul Courtright edited, *From the Margins of Hindu Marriage*, Oxford University Press.

Cronin, Vincent. 1959. *A Pearl to India. The Life of Roberto de Nobili*, Rupert Hart-Davis.

Crowell, Lorenzo, M. 1990. "Military Professionalism in a Colonial Context: The Madras Army, circa 1832," in *Modern Asian Studies*, 24, 2.

Dalmia, Vasudha. 2007. *Orienting India. European Knowledge Formation in the Eighteenth and Nineteenth Centuries*, Three Essays Collective.

Dasgupta, Subrata. 2007. *The Bengal Renaissance*, Oxford University Press.

Das, Sisir Kumar. 1974. *The Shadow of the Cross*, Munshiram Manoharlal Publishers Pvt. Ltd.

———. 1978. *Sahibs and Munshis: An Account of the College of Fort William*, Orion Publications.

Datta, V.N. 1988. *Sati, A Historical, Social and Philosophical Enquiry into the Hindu Rite of Widow Burning*, Manohar.

Davies, Nigel. 1981. *Human Sacrifice: In History and Today*, William Morrow.

Derrett, Duncan J. 1968. *Religion, Law and the State in India*, Faber and Faber.

Desika Char, S.V. 1983. Edited. *Readings in the Constitutional History of India 1757–1947*, Oxford University Press.

Dhagamwar, Vasudha. 1988. "Saint, Victim or Criminal," in *Seminar*, February.

Dharampal. 1983. *Indian Science and Technology in the Eighteenth Century*, Academy of Gandhian Studies.

——. 2000. *Some European Narratives On India: c.1600–1800*, Vol. I, Ashram Pratishtan, Sevagram.

Dirks, Nicholas B. 2007. *The Scandal of Empire*, Permanent Black.

Dodson, Michael S. 2011a. *Orientalism, Empire, and National Culture. India, 1770–1880*, Cambridge University Press.

——. 2011b. "Thomas Maurice and Domestic Orientalism, c. 1790–1820," in Cynthia Talbot edited, *Knowing India. Colonial and Modern Constructions of the Past*, Yoda Press.

Drewery, Mary. 1978. *William Carey, Shoemaker and Missionary*, Hodder & Stoughton.

Dutt, Romesh. 1970. *The Economic History of India*, 2 vols., Publications Division.

Dyson, Ketaki K. 1978. *A Various Universe*, Oxford University Press.

Edwards, Michael. 1972. *Ralph Fitch. Elizabethan in India*, Faber and Faber.

Embree, Ainslie. 1962. *Charles Grant and British Rule in India*, George Allen & Unwin Ltd.

Farquhar, J.N. 1967. *Modern Religious Movements in India*, Munshiram Manoharlal, first published in 1914.

Fisch, Jorg. 1985. "A Solitary Vindicator of the Hindus: The Life and Writings of General Charles Stuart (1757/58–1828)," in *Journal of the Royal Asiatic Society of Great Britain & Ireland*.

——. 1985. "A Pamphlet War On Christian Missions in India 1807–1809," in *Journal of Asian History*, Vol. 19, No. 1.

——. 1998/2005. *Immolating Women*, Permanent Black.

Frykenberg, Robert E. 1999. "India to 1858," in *Historiography, The Oxford History of the British Empire, Vol., V*, ed. Robin W. Winks, Oxford University Press.

Furber, Holden. 1970. *John Company at Work. A Study of European Expansion in India in the Late Eighteenth Century*, Octagon Books, first published 1948.

Gaitonde, P.D., 1983. *Portuguese Pioneers in India*, Popular Books.

Ganguly, N.C. 1934. *Raja Rammohun Roy*, YMCA Publishing House.

Ghose, J.C. 1982. Edited. *The English Works of Raja Rammohun Roy*, Cosmo Publications, first published in 1906.

Ghosh, Durba. 2008. *Sex and the Family in Colonial India*, Cambridge University Press.

Ghosh, Suresh Chandra. 1998. *The British in Bengal. A Study of the British Society and Life in the Late Eighteenth Century*, Munshiram Manoharlal.

——. 2001. *Birth of a New India. Fresh Light on the Contributions Made by Bentinck, Dalhousie and Curzon in the Nineteenth Century,* Originals.

Green, J.R. 1875. *A Short History of the English People,* Macmillan and Co.

Griffin, Sir Lepel. 1957. *Ranjit Singh,* S. Chand & Co., first published in 1892.

Gupta, Brijen K. 1966. *Sirajuddaullah and the East India Company, 1756–1757: Background to the Foundation of British Power in India,* E.J. Brill

Gupta, Sanjukta and Richard Gombrich. 1984. "Another View of Widow-burning and Womanliness in Indian Public Culture," in *The Journal of Commonwealth and Comparative Politics,* Vol. XXII, No. 1.

Halevy, Elie. 1949. *England in 1815,* Ernest Benn Limited, first published in 1913.

Hardgrave, Robert. 1998. "The Representation of Sati: Four Eighteenth Century Etchings by Baltazard Solvyns," in *Bengal, Past and Present.*

Harlan, Lindsey. 1992. *Religion and Rajput women. The ethics of protection in contemporary narratives,* University of California Press.

——. 1994. "Perfection and Devotion: Sati Tradition in Rajasthan," in John S. Hawley edited, *Sati, the Blessing and the Curse,* Oxford University Press.

Harlan, Lindsey and Paul B. Courtright. 1995. Edited. *From the Margins of Hindu Marriage,* Oxford University Press.

Hawley, John S. 1994. Edited. *Sati, the Blessing and the Curse,* Oxford University Press.

Hiltebeitel, Alf. 2011. *When the Goddess was a Woman. Mahabharata Ethnographies.* Essays by Alf Hiltebeitel, Vol. II, Edited by Vishwa Adluri and Joydeep Bagchee, Brill.

Hobson-Jobson: A Glossary of Anglo-Indian Words and Phrases, edited by Henry Yule and Arthur Coke Burnell, Reprinted: 1968, Munshiram Manoharlal.

Holcomb, Helen H. 1901. *Men of Might in India Missions,* Oliphant, Anderson & Ferrier.

Horstmann, Monica. 2000. "The Sati Debate in the Rajputana Agency," in Jamal Malik edited, *Perspectives of Mutual Encounters in South Asian History,* Brill.

Howse, Ernest Marshall. 1960. *Saints in Politics. The 'Clapham Sect' and the Growth of Freedom,* George Allen & Unwin Ltd.

Husain, Shahanara. 1985. *The Social Life of Women in Early Medieval Bengal,* Asiatic Society of Bangladesh.

Hutchins, Francis G. 1967. *The Illusion of Permanence. British Imperialism in India,* Princeton University Press.

Ingham, Kenneth. 1956. *Reformers in India 1793–1833. An Account of the Work of Christian Missionaries on Behalf of Social Reform,* Cambridge University Press.

Jacobsen, K.A. 2011. Edited. *Brill's Encyclopedia of Hinduism,* Brill.

Jain, Meenakshi. 2011. *The India They Saw, Foreign Accounts: 18th– mid 19th century,* Ocean Books.

Jain, Sharda, Nirja Misra and Kavita Srivastava. 1987. "Deorala Episode: Women's Protest in Rajasthan," in *Economic and Political Weekly,* 22: 4, November 7.

Joshi, V.C. 1975. Edited. *Rammohun Roy and the Process of Modernization,* Vikas Publishing House.

Kane, P.V. 1997. *History of Dharmasastra,* Vol. II, Part I, Bhandarkar Oriental Research Institute.

Kasturi, Malavika. 2002. *Embattled Identities: Rajput Lineages and the Colonial State in Nineteenth Century North India,* Oxford University Press.

Kejariwal, O.P. 1988. *The Asiatic Society of Bengal and the Discovery of India's Past,* Oxford University Press.

Kincaid, Dennis. 1973. *British Social Life in India, 1608–1937,* Routledge & Kegan Paul, first published in 1938.

Kling, Blair B. 1976. *Partner in Empire. Dwarkanath Tagore and the Age of Enlightenment in Eastern India,* University of California Press.

Knowles, Adam. 2011. "Conjecturing Rudeness: James Mill's Utilitarian Philosophy of History and the British Civilizing Mission," in Carey A. Watt and Michael Mann eds., *Civilizing Missions in Colonial and Postcolonial South Asia,* Anthem Press.

Kopf, David. 1969. *British Orientalism and the Bengal Renaissance,* Firma K.L. Mukhopadhyay.

Kulkarni, A.R. 1996. "Sati in the Maratha Country," in Anne Feldhaus ed., *Images of Women in Maharashtrian Literature and Religion,* SUNY.

Laird, M.A. 1972. *Missionaries and Education in Bengal 1793–1837*, Clarendon Press.

Lawson, Philip. 1993. *The East India Company: A History*, Longman.

Lecky, W.E.H. 1883. *A History of England in the Eighteenth Century*, Longmans, Green, and Co.

Leifer, Walter. 1971. *India and the Germans: 500 Years of Indo-German Contacts*, Shakuntala Publishing House.

Leslie, Julia. 1989. *The Perfect Wife: The Orthodox Hindu Woman according to the Stridharmapaddhati of Tryambakarajan*, Oxford University Press.

———. 1991. Edited. *Roles and Rituals for Hindu Women*, Printer Publishers.

———. 1993. "Suttee or Sati: Victim Or Victor," in David Arnold and Peter Robb edited, *Institutions and Ideologies*, Curzon Press.

Lewis, C.B. 1873. *The Life of John Thomas*, Macmillan & Co.

Lingat, Robert. 2004. *The Classical Law of India*, Oxford University Press, reprint.

Loomba, Ania. 1993. "Dead Women Tell No Tales: Issues of Female Subjectivity, Subaltern Agency and Tradition in Colonial and Post-Colonial Writings on Widow Immolation in India," in *History Workshop Journal*, No. 36.

Ludden, David. 1993. "Orientalist Empiricism: Transformations of Colonial Knowledge," in Carol A. Breckenridge and Peter van der Veer edited, *Orientalism and the Postcolonial Predicament*, University of Pennsylvania Press.

Madra, Amandeep Singh and Paramjit Singh. 2004. Edited. *"Sicques, Tigers, Or Thieves": Eyewitness Accounts of the Sikhs (1606–1809)*, Palgrave.

Majeed, Javed. 1992. *Ungoverned Imaginings, James Mill's The History of British India and Orientalism*, Clarendon Press.

Major, Andrea. 2006. *Pious Flames. European Encounters with Sati*, Oxford University Press.

———. 2007. Edited. *Sati, A Historical Anthology*, Oxford University Press.

———. 2011. *Sovereignty and Social Reform in India. British Colonialism and the Campaign against Sati, 1830–60*, Routledge.

———. 2012. "Contested Sacrifice. Sati, Sovereignty and Social Reform in Colonial India," in Charu Gupta ed., *Gendering Colonial India*, Orient Blackswan.

Majumdar, J.K. 1941. Edited. *Rammohun Roy and Progressive Movement in India. Selections From Records (1775–1845)*, Art Press.

Majumdar, R.C. 1972. "Raja Rammohun Roy — A Historical Review," in *The Calcutta Review*, Vol. III, January-March.

——. 1973. *The History of Mediaeval Bengal*, G. Bharadwaj & Co.

——. 1984. reprint. *On Rammohan Roy*, The Asiatic Society.

Mani, Lata. 1990. "Multiple Mediations: Feminist Scholarship in the Age of Multinational Reception," in *Feminist Review* 35.

——. 1993. "The Female Subject, the Colonial Gaze: Reading Eyewitness Accounts of Widow Burning," in Tejaswini Niranjana, P. Sudhir, Vivek Dhareshwar edited, *Interrogating Modernity*, Seagull Books.

——. 1998. *Contentious Traditions. The Debate on Sati in Colonial India*, Oxford University Press.

——. 1999. "Contentious Traditions. The Debate on Sati in Colonial India," in Kumkum Sangari and Sudesh Vaid edited, *Recasting Women, Essays in Colonial History*, Zubaan.

——. 2007. "Production of an Official Discourse on Sati in Early-Nineteenth-Century Bengal," in Sumit Sarkar and Tanika Sarkar edited, *Women and Social Reform in Modern India*, Permanent Black, first published in *Economic and Political Weekly*, Vol. XXI No. 17, April 1986, WS 32-40.

Marshall, P.J. 1968. *Problems of Empire. Britain and India 1757–1813*, George Allen & Unwin.

——. 1970. *The British Discovery of Hinduism in the Eighteenth Century*, Cambridge University Press.

——. 1976. *East India Fortunes. The British in Bengal in the Eighteenth Century*, Clarendon Press.

——. 1986. "The Moral Swing to the East: British Humanitarianism, India and the West Indies," in K. Ballhatchet and J. Harrison edited, *East India Company Studies: Papers Presented to Prof. Cyril Philips*, Asian Research Service.

Mayhew, Arthur. 1929. *Christianity and the Government of India*, Laber & Gwyer.

Mehta, Uday Singh. 1999. *Liberalism and Empire. A Study in Nineteenth-Century British Liberal Thought*, The University of Chicago Press.

Menon, Meena, Geeta Seshu and Sujata Anandan. 1987. *Trial by Fire: A Report on Roop Kanwar's Death*, Bombay Union of Journalists.

Metcalf, Thomas R. 1995. *Ideologies of the Raj*, Cambridge University Press.

Misra, B.B. 1959. *The Central Administration of the East India Company 1773–1834*, Oxford University Press.

Mittra, Peary Chand. 1880. *Life of Dewan Ramcomul Sen*, I.C. Bose & Co.

Moon, Penderel. 1947. *Warren Hastings and British India*, Hodder and Stoughton.

Moor, Edward. 1968. *The Hindu Pantheon*, Indological Book House, first published in 1811.

Morris, Henry. 1904. *The Life of Charles Grant*, John Murray.

Mukherjee, S.N. 1968. *Sir William Jones: A Study in Eighteenth-Century British Attitudes to India*, Cambridge University Press.

——. 1977. *Calcutta: Myths and History*, Subarnarekha.

——. 1982. "Raja Rammohun Roy and the Status of Women in Bengal in the Nineteenth Century," in Michael Allen and S.N. Mukherjee edited, *Women in India and Nepal*, ANU.

Mukherjee, Amitabha. 1968. *Reform and Regeneration in Bengal, 1774–1823*, Rabindra Bharati University.

Mukhopadhyay, Amitabha. 1957. "Sati as a Social Institution in Bengal," in *Bengal Past & Present*.

——. 1958. "Movement For the Abolition of Sati in Bengal," in *Bengal Past & Present*.

Nag, Jamuna. 1972. *Raja Rammohun Roy*, Sterling Publishers.

Nair, P. Thankappan. 1983. Edited. *British Social Life in Ancient Calcutta 1750 to 1850*, Sanskrit Pustak Bhandar.

——. 1984. *Calcutta in the 18th Century. Impressions of Travellers*, Firma KLM Private Ltd.

——. 1989. *Calcutta in the 19th Century*, Firma K.L. Mukhopadhyay Ltd.

Nandy, Ashis. 1975. "Sati: A Nineteenth Century Tale of Women, Violence and Protest," in V.C. Joshi edited, *Rammohan Roy and the Process of Modernization in India*, Vikas Publishing House.

——. 1994. "Sati as Profit Verses Sati as a Spectacle: The Public Debate on Roop Kanwar's Death," in John S. Hawley edited *Sati, the Blessing and the Curse*, Oxford University Press.

Narasimha, Sakuntala. 1990. *Sati. A Study of Widow Burning in India*, Viking.

Neill, Stephen. 1984. *A History of Christianity in India*, Cambridge University Press.

Nevile, Pran. 2010. *Sahib's India. Vignettes from the Raj*, Penguin Books.

Noble, William A. and A.D. Ram Sankhyan. 2001. "Signs of the Divine: Sati Memorials and Sati Worship in Rajasthan," in Karine Schomer, Joan L. Erdman, Deryck O. Lodrick and Lloyd I. Rudolph edited, *Idea of Rajasthan*, Vol. I, Manohar.

Oddie, Geoffrey. 2006. *Imagined Hinduism. British Protestant Missionary Constructions of Hinduism, 1793–1900*, Sage Publications.

Oldenburg, Veena Talwar. 1994. "The Continuing Invention of the Sati Tradition," in John S. Hawley edited, *Sati, the Blessing and the Curse*, Oxford University Press.

O'Malley, L.S.S. 1931. *The Indian Civil Service 1601–1930*, John Murray.

Panda, Nandini Bhattacharyya. 2008. *Appropriation and Invention of Tradition. The East India Company and Hindu Law in Early Colonial Bengal*, Oxford University Press.

Pels, Peter. 1999. "The Rise and Fall of the Indian Aborigines. Orientalism, Anglicism, and the Emergence of an Ethnology of India, 1833–1869," in Peter Pels and Oscar Salemink edited, *Colonial Subjects. Essays on the Practical History of Anthropology*, The University of Michigan Press.

Penner, Peter and Richard Dale MacLean. 1983. *The Rebel Bureaucrat. Frederick John Shore (1799–1837) as Critic of William Bentinck's India*, Chanakya Publications.

Penner, Peter. 1986. *The Patronage Bureaucracy in North India. The Robert M. Bird and James Thomason School, 1820–1870*, Chanakya.

Phadke, H.A. 1996. "Sati: A Historical Survey of the Practice of Widow Immolation in Ancient India," in C. Margabandhu and K.S. Ramachandran edited, *Spectrum of Indian Culture*, Vol. II, Agam Kala Prakashan.

Philips, C.H. 1961. *The East India Company, 1784–1834*, Manchester University Press, first published in 1940.

———. 1967. "James Mill, Mountstuart Elphinstone, and the History of India," in C.H. Philips edited, *Historians of India, Pakistan and Ceylon*, Oxford University Press.

Porter, Andrew. 1999. "Religion, Missionary Enthusiasm, and Empire," in *The Oxford History of the British Empire, Vol. III. The Nineteenth Century*, edited by Andrew Porter, Oxford University Press.

Potts, Daniel E. 1967. *British Baptist Missionaries in India 1793–1837*, Cambridge University Press.

Rajan, Rajeswari Sunder. 1993. "The Subject of Sati," in Tejaswini Niranjana, P. Sudhir, Vivek Dhareshwar edited, *Interrogating Modernity*, Seagull Books, first published in *Yale Journal of Criticism*, 1990, 3.2.

———. 1993a. *Real and Imagined Women: Gender, Culture and Postcolonialism*, Routledge.

Rangachari, Devika. 2009. *Invisible Women Visible Histories*, Manohar.

Ray, A.K. 1985. *Widows are not for Burning*, ABC Publishing House.

Rege, M.P. 1987. "Editorial," in *New Quest*, September-October.

Robb, Peter. 2007. *Liberalism, Modernity, and the Nation*, Oxford University Press.

Robertson, B.C. 1999. *The Essential Writings of Raja Rammohan Roy*, Oxford University Press.

Rocher, Rosane. 1983. *Orientalism, poetry and the millennium: The chequered life of Nathanial Brassey Halhed, 1751–1830*, Motilal Banarsidass.

———. 1984. "The Early Enchantment of India's Past," in *South Asian Review*, 8, 5.

———. 1989. "The Career of Radhakanta Tarkavagisa: An Eighteenth Century Pandit in British Employ," in *Journal of the American Oriental Society*, 109.

———. 1993. "British Orientalism in the Eighteenth Century: The Dialectics of Knowledge and Government," in Carol A. Breckenridge and Peter van der Veer edited, *Orientalism and the Postcolonial Predicament*, University of Pennsylvania Press.

Rocher, Rosane and Ludo Rocher. 2012. *The Making of Western Indology. Henry Thomas Colebrooke and the East India Company*, Routledge.

Rose, Vincent. 1990. *The French in India*, Popular Prakashan.

Rosselli, John. 1974. *Lord William Bentinck. The Making of a Liberal Imperialist 1774–1839*, Thomson Press.

Roy, Benoy Bhusan. 1987. *Socioeconomic Impact of Sati in Bengal and the Role of Raja Rammohun Roy*, Naya Prokash.

Sangari, Kumkum and Uma Chakravarti. 1999. Edited. *From Myths to Markets: Essays on Gender*, Manohar.

Sapra, Rahul. 2011. *The Limits of Orientalism*, University of Delaware.

Sardesai. G.S. 1958. *New History of the Marathas*, Vol. II, Phoenix Publications.

Sastri, Nilakanta. 1966. *A History of South India*, Oxford University Press, first published in 1947.

———. 1975. *The Colas*, University of Madras, reprint.

Saxsena, R.K. 1975. *Social Reform: Infanticide and Sati*, Trimurti.

Schwab, Raymond. 1984. *The Oriental Renaissance,* Columbia University Press.

Sen Gupta, Kanti Prasanna. 1971. *The Christian Missionaries in Bengal 1793–1833*, Firma K.L. Mukhopadhyay.

Settar, S. and G. Sontheimer. 1982. *Memorial Stones, a study of their origin, significance and variety*, Institute of Indian Art History, Karnatak University.

Sharma, Arvind. 1978. "Suttee: A Study in Western Reactions," in his *Threshold of Hindu-Buddhist Studies*, Minerva.

———. 1988. Edited. *Sati, Historical and Phenomenological Essays*, Motilal Banarsidass.

Sharma, Dasharatha. 1935. *Early Chauhan Dynasties*, S. Chand & Co.

Seed, Geoffrey. 1955. "The Abolition of Suttee in Bengal," in *History* (n.s.) 40 (140).

Singh, Iqbal. 1987. *Rammohun Roy. A biographical inquiry into the making of modern India*, Vols. II and III, Asia Publishing House.

Sinha, H. N. 1954. *Rise of the Peshwas*, The Indian Press Ltd.

Smith, G. 1885. *Life of William Carey*, D.D., John Murray.

Spear, Percival. 1980. *The Nabobs*, Curzon Press, first published 1932.

———. 2003. *A History of Delhi Under the Later Mughuls,* Low Price Publications, first published in 1951.

Spivak, Gayatri Chakravorty. 1988. "Can the Subaltern Speak? Speculations on Widow-Sacrifice," in Cary Nelson and Lawrence Grossberg edited, *Marxism and the interpretation of culture*, Urbana, Illinois.

Sramek, Joseph. 2011. *Gender, Morality, and Race in Company India, 1765–1858*, Palgrave.

Stein, Dorothy. 1978. "Women to Burn: Suttee as a Normative Institution," in *Signs* 4 (2).

———. 1988. "Burning Widows, Burning Brides: The Perils of Daughterhood in India," in *Pacific Affairs*, Vol. 61, No. 3.

Stokes, Eric. 1982. *The English Utilitarians and India*, Oxford University Press, first published in 1959.

Storm, Mary. 2013. *Head and Heart. Valour and Self-Sacrifice in the Art of India*, Routledge.

Sturman, Rachel. 2013. *The Government of Social Life in Colonial India. Liberalism, Religious Law, and Women's Rights*, Cambridge University Press.

Stutchbury, Elizabeth L. 1982. "Blood, Fire and Mediation: Human Sacrifice and Widow Burning in Nineteenth Century India," in Michael Allen and S.N. Mukherjee edited, *Women in India and Nepal*, ANU.

Teltscher, K. 1995. *India Inscribed: European and British Writing on India, 1600–1800*, Oxford University Press.

Thakur, U. 1963. *The History of Suicide in India*, Munshiram Manoharlal.

Thompson, Edward. 1928. *Suttee: A Historical and Philosophical Enquiry into the Hindu Rite of Widow Burning*, George Allen and Unwin.

Tomkins, Stephen. 2010. *The Clapham Sect*, Lion Hudson.

Trautmann, Thomas R. 2004. *Aryans and British India*, Yoda Press.

Travers, Robert. 2008. *Ideology and Empire in Eighteenth-Century India*, Cambridge University Press.

Trevelyan, G.M. 1926. *History of England*, Longman.

———. 1944. *British History in the Nineteenth Century and after (1782–1919)*, Longmans, Green and Co.

Tschurenev, Jana. 2004. "Between Non-interference in Matters of Religion and the Civilizing Mission: The Prohibition of Suttee in 1829," in Harald Fischer-Tine and Michael Mann edited, *Colonialism as Civilizing Mission. Cultural Ideology in British India*, Anthem Press.

Tully, Mark. 1991. *No Full Stops in India*, Viking.

Upreti, H.C. and Nandini Upreti. 1991. *The Myth of Sati*, Himalaya Publishing House.

Vaid, Sudesh and Kumkum Sangari. 1991. "Institutions, Beliefs, Ideologies. Widow Immolation in Contemporary Rajasthan," in *Economic and Political Weekly*, 27 April.

Venkata Ramanayya, N. 1986. *Studies in the Third Dynasty of Vijayanagara*, Gian Publishing House, first published in 1935.

Verghese, Anila. 2000. *Archaeology, Art and Religion. New Perspectives on Vijayanagara*, Oxford University Press.

Viswanathan, Gauri. 2009. *Masks of Conquest. Literary Study and British Rule in India*, Oxford University Press.

Washbrook, D.A. 1999. "India, 1818–1860: The Two Faces of Colonialism," in Andrew Porter edited, *The Oxford History of the British Empire, Vol. III, The Nineteenth Century*, Oxford University Press.

——. 2004. "South India 1770–1840: The Colonial Transition," in *Modern Asian Studies*, 38, 3.

Weinberger-Thomas, Catherine. 2000. *Ashes of Immortality, Widow Burning in India*, Oxford University Press.

Willson, Leslie A. 1964. *A Mythical Image: The ideal of India in German Romanticism*, Duke University Press.

Wilson, Jon E. 2010. "Anxieties of Distance: Codification in Early Colonial Bengal," in Shruti Kapila edited, *An Intellectual History for India*, Cambridge University Press.

Woodruff, Philip. 1963. *The Men Who Ruled India, the Founders*, Jonathan Cape.

Woodward, Sir Llewellyn. 1962. *The Age of Reform 1815–1870*, Clarendon Press.

Yang, Anand A. 2007. "Whose Sati? Widow Burning in Early-Nineteenth Century India," in Sumit Sarkar and Tanika Sarkar edited, *Women and Social Reform in Modern India*, permanent black.

Zastoupil, Lynn. 2011. *Rammohun Roy and the Making of Victorian Britain*, Palgrave.

Zupanov, Ines G. 2001. *Disputed Mission*, Oxford University Press.

Index

A Memoir of the Expediency of an Ecclesiastical Establishment for British India 122, 156

Account of the Writings, Religion and Manners of the Hindoos 160

Adam, John 196

Adam, William 84

Akbar (Emperor) 14, 19

Alberuni 26, 228

Amherst, Lord 174, 203, 413

An Apology for Christianity in India 191

Anquetil-Duperron 213, 282

Archer, Major Edward C. 219, 397

Asiatic Researches 5, 53, 55, 56, 58

Asiatic Society of Bengal 53, 58

Atkinson, James 35

Bana 7

Baptist Magazine 160

Baptist missionaries xvii, xviii, 40, 116, 146, 178, 183, 186, 373

Baptist Missionary Society (BMS) 117, 137, 178, 185

Baptists xviii, 20, 41, 84, 115, 126-27, 134, 148, 155-56, 169-70, 172, 180, 184-85, 194, 196

Barbosa, Duarte 28, 235

Barker, Sir Robert 61

Barlow, George 126-27, 129, 131

Belaturu Inscription 11

Bengali New Testament 120

Bentham, Jeremy 105, 109

Bentinck, William xv, 109, 128, 204, 208, 336, 403

Bernier, Francois 18, 267

Black Hole 85

Board of Control 72, 98, 134, 163
Bowen, John 172
Brahmin(s) vii, viii, 13, 16, 19-
    20, 40, 46-47, 49, 51, 62, 72,
    131, 137, 147-49, 177, 190-92,
    207-08, 216, 234, 243-44, 263,
    275, 281, 289-90, 300-01, 305,
    318-20, 336, 339-41, 346-47,
    365-67, 374, 389, 409-10
British and Foreign Bible Society
    90, 110, 195, 204
Brown, Rev. David 91, 94-96,
    116, 118, 121, 130, 158, 183,
    366
Buchanan, Claudius 84, 92, 95,
    99, 104, 119, 121-22, 126, 129,
    133, 135, 138, 152-53, 155-56,
    161, 163, 168, 174, 177-78,
    180, 183, 191-92, 366-67
Buckingham, James Silk 196
Buxton, Thomas Fowell 91-92,
    200

Carey, Eustace 79, 150-51
Carey, William xix, 39, 79, 82,
    89, 116-18, 120, 123, 127, 133,
    147-53, 155, 177-78, 181, 206,
    354
Chambers, William 93-95, 115-
    16, 118, 177, 180, 183
Changu Narayana temple 10
Charnock, Job 18, 71, 277
Charter Act of xviii, 1813 139,
    162
Christian Researches in Asia 157,
    183
Church Missionary Society 82,
    90, 92, 157, 184-85
Clapham (sect) 91-93, 98, 103,
    112, 130, 162-63, 170, 172, 200

Clarke, Rev. T. 95
Colebrooke, H.T. 5, 50, 56-57,
    179, 192, 202, 215
College of Fort William 120, 123,
    356
Commission of Sati (Prevention)
    Act of 1987 xv
Company Charter – 1793 101
Conti, Nicolo 27, 231
converts 127
Cornwallis, Lord xix, 58, 72, 83,
    96, 201
Costard, George 39, 51, 292
Court of Directors xvii, 50, 71-
    72, 99, 115, 123, 127, 130, 133,
    139, 161, 163, 165, 183, 200,
    203, 336
Craufurd, Quintin 59, 215
Crowninshield, Benjamin 39

dastaks 73-74
Dayabhaga 17, 57, 192-93
Deb, Radhakant 209-10
Dharmasutras 5
Dholpur inscription 14
Diodorus xviii, 9, 25, 27, 225,
    394
Dow, Alexander 47, 214, 390
Dubois, Abbe 206, 216
Duncan, Jonathan 50, 58, 177
Dundas, Henry 72, 98, 101, 104
Dundas, Robert 134

East, Sir Hyde 200
Economic and Political Weekly viii
Elphinstone, Mountstuart 202,
    216, 394
Eran Stone Pillar Inscription 10
Evangelical(s) xvii, xviii, 3, 40,
    44, 63, 68, 79, 85, 89-95, 99,

101, 105, 110-13, 116, 130, 146, 155, 157, 162, 166, 172, 174, 177, 179, 182, 185, 190, 194, 213, 221
Evangelical movement 89-90

Fay, Eliza 81, 215, 294
Federici, Caesaro 30, 240
Female infanticide xviii, 85, 153, 216, 325, 393
Forbes, James 215
Forbes, Sir Charles 200
Foreign and Bible Society 137
Forster, George 48, 214, 390
Fox, Charles James 103
France xix, 84, 89-90, 98, 103, 105, 112, 207, 388
Friar Odoric of Pordenone 27, 228
Friend of India 20, 146, 196, 367
Fuller, Andrew 117, 124, 137, 147, 152

Ghatiyala inscription 14
Ghaut murders 153
Graham, Maria 60
Grandpre, La De 18, 215, 297
Grant, Charles xvii, 71, 92-98, 106, 109, 111-12, 115-16, 118, 121, 130, 146, 170, 177, 183
Grimshawe, Rev. T.S. 196
Grose, John 37, 44
Guyon, Abbe de 20, 280

Haileybury College xix, 106
Halhed, Nathaniel 39, 50-51, 292
Halliday, Frederick 41, 334
Hamilton, Alexander 32, 71, 277

Hamilton, Robert 218
Harsacarita 11
Harsha 10, 11
Hastings, Lord Warren xvii, 49-50, 52-53, 83-84, 100, 130, 135, 165, 173-74, 196, 202, 412-13
Hawkins, William 31, 244
Herbert, Thomas 33, 257
Hickey, James 79
Hindu religion 49, 58, 147, 160, 407-08, 421
Hinduism xvii, xix, 44, 58, 68, 79, 113, 136, 146, 153, 155, 160-61, 177, 202, 218
History of British India 106-08
Holkar, Ahalya Bai 16, 305
Holwell, John Z. 38, 46
hook swinging 85, 151
Huggins, William 218, 391

Ibn Battuta 27, 229
Idolatry 57, 149-51, 155, 160, 204
Image-worship 149-50
Infanticide xviii, 85, 152-53, 170, 178, 216, 325, 393-94, 409
Irwin, Eyles 35

Jagannath temple 155, 158
jauhar 14, 220
Jimutavahana 17, 192-93
Johns, William 134, 194
Jones, William 5, 50, 53-54, 58, 107, 111-12, 153, 302
Jordanus, Friar 27, 229

Kanwar, Roop v, vii-viii, x-xi, xv

Kaye, Sir John 83, 220
Kettle, Tilly 35
Khan, Muhammad Reza 75-76
Kircher, Athanasius 34
Knox, Alex 36

London Missionary Society 90, 379
Long, Rev. James 82, 160
Lord, Rev. Henry 32, 214, 257
Lushington, Charles 186
Lushington, Sir Stephen 168

Macintosh, William 59
Macnaughten, Sir William 203
Mahabharata ix, 6, 54
Malcolm, Sir John 100, 110, 128, 173, 216, 393
Malet, Sir Charles 177, 306
Manu Smriti 5
Manushi v, viii-ix
Marquis of Hastings 113, 173
Marsh, Charles 168-69
Marshman, Joshua 116-17, 147, 177, 184, 196
Martin, Francois 214, 274
Martin, Montgomery 218
Medhatithi 7
memorial stones 4, 12-13, 29, 242
Methwold, William 32, 250
Mill, James 105-06, 109-12, 160
Minto, Lord 131-33, 161, 174, 202
Minute on Sati 196, 205, 209, 403
Mir Jafar 74-76
Mir Kasim 74
Mission to Bengal 95

Missionaries xi, xvii-xix, 9, 34, 40-41, 60-61, 89, 93, 95-96, 102, 104, 108, 112, 115-19, 123-39, 146-49, 161-63, 166-68, 170, 174, 177-80, 183-86, 190, 193-94, 200, 205-06, 208, 210, 217, 221, 375, 394
Missionary Papers 160, 185
Missionary Register 160, 164, 184-85
Missionary Society 82, 90, 92, 98, 117, 137, 157, 163, 170, 178, 184-85, 379
Mitaksara 8, 57, 192
Montgomery, Sir Henry 168
Munro, Thomas 167

Nau'i, Muhammad Riza 19
Nayaka of Madurai 30-31
Nobili, Roberto de 31
Nuniz, Fernao 29, 238

Observations on the State of Society among the Asiatic Subjects of Great Britain xvii, 98-99
Orme, Robert 48, 77
Ovington, John 36
Owen, Rev. John 137

Paes, Domingo 30
Pamphlet war 134, 136
Parkes, Fanny 219, 326, 392
patriarchy viii
patronage powers 71
Peggs, James 197
Pelsaert, Francisco 31, 214, 248
Periodical Accounts 185
Picart, Bernard 36, 279
Pious Clause 102-03

Pires, Tome 28, 235
Playfair, John 62
Polo, Marco 26, 228
Prinsep, James 50
Promotion of Christian Knowledge (SPCK) 94-95, 129, 164

Raghunandana 4, 8, 17
Rajputana 14-15
Ramayana ix, 7, 125
Rani Sati temple vii
Razzak, Abdur 30
Regulation XVII of 4 December 1829 xv
Rig Veda 4-5, 59
Robertson, William 59
Roger, Abraham 34
Roy, Rammohan ix, 110, 192, 205, 208-10

Sanskrit xiv, 21-22, 47, 51-54, 57-59, 112, 124-25, 153, 215
Sati v-xviii, 3-4, 7-8, 12-13, 15, 21-22, 25, 29-30, 35, 40-41, 85, 177-78, 185, 188, 196, 200, 205-06, 209, 213, 223, 225, 227-29, 231-32, 234-35, 238, 240, 243-48, 250-53, 257-58, 260, 262-65, 270-74, 276, 278, 282, 285, 295, 305, 307, 312, 314, 318, 320-21, 326, 329, 334, 336, 338-39, 342, 344, 346-47, 349-50, 373, 377, 390-91, 403, 419, 423, 425-26, 431
sati *mata* vi-vii
Sati stones 13, 15, 22
Schwartz, Rev. Frederick 116
Scrafton, Luke 37, 45, 281

Serampore 89, 116-20, 123-26, 130-32, 134, 149, 160, 178-79, 181, 183, 191, 194, 210, 351, 356, 359, 365, 367, 411
Serampore mission 89, 117-18, 123-24, 126, 134, 149, 183
Shore, Frederick John 78, 80, 83, 85, 92-93, 101, 112, 177, 201, 219, 396
Sleeman, W.H. 41, 329
Smith, Sydney 137
Solvyns, Francois Baltazard 35
Sonnerat, Pierre 37, 281
Stavorinus, J.S. 38, 288
Stewart, Col. 136
Stridharmapaddhati 9

Tavernier, Jean Baptiste 33
Teignmouth, Lord 93, 138, 165, 166
Tennant, William 39, 365
Terry, Edward 32, 247
The Light of the World 157
The Nabob 78, 277, 313
The Star in the East 157
Thiruk-koyilur inscription 12
Thomas, John 98, 115-18, 123, 178, 351
Thompson, Edward 3, 42, 210
Tod, James 14-15
Twining, Thomas 19, 130, 134, 307

Udny, George 94-95, 118, 152, 177-78, 180
Utilitarians 105, 109-13

Valle, Pietro Della 32-33, 214, 252-53
Vansittart, Henry 74, 76

Varthema, Ludovico di 28, 30, 234

Vellore Mutiny 128, 131, 134, 139, 202

Vidyalankar, Mrityunjaya 208

Virvinod 16

Vishnusmriti 7

Ward, William 49, 116-17, 120, 127, 131, 147, 150, 152, 154-55, 160, 177, 180-81, 191, 194-95, 206-07, 356, 381

Waring, Major Scott 135

Wilberforce, William 85, 91, 96, 98, 162, 177, 184

Wilkins, Charles 50, 52

Williamson, Captain Thomas 60, 80

Wilson, H.H. 5, 50, 58, 107, 153, 205

Withington, Nicholas 31, 245

Yajnavalkya Smriti 6, 8

Yasomati (Queen) 10

Zoffany, Johann 35